EXILED CUBA

CUBA Y SUS JUECES COLLECTION

EDICIONES UNIVERSAL, Miami, Florida 2012

A massive march by Cuban exiles in
Little Havana in the 1990s.

RAÚL EDUARDO CHAO

EXILED CUBA

A Chronicle of the Years of Exile from 1959 to the Present

...EDICIONES UNIVERSAL

First Edition, 2012

EDICIONES UNIVERSAL
P.O. Box 450353 (Shenandoah Station)
Miami, FL 33245-0353. USA
Phone: (305) 642-3234   Fax: (305) 642-7978
e-mail: ediciones@ediciones.com
http://www.ediciones.com

Library of Congress Catalog Card No.: 2012946160
ISBN-10: 1-59388-240-8
ISBN-13: 978-1-59388-240-2

Chao, Raúl Eduardo, 1939-
EXILED CUBA / Raúl Eduardo Chao

Front Cover:
The *Freedom Tower*, Miami.
Back Cover:
Estampida, acrylic on canvas by Gustavo Acosta; a view of
Biscayne Boulevard, north, from the Freedom Tower stairs.

To Carolina Isabel

SOME DAY, WHEN
THOSE OF YOUR GENERATION
READ THIS BOOK,
THEY WILL KNOW WHY THEIR
ABUELOS AND *ABUELAS*
WERE AT THE SAME TIME
PROUD AMERICANS
AND PASSIONATE SUPPORTERS
OF FREEDOM FOR
THE COUNTRY OF
THEIR BIRTH.

Cuban exiles in Paris, at a demonstration
in *Trocadero*, calling for human rights in Cuba.

Index

Appendices

Foreword

THIS BOOK SHARES with *Republican Cuba* * the desire of the author to provide a record of many years of patriotic and unselfish efforts by hundreds of Cubans to develop and build-up Cuba, first as active citizens of the Republic and later as unwilling members of the Exile. Many Cubans who witnessed, studied or participated in these episodes, always with profound devotion to their country of birth, have tried to leave behind a trail of their knowledgeable accounts of these constitutive events for future historians to interpret. Hopefully, this book brings together as many contributions to that effort as possible.

A book with these aspirations is by necessity a collective project. The author feels indebted to the numerous writers, analysts, historians, academics, librarians, journalists, scholars, cartoonists and political pundits that have written incessantly about Republican Cuba and its 50 plus years exiled Diaspora. Their contributions will never be forgotten and are a priceless portrayal of the Cuban drama. Any and all flawed interpretations of their testimonies and accounts can be fairly imputed only to this author.

Given the nature of the many digressions, wanderings and rambles of Cuban history over the last century, it is not easy to anticipate where Cuba is headed at the time this book is published. Optimists believe that the basic strengths of the Cuban ethos will overcome the physical and moral devastation, the ideological confusion and the damage done to the Cuban soul by a cruel and vulgar totalitarian credo foreign to our spirit; if this is the case, a recuperation of our real character will be insured and Cuba will return to the honorable course of its true destiny. Others, however, feel that half a century of indoctrination, repression and captivity have caused irreparable damage to the nation, and that Cuba may evolve in unknown ways but will never recover its original imprint and spirit.

What the future holds for Cuba is known only to God.

Raúl Eduardo Chao
Coral Gables, Fall of 2012.

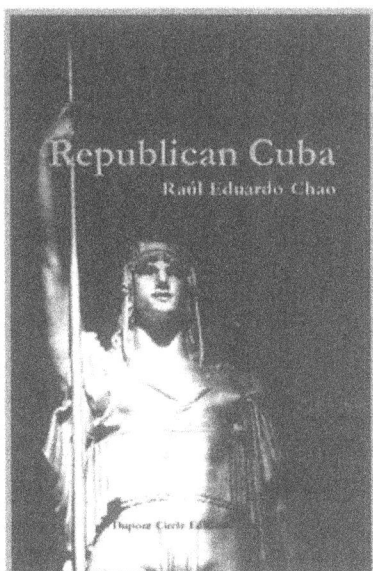

* Republican Cuba, Raúl Eduardo Chao, published by *Dupont Circle Editions*, 2011. (ISBN 978-0-9791777-8-1)

Introduction

ex·ile. *[egzīl].* **n.** The state of being barred from one's native country,
typically for political or punitive reasons.
The enforced removal from one's native country.
Self imposed absence from one's country.
tr.v. to send into exile; to banish.

im·mi·grant. *['imigrənt].* **n/adj.** A person who has come
into a foreign country to live there permanently,
not as a tourist or visitor. A person who migrates
to another country, usually in search of economic betterment.

EXILES ARE UBIQUITOUS in history. They first came into
the world side by side with the first recognitions of authority
by groups of individuals in pre-historic times. The term *"exile"*
became instantly embedded in the annals of all cultures and
civilizations. Many other constructs are contemporaneous with
the notion of exile defined above: *ostracism, diaspora, deportation,
extradition, asylum, refuge* and *ghetto* to mention a few. Together
they mostly tell a sad and deplorable story about the human
condition. It is appalling that the more civilizations develop
and expand the more exile, ostracism and forced migrations
occur.

The Exile Experience.

Interestingly, most exile experiences throughout history
share significant similar circumstances and events. This book
has the purpose of exploring what has been in many ways one
of the most remarkable examples of exile: the Cuban exile experience of the second half of the XX century.

The first well documented instance of a nation in exile belongs to the Jewish people. After they revolted against the rulers of the Chaldean (or Neo-Babylonian) Empire, they were
deported from the Kingdom of Judah to Babylon by king Neb-
uchadnezzar II in 597 BC, a few years after the destruction of

the First Temple. The deported Jews were allowed to stay in a tight community in Babylon; they remained in contact with two other closely-knit communities of Jewish exiles, one in Egypt and a second one in conquered Judea. In the same fashion, a millennium later, in Renaissance Italy, it became customary for men punished into exile after power struggles to seek each other's support by also clustering into tightly bound groups seeking to undermine the regime back home.

It was not unexpected that Cuban exiles made a similar decision in the XX century by staging themselves in close-woven communities in Miami, Madrid, the New York area, Paris and other capitals, hoping to jointly undermine, rattle and subvert the regime in Havana. In fact, they had a precedent: many Cuban liberals had escaped the repression established in the island during the last days of the XIX century by going into exile in the United States, specifically in the great port cities of New Orleans, Philadelphia and New York.

The Diaspora.

It was in Roman times that the term *"Diaspora"* (from the Greek διασπορά, scattering, dispersion) was coined. It was originally capitalized and referred exclusively to the Jewish dispersal. After WWII, the term was widely assimilated into Western culture as «*the movement, migration, or scattering of people away from an established or traditional homeland, as long as they have a hope, or at least a desire, to return to their homeland if it still exists in any meaningful sense.*»

Most of the time, of course, communities which were remotely separated from their original roots evolved separately and changed their cultural traits, traditions, language, and other factors. The last vestiges of cultural affiliation in a Diaspora is often found when there is a community resistance to completely discard their original language, to forsake their fondness for their traditional foods and to abandon the political persuasions that led them into exile.

Additional less documented exile experiences throughout history are too many to mention, but the best known in antiquity were probably these two: In 8 AD, Emperor Augustus, sentenced the refined and sophisticated Roman poet Ovid to permanent exile in Tomis, on the Rumanian coast of the Black Sea. And in 70 AD, after the Roman occupation of their land and their rebellion against Roman rule, the Jews were again sent into exile from the region of Judah. This time the second Temple in Jerusalem (Herod's) was destroyed and Roman Emperor Hadrian attempted to erase all connections of Jews with the land by changing the name of the province from Roman Judaea (formerly Judah or Judea) to Syria-Palestina.

As the expulsion of Ovid from Rome, the 1959 Cuban Revolution also sent into exile some of the best Cuban talent of the times (artistic, managerial, creative, scientific) and tried for many years to erase the connection of Cubans in exile with their families and friends in Cuba through closed borders, total isolation and a propaganda war waged against exiles depicting them as "*gusanos,*" a greedy and amoral group.

The illegitimate and tyrannical regime that produced the exile of hundreds of thousands of Cubans in the second half of the XX century was an exception to the tradition of ultimate life-saving tolerance (*tirar una toalla* or "throw a towel" —a boxing term in Cuban slang) that ran throughout most of Cuban republican history.

To the amazement of many anthropologists, sociologists and political pundits, the Cuban Diaspora has probably been the most resilient in history when it comes to its persistence to retain and pass on to other generations its dreams and passion to see Cuba free from the grip of its captors.

The Anguish and Agony of Exile.

The condition of exile has always been extremely hard and incredibly painful. In 399 BC, for instance, 70-year old Socrates, having been found guilty of corrupting the youth of Athens, preferred death over the alternative of exile and willingly drank his hemlock. Years later, during the Roman Empire, deportation to certain islands was a favorite form of sending political opponents into exile. Roman Senators could either remain in town facing punishment and perhaps death, or go into voluntary exile and avoid a trial. Exile, a sort of formal penalty contained in the statutes, was seldom the choice.

The painful nature of the exile experience was shown in some of the literature about exiles that came from Italy in the XVI century; it was extraordinarily pessimistic and full of lamentations and has been known since as the *consolatoria*:

«*The man living in exile from his homeland is a dead man, and lives in a sepulcher, dying every day,*» «*nothing can be more desperate and miserable than exile,*» «*exile is the supreme example of misfortune.*»

In the context of the Cuban exiles, the pain and anguish that was brought to hundreds of Cuban families has been extraordinary for over half a century. Entire families of honest and hard working men and women left behind and lost many of their kin, their possessions, their homes and their careers to start anew in a foreign land that —however friendly— was completely unfamiliar in its culture, language and mores. Most of them took the road to exile thinking it was to be short and bearable; as the Romans, perhaps they would have done otherwise if they had known it would last their lifetimes.

Individual and Collective Exile.

Cuba never suffered a collective exile before 1959, although Cubans witnessed the exile of its rebellious youth and intellectuals years before their independence from Spain. Many Spaniards escaped the peninsula and took refuge in France during the Inquisition and after the French Revolution. Teresa Cabarrús, for instance, also known as *Notre-Dame de Thermidor*, was a Spanish exiled lady who played an important role in the fall of Robespierre and the empowering of the Directory in Paris. The Spanish Royal family (Carlos IV and María Luisa de Parma), with Manuel Godoy, duque de Alcudia (Prime Minister to Carlos IV and lover to María Luisa) took refuge in France with a large entourage; their son Fernando VII also sought and obtained refugee status and protection from Napoleon. It was a time when the French Pyrenees accommodated over 60,000 Spanish residents, refugees, fugitives, deserters, and prisoners of war.

Exile in XIX century Cuba, however, was mostly a one-by-one compulsory exclusion of those resisting political impositions: Martí, Estrada Palma, Maceo, Calixto García, Del Monte, among many others. They were compelled or pressed to leave Cuba and were unable to return until a change of political conditions took place (the Independence War, for instance). At times, as an exception, exile was almost self-imposed; such was the case of Varela, Saco, Aldama, Aguilera and Heredia. As members of the economic or intellectual elite, exile was their response to a limitation of their political and individual rights.

One-by-one exiles continued to leave XX century republican Cuba. As in the previous century they involved people directly persecuted by the authorities or by *vigilante* or para-military organizations that forced opponents into exile (forced exile), or by citizens that felt an existential threat to their lives (self exiles). But it can be fairly said that not until 1959 Cuba experienced a collective exile.

Exile, of course, never occurs in democratic societies. There was no need for Nixon to go into exile in 1974 after his almost impeachment, or for Winston Churchill to leave London after WWII or for Charles de Gaulle to return to England in 1946 after they both lost their elections. Exceptions do occur (mostly upon realization of one's waning influence), as when Luis Muñoz Marín left Puerto Rico in 1970 after the Pro-Statehood party won the governorship of the island. Many self imposed exiles abound in Latin America, usually due to the inconformity of great men as they see their dreams in peril when they fall in the hands of lesser figures. Such was almost certainly the case of José de San Martín and Jorge Luis Borges in Argentina. They both retired into exile and died in Europe.

Massive or collective exiles are compulsory phenomena resulting from authoritarian political systems that are unwilling or unable to create pluralistic, tolerant and inclusive structures of citizen participation.

The Spanish kings forcefully expelled the Jews in the 1490s and the Muslims in the early XIV century (forced collective exiles). Spain again produced the most numerous, long-lasting and painful exile known until then; the 1936-1939 Spanish Civil War provoked an unprecedented political exile of republicans escaping the repression of post-war Spain. Close to 750,000 persons were displaced (600,000 eventually returned to Spain), half a million of which crossed the French border in 1939. They included many internationally known scientists, musicians, artists, writers and poets, journalists, philosophers and pedagogues. Similar cruel human dislocations (not quite considered exiles, however) were effected by the British, the Spaniards and the Portuguese when they unyieldingly displaced thousands of Africans to America as slaves.

It is interesting to know that Spain began as a country that drove out immigrants (6.5 million from 1492 to 1800; 4.1 million from 1800 to 1930 and close to 1 million from 1930 to 2000) and ended up as a country of immigration uptake (6 million from 1990 to the present). Cuba on the other hand began as a magnet for immigration (2.1 million from 1492 to 1958) and ended up as an expeller of exiles and immigrants (1.1 million since 1959).

In recent times, Spain has had a difficult time explaining why its hard-working yesteryear immigrants to America, all deserve a proud and gallant image while its current immigrants from America all merit a negative profile as undesirables. A similar situation is occurring in Cuba. For many years the Cuban tradition was to recognize that the independence of the country was almost 100% due to the value, political savvy and generosity of exiles. Since 1959, however, the political discourse of the Revolution (enunciated by practically all leaders, educators, artists, and literary men in the island) is that current exiles are all former economic exploiters, worthless "worms" and unpatriotic agents of the US.

The reality of massive exile has been, by and large, a phenomenon characteristic of XX century totalitarian regimes, particularly in Hispanic America, Eastern Europe and Africa. In that regard, no exile in Hispanic America comes close in its dimensions and its tragedy to the half century heartbreaking event of the Cuban exile.

The Cuban Exile Experience.

In this book we try to explain how the Cuban exile has affected the lives of thousands of honest citizens that were displaced from their land by what has turned out to be a brutal fascist dictatorship led by a group of egotistical and authoritarian compatriots with an insatiable appetite for power. We also deal in this book with the personal and collective experiences of the exiles, their interactions with their host societies and their frustrations with the global political realities that left them on the sidelines, at the mercy of a convulsed world that very quickly turned deaf ears to their pleas for help. We also present the resourcefulness of Cubans, lifting themselves by their bootstraps, counting on their own resources and the support of each other, and turning their fate from desolation to success. Their accomplishments and home-grown prosperity have been a well deserved tribute to the generosity of those around the world who trusted and helped them, particularly the people of the United States.

CUBA PATIENTLY AWAITS
by Garrinche

Two preludes to
The story of the Cuban Exile of
1959 and beyond:

- *The nature of the Cuban*
  political character, and
- *The story of the city of Miami,*
  where the exiles
  sought and received refuge
  and assistance.

The nature of the Cuban political character

The histories of both **Republican Cuba** and **Exiled Cuba** have been a logical consequence of the political passions that have characterized Cubans over the last two centuries. Historically, they have been blind to the reasoning of others with whom they share their dreams, and have always been willing to risk the success of their efforts in order to prevail and win arguments. A case in point was the second meeting of Martí, Maceo and Gómez in Oriente province, Cuba, which resulted in a repetition of the failed meeting of the same three leaders on October 2nd, 1884, at the **Hotel Griffou** in Manhattan (21 West 9th Street, New York).

On May 5, 1895, this second meeting took place at the **Ingenio La Mejorana**, near the town of *Dos Caminos*, on the banks of the *Ullao* and *Guanínico* Rivers, in the municipality of *San Luis*, in Eastern Cuba. It was attended by **José Martí**, **Antonio Maceo** and **Máximo Gómez**. The purpose of the meeting was to discuss the roles and responsibilities of each in the war of 1895. According to Rafael Estenger...

> **Martí** attended the meeting «*wearing a blue chamarreta and blue trousers, black hat and casual shoes; in his hands, as always, was the wrought iron ring made with one of the chain links that he had worn in prison when he was 16 years old*». **Maceo** dressed in a «*Holland gray uniform, arrived mounted on a beautiful golden chestnut horse, saddled with a graceful leather chair festoned with silver stars*». **Gómez**, «*happy as if he was going to a party, looked like an agile but small old man, sporting a neat white beard and a leafy Panama hat*».

Martí was 31 years old. He became upset when Gómez took a bath in the middle of the meeting. At the end, Martí left the meeting «*slamming the room door*», while Maceo commented to Gómez «*este hombre se va disgustado con nosotros.*»

(Continued)

Photos below, left to right: Manhattan's **Hotel Griffou** in 1884 and today.

(Continuation)

The **Martí-Maceo-Gómez** meeting at **La Mejorana** produced no agreement that would benefit the impending war. At the outset, all three agreed that Gómez would be the **Commander in Chief**, Maceo his **Lieutenant General** and Martí the **Delegate** (President) of the *Cuban Revolutionary Party*. The first signs of disagreement occurred when Martí insisted that during the war, the supreme power should rest on a civilian government; Maceo argued that the supreme command had to be a military junta holding total and absolute control over the war.

After several civilized clashes, Martí became angry with Maceo, who had threatened to leave the meeting in more than one occasion. Maceo also suggested that Martí should not stay in Cuba but return to New York to raise funds and manage the war politically. Maceo then lost patience with Martí and asked him if after the meeting he was planning to go with him or with Gómez's troops.

At one point everyone noticed that Maceo was visibly disgusted with Martí; he even reproached Martí for having sent the funds for their journey from Central America to Flor Crombet and not to him. Martí also ended up uneasy and wrote in his diary «*I like Maceo now less than I used to,*» adding «*Maceo hurts me and disgusts me; he is trying to define me as a petty civilian-obsessed man who is unbearably hostile to the military movement.*»

Towards the end of the meeting Maceo began to feel in a hurry to leave, saying the night was about to fall and he had six hours on horseback to get to his headquarters. Martí felt deceived knowing that Maceo's troops were close, yet he had not invited him or Gómez to visit them. Martí also did not like that Maceo, about four in the afternoon, had taken him and Gómez outside the camp and told them where they would be spending the night «*alone and helpless, escorted by just 20 men poorly trained and poorly armed*».

Interestingly, four pages of **Martí's Journal**, from page 18 to page 21, dealing with the May 6, 1895 meeting in **La Mejorana**, have disappeared. The Journal was guarded by Máximo Gómez after the death of Martí in **Dos Rios**. Almost certainly, it was Gómez who decided to tear those pages to remove evidence of the rift between Martí and Maceo.

Photo below: the meeting at **La Mejorana** on May 5th, 1895. (Oil on Canvas by Juan Emilio Hernández Giró)

Cuban exiles were not exempted from jealousy and resentment in the years before the Independence War of 1895. Below are some excerpts of the infamous letter of **Enrique Collazo** (from his home in Cuba) to **José Martí** (on exile in New York). Collazo was a veteran of the 1868 War. Martí was 13 years old when Céspedes proclaimed the *Grito de Yara* in 1868 and was deported to Spain in 1870. *On the right, a stamp with a picture of Enrique Collazo.*

Habana, 6 de Enero de 1892
Sr. D. José Martí, en la Emigración.

Muy Señor Mío:

«Los que militamos en la revolución y vivimos ahora en Cuba tenemos hoy el mismo criterio que ayer tuvimos, y, a pesar del tiempo transcurrido, mantenemos los vínculos que nos unieron a la década del sacrificio. Nuestro juicio sobre la emigración, por la conducta que observó durante la guerra, [...es muy mala].»

«Después de la guerra hemos perseverado en esa opinión, abonada por los hechos; pero nunca imaginamos tan ruin a esa emigración como usted la hace aparecer en su discurso. ¡Cómo! ¿Con qué?; a pesar de los años transcurridos, ¿todavía puede asustarse esa emigración con el relato fiel de las privaciones, trabajos y desventuras que afrontamos durante diez años?»

« ¿Cree usted, señor Martí, que los que, a impulso del deber, arrostren el peligro de hacer patria, deben ir ciegos o engañados como el soldado mercenario a quien se emborracha para que sirva de carne de cañón? ¿Tan ruin imagina usted la generación presente, que la cree incapaz de ir al sacrificio con plena conciencia de lo que va a hacer, con el mismo valor y estoicismo con que arrostraron la muerte, en el campo y en el patíbulo, los hombres del 68?»

«El que con ofensas más que suficientes -el grillete-, con edad sobrada, no cumplió con los deberes de cubano cuando Cuba clamaba por el esfuerzo de todos sus hijos; el que prefirió continuar primero sus estudios en Madrid, casarse luego en México, ejercer en la Habana su profesión de abogado, solicitar más tarde, como representante del Partido Liberal, un asiento en el Congreso de los Diputados, por Puerto Príncipe o por Cuba, el que prefirió servir a la Madre Patria, o alejar su persona del peligro, en vez de empuñar un rifle para vengar ofensas personales aquí recibidas, ése, usted, señor Martí, no es posible que comprenda el espíritu de *A Pie y Descalzo*. [1] Aún le dura el miedo de antaño....»

«Si de nuevo llegase la hora del sacrificio, tal vez no podríamos estrechar la mano de usted en la manigua de Cuba; seguramente porque entonces continuará usted dando lecciones de patriotismo en la emigración, a la sombra de la bandera americana.»

---

(1) A 1890 book by Ramón Roa, with not very positive comments by Martí in a 1891 review. Ramón Roa was the father of Raúl Roa, Foreign Relations Minister of the Castro government in 1959.

	A	B	C	D	
1	Queridos compañeros	la realización de las premisas del programa	nos obliga a un exhaustivo análisis	de las condiciones financieras y administrativas existentes	1
2	Por otra parte y dados los condicionamientos actuales	la complejidad de los estudios de los dirigentes	cumple un rol esencial en la formación	de las directivas de desarrollo para el futuro	2
3	Asimismo	el aumento constante en cantidad y en calidad de nuestra actividad	exige la precisión y la determinación	del sistema de participación general	3
4	Sin embargo no hemos de olvidar que	la estructura actual de la organización	ayuda a la preparación y a la realización	de las actitudes de los miembros hacia sus deberes ineludibles	4
5	De igual manera	el nuevo modelo de actividad de la organización	garantiza la participación de un grupo importante en la formación	de las nuevas proposiciones	5
6	La prática de la vida cotidiana prueba que	el desarrollo continuo de distintas formas de actividad	cumple deberes importantes en la determinación	de las direcciones educativas en el sentido del progreso	6
7	No es indispensable argumentar el peso y la significación de estos problemas ya que	nuestra actividad de información y de propaganda	facilita la creación	del sistema de formación de cuadros que corresponda a las necesidades	7
8	Las experiencias ricas y diversas muestran que	el reforzamiento y desarrollo de las estructuras	obstaculiza la apreciación de la importancia	de las condiciones de las actividades apropiadas	8
9	El afán de organización, pero sobre todo	la consulta con los numerosos militantes	ofrece un ensayo interesante de verificación	del modelo de desarrollo.	9
10	Los superiores principios ideológicos condicionan que	el inicio de la acción general de formación de las actitudes	implica el proceso de reestructuración y de modernización	de las formas de acción	10
11	Incluso bien pudiéramos atrevernos a sugerir que	un aplazamiento específico de todos los sectores implicados	habrá de significar un auténtico y eficaz punto de partida	de las básicas premisas adoptadas	11
12	Es obvio señalar que	la superación de experiencias particulares	permite en todo caso explicar las razones fundamentales	de toda una casuística de amplio espectro	12
13	Pero pecaramos de insinceros si soslayasemos que	una aplicación indiscriminada de los factores concluyentes	asegura en todo caso un proceso insensible de inversión	de los elementos generadores	13
14	Por último y como definitivo elemento esclarecedor cabe añadir que	el proceso consensurado de unas y otras aplicaciones concurrentes	deriva en una directa incidencia superadora	de toda una serie de criterios ideológicamente sistematizados en un frente común de actuación generadora.	14
	A	B	C	D	

During the 1952 national elections in Cuba, a comedy writer (rumors were that it was **Castor Vispo**, the writer of *La Tremenda Corte*), tired of listening to political speeches, published a **guide to partisan preaching** that even the most inarticulate candidate could use to produce good-sounding political appeals. His instructions were simple: 1- Choose four combinations of letters (A to D) and numbers (1 to 14) and put them together from A to D. 2- Repeat the process as many times as necessary. One such sentence, for example, could be A6-B4-C3-D12, where numbers 6, 4, 3 and 12 would be chosen *at random*. This would produce the sentence «*La práctica de la vida cotidiana prueba que – la estructura actual de la organización – exige la precisión y la determinación - de toda una casuística de amplio espectro*». WHOA!

The Story of the City of Miami

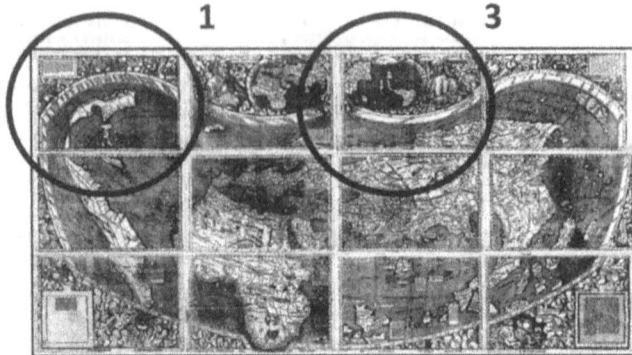

The joint fate of Florida and Cuba was apparently sealed over 500 years àgo when **Martin Waldseemüller (1470-1521)**, a German monk, produced in France, in 1507, a map of the new world incorporating all geographical knowledge of the times. This map gave the continent its name of **"America,"** as shown in panel number 3 above. The only thing known of North America in 1507 was a slice of the East coast from the Chesapeake Bay to Florida. Miami did not exist yet, but the tip of Florida was duly drawn in the map. Cuba, on the other hand, was clearly identified as **Isabella Insula**.

Maps above: the twelve-panel **Waldseemüller map** of 1507, showing panels 1 and 3 circled; panel 1 shows the tip of *Florida*, and an almost perfect Europe; panel 3 shows *Cuba*, the US East coast and the title *"Americi"* that gave the continent its name.

The Story of the City of Miami

The builders of Miami, left to right:

Carl Fisher, real estate developer in *Miami Beach*, lost his $100 million fortune in the *Stock Market Crash* of 1929.

William Brickell, former owner of *Coconut Grove*, opened a trading post near the Miami River, close friend of Julia Tuttle.

Henry Flagler, American tycoon, partner of John Rockefeller, thought of South Florida as the American Riviera; opened a railway to what was a «*wilderness of waterless sand*» (Miami).

Julia Tuttle, entrepreneur and citrus farmer, original owner of *the land where Miami is today*; moved Flagler to build the highway to Miami; was broke when she died of meningitis at age 49.

George Merrick, planner and builder of *Coral Gables*, founder of the University of Miami, ruined by the *Labor Day Hurricane* of 1935.

Photo below: **John S.Collins**, land developer, at age 74 built the *Collins Bridge* across Biscayne Bay and almost went bankrupt.

The city of **Miami** after Flagler extended his railroad south in 1896.

The inauguration of the **Collins Bridge** (today's *Venetian Causeway*) in 1913.

John S. Collins, the builder of **Collins Bridge,** on the beach, across the intracoastal waters

(Continued)

(Continuation)

(Continued)

Photos above, top to bottom:
Seminole Indians in the *Miami River* in 1910; A **Bathing Casino** on
23 Street in *Miami Beach* in 1912; an Ad for **Florida Real Estate** in
1920; lots for sale in **Miami Beach** in 1915; in **Coral Gables**, the
future land for the *University of Miami* alongside US Route 1.

(Continuation)

Coral Gables'
Biltmore Hotel
under construction
in 1926.

**Pan Am Dixie
Clipper** (Boeing
314) taking off in
Miami in 1950.

The old
Miami Public Library
In *Bayfront Park* in
1951.

Arthur Godfrey, the
man who popularized
Miami and Miami Beach in
the 1950s and 1960s and
for whom the causeway
into 41st Street in Miami
Beach is named.

(Continued)

(Continuation)

Wolfie's, the **Delano** and **di Lido Hotels** in Miami Beach in the early 1950s.

Ana Gloria y **Rolando** entertaining tourists aboard flights to Cuba in the 1950s.

The **Fountainbleau Hotel** in Miami Beach under construction in 1954.

An Ad for **Cubana Airlines** flights Havana-New York in the 1950s.

(Continued)

from *NEW YORK* to *HAVANA* NON-STOP

luxurious **SUPER-G CONSTELLATION**

DAILY EXCEPT TUESDAY - 4 HOURS 35 MINUTES

TOURIST CLASS
$152.71 round trip

FIRST CLASS EXCURSION
$207.00 round trip
30 day limit

FIRST CLASS
$180.00 round trip

CUBANA AIRLINES

Miami in 1902, at the time of Cuban independence.

Downtown *Miami* in the 1920s.

The skyline of *Miami* in the 1930s.

Miami's Courthouse, known by the Cubans as *Cielito Lindo*, during construction in the 1940s.

(Continued)

(Continuation)

The entrance to
the road for
Miami Airport,
at the end of
Le Jeune Road,
in the 1940s.

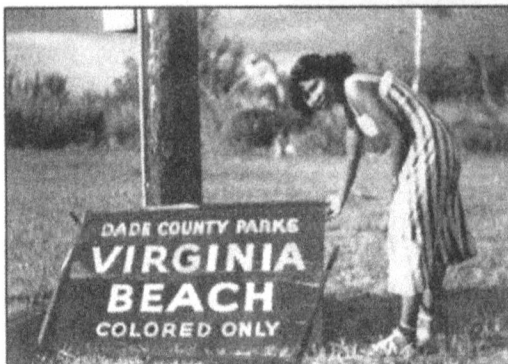

The entrance
sign for
Virginia Beach
in Miami, in the
1950s.

The **Dog Racing
Track** at
South Miami Beach
in the 1950s.

The **Nautilius Hotel**,
in *1959 Miami Beach*,
currently the location
of *Mount Sinai
Hospital*.

I

A Long Tradition of Political Exile

> «The newspaper *La Verdad* wants all Cubans to join
> the independence struggle, to break once and forever
> with Spain and, as owners of their own destiny, to decide
> what else can suit them for the future.
> *La Verdad* will not oppose the desire of most Cubans. »
>
> GASPAR BETANCOURT CISNEROS (AN ARDENT ANNEXIONIST EXILE)
> AS HE EMBRACED INDEPENDENTISM IN OCTOBER 1859.

> «This newspaper is born in the hour of danger,
> to keep a vigil on freedom, to insure that unity makes
> our forces invincible, and to prevent the enemy
> from beating us again due to our own disarray. »
>
> JOSÉ MARTÍ, PAGE 3 OF THE FIRST ISSUE OF
> HIS NEWSPAPER *PATRIA*, NEW YORK, MARCH 14, 1892.

ON SEPTEMBER 1, 1853, a few months after José Martí's birth in Havana, Cuban exiles met in New York City at 600 Broadway, just south of Hudson Street, after a Requiem Mass at the old St. Patrick's Cathedral in Mott Street. They were honoring Narciso López and the men *«who lost their lives while attempting to revolutionise (sic) the Government of Cuba,»* according to the heading *"The Cuban Invaders"* in the *New York Times* of September 3, 1852. The speakers were Miguel Tourbe Tolón, Francisco Agüero y Estrada, Tomás de Armas and Manuel de Arango.

«They all spoke warmly of the wrongs inflicted by the Mother Country... and lamented the loss of the brave men who had laid down their lives in the effort to liberate Cuba from her bondage,»

concluded the *Times*. It was not the first time that Cuban exiles would make their presence felt on behalf of Cuban independence, and would certainly not be the last.

Cuban Exiles in the XIX Century.

In the US, the second half of the XIX century witnessed the growth of a handful of Cuban exile communities that were determined to represent and support the noblest wishes of Cubans to be independent. Many such communities became coordinating centers for the Wars of Independence, and rendered invaluable assistance to the men fighting in Cuba (expeditions, shipment of weapons, procurement of funds, legal aid and jobs for new exiles). Perhaps the deeds of Narciso López and his *filibusteros* (1848, 1849, 1850, 1851) did not provide the most legitimate, inspiring and optimal initial impulse to the cause of independence (they did not get support from Cubans in the island because most of Lopez' men were adventurers who were not even able to communicate in Spanish), but it was a start that would be followed many years later by the men of 1868 and those of 1895.

Between the 1850s and 1895, Cubans in the US —many but not all of them political exiles— evolved from **annexionism** (at one time only comprising sugar baron émigrés, Cubans invested in the slave trade, thriving merchants and Spain decorated aristocrats) into **independentism** (which was initially supported only by tobacco workers, teachers, writers and intellectual émigrés). This transition was encouraged and affirmed by a lively community of Cuban exiles and a strong, free and vigorous exile press (Félix Varela's *El Habanero*, Cirilo Villaverde's *El Espejo*, Gaspar Betancourt Cisneros' *La Verdad*, among others), of which many of its brightest issues have been lost to history.

Needless to say, the transformation of pro-annexionists into pro-independentists was also a direct consequence of events happening in Cuba (the *Rayos y Soles de Bolivar* (1823) and the *Escalera* (1843) conspiracies, the *reformist* movement in Cuba, the *1868 War of Independence*, the accidental *sinking of the Maine* and others), in the US (the *Monroe Doctrine* in 1823, President Grant's initial sympathy for the cause of Cuban independence, for instance) and elsewhere (the Haitian revolt of 1791, the disastrous experiences of the former Spanish colonies after independence from Spain, the removal of Fernando VII from the Spanish throne, the Spanish *1812 Constitution*, among others).

As early as the 1820s there were Cuban exile or émigré communities in the US, particularly in New York, New Orleans, Key West and Philadelphia. It was a decade when, for the first time, Cuban exports to the US exceeded in volume the trade with Spain. Americans began to establish themselves in Cuba during those years (sugar barons and merchants) while Cubans began to move to the US. Some saw in the US a Mecca for education, second only to Europe, others were seeking improved job opportunities.

The US Civil War only interrupted this two-way flow momentarily; it regained impetus and attracted a wider representation of both societal flows after Lee's surrender to Grant at Appomattox Court House on April 9, 1865. It was after the Civil War that Cuban cigars became immensely popular worldwide and required expert hands in Key West and Tampa (to manufacture smokes in the US rather than having to import them from Cuba under the burden of US protective tariffs). By the end of the Cuban War of 1868-1878, there were 2,000 Cubans in Key West, 1,200 in Tampa, 3,500 in New Orleans and 4,800 in New York, plus about 3,000 in the rest of the nation. The production of cigars in Florida was to grow from 8 million in 1869 to 115 million by 1890. By then, the body of exiles included all professions: merchants, cigar makers, construction workers, industrial workers, physicians, teachers, journalists, clerics, cooks, sailors and even Cubans that enlisted as US soldiers.

The Exiles during the 10 Year War (1868-1878).

On October 10, 1868, almost as soon as Carlos Manuel de Céspedes, Francisco Vicente Aguilera, Perucho Figueredo and others, launched the insurrection in *La Demajagua*, near Yara,

Cuban exiles in New York formed the *Junta Revolucionaria de la Isla de Cuba* and issued a manifesto joining the *alzamiento*. Between the end of November and June of 1869 hundreds of Cuban exiles joined US based support groups and on December 10 of that year, the steamer *Galvanic* reached Cuba with the first contingent of rebels seeking the independence of Cuba. In total, close to 15 expeditions were organized and funded by Cuban exiles in the US. By January there were pro-independence committees in New Orleans, Key West and Philadelphia. Almost immediately a wave of exiles went to the US, particularly after the events at the *Villanueva* Theater in Havana, when pro-Spanish *voluntarios* stormed the theater in the middle of a function, launching three days of riots and terror in Havana.

All told, however, Cuban exiles during the War of 1868-1878 were a disappointment to the Cubans in the *manigua*. In New York, Key West and Tampa, Cuban exiles engaged in numerous unproductive discussions, internal fights and bitter polemics that eroded their ability to provide funds, men and materials for the war effort. All were unanimous in their desire to liberate Cuba from Spain, but they fought each other for popular supremacy (what today is called *protagonismo*) once the initial enthusiasm had produced tangible results. The internal struggles in New York between exiles supporting Manuel de Quesada (*Quesadistas*) or Miguel de Aldama (*Aldamistas*) became a serious division that would eventually end the support of the exiles to the fight in Cuba. By 1878 the war had been almost forgotten in New York and all that remained were pamphlets, speeches and proclamations of plans that were never taken seriously. Leadership had changed hands too many times. Serious political and military analysis disappeared, giving room to mistrust and insurmountable differences. Cirilo Villaverde resumed the situation with these words:

> «*Anexionistas, Concesionistas, Reformistas, Autonomistas, Independentistas... tarde o temprano todos les han vuelto la espalda a los hombres de acción en la hora de prueba.*»

Something similar also occurred in Cuba.

General Antonio Maceo had to reprimand General Vicente García for his divisionism and seditious actions in *Lagunas de*

Varona (1875) and *Santa Rita* (1877) against President Cisneros. In fact, the *Lagunas de Varona* revolt against President Cisneros has been viewed as a major contributing factor to the defeat of the rebel cause in the 10 Year War, because it interfered with General Máximo Gomez's advance to Western Cuba.

The *mambises* were reluctant to fight anywhere but in their own geographical areas and only under leaders known to them (Tuneros in the north of Oriente, Camagüeyanos in their province, Bayameses in southern Oriente), a condition that the leaders could never overcome. Céspedes became a victim of internal strife and was deposed as President of the Republic at Arms.

Finally, the *Comité del Centro* arranged for a surrender (*Pacto del Zanjón*) without consulting leaders like Generals Antonio Maceo, Guillermón Moncada, Flor Crombet, Tita Calvar and Jesús Rabí, among others.

As these things were happening in Cuba, the same lack of discipline was evident in New York. As would happen again many years later, the dissention among exiles went beyond a rivalry resulting from personal antagonisms, protagonism or strategic differences; the rivalries had profound ideological roots, and were probably impacted by serious economic and social differences among the exiles. So strong were these differences that they disengaged the exile communities in the US from the men and women fighting and risking their lives in Cuba. Two examples of lack of discipline and ideological differences follow:

Juan Clemente Zenea, after obtaining letters of recommendation from Miguel de Aldama and José Manuel Mestre, both important leaders of the *Cuban Exiles Junta* in New York, met behind their backs with the Spanish Minister in Washington, departed to Cuba and met with Carlos Manuel de Céspedes. There he argued in favor of **autonomy** rather than **independence**, expressing the opinion that little could be expected from the Cuban exiles in New York. This maneuver discouraged and disheartened many *mambises* in Cuba and resulted in a wave of surrenders to the Spanish troops.

On a similar vein, in the summer of 1871, Juan Macías, a member of the *Cuban Exiles Junta* and a close friend of José Morales Lemus, José Manuel Mestre and José Antonio Echeverría, received an appointment as official Cuban agent in London. On arriving in Great Britain, Macías decided on his own that, since England was a colonial power itself, it was not likely to support the *mambises* in their efforts to prevail over Spain. Without consulting with anyone, he published a pamphlet (*Cuba in Revolution*) favoring **autonomy** and used it to approach the British with the notion that

« Cubans were open to the establishment of a protectorate in the island similar to Canada, under the regis and guarantees of a great power such as England,»

to which Echeverría in New York responded that

«Cubans would be very foolish if they would allow to be imposed a new yoke, even if such imposition were to be under the guarantees of all the powers of Europe.»

This, of course, discredited the *Junta* in the eyes of Cuban exiles all over the world. Within hours of Echeverría's letter to Macías, he, Mestre and Aldama resigned their positions as members of the *Junta* and as diplomatic representatives of the Cuban Republic in Arms. This led to the appointment of Manuel de Quesada to the *Junta*—he was Céspedes brother-in-law and was already in New York— and the tragic incident of the *Virginius* (Quesada's follow-up to his *Galvanic* expedition) in October of 1873.

The Exiles between the Two Wars of Independence.

During the period between the two large Wars of Independence (1878-1895), **autonomismo** never recovered its prestige and many **independentistas** turned **reformistas** and joined ranks with a renewed Liberal Party. An initial attempt by exiles to back Antonio Maceo after his *Protesta de Baraguá* failed. Quesada, Aldama, Vicente García, Echeverría and, of course, Céspedes, were lost to the independence of Cuba. In New York the former opponents of Aldama took control of the *Junta*. In Key West the son of Carlos Manuel de Céspedes, José Poyo, Fernando Figueredo and others continued to meet. Calixto García (now in his 40s) moved to New York and assumed a position of leadership. In many US cities Cuban exiles continued to organize and so did revolutionary groups in the island of Cuba. But the disorder among Cuban exiles effectively ended all opportunities to initiate a new fight against Spain.

The first attempt to renew hostilities, la *Guerra Chiquita*, also failed. It involved close to 5,000 rebels under the command of Calixto García and Emilio Núñez. Cubans in the island did not support the exile-led movement since it only consisted of two very humble expeditions. After this failure the exiles lost whatever little enthusiasm they had; many revolutionary clubs disbanded, exile newspapers ceased publication, meetings and assemblies were infrequent and independence activity almost ceased to exist.

The Independence War of 1895.

It was not until 1880 that things began to change among the exiles. José Martí arrived in New York via Paris after having been deported from Havana. He became the leader of the *Club Revolucionario* after Calixto García left for the *manigua* in Cuba. Ramón Leocadio Bonachea arrived in Key West in 1883. He was the last man fighting in the War of 1868-1878, having never surrendered; he simply buried his weapons and went home. He was joined the same year by Carlos Agüero, a former aide-de-camp of General Julio Sanguily in the Ten Years War. Cuban exiles, for the first time in years of inaction, joined forces and threatened to riot when Agüero, at the request of the Spanish consul, was detained as a "*guerillero*" by federal authorities. Key West mayor, Livingston Bethel, fearful to lose his position, joined the Cuban exiles to press the federal government to release Agüero. On February 21, the US District Judge, also fearing to be voted out of his position, ordered the release of Agüero. Cubans from everywhere in Florida travelled to Key West and organized a 5,000 men demonstration celebrating the release of Agüero. Florida's Lieutenant Governor took part in the celebration, anticipating things to come over the next century. After his release, Agüero joined Bonachea and entered Cuba ready to fight for its independence.

When José Martí arrived in New York the prevailing opinion among Cuban exiles in the US was that a war in Cuba was unlikely to resolve the issue of Cuban independence and that the exiled community was ill prepared (mentally, strategically and physically) to carry out a successful struggle in Cuba. In Key West and Tampa the patriotic fervor of the exile leadership was competing with workers-rights issues in the midst of a deep US depression that had started in the late 1870s. Martín Morúa Delgado, for instance, (aged 24 at the time, son of an African slave mother, later to be elected first President of the Cuban Senate in 1901), joined and became a leader of the *Knights of Labor* movement (champions of the eight-hour day, end of child labor, rejection of strikes and supporters of workers cooperatives). Opposing Morúa were *"the three Enriqueses"* (Roig de San Martín, Messonier and Creci), who were competing for the loyalty of the Cuban cigar workers from the tribunes of *Alianza Obrera*, the Spanish anarchist organization. Cuban exiles in Florida began to move their interests from conspiratorial undertakings to the pressing socio-economic issues of the working classes.

Enter José Martí. With Cuban revolutionary fervor at a low ebb in Florida and the *Cuban Clubs* having lost 80% of their 1880 membership, Martí revitalized the patriotic fervor. In fact, he had to contend with two other pressing issues: a resurgence of sympathies for **annexionism** among Cuban exile professionals in the northern communities, Philadelphia, Washington and New York. Even former President Cisneros had told his friends that *annexionism* was still a valid option. In addition, he knew the *age of expansionism* was culminating and many in the US were working incessantly to expand the frontiers of the young nation. In the 1880s, from the perspective of the Cuban exiles, instead of fears of slave uprisings or a black republic, the neo-annexionists were exploiting the fear of a repetition of the destructiveness of the Ten Year War and the sorry spectacle of the fate of the former Spanish colonies in the rest of America.

Martí began his mission by denouncing the *1889 Pan American Conference* that President Benjamin Harrison had organized in Washington, DC. Harrison had attempted to annex Hawaii and the Samoan Islands and was a firm supporter of Cuba's annexation to the US. In a letter to Gonzalo de Quesada (who was acting as Secretary of the Argentine delegation to the Conference) Martí for the first time addressed the lack of support of the Hispanic republics towards Cuba, an issue that would continue to be significant 100 years later:

> «A large number of Hispano-American nations, for our large and incredible misfortune, are prone to ignore Cuba and assist the government of the United States to take over our country, leaving the key to the other America in strange hands.»

José Martí as the Master Strategist.

The strategist in José Martí told him that the key to stop pro-*annexionism* in the north and revitalize the pro-independence fervor in the south was to spend a lot of his time in Key West. He felt ready to undertake this mission and battle the annexionists with the same zeal that Céspedes, Aguilera and Agramonte had shown in the 1860s. At the San Carlos Club in Key West, in May of 1888, Fernando Figueredo, inspired by Martí, organized a massive meeting of Cuban exiles and began to collect funds. Women offered their jewels, cigar workers pledged a weekly portion of their earnings, and the rich dropped gold coins in an improvised safe box. Almost simultaneously Martí joined forces with Flor Crombet and Benjamín Guerra in New York and founded the *Club de los Independientes*. After Martí's pledge of a new insurrection, the New Yorkers were as generous as the Floridians. In Tampa and Ybor City the *Liga Patriótica Cubana* and the *Club Ignacio Agramonte* were born in December of 1890. By early 1892 Martí had revitalized all Cuban Clubs and the patriotic fervor was on the upswing.

Never in history had the Cuban exiles be so unanimously united. Martí knew his Cuban history very well. During the Ten Year War Céspedes had appointed his Cabinet without consulting the exiles. In 1880, Calixto García had organized the *Guerra Chiquita* in New York without consulting the exiles in Florida. In the early 1890s, when Máximo Gómez and Antonio Maceo tried to launch a new war of independence, they never thought of securing a full exile consensus. Martí, however, created the *Partido Revolucionario Cubano*, recruiting its ranks from the *Cuban Clubs* in New York, Philadelphia, Washington, Mexico City, Caracas, Ocala, New Orleans, Tampa, Jamaica, Panamá, Costa Rica, Santo Domingo, Key West and practically everywhere there was a Cuban exile to include.

He remained in constant correspondence with everyone, including his inveterate opposite Enrique Trujillo, editor of the New York newspaper *El Porvenir*. Trujillo believed the moment was ripe for «*incubation and not for war;*» preached that caution was required and insisted that the exiles should not be too militant so as to alienate pacific Cubans in the island. Deep down, however, Trujillo was envious of Martí's untiring vitality and charisma, «*capable to attract almost total loyalty from his followers,*» as Gonzalo de Quesada had expressed. He also disagreed with Martí's emphasis in Florida exiles, at the expense of those in the north of the US. For exposing these ideas, the *Consejo de Cuban Clubs de New York* denounced Trujillo for his divisionist writings and expelled him from its ranks.

Cuba in the 1890s, of course, was imploding; Spain could not contain the process of internal decomposition and the island was more and more economically dependent on the US for its survival. With a desperate short vision, the Madrid government was increasing tariffs, oblivious to a threatened US retaliation in the form of the 1890 McKinley Tariffs. Spain's 1879 Electoral Law (giving Cubans a place in the Spanish Cortes), and the full suffrage laws of 1890 (granting voting rights to all males only), turned out to be meaningless efforts. The Madrid appointed Captain General remained in full charge of Cuba's destiny.

Ignoring Trujillo's attacks, Martí expanded the support for a definitive war in 1895. He corresponded and met with veterans of the 1868 War like Carlos Roloff, Serafín Sánchez, Fernando Figueredo, Máximo Gómez, Piedad Figueredo, Juan Gualberto Gómez, Antonio Maceo, José and Rosario Lamadriz, José Dolores Poyo and Eduardo Gato. All the while he continued to raise funds, purchase weapons and ammunition and meet with *Cuban Clubs* every time he had an opportunity.

It did not mean he did not find difficulties and opponents, even among patriotic people like Juan Bellido de Luna, who from his leaning position towards *annexionism*, never backed the *Partido Revolucionario Cubano (PRC)*. Martí also had to respond to attacks from enemies of the PRC, like José Ignacio Rodríguez, a friend of Enrique Trujillo and also an annexionist, who not only called Martí *"un loco peligroso, eminentemente socialista y anárquico"* but accused him of

> «preaching hatred of Spain, hatred of cultivated and conservative rich men, having introduced in Cuba an element that had hitherto been unknown, for all movements of the country had always come from the upper class and the wealthy, and hatred for the United States, calling it an insolent race, which dominated the other countries of continental America, and against which he had pledged to fight without rest.»

The final spark that ignited the War of 1895, aside from Martí's escalating and relentless efforts, was the rejection of the plan of Antonio Maura, *Ministro Español de Ultramar*, who had presented a reform law to the Spanish Courts in 1894.

Cuba was ready for revolution and Martí responded with the *Fernandina Plan*. Its failure (ships and weapons were intercepted by the US Federal government), rather than a setback, created an unusual eagerness in Cuba. Within hours the enthusiasm that had been accumulating among Cuban exiles since 1868 exploded. Martí, Gómez and Maceo were received with great excitement in Cuba. The exile community responded without concern for race, wealth or political preferences. Slavery, past credentials from the 1868 War, previous loyalties to anarchism or socialism and workers rights became non-issues. Cuban exile polarizations between separatism, annexionism, reformism or autonomism were forgotten. New Patriotic Clubs were formed; the PRC was embraced almost universally by all exiles. The Cuban exile errors during the Ten Year War and the Guerra Chiquita were not repeated.

It was a radiant and promising moment for the independence of Cuba. Never again, throughout Republican times up to the fateful year of 1959, Cuban exiles were as necessary and had such a decisive importance in the future of Cuba.

Cuban Exiles
before 1959

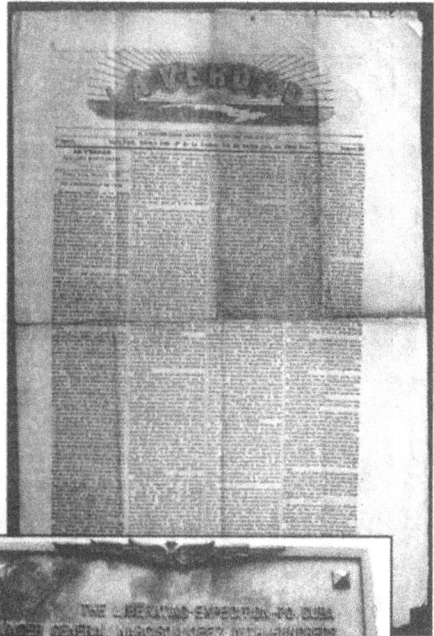

Cuban exiles in the mid 1800s.

Photos above, top to bottom, left to right:

José María Heredia; first exiled in Mexico in 1825, and again in 1837; a copy of the newspaper **La Verdad**, March 1, 1849, published by Miguel Teurbe Tolón; **Father Félix Varela**, forced to flee Spain through Gibraltar after speaking out against slavery while a member of the Spanish Cortes; a plaque commemorating the **Narciso López expedition** aboard the Creole, that left New Orleans on May 11, 1850; **Miguel Teurbe Tolón** in 1852; **Cirilo Villaverde**, editor of the newspaper *El Espejo* and author of *Cecilia Valdés*.

Photos above, top to bottom, left to right:

Francisco Vicente Aguilera, one of the wealthiest men in Cuba who gave his entire fortune to the War of 1868 and died poor as an exile in New York City; **Manuel Sanguily**, in January of 1868 landed in Cayo Romano from the *Galvanic* and rowed to Guanaja to join the Independence troops; **Manuel de Quesada Loynaz**, first war general landing in Cuba aboard the *Galvanic* in 1867; **Ana de Quesada**, sister to Manuel, second wife of Carlos Manuel de Céspedes; **Quesada** (l), **Aldama** (r) and **Céspedes** (seated) in 1864; the remains of the *Goleta Galvanic* in Matanzas in 1926.

One of the most prestigious Cuban families in exile was the **Loynaz del Castillo** family. They were linked by blood to Mayor General *Ignacio Agramonte Loynaz* and *Carlos Manuel de Céspedes del Castillo*, as well as General *Manuel de Quesada Loynaz, Salvador Cisneros Betancourt* and *Manuel Cardenal Arteaga*.

The family patriarch was **Don Enrique Loynaz Arteaga**, who owned the *Goleta Galvanic* and lent it to New York revolutionaries in 1868 for the first expedition supporting the uprising of October 10, 1868 in Oriente, Cuba. Don Enrique had bought the Goleta for $85,000 after winning the Brooklyn lottery on March 1, 1867. On the first of two trips to Cuba, the *Galvanic*, following a course Nassau-Cayo Romano-Guanaja, landed successfully with 1 cannon, 300 grenades, 2,600 Enfield rifles, 150 Spencer rifles, as well as ample quantities of ammunitions and dynamite. It was all bought with Lottery proceedings.

A second trip with the same itinerary on January 13, 1869, failed when the Spanish steamer *Conde de Venadito* was expecting it at Cayo Romano. The *Galvanic* eventually became a merchant ship in the coasts of Cuba and sank during the 1926 hurricane in Matanzas Bay.

Photos above:

The **Loynaz del Castillo** family in 1889, around Don Enrique (in a circle).
On the left, **Enrique Loynaz del Castillo**, oldest son, who met Martí in New York and Maceo in Costa Rica. He earned his Brigadier General rank in the Battles of *Mal Tiempo, Coliseo* and *Calimete* and authored the *Himno Invasor de Cuba*. To his right, his daughter **Dulce María Loynaz**, winner of the *Miguel de Cervantes Award*, the top honor in Spanish letters.

Cubans began again to seek asylum in the US during the start of the 1868 War of Independence. The pattern was well established in those years: the primary reason was to escape political persecution; the sanctuary was the US, a big, secure, prosperous and nearby country to the north, with its favorable climate and from where it was easy and fast to get back to Cuba openly or secretly. Exile always meant a short period of time after which things were back to normal in Cuba and conditions were favorable for a safe return.

*Photos: above, **José Martí** meeting with cigar workers at the cigar factory of **Vicente Martinez Ybor** in Ybor City in 1893; the Cigar Factory of **Eduardo Hidalgo Gato** in Key West; the Key West Cuban Club in 1895.*

The economic panic in the US in 1857 precipitated a pressure to raise tariffs to all items manufactured abroad. Cuba was not exempt of these decisions. Its exports to the US in the form of finished cigars were taxed at a rate of 40%. It strengthened the resolve of cigar manufacturers to open operations in American territory. Since Cuban manpower was readily available because of the uncertain security in Cuba, the solution was clear. It prompted a swelling of the exile population in Florida and a bonanza of entrepreneurs willing to open jobs for them in a foreign land.

After the *Pacto del Zanjón* capitulation at the end of the 1868 to 1878 Independence War in Cuba, those exiles viewed their return to Cuba with increased reservations. They had lived through an era of militancy among cigar workers and they began to support and sponsor the creation of powerful workers unions in Cuba. The *Workingmen's Mutual Aid Society of Havana*, the *Workers Brotherhood of Santiago de las Vegas*, the *Workingmen's Society of San Antonio de los Baños*, the *Gremio de Escogedores de la Habana* (in 1872), the *Unión Cubana de Rezagadores* (in 1880) and the *Gremio de Fileteadores de Cuba* (in 1886), to mention a few.

To close the loop, the Havana societies of workers began to influence and validate the exile communities in Florida, particularly in Key West. A prolonged and violent strike in 1889 and a well organized work stoppage in 1894 broke the back of many Southern cigar manufacturers and led many of the survivors to settle in the Tampa area.

All along, the cigar workers maintained their passion for the independence of Cuba. They inspired Martí in this task as much as Martí inspired them. Unlike the 1868 War, the new effort in 1895 was firmly and decidedly supported by the working class in exile. It made all the difference and distinguished the 1895 Cuban exiles as the most mature and active of all the exile groups that Cuba had in almost 100 years of its history.

Photo above: A meeting of the *Cigar Factory Workers of Tampa,* mostly Cuban exiles or Cuban exile descendants, as they went on strike in 1920.

The exiles during the 1868-1878 War took advantage of the presence of that supporting Cuban community in the US —mostly in Florida— that had emigrated due to the excessive taxes from Spain and the US taxes to the tobacco industry. That community was first established in Key West by men like **Vicente Martínez Ybor (1818-1896)**, a Spanish cigar manufacturer who moved his operations from Havana to the Floridian key in 1869. *His photo is at left.*

The two significant industries in Key West during the second part of the 1800s were cigar making and the trade based on shipwrecks. Both attracted a large number of Cuban exiles. Over the years cigar manufacturing gave rise to *Gatoville*, a prosperous industrial community that included housing, recreational areas, hospitals and schools, all built around the tobacco factories of **Eduardo Hidalgo Gato (1839-1926)**. Only the communities of Hershey in Pennsylvania (chocolate) and Lynn in Massachusetts (shoes) approached the scope of what Hidalgo Gato, a good friend and benefactor of José Martí had achieved in Key West.

Hidalgo Gato was one of the largest financial sponsors of the Cuban Independence War of 1895. He had been born in Cuba and fled to Key West to avoid imprisonment during the Ten Year War of 1868 for his support of the *mambises*. Originally he tried to start a cigar factory in New York City because of its closeness to the most attractive markets. He could not find the proper manpower and in 1874 moved to Key West. Soon he became involved with Monroe County politics and became the largest industrial tycoon in Florida. When other tobacco industries moved to Tampa, he remained in Key West and became one of the largest sponsors of the San Carlos Institute, founded in 1871.

Photos at right: **Hidalgo Gato** and Gatoville in 1891.

By mid 1870, there were over 65,000 Cubans living in the state of Florida, most of them of course, cigar workers. Perhaps as many as 1,200 aristocrats had settled in Europe and 2,000 middle class businessmen and professionals had emigrated to New York, Philadelphia, New Orleans, Atlanta and Boston. In places like Key West, Cubans soon became a majority of the population. All were not political refugees but most had clearly emigrated from Cuba for political reasons and —on both sides of the Atlantic— were imbued with revolutionary fervor.

Aside from their devotion to Cuban independence, the Florida exiles became participants in the political life of Southern Florida. By the time the 1868-1878 War ended, there were over a thousand Cuban exiles with US citizenship exercising their right to vote in Florida. In Key West, for instance, they elected **Fernando Figueredo Socarrás (1846-1929)** to the Florida House of Representatives from Monroe County. The man who had been secretary of Carlos Manuel de Céspedes, the President of the Cuban Republic in Arms, became the pioneer of many lobbying efforts on behalf of Cuban independence. *His photo is at right.*

. THE ISLAND OF KEY WEST.

. THE ISLAND OF KEY WEST.

Situated in Havana waters, was ceded to the United States in the year 1821, and utilized for a naval and coaling station for our Southern squadron.

Up to 1869 the island had but a few Cuban inhabitants supporting themselves upon the wrecks cast upon the reefs of the Florida Keys. About that year, Mr. Robert E. Kelly, a wealthy New York merchant, seeing the advantages of the Havana climate being the same as the climate of Key West, so essential to the manufacture of fine cigars, at once commenced to make Havana Cigars there. The island being United States territory, the excessive duty is saved on these cigars, and therefore can be sold cheaper than those imported from the Island of Cuba, but a little ways across.

Key West Cigar Factories.

A Key West correspondent of the Tribune writes that the business of cigar making from Havana tobacco at that place, is almost entirely in the hands of Cuban refugees. There are about 15 factories, large and small (mostly small,) and they employ about 1,200 hands. The wages vary from $18 to $45 a week, and as not only men but women and children are employed, many families have a respectable income. The cigar made may well be mistaken for a genuine Havana, and is intended to compete with it. No pains are spared to make it first-class and Havana-like. The Havana tobacco is used, Havana hands manipulate it, and in some cases even the water used in the manufacture of the cigar is imported from Havana. The result is an article which proves a most acceptable substitute, and would deceive 99 smokers out of a 100. It is sold at 33 per cent. less than the best Havana brands, and then proves remunerative. The average monthly product of the factories is about 1,000,000 cigars.

Photos: Two accounts of Key West and its Cuban refugees in the 1800s. *Left, San Francisco Evening Bulletin*, May 15, 1880. *Right: Georgia Journal & Messenger*, December 23, 1873.

By the time the 1895 Cuban War of Independence broke out, the Cuban refugees became a reliable source of funds for the Cuban struggle for independence.

Photo above: **José Martí** and the founders of the *Partido Revolucionario Cubano* in Key West.
Standing, left to right: Genaro Hernández, Serafín Bello, Aurelio Rodríguez, José G. Pompéz, Frank E. Bolio, Francisco M. González.
Seated: Gualterio García, José Martí, Angel Peláez.

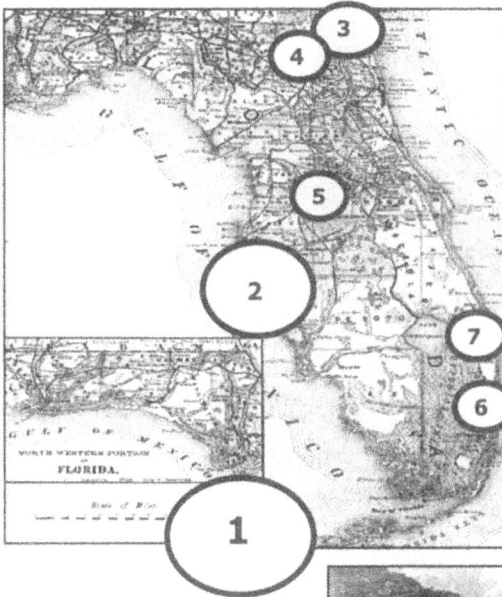

Graphic on the left:
Monetary Contributions of the Cuban refugees in Florida to the 1895 War of Independence. The size of the circles represent their relative contributions:

1- Key West
2- Tampa
3- San Agustín
4- Gainesville
5- Ocala
6- Miami
7- Fort Lauderdale

After the independence of Cuba, from the 1920s to the 1950s, Miami grew by leaps and bounds with the help of small groups of Cubans that came to the city as tourists —all year around. There were also many political refugees escaping from the turbulence in Cuba, mostly during the governments of Gerardo Machado and Fulgencio Batista. The city became a sanctuary for ever present political refugees from Cuba, a tradition that would last for over a century.

Photos above: the Miami River area in the 1920s and the Bayfront area in the 1950s.

A lifetime of political militancy of Cuban exiles in Miami.

Mario Garcia Menocal (1866-1941), the third President of Republican Cuba (1913-1921) went into exile in Miami in 1931 after running for President in 1924 against Machado. He had failed to start a revolution after Machado's re-election victory and moved to a stone mansion with tiled roof in Miami Beach, at Collins Avenue corner of Lincoln Road. From there on, Miami became the closest and friendliest place to be in exile while conspiring against the *status quo* in Cuba.

Gerardo Machado (1871-1939), Cuba's fifth President (1925-1933) went initially to Montreal and Paris but in 1934, as did many of his followers, established his residency in Coral Gables, on Anastasia Street near the *Biltmore Hotel*, until he died in 1939.

Carlos Prío Socarrás (1903-1977), Cuba's 17th and last Constitutional President (1948-1952) went into exile in Mexico and Miami in 1952, returning to Cuba in 1956 after Batista granted a general amnesty. He was soon forced back to Miami at gunpoint, returning to Cuba in January 1959 after the success of the 1959 revolution he had generously supported. His last Miami exile took place in December 1959, and lasted until his death in 1977.

Photos above: Cuban exiles meet at **President Menocal's** residence in Miami Beach in 1931; **President Machado** at his garden; and **President Carlos Prío** during his arrest at gunpoint in *La Chata*, his countryside home, by forces of General Batista in 1956.

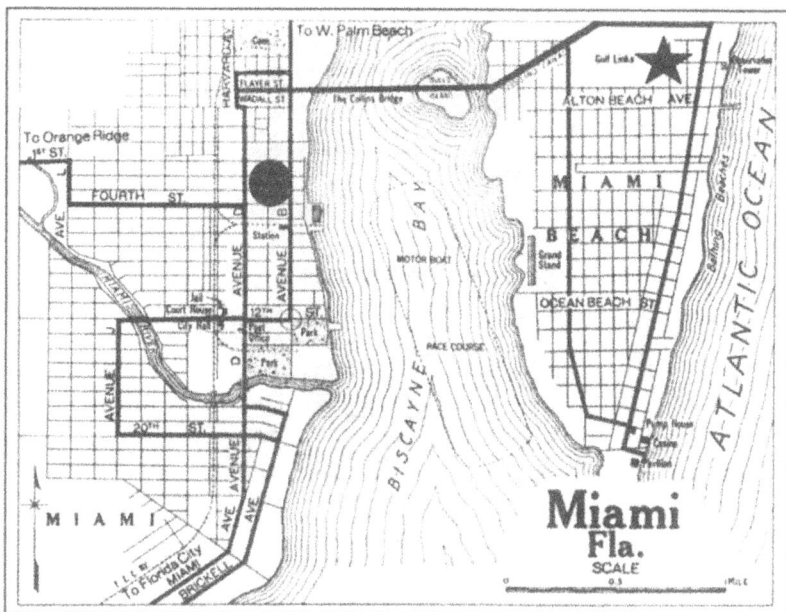

● Area of homes of Members of
the Directorio: around NE 1st
Avenue and 11th Terrace.

★ Mario García
Menocal's Home:
Collins and Lincoln Road.

While Menocal was quietly enjoying his 1931 exile a large group of Cuban refugees began to move to Miami as the government of Machado tightened its control of political life in Cuba. This second group—actually and literally the first *balseros* in Cuban history—concentrated on the Miami side of the intracoastal, living in inexpensive and crowded housing near the corner of 1st Avenue and 11th Terrace in the Northeast (see map of Miami above).

The group, mostly students from the University of Havana, was led by Carlos Prío, Tony Varona and Rubio Padilla, all members of the *Directorio Estudiantil Universitario (DEU)*. The DEU condemned both US intervention in Cuba and any US support for the Machado government. Those views were not popular among other exiles, hence contributions to their cause were meager, particularly from Menocal and his ever present friends. The DEU soon became a burden to the city government. Within a year their members increased and reached several thousands, enough to support or disrupt any political move in the city.

Eventually, Menocal won over the students by joining their cause: no US intervention, no US support for Machado. That move cost Menocal the backing of the NY Machado opponents rallied by former President Carlos Mendieta as a government in exile. Menocal, a refined gentleman with many connections among the Miami elite, got the DEU members the sponsorship of the *Pan American League of Miami*, an organization focused on the promotion of peace and understanding among all the American republics.

Carlos Prío, Antonio de Varona and Juan A. Rubio Padilla were in the 1930s outside the mainstream of Cuban politics when they sustained that most of the ills of Cuba were the product of a continuous dependency on US interventions. They described themselves as «*the purest and most cohesive of all the revolutionary groups.*» Once Menocal renounced the concept of seeking peace in Cuba by appealing to the assistance of a US intervention, the young Cuban exiles following the principles of the DEU began to receive the support they had been requesting from Miami's VIPs.

The affirmation came from Menocal, the smart and debonair Cuban millionaire from Miami Beach when he opened the doors of the *Pan American League of Miami* to the young exiles. The organization had been founded in 1930 as a non-political, non-profit and non-sectarian effort to promote friendship among all American republics. It had been founded by Mrs. Clark Stearns (of Bear-Stearns fame) with the support of Marjorie Stoneman Douglass. The League, at the request of Menocal, sponsored a fund raising affair at the home of Mrs. Hugh Matheson in Coconut Grove (the Church of Saint Hugh's was named after Mr. Matheson after a providential monetary contribution in 1929).

All VIPs in the city attended, with the exception of Frank Katentine, the mayor of Miami Beach. He alleged that «*the refugees were political enemies of the legitimate government of Cuba, and since the United States still recognized that government he felt that his name should not be used to encourage political strife between factions in any other countries.*»

(Continued)

Photos above: on top, the Matheson's residence in Coconut Grove and *Marjorie Stoneman Douglass. Below, Carlos Prío, Antonio de Varona and Juan A. Rubio Padilla.*

(Continuation)

Miami Beach Mayor Frank Katentine found out during a fund raiser for the *Pan American League of Miami* that a house on Collins and Lincoln was not only a magnificent residence but also a center for meetings, strategic sessions and money collections for the over-throw of the Cuban government. He became terrified and despond-ent fearing that the cultivated good will of Miami Beach hoteliers towards Cuban tourists could be affected. In 1931 Cuba accounted for close to 35% of the tourist business in Miami. In addition, Ma-chado was still in power and, in fact, an enthusiastic customer of the beach hotels.

At the time Judge Frank Stoneman, Marjorie Stoneman Douglass father, was the founder, editor in chief and foreign editor of *The Mi-ami Herald*. The *Herald* decided to ignore any news that could be read in Havana about the Miami Cuban refugees. It ignored its own customer's complaints by Miami Beach subscribers about daily meetings and noisy demonstrations along Lincoln Road. It ignored news of guns from the Miami National Guard Armory that had been stolen and shipped to Cuba. In fact, during early 1931 to late 1933, anybody wanting to find out what was happening in Miami with the several thousands of Cubans refugees had to read *The New York Times*. Aside from the apprehension of Judge Stoneman about the business of the Miami Beach hoteliers, a probable inducement to suppress the news about the Cuban exiles was that every Sunday the *Herald* was publishing five or more pages of advertising paid by the Machado government.

Photos above: Lincoln Road at Alton Road, looking East, in Miami Beach in 1931; the logo of the *Pan American League* of **Marjorie Stoneman Douglass**; ex-President **Mario García Menocal** on the side of his home; the Stoneman family in the 1890s, the Judge holding baby Marjorie (circle).

While the Cuban exiles formed alliances first with Menocal and later with both Menocal and Mendieta, the Cuban government was anxious to bring a solution to the Cuban crisis. Machado surprised everyone taking an amphibian *Sikorsy* aircraft to Nassau and later to Montreal, leaving behind his wife, who would be meeting him in Miami. It was up to Secretary of State, Orestes Ferrara, to face the succession crisis. Ferrara asked US Ambassador Sumner Welles to prevent bloodshed by mediating with the mobs celebrating the fall of Machado in the streets of Havana. Secretary Ferrara, a distinguished diplomat that had served as a colonel in the 1895 War of Independence, joined then the Cuban exiles in Miami, not without risking his life and his wife's, both in Havana during his departure on a *Pan Am clipper*, and also at his arrival in Miami.

In Miami, at Dinner Key Harbor, an angry mob of refugees was waiting for Ferrara and his wife shouting *carnicero, asesino, criminal...* (butcher, assassin, murderer). The Italian character in Ferrara could not resist confronting the Cuban exiles with even worst insults. His wife María Luisa, a beautiful lady to whom José Martí had dedicated a poem on a visit to Tampa, had to rescue him from the mob. Under heavy police protection Ferrara hired a taxi and rode to the Hollywood train station in Broward County where he boarded a Pullman for New York.

*Photos above: **Gerardo Machado**; **Orestes Ferrara** and his wife Maria Luisa; and Dinner Key Harbor in Coconut Grove, Miami, where hundreds of Cuban refugees waited for and harassed Ferrara in 1933. All photos from 1933.*

A slightly milder scene occurred in Miami upon the arrival of Machado's family. The Chief of Police had to use billy clubs to control the screaming crowd embarrassing Mrs. Machado. Ten exiles were arrested. The papers reported Chief Scarburo saying *«Anyone who wants to fight and raise hell should go back to Cuba. »*

Days later the *Herald* reported that *«some of these Cubans have been responsible for thefts of machine guns and pistols from U.S. armories that have found their way to Havana. »* In order to bring a quick solution to the Miami-Havana rift, the revolutionary government of Carlos Manuel de Céspedes sent a ship to Miami to return to Cuba the ten arrested exiles. The *Herald*, meantime, editorialized what a sensible loss to Miami had been the loss of so many valuable Cuban refugees at the same time. It added *«Miami's gates will always be open to Cubans, should the time ever come again when they need a refuge.»*

After 1933, the population of Miami began to fluctuate in numbers depending on the changes of government in Cuba. Over the years, as many Cubans decided to stay even after the causes for their exile had disappeared, the Cuban population of Miami continued to grow until it reached over 100,000 strong in 1958.

Machado's wife, Elvira Machado Nodal, and their three daughters Laudelina (Nena), Ángela Elvira, and Berta, eventually settled in New York. Machado, however, went to Nassau since he was fearful he would be extradited to Cuba. In 1934 he traveled to the Dominican Republic and Paris, and in 1936, he joined his family in New York, and then moved to Miami Beach. On 29 March 1939, Gerardo Machado passed away. He is buried in Miami's Woodlawn Cemetery.

*Photos: above, left to right: **Elvira Machado**; the Machado family in Nassau, days before the President's death in 1939: Nena and Angela Elvira standing up, Nenita, Mrs. Machado and Gerardo Machado seated, Angela Elvira's daughters on the ground; **President Gerardo Machado** in 1933 in Bermuda.*

In spite of anecdotic stories about hundreds of exiles during the Gerardo Machado presidency (1921-1933), the truth is that the flow of Cubans to the US during those years was lower than during the years 1902 to 1921, when the grounds for emigration to the US were mostly economic —taxation issues and severe crises in the sugar and tobacco industries— and not political.

During the second and third decades of Republican Cuba the political exiles were probably less numerous than those Cuban immigrating to the US to protect themselves from the perils of the great worldwide depression. All through the 1930s less than 10,000 Cubans went to the US, many of them to New York rather than Miami. Less than 1,000 made it to Europe, particularly Spain and France.

During the 1940s and 1950s, however, over 80,000 moved — probably permanently— north to the US, a fact well recorded years later (1989) in Oscar Hijuelos' *The Mambo Kings Play Songs of Love*. Many of these found comfort in the large migration of artists, musicians, radio personalities and athletes that made possible to live in a Cuban-friendly environment outside Cuba. By the time the great escape due to the revolution of 1958 occurred, close to 50,000 Cuban émigrés lived in the US in Manhattan, Queens, Brooklyn and Staten Island; 100,00 of them lived in the Miami area, probably 15,000 in Chicago, San Juan and Los Angeles and some 2,000 in Europe, mostly in Paris.

Photos above: Cuban entertainers in the US in the 1940s and early 1950s.
On the left, **Miguel Asante**, **Desi Arnaz Jr**. and **Antonio Banderas** as they were portrait in *The Mambo Kings Play Songs of Love*;
On the right, **Machito** and his Afrocubans in NY in 1946.

The comfortable exodus of Cubans to the US and Europe changed radically in the late 1950s. Cuban exiles worldwide moved to make the tragedy of Cuba known to everyone in Miami, Tampa, Paris and New York, among other places.

Photos above: a march of Cuban exiles along Flagler Street in Miami November 20, 1957; a *Tampa* newspaper reported the arrest of **Carlos Prío** and **Segundo Curti** for violating the *US Law of Neutrality* exporting weapons outside the US; a group of exiled Cuban ladies protesting in front of *Saint Patrick Cathedral* in Fifth Avenue, New York, in 1958; regular protest meetings took place at the *Place José Martí* in Paris during the late 1950s; Segundo Curti, Cuban Minister of Interior in the 1948 Prío Cabinet.

SInv SIM
Nro 955.

Quartel "Coronel Blanco Rico"
Ciudad Militar, 5 Agosto 957.

Al Señor Ministro de Estado,
Ministerio de Estado,
La Habana.

Señor:

Tengo el honor de relacionarle a continuación, las actividades de índole insurreccional que ha desarrollado hasta el presente CARLOS PRIO SOCARRAS, según datos que obran en nuestros Archivos:

6 Oct 1952:- Compró armas de varios tipos, así como gran cantidad de parque, y los trasladó para Costa Rica.

22 Oct 1952:- Le informó personalmente al comentarista y Periodista Norteamericano Walter Winchel, que había comprado armamentos en el Canada por valor de $195,000.00.

13 Feb 1953:- Le entregó $500,000.00 a Eufemio Fernández Ortega, para gastos de la revolución.

15 May 1953:- Se declaró como jefe máximo de la Organización secreta Triple A, y citó para una reunión en New York, a dirigentes de Partidos de Oposición del Gobierno de Cuba.

18 Ago 1953:- Elementos encabezados por Prío Socarrás, en combinación con otros elementos extranjeros, han adquirido gran cantidad de armamentos, destinados a una revolución en Cuba, habiéndolos ocultados en Haití, en cuya adquisición participó Aureliano Sánchez Arango.

26 Ago 1953:- El 30 de Jul de 1953, se reunió en su casa de Miami, con varios amigos y expresó que no descansaría hasta derrocar el Gobierno de Cuba, expresando que el próximo ataque sería al Palacio Presidencial, a la Cabaña y a la Ciudad Militar.

30 Ago 1953:- Prío Socarrás y Aureliano Sánchez Arango, comenzaron a planear un golpe de estado en las 6 Provincias de Cuba, siendo su principal objetivo un bombardeo aéreo a la Ciudad de la Habana.

9 Nov 1953:- Sostuvo una reunión con elementos insurreccionalistas, y entre otras cosas acordaron poner en marcha un plan de entorpecimiento a la zafra azucarera.

4 Dic 1953:- Fué arrestado en Miami en unión de Segundo Curti Messina, acusados de Contrabando de Armas con destino a una revolución en Cuba. Se le tomaron las impresiones digitales, siendo fichados y puestos en libertad bajo fianza de $50,000.00, teniendo que comparecer ante el Gran Jurado de New York para ser juzgados.

(Continúa en la hoja No 3)

Carlos M Cantillo, MSNP,
Coronel, Jefe del S.I.M.

joaf.

The proximity of Miami to Havana was a blessing that carried many risks. The Spaniards had sent spies to Florida during the independence wars. So did **Machado**, **Batista** and, most of all, the Communist regime from 1959 on. As many others, former President **Carlos Prío**, a main contributor to the struggle against his nemesis Fulgencio Batista from 1952 to 1959, was closely watched during his entire exile in Miami by Batista undercover agents.

Photo above: a copy of the 9 page report on all activities of **Carlos Prío** since 1952 presented to the government of **Fulgencio Batista** by **Carlos Cantillo**, head of the Cuban *Servicio de Inteligencia Militar (SIM)* in 1957.

The most dramatic effort of the Cuban exiles to overthrow the Batista government during the years 1952 to 1958 was the expedition of the *Corinthia* on May 19, 1957. At that time the *Movimiento 26 de Julio* of Fidel Castro had not been organized yet; its first public declarations were not made until July 12 of that year.

Former President Carlos Prío financed the military force that left Biscayne Bay headed for Cuba under the leadership of **Juan Calixto Sánchez Whyte (1924-1957)**, a former pilot of *Cubana de Aviación;* he had been born in Scotland while his father was a diplomat there in 1924. The expedition consisted of 27 members of *Organización Auténtica (O/A)* that landed in Cabonico, near Mayarí, Oriente, on May 23 without knowing that a *guardia rural* had spotted the ship and warned **Colonel Fermín Cowley**, the man in charge of the Holguín garrison. Through a spy, Cowley even knew the names of all the expeditionaries.

Calixto Sánchez' men (an advance group) were massacred after disembarking in Cuba as they crossed the *Brazo Grande River* on course for the *Sierra Maestra* Mountains. The *New York Times* falsely reported that sixteen rebels were killed in a battle; that they were all armed with rifles equipped with telescopic sights and machine guns and that the number of attackers had been 150.

A confidential report of Havana's *American Embassy Foreign Service Dispatch,* dated May 29, 1957, indicated that the capture of two rebels had been confirmed and that they had declared that «*they had no connection with Fidel Castro because he is a communist...*»

Photos above, from left to right: **Juan Calixto Sánchez Whyte**, 33, chief of the *Corinthia* expedition against Batista in 1957; the killing field at Cabonico, where the expeditionaries were assassinated after surrendering; Col. **Fermín Cowley**, chief of the Holguín barracks, who was murdered in the streets of Holguín a few weeks later.

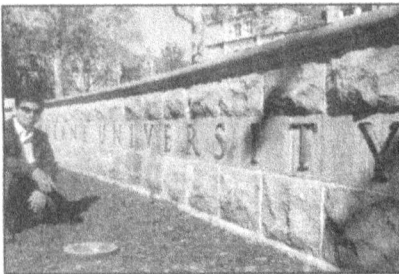

Many young Cubans in exile in the late 1950s took advantage of their situation to advance their education, a prized asset for most Cuban families.

Photos, top to bottom, left to right: some of the most popular and prestigious Colleges and Universities traditionally favored by Cubans in the 1950s: *International University in Paris, University of Florida* at Gainesville, the *Sorbonne* in Paris, *Georgia Institute of Technology, University of Miami, Tulane* in New Orleans and *University of Puerto Rico*.

In spite of previous outflows of refugees to Florida during the constitutional governments of **Fulgencio Batista** (1940-1944), **Grau San Martín** (1944-1948), **Carlos Prío** (1948-1952) and the unconstitutional government of **Fulgencio Batista** (1952-1958), nothing prepared the state of Florida for the largest migration of refugees to its shores, triggered by the events of late 1958, when the Cuban army disintegrated and opened Cuba's fate to the rebels of the *Sierra Maestra*.

Photo on the right: the startling NY Times photo of **Herbert Mathews** interviewing **Castro** in the Sierra Maestra on Feb. 24, 1957; *below*: Castro and Mathews in NY a few months later.

It was not difficult to anticipate a surge of Cubans leaving their country as the revolution became triumphant. Hundreds of middle class families began to retrieve their savings from the banks, either because they expected some sort of confiscation or because they secretly planned to leave the island. As the year 1958 was coming to a close, most of the upper classes had already placed abroad a good portion of their capital.

Photo above: middle class Cubans waiting in Havana for the doors of **Banco Godoy-Sayán** to open to take their money from their savings and checking accounts.

Starting in late 1958, all the way through October of 1962, Americans could drive their cars onto the *City of Havana* ferry at Stock Island, in Key West and, seven hours later, drive off the ship in Havana. By the same route Cubans of means could safely drive their cars into the US with all their possessions. A terminal, port and channel had been constructed at Stock Island at a cost of more than a million dollars; Americans referred to the ferry service as *"an extension of U.S. Highway 1"*; Cubans spoke of it as the *"continuation of Havana's Avenida del Puerto."*

Travelers were offered all sorts of accommodations, including lounge, snack bar, beverage bar and staterooms, all fully air conditioned. The 472-foot long ship had accommodations for 500 passengers, 125 automobiles and eight railroad cars. Round trip fare Key West to Havana or vice versa was $23.50 per person, with a charge of $76 per car. Staterooms could be reserved at a rate of $10 per room each way. Special travel packages were available, including four- or five-night stays complete with sightseeing and nightlife tours. There were three weekly departures from Key West and three from Havana.

All through 1958 and as late as 1962, rich Cuban families made use of the services of the ferry to take their assets to the US. In 1962, with diplomatic relations between the United States and Cuba coming to an end, the ferry was filled for a final trip with families and employees of the U.S. Embassy in Havana. The last trip out, made on October 31, carried 287 passengers 232 of whom were citizens of Cuba possessing U.S. residence permits. The remainder consisted of personnel of several Latin American States and the US State Department. Most of the 86 automobiles on board belonged to the American Embassy.

Photos above: An Ad for the *Key West to Havana* ferry;
the ferry boat and its terminal in Havana

The US government had experienced a similar inflow of political refugees after the 1956 events in Hungary, when hundreds of Hungarian dissidents sought refuge in the US after the Soviet Tanks had wiped out their comrades in the streets of Budapest. In fact, the US assigned the same man who organized the admission of Hungarians in 1956 to prepare for a possible uncontrolled incursion of Cubans in Miami after the fall of Batista: Under Secretary of the Army **Tracy Stebbins Voorhees (1890-1974)**.

Photos below: the tanks in Budapest as they were initially controlled by the rebellious Hungarians; a portrait of Tracy S. Voorhees in 1959.

Tracy S. Voorhees ended up serving from 1959 to 1961 as *President Eisenhower's Personal Representative for Cuban Refugees*. In his report to President Eisenhower at the end of his mission, on January 18, 1961, barely two years into the 1959 exodus of Cubans into the US, he commented:

«*The influx of Cuban refugees has approached almost 40,000 and continues at a rate of more than 1,000 a week. The principal port of entry has been and will continue to be Miami. Although there has been a large spillover to the New York area, including New Jersey, and to a relatively small extent to other cities, the majority will remain in the Miami area...*

«*About 6,500 Cuban students are going to the Miami public and parochial schools. 93% of them have been exempted from the $50 fee provided under Florida State Law; 18% have been exempted of necessity from school charges for instructional supplies; 6% have been exempted from lunch charges. School administrators report that many students are getting their only hot meal of the day at school...*

«*Teachers and administrators describe these young people as generally a very high type of student from ambitious, education-minded families... as many as two thirds of the students are unable to speak English... most of them aspire to a college education.*

«*These students have seen and heard much of fear and violence and are eager to adjust and learn... students that register with frightened faces one day are purposeful and adapted in a only a few days... there are a lot of very fine people coming into our schools. They will be fine potential citizens of the United States or fine ambassadors for us when or if they get to return to Cuba.*»

Despite the jocular commentary of many Cubans in later years, Miami was a city already undergoing a healthy development and fast growth when Cuban Refugees began to arrive in droves after 1959. It was true nevertheless, that it was blessed by the contributions of a new class of citizens that brought know-how, dedication and a sense of innovation and entrepreneurship to a city mostly famous as a winter paradise.

On the left: **Miami** in the 1910s, when it was indeed a swamp.

Right: **Biscayne Boulevard** looking south in the 1940s.

Left: **Biscayne Boulevard** looking north in the 1940s.

On the right: **Hotel Row** in Miami Beach during the 1950s.

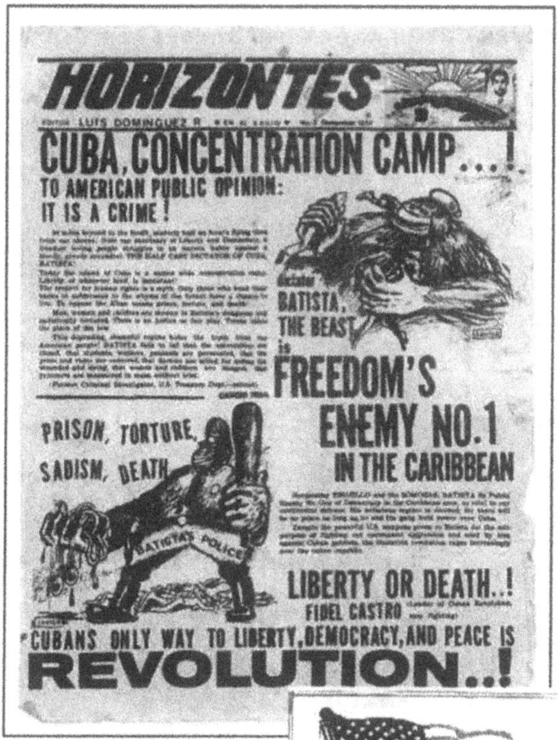

HORIZONTES

CUBA, CONCENTRATION CAMP...!

TO AMERICAN PUBLIC OPINION: IT IS A CRIME!

dictator **BATISTA, THE BEAST** is

FREEDOM'S ENEMY NO.1 IN THE CARIBBEAN

PRISON, TORTURE, SADISM, DEATH

BATISTA'S POLICE

LIBERTY OR DEATH..!
FIDEL CASTRO

"CUBANS ONLY WAY TO LIBERTY, DEMOCRACY, AND PEACE IS

REVOLUTION..!

AMERICANS:

In Cuba, 90 miles from the United States, there is a military base that threatens your security, and a subversion "sanctuary" that foments terrorism in the U. S. A.

Don't tolerate it any longer. We Cubans don't ask your money nor your army. We ask only recognition of the CUBAN INVASION GOVERNMENT, with former Cuban Supreme Court Justice Francisco Alabau Trelles as its President.

With your help, we Cubans can expel communism from Cuba and save America from the Russian peril.

SUPPORT THE

Cuban Invasion Government

After January 1st, 1959, the old posters appealing for help in the fight against Batista were replaced by flyers asking for support against the Communist takeover of the island. Most Miamians duly complied and opened their doors to thousands of Cuban refugees coming to Miami in unprecedented numbers.

1958 Miami: the Places Cuban Exiles will always remember.

Gesu Church,
First Avenue NE
and 2nd Street.

El Refugio
(earlier the Miami
News Building,
later the
Freedom Tower).

*Miami's Baptist
Hospital*, at
8900 N Kendall
Drive, before the
grounds were
finished in 1959.

Miami Amphitheater in *Bayfront Park.*

Miami Orange Stadium in 1958.

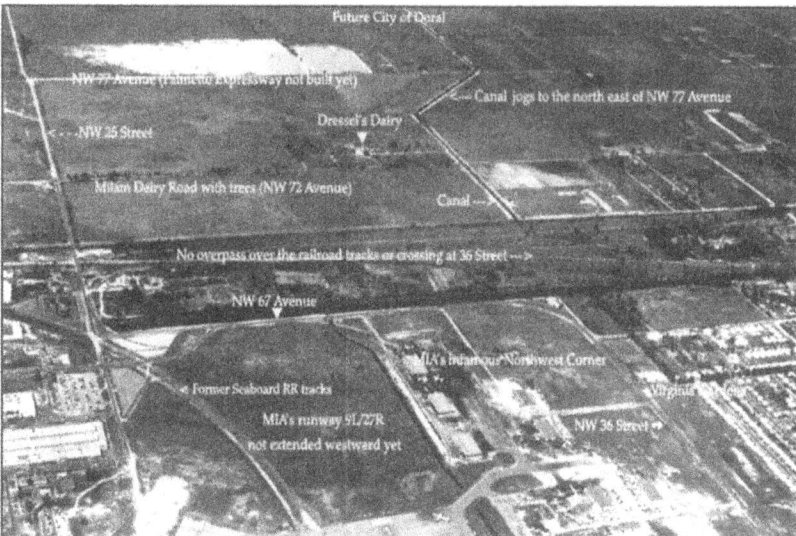

The area west of **Miami Airport**.

Miami Senior High School.

Cielito Lindo
Courthouse.

Lincoln Road Mall in
Miami Beach.

An Ad for **Royal Castle**.

Tower Theater on calle Ocho.

Dadeland Mall.

1958: Other Places Cuban Exiles will always remember.

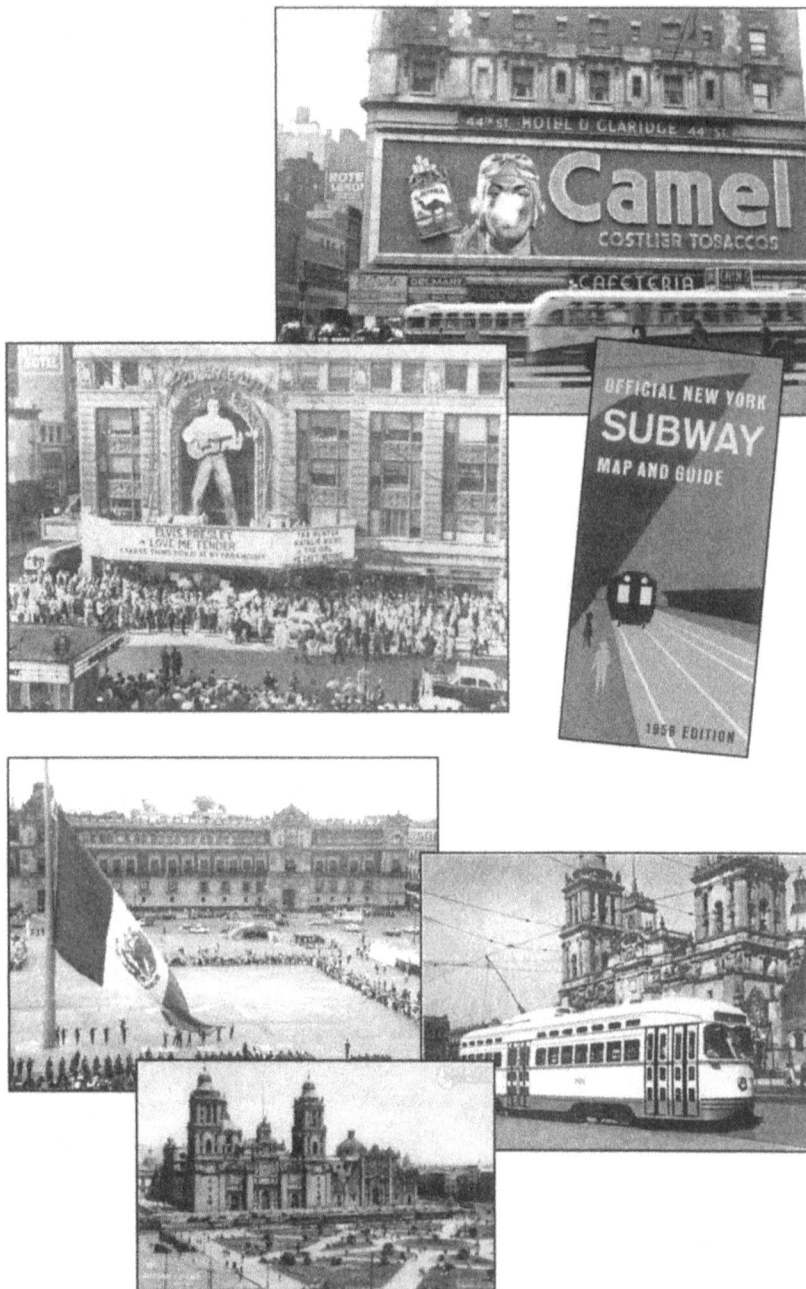

Photos above, from top to bottom: The smoking **Camel** billboard at Times Square in New York; the **Paramount Theater**; a 1958 **Subway Guide**.

Below: **Plaza del Zócalo** in Mexico City; the **Cathedral of Mexico** in 1957.

Photos above, from top to bottom:

A 1955 ***Citröen*** stationed by the Seine River;
Maison de Cuba at the Campus of the ***Cité Universitaire*** in Paris;
the ***Correos*** (Post Office) building in Madrid, by the ***Cibeles Fountain***;
Antonio Mingote, the popular Spanish caricaturist in 1958.

II

1959 and the Crucial 1960s
Times of Unexpected Deceit and Treason

«I know not what sweetness our native soil draws in all of us,
and never allows us to forget."»
OVID, THE POEMS OF EXILE.

«Let those who desire a secure homeland conquer it.
Let those who do not conquer it live under the whip and in exile,
watched over like wild animals, cast from one country to another,
concealing the death of their souls with a
beggar's smile from the scorn of free men.»

JOSÉ MARTÍ, APOSTLE OF CUBAN INDEPENDENCE.

EXCLUSION OF THE OPPOSITION has always been the natural outcome of all authoritarian rulers and tyrants. It is only in despotic and totalitarian regimes that those fallen from power or clearly in the opposition, are inevitably forced to take the roads of confinement and exile; so has been the case in Cuba since 1959. Cuban politics after 1959 has been a game of exclusion, unparallel cruelty, criminality, radical and undeserved loyalty, patronage and favoritism.

Exile, however painful, has traditionally been a formative and maturing political and humanistic experience. Such has been the experience of almost all nations in world history. During colonial times and the first half century of the Cuban republic, for instance, occasional exile periods always played a vital part in shaping the form and styles of the political condition of the nation. It has been the case in most exiles in world history. The examples abound: José Martí, Rómulo Betancourt, Alexander Solzhenitsyn, Frédéric Chopin, Leon Trotsky, Sigmund Freud, Friedrich von Hayek, Dante Alighieri and Victor Hugo, to mention a few. After 1959, however, the new Cuban political regime became so excluding, heartless and brutal that the exile it provoked was and has been to this day completely marginalized from the development of a future Cuban society.

The First Exiles in 1959

Following the fall of Santa Clara, the flight of Fulgencio Batista and his men and the general strike summoned by the Castros from *Sierra Maestra* on January 1, 1959, hundreds of former officials from the armed forces and the government (many of them, but not all complicit with the *Batistato*) began a strategic mass escape from Cuba prompted by real physical or psychological fear for their lives and certainly for their lifestyles.

These initial exiles were accompanied by some law-abiding civilians that had not been involved in any political or military actions but were driven by a collective intuition that things were going to get very bad in Cuba. By mid 1959, however, the would-be-refugees had more than just their intuition to justify their escape from Cuba. The Castro brothers began to institutionalize in the Cuban judicial system a practice that had a well established precedent in the *Sierra Maestra* during the years 1957 and 1958, when the Castro brothers and Ernesto Guevara acted as prosecutors, juries and executioners of those *camaradas* they found less than enthusiastic about the motives and strategies of the revolution. In the relative obscurity of the jungles of Oriente Mountains there were many death sentences after precipitous and slap-bang summary trials for which there were never any appeals and no rational and competent defenses for the accused. These practices were carried to the Cuban cities early in 1959. Hundreds of young students began to fall into the hands of Ernesto Guevara and were shot in the prison of *La Cabaña*, in Havana, as dozens of military men had their trials in a circus atmosphere at the *Sport Coliseum* in Havana and other public venues, followed by executions filmed and presented in the movie theaters all across Cuba as a warning that the revolution meant business.

Given those distressing and well publicized events, would-be-refugees began to escape the island, even when it became known that most of their properties and belongings would be seized by the government. They knowingly and willingly discarded their homes, savings, jobs, friends, families and lifetime memories. They were more than amenable to face an uncertain future in a foreign country rather than suffer the despair and hopelessness that many of them had known from exiles that had come to Cuba from Eastern Europe after World War II. They were not willing to bind their future to the uncertainties of the Castro regime, or the known abuses of Communist regimes in Europe.

Initially the majority of civilian exiles from Cuba belonged to the upper crust and to the middle layers of society: professionals in business, science, medicine and the law. Intellectuals and artists fled the island as well. All those who had worked for their own future began to be seriously threatened by the Communist (or Castrist) takeover. Soon, however, the exodus (still in its infancy) involved people from all walks of life and all parts of Cuba. Small business owners, clerks, teachers, homemakers, union members, fishermen, dockworkers, everyone who knew of the 1956 Hungarian revolt, had listened to the dreadful stories about massacres in the Soviet gulags or knew of the violence of the Russian Revolution. They began to have strong reservations about remaining in Cuba if there were alternatives. It became a reprisal (in reverse) of what had happened in Spain after the front at the Ebro River collapsed in 1939 and the Republican Government ordered the evacuation of Barcelona. It was still a sort of a preventive movement, sparked by an intuitive concern for things to come. People trying to depart before the situation worsened, while there was still time to leave peacefully, with some capital and easy to remove personal and family belongings.

The Regime Begins to Show its Intentions

By the fall of 1960, however, the first severe blow of Communism to the island of Cuba took place: the nationalization of all corporations, industries, farms, real estate and most of the small businesses in the country. With a callous concern for Cuba's future, the Communists precipitated the flight of thousands of Cubans that managed and made a living in Cuban-owned work centers; it represented the largest and swiftest loss of know-how ever recorded by any developing country in modern times. It lasted some twenty years, well into the 1980s.

Cuba has never been able to make up the loss of well educated and skillful citizens during that savage mistake. In time, the losses proved to be irreparable. Successful achievers like Roberto Goizueta, the entire Bacardí family, Jorge Pérez and Felipe Pazos in business and finance; Nicolás Quintana and Max Borges in architecture; Marcelo Alonso, José Ramón de la Vega and Manuel Suárez Carreño in the sciences and engineering; Roberto Estopiñán and Gay García in Sculpture; Nivaria Tejera, Guillermo Cabrera Infante, Enrique Labrador Ruiz, Heberto Padilla and Severo Sardui among the writers; Agustín Acosta, José Angel Buesa and Luis Mario in poetry; Marta Pérez, Olga Guillot and Celia Cruz in the vocal arts; Rosendo Rossell and Rolando Barral in the scenic arts; Jorge Camacho, Rafael Soriano, José Mijares, Agustín Fernández, Joaquín Ferrer and Gina Pellón among the painters; León Ichaso, Nestor Almendros, Mari Rodríguez Ichaso and Andy García in film making; Juan Clark, Carlos Alberto Montaner, José Ignacio Lasaga, Jaime Suchlicki among political and social analysts; Jorge Bolet, Paquito d'Rivera, Israel Cachao López and Arturo Sandoval in music; Nilo Cruz, Oscar Hijuelos and Carlos Eire among future Pulitzer and National Book Award winners-to-be; Fernando Bujones in classical dancing, to mention just very few. For many of them, Miami or New York, rather than Havana, became the cities where they wanted to live, work, play and share their lives with their compatriots. It was a gigantic loss to Cuba.

A Complete Change of Game in 1961

When the exiled-backed *Bay of Pigs* invasion failed in 1961, things got even darker and a new wave of exiles left Cuba. Until then many Cubans in the island were either making up their minds, or waiting for the right time to act or actively trying to escape. After April 18, 1961 those patient souls that had hoped for a quick resolution of the miserable experience that Cuba was suffering decided to leave. Cubans going into exile, now in greater numbers than in 1959, became a great source of quality manpower and responsible citizenship for the US, as well as a safety valve for the revolution in Cuba. The Cuban middle class was now decimated: clerical workers, butchers, masons, middle managers, trade specialists, lawyers, teachers, engineers and thousands of students took advantage of freedom flights, secured visa waivers and escaped to the US and Europe. Many of them had initially supported the revolution but now were certain that the exit doors to Cuba would soon be closed. In retrospect the unstoppable wave of refugees after 1961 drained the capability of Cuba to function as a viable society but also removed a vast majority of disaffected citizens that would have weakened and subverted the revolution. Many Cubans, before and after Girón fought valiantly against the imposition of Communism in Cuba. On balance, however, the flight of refugees impaired forever the future of Cuba while making the revolution immeasurably stronger.

The New Order takes hold in Cuba

In the rest of the 1960s, the *Escambray Mountains* of Cuba briefly became the fighting landscape for many disillusioned former members of the revolutionary government. The steep and intricate slopes of the mountains between Cienfuegos, Trinidad and Sancti Spíritus soon turned into the killing fields of the revolution. The Castro regime emptied the *Escambray* of all its inhabitants to have a clear shot at the belligerents. It was a move clearly inspired by Valeriano Weyler's reconcentration strategies during the 1895 War of Independence and by Hitler's *völkermord* during WWII. The *Escambray* witnessed the last heroic fighting moves striving to defend Cuba from the usurpers that were imposing a "new order." It was a ferocious display of what the Castro regime would become; it was genocide.

Finally, as the decade was closing, the exit ramps to escape the revolution were shut down and Cuba became a land so far distant from the exiles as if it were at the end of the civilized world. Families were caught with an impregnable wall that separated those who stayed in Cuba from those who fled. Phone communications were curtailed and limited only to official government business. Correspondence between brothers and sisters, mothers and children, old men and women with their little ones, was interfered and sometimes purposely thrown away. Not one of the Hispanic American countries tried to intervene on behalf of the Cuban people. In the words of *Nestor Almendros*, a genial Oscar-winning Cuban exile cinematographer, *"nadie escuchaba."*

In this and the following chapters, it is important to recognize that the changing themes of the exile's reactions have to be seen through the lens of what was happening in Cuba at the time; hence our emphasis in describing the contemporary realities in the island when describing the feelings, thoughts and behaviors of the exiles across the seas.

MAY I HAVE YOUR ATTENTION
by Garrinche

1959 and the 1960s

The world press recorded the fall of Batista and the triumph of the revolution in Cuba on January 1, 1959.

The New York Times.

BATISTA AND REGIME FLEE CUBA;
CASTRO MOVING TO TAKE POWER;
MOBS RIOT AND LOOT IN HAVANA

The most important account of the fall of Batista —for obvious political reasons— was probably the endorsement of Castro by the *New York Times*, which after all had been instrumental in getting Castro's forces to prevail in Cuba.

Photos above: the Jan 2, 1959 edition of the *NY Times* and the humorous advertisement of the *Times* in the *NY Subways* throughout most of 1959.

As soon as the revolutionary government was installed in Cuba in January of 1959 it began to characterize its opponents as evildoers and criminals or former *batistianos* seeking revenge for their having been thrown out of power. Many former revolutionaries, however, were dismayed by the efforts to turn Cuba into a Marxist country and began to oppose the Communists inside Cuba or go into exile to resist what they perceived as an unrelenting drifting of Cuba into Communism. ***Many organizations were founded in those months between 1959 and 1961. By all accounts there were too many of them.*** It unquestionably explains the main reason they did not succeed in stopping the fall of Cuba into the claws of the Soviets. Because of their patriotic intentions and inspirations, however, their actions, their generous sacrifice and their presence are worth mentioning here:

- At the end of January of 1959 **Salvador Díaz Versón** denounced the presence of numerous international Communists in Cuba at a Journalist's Congress in San José, Costa Rica.
- Former members of Castro's Rebel Army joined forces and organized the *Legión Democrática Constitucional* under the leadership of **Evelio Duque Miyar**, who would later take up arms in the *Sierra del Escambray*.
- Cuban Air Force Commander **Pedro Luis Díaz-Lanz** escaped with his plane to the US and denounced the presence of Communists in Cuba at a session of the US Congress.
- In December 1959 three important anti-Castro organizations were founded in Havana: the *Movimiento de Recuperación Revolucionaria* (MRR), with **Manuel Artime** as leader, the *Movimiento Demócrata Cristiano* (MDC), with **José Ignacio Lasaga** as leader and the *Frente Nacional Democrático Triple A (FND AAA),*whose leader was **Aureliano Sánchez Arango**.
- In February of 1960 sixteen *University of Havana* students were arrested after they removed from the statue of *José Martí* in Havana the flowers deposited there by **Anastas Mikoyán**, Vice Premier of the USSR.
- All through 1959 and 1960 numerous efforts to challenge the control and success of the Communist economy in Cuba (mostly burning of cane fields and city shops) culminated in the explosion of a French cargo ship, **Le Coubre**, at the *Pan American Docks* in Havana harbor.

(Continued)

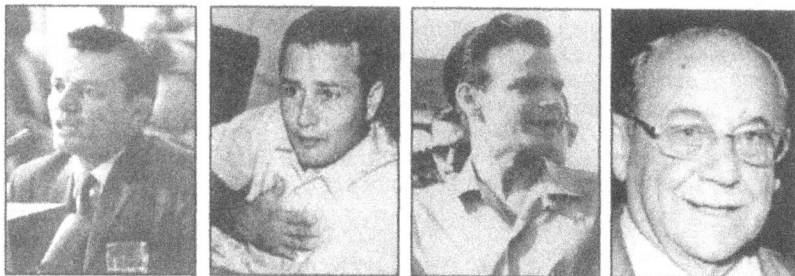

Photos above, left to right:
Pedro Luis Díaz-Lanz testifying before the US Senate's Internal Security Committee on July 14th 1959; **Evelio Duque Miyar**, one of the first men who fought Castro in the *Escambray Mountains*; **Manuel Artime Buesa**, founder of the **MRR** and political leader of the *Brigade 2506* during the *Bay of Pigs*; **José Ignacio Rasco**, classmate of Castro, prestigious journalist and historian.

(Continuation)

- In March 1960, the *November 30 Movement (M-30-11)* was founded, with **David Salvador**, a former labor leader, as its leader. Several organizations joined forces under the umbrella of the *Frente Revolucionario Democrático (FRD)*, with **Enrique Ros** as the National Coordinator
- In May the *Frente Estudiantil Universitario Democrático (FEUD)*, later known as the *Directorio Estudiantil Revolucionario (DER)*, was founded in Havana with **Juan Manuel Salvat**, **Alberto Muller** and **Luis Fernández Rocha** as its leaders. Also founded in May were the *Movimiento de Rescate Revolucionario Democrático (MRRD)*, with **Manuel Antonio de Varona** as the leader and *Agrupación Montecristi (AM)* with **Justo Carrillo** as the leader.
- In June **Pedro Luis Díaz-Lanz** became the founder of *Movimiento Cruzada Cubana Constitucional (MCCC)*.
- In July, the *Colegio de Periodistas de Cuba en el Exilio* was founded in Miami by some of Cuba's most prestigious journalists: **Armando García Sifredo**, **Francisco Chao Hermida**, **Ernesto Montaner** and **Salvador Díaz Versón**.
- In the month of August of 1960 several organizations (*30 de Julio, Resistencia Cívica, Acción Democrtática Revolucionaria and Verde Olivo*, among others) joined forces to form the *Movimiento Revolucionario del Pueblo (MRP)*, with **Manuel Ray, Felipe Pazos, Raúl Chibás, Rogelio Cisneros, Amalio Fiallo, Reynol González** and **Rufo López Fresquet** (all former supporters of the revolution) as leaders.
- Also during August, the *MRR, Organización Auténtica*, the *Frente Anticomunista Cubano* and *Cruzada Constitucional*, joined forces as *Alianza por la Liberación de Cuba*.
- In September, during training exercises in Guatemala, **Carlos Rodríguez Santana**, (Carlay), died. He was a student of Medicine, member of the MRR and the brigade that had plans to invade Cuba. His ID number was **2506**, and the Brigade took that number in homage to him.

(Continued)

Photos above, left to right:
Carlos Rodríguez Santana (1938-1960), a member of the MRR, who died in Guatemala while on training for an invasion of Cuba that resulted in the *Bay of Pigs*; **Manuel Ray**, former Project Manager for the construction of the *Havana Hilton* and founder of the MRP in exile; the founding members of the *Frente Revolucionario Democrático*: left to right, **Manuel Artime, Antonio Varona, José Ignacio Rasco, Aureliano Sánchez Arango** and **Justo Carrillo**.

(Continuation)

- In September, several organizations joined the *Frente Revolucionario Democrático (FRD)*: *Movimiento Institucional Democrático (MID)*, *Movimiento Acción Recuperadora (MAR)*, *Comité de Liberación de Cuba (CLC)*, and the *Bloque de Organizaciones Anticomunistas (BOAC)*. Also, the *Movimiento de Rescate Revolucionario (MRR)* was founded under the leadership of **Laureano Batista Falla** and **Luis Aguilar León**.
- In October Cuban union activists in Miami organized with **Pascasio Linares** the *Frente Obrero Revolucionario Democrático (FORD)*.
- During the first days in November, a new organization, *Unión Nacional Democrática 20 de Mayo (UND-20-05)* issued a manifesto asking for unity. It was signed by its leader **Andrés Vargas Gómez**.
- At the end of November, the *Directorio Magisterial Revolucionario* was organized in Miami under the leadership of **Oscar de la Vega Torres**.
- Early in December, the *Colegio Nacional de Locutores de Cuba en el Exilio* was founded in Miami by **Ramiro Boza Valdés** and **Juan Amador Rodríguez** and the *Colegio de Abogados de la Habana* met in Miami under the presidency of its Dean, **Silvio Sanabria**.
- In September of 1960, a group of students from the University of Havana organized in Miami the *Directorio Revolucionario Estudiantil en el Exilio*. A communiqué was issued, signed by **Alberto Muller**, **Ernesto Fernández Travieso**, **Jorge Mas** and others. Several organizations joined efforts under the *Movimiento Unidad Revolucionaria*, led by **Octavio Barroso**.
- On December 20, the *Asociación del Poder Judicial de Cuba en el* Exilio was founded under the leadership of **Francisco Alabau Trelles**.
- Two days later, on the 22nd, 23 clandestine groups in Havana joined forces to form *Unidad Revolucionaria*, under the leadership of **Rafael Díaz Hanscon, Marcial Arufe** and **Octavio Barroso**. Barroso and Arufe would soon be killed by forces of the Cuban State Security.

Altogether, close to **45 libertarian and democratic organizations** were founded in Havana and Miami during the first two years of the Cuban revolution. They were integrated mostly by idealistic young Cubans trying to contain the slide of their country into Communism. None had political aims; none of those mentioned above were staffed by pro-Batista followers; less than a handful of these groups included former Cuban political or military personalities.

(Continued)

Photos above, left to right:
Luis Aguilar León, professor to *Bill Clinton* at *Georgetown University* and a classmate of *Fidel Castro* in Cuba; **Andrés Vargas Gómez**, captured after slipping back to Cuba, served 20 years in jail; **Alberto Muller**, student leader, professor at the *University of Miami*, suffered 15 years in prison in Cuba; **Justo Carrillo**, old opponent of Machado and Batista, very respected as an economist during Cuba's republican period.

(Continuation)

Over the last half of the 20th century, while hundreds of Cubans were taking the road to exile, many outspoken men and women of letters, journalists, artists and politicians became intoxicated and enraptured by the words of Fidel Castro and Ernesto Guevara; they worshiped both as inspiring romantic revolutionaries and could not resist their instigating and inflammatory rhetoric.

Castro's sympathizers included people like **Jean Paul Sartre**, **Simone de Beauvoir**, **Waldo Frank**, **Wright Mills**, **Gabriel García Márquez**, **Guayasamín**, **José Samarago**, **Ernest Hemingway**, **Pierre Trudeau** and **Juan Carlos Onetti**, to mention a few. Many of them came to be fellow travelers of the Castros and Guevara through the influence and exposure to **Jorge Ricardo Masetti's** *Prensa Latina,* an international press agency doubling as a propaganda vehicle for Castro and his revolution. *Prensa Latina* was founded in Cuba in 1959 by Masetti, an Argentinean journalist turned revolutionary leader; a tragic figure, he died in 1964 after blindly following Ernesto Guevara in his revolutionary adventures.

Over the years Masetti was sometimes portrayed as a virulent anti-imperialist, a former Argentinean *Montonero*, Nazi sympathizer and avowed Peronist, who later denounced and abandoned each of these credos, as was the testimony of **Rodolfo Walsh**, an Argentine journalist co-founder of *Prensa Latina*; other times he was presented as a young tango vocalist and light-weight journalist who married Celia Dorita Jury, his first sweetheart, and every Sunday went with her to Mass at 11:00 am, according to **Conrado Yasenza**, a prize winning Argentinean poet and journalist. Yasenza even quoted Masetti's reasons for going to Cuba in 1958: «*Sé que Batista es lo peor. Pero hay que ver si los otros son o no son comunistas,*» (I know Batista is bad but I have to check if the others are or are not Communists).

(Continued)

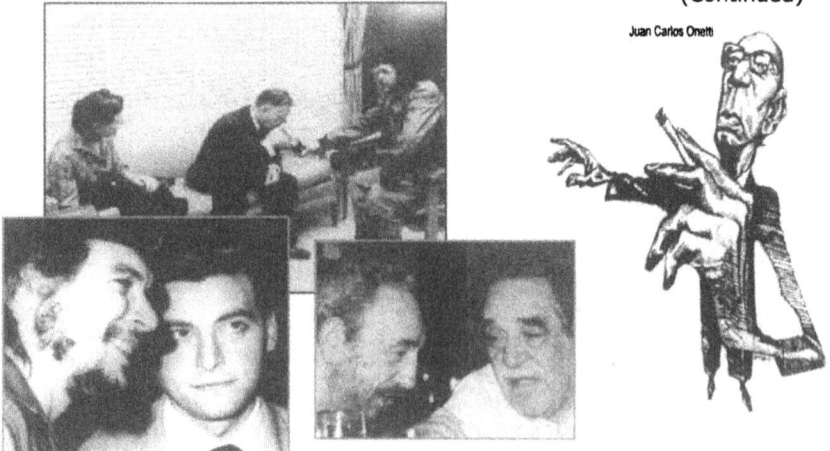

Juan Carlos Onetti

Photos above, left to right:
Jean Paul Sartre and **Simone de Beauvoir** with Guevara in Havana,
Masetti with Guevara; Castro with **García Márquez** and a
Cartoon of **Juan Carlos Onetti**.

(Continuation)

A year after founding **Prensa Latina** in June of 1959, Masetti abandoned his wife for Concepción Dumois, his Cuban secretary; six months later he was separated from the direction of **Prensa Latina** and began to follow Guevara and his revolutionary escapades. In 1962 his orders were to secure help for **Houari Boumediene** and his *Algeria National Liberation Front*; in 1963 he infiltrated and led —as *Comandante Segundo*—the guerillas in northern Argentina. His name **Segundo** (second) alluded to a **Primero** (first), Guevara himself, who was supposed to join him as the main guerrilla leader. To Masetti's dismay, Guevara never showed up and Masetti escaped to the jungles of *Salta*, Argentina, where he was killed.

Prensa Latina, however, continued its lurid and murky mission for many years and became the main assault instrument of the Cuban government against Cuban exiles and against the leaders of free nations in Latin America and Africa.

Photos above, top to bottom, left to right:
Three pro-Castro books from the 1960s by *Jorge Masetti*, *C. Wright Mills*
and *Robert Wright*; Castro with Ecuadorian painter *Guayasamín*,
and with *Nobel Prize* writers *José Samarago* from Portugal
and *Hemingway* from the US.

(Continuation)

In spite of serious setbacks by the anti-Communist guerrillas operating in Cuba since early 1959, Cuban exiles and opponents of the
Revolution in the island were cooperating in preparing the invasion
to Cuba from somewhere in Central America. In the meantime, the
events in Cuba were occurring at an accelerated pace:

- On January 4, 1961, **Pedro Luis Boitel**, who had been denied the presidency of the *Federation Estudiantil Universitaria (FEU)* through government pressure, was sentenced to a long prison term. He died in prison
  many years later after a valiant hunger strike.
- The following day, January 5th, the freedom guerrillas at the *Escambray
  Mountains* took **Conrado Benitez**, an informer infiltrated in their lines, to
  a firing squadron after a summary trial.
- In February the *Colegio Nacional de Procuradores Cubanos en el Exilio*
  and the *Asociación de Ingenieros Eléctricos en el Exilio* were organized in
  Miami.
- On February 11, on the 33rd anniversary of the founding of the *Juventudes
  de Acción Católica*, a celebration took place in Miami while a similar gath-
  ering in the *La Salle del Vedado*, in Havana, was attacked by fanatics.
- The *Agrupación de Obreros del Transporte en el Exilio* was organized in
  Miami under the leadership of **Marcos Irigoyen**, a former Communist
  and AFL-CIO activist turned passionately Anti-Communist.
- **Nazario Sargén** founded in Havana the *Alpha 66* organization.
- The *Asociación Patriótica José Martí* was founded in Caracas by **José de
  Jesús Planas**, a former leader of the *Juventud Obrera Católica,* with the
  participation of **Marino Pérez Durán**, **Justo Carrillo**, **Leví Marrero**,
  Jorge Quintana and **Félix Mondejar**.
- During March the *Consejo Revolucionario Cubano* was organized in Miami,
  presided by **José Miró Cardona**.
- **Rolando Espinosa** organized in Miami the *Colegio Nacional de Pedagogos*
  and **Aidé Velasco Ortega** the *Colegio de Enfermeras en el Exilio*.

(Continued)

Photos below, left to right:

Pedro Luis Boitel Abraham, who died in *El Principe* prison in Havana, on
May 25, 1972, after a 53 day hunger strike, at age 33; **José de Jesús
Planas**, former leader of the *Juventud Católica Cubana*, a member of the
National Committee of the CTC in 1959, was soon exiled in Caracas; **Levi
Marrero**, pre-eminent Cuban historian, economist and geographer, left Cuba
for exile in Venezuela and Puerto Rico in 1961; **José Miró Cardona**, professor of Law at the University of Havana, Prime Minister in 1959, Cuban Ambassador to Spain in May 1960, went into exile in the US by July 1961, disillusioned with Castro. He became head of the Cuban Revolutionary Council.

(Continuation)

- On April 8, several small boats failed to go ashore in Moa, Oriente, with **José Ignacio Rasco, Pedro Luis Díaz Lanz, Laureano Batista, Enrique Ros, Clemente Inclán** and **Luis Aguilar León**, among others, in what was apparently an effort to place in Cuba a group of exile leaders in anticipation of the *Bay of Pigs* invasion.

- On April 13th, the *2506 Brigade* invasion force left Puerto Cabezas, Nicaragua, under the direction of **José Pérez San Román**. His second in command was **Erneido Oliva González**. It carried 1,143 men, 72 tons of weapons, munitions and vehicles. The same day *El Encanto* department store in Havana was set on fire by **Carlos González Vidal**. The operation was purposely carried out at night but one lady employee was inside the store and died. González Vidal was executed on September 20, 1961.

- On April 18th, while the *Brigada 2506* tried to fight its way into the *Bay of Pigs*, at *La Cabaña* fortress in Havana, after a twenty minute trial with no appeals, the government took revenge for the invasion by executing nine members of *Rescate Revolucionario* and the *Directorio Revolucionario Estudiantil*, including **Virgilio Campanería** and **Alberto Tapia Ruano**.

- On April 20th, eight more opponents were executed at La Cabaña in cowardly retaliation for the invasion; the group included **Rogelio González Corso, Eugenio Fernández, Humberto Sorí Marín**, former commander at the *Sierra Maestra* and *Minister of Agriculture* in 1959; Sorí Marín had returned to Cuba from Miami to coordinate the *Brigade 2506* landing.

- During the summer of 1961 groups of exiles in Miami denounced the abuses committed against women prisoners in the *Guanabacoa* and *Guanajay* prisons; exiles from New York began a campaign to denounce the Cuban Communist government, including interrupting mayor league games by descending to the playing field with flags and placards.

- Cuban labor leader **Angel Cofiño** denounced the lack of rights in Cuba at the *Organización Regional e Internacional de Trabajadores* (ORIT) congress in Sao Paulo. The organization condemned the Cuban regime.

(Continued)

Photos above, left to right:

Erneido Oliva González, José Pérez San Román and **Manuel Artime** in the days of the *Bay of Pigs* invasion; **Virgilio Campanería**, a former student at *Belén, La Salle, Baldor, Havana Military Academy* and the *University of Villanueva* in Havana, founder of **Salvar a Cuba** (SAC), executed in 1961; **Humberto Sorí Marín**; he began to conspire against the government in 1961, was betrayed on March 18th and shot on April 20th.

(Continuation)

- Members of the *Directorio Revolucionario Estudiantil* denounced the tyranny of Cuba at the **IV Latinamerican Student Congress** in Natal, Brazil; the Congress censured the Cuban regime by unanimous vote.

- In Madrid, on October 23rd, the *Grupo Cubano Patriótico Luz de Yara* was founded. The following day, Pope John XXIII received **Mons. Eduardo Boza Masvidal** who gave him a large summary of the Cuban situation.

- In November, the *Confederación de Trabajadores de Cuba en el Exilio (CTC)* was founded in Miami by **Jesús Artigas Carbonell**; also in Miami **Alberto J. Suñé** founded the *Movimiento Insurreccional Libertad,* and **Ramón Blanco Jiménez**, the *Asociación de Prensa de Cuba*.

- In August of 1962, after news of a party at which Fidel Castro would be present, **Isidro Borja, Bernabé Peña, José Basulto, Carlos Hernández, Juan Manuel Salvat** and other **DRE** members, attacked from the sea the *Rosita de Hornedo Hotel* in Havana.

- **Manolo Guillot Castellanos**, one of the leaders of the February 1960 protest by *University of Havana* students against *Mikoyan*, was executed in *La Cabaña*; it was the beginning of what was called the *Conspiración del 30 de Agosto*. *"Monty"* Guillot had often entered and left Cuba.

- In September, **Manolo Ray**, founder of the MRP and former *Minister of Public Works* in 1959, founded the *Junta Revolucionaria Cubana (JURE)* in Río Cañas, Puerto Rico.

- Based in Miami and Puerto Rico, **Alpha 66** began its attacks on military installations in Caibarién, Las Villas in September of 1962, as well as a Cuban Merchant ship, a British cargo vessel, *New Lane*, loading sugar in *Cayo Francés* and the *Instituto de Amistad con los Pueblos (ICAP)* in Havana. In October **Alpha 66** assaulted a Russian encampment at *Isabela de Sagua* and blasted a Cuban patrol boat in Nueva Gerona. Two of the most visible leaders were **Nazario Sargén** and **Antonio Veciana**.

- While President *John F. Kennedy* dealt with *Khrushchev* during the *Missile Crisis of 1962*, the executions of infiltrated exiles continued in Cuba, as well as many acts of sabotage that originated in Miami and San Juan.

(Continued)

Photos below, left to right:

Msrg. Eduardo Boza Masvidal, expelled from Cuba in 1961, founder of the *Unión de Cubanos en el Exilio*, a fraternal rather than a political or military organization; **Nazario Sargén** and **Antonio Veciana**, leaders of *Alpha 66*; **Manuel Guillot Castellanos (Manolín)**, an alumnus of *La Salle*, leader in Cuba of the *Movimiento de Recuperación Revolucionaria*, went into exile and stealthily returned several times to Cutimes. He was betrayed and caught in Cuba leaving a Church after Mass.

(Continuation)

- The year 1962 ends with **Mons. Eduardo Boza Masvidal** founding in Miami the *Unión de Cubanos en el Exilio (UCE)*; it will soon have chapters in San Juan, PR, New York, Chicago, Los Angeles, Houston, New Orleans and practically every important city in the US.
- The support of Cuban exiles to the forces fighting against the Communist regime in Cuba continued unabated during 1963. The government recognized that in January of 1963 there were at least *1600 fighters* in *180 different groups* in the mountains of Cuba. Thousands of revolutionary troops, over 120,000 by some accounts, continued trying to surround and defeat them.
- On March 7, several organizations in Cuba and in exile started to coordinate an attempt against Castro during the commemoration of the March 13th 1963 attack to Palacio and Radio Reloj, when José Antonio Echeverría and Menelao Mora were killed. The magnicide would have been a shot to the presiding tribune with a bazooka but it failed.
- From Miami, **Alpha 66** attacks the Soviet ship *LGow*, loading sugar in the town of Isabela de Sagua; a boat with exile fighters reaches the *Tarará River* and attacks a government patrol; **Comandos L** forces led by **Tony Cuesta** try to sink the soviet ship *Bakú* in the port of Caibarién.
- In Veracruz, Mexico, during the month of June, three Cuban ships loading supplies bound for Cuba were attacked by Cuban exile fighters who were taken under custody by the Mexican government.
- Cuban exile leaders in Miami and New York denounced that the government of Cuba was conducting massive execution operations by taking groups of prisoners in military transports to remote locations at night and executing them under the lights of the vehicles.
- Originating from a point in Central America, troops from **Comandos Mambises** reached *Casilda*, near Trinidad in Cuba, aboard the ships *Lavo*, *Leda* and *Bee*, and destroyed a large fuel depot and a railroad tank farm. Days later they reached Puerto Maraví, near Baracoa, and destroyed a large sawmill. The same day, a plane manned by **MIRR** combatants dropped five powerful bombs in *Central Jaronú*, in north Camagüey.

(Continued)

Photos above, left to right:

US journalist **Andrew St. George**, who had interviewed Castro twice in the *Sierra Maestra*, meeting with members of **Comandos L** in 1963; the logotypes of the **Unión de Cubanos en el Exilio (UCE)** and **Comandos Mambises**.

(Continuation)

- By the end of 1963 every active belligerent caught in Cuba and every infiltrated exile found in the island was submitted to standing orders by the government to be executed rather than taken prisoner.
- At the end of the year frogmen from **Comandos Mambises**, operating out of the ship *Reefer*, sank the government torpedo boat LT-385 at Siguanea, Isla de Pinos.
- In March of 1964, **Angel Cuadra** began to clandestinely publish in Cuba, with the support of the Unidad Nacional Revolucionaria (UNARE), the literary magazine *La Poesía Cubana frente al Comunismo*.
- On April 29, Alberto Delgado Delgado, aka **El Hombre de Maisinicú**, faced a firing squad under the command of **José "Cheito" León**, an important leader of anti-Castro fighters in the Escambray. Delgado was an informer that had caused the capture of numerous freedom fighters.
- On May 25, **José "Cheito" León**, the last guerrilla leader in Sierra del Escambray, fell on a battle at a farm near Jabira, Las Villas. He was 22 years old.
- In July, hundreds of opponents jailed at Presidio Modelo de Isla de Pinos formed the **Bloque de Organizaciones Revolucionarias (BOR)**, to coordinate their boycott to the government plan to force prisoners to work. The prison political population included members of **MRR, M-30-11 Movement, MRP, Unidad Revolucionaria, DRE** and **MDC**.
- In New Orleans, federal authorities confiscated over a ton of explosives destined to the war in Cuba.
- In August, a group of exiles attacked the María Teresa, a Cuban merchant ship taking goods to Cuba from the port of Montreal, Canada.
- On September 18, two distinguished journalists, **Emilio Adolfo Rivero Caro** and **Alfredo Izaguirre de la Riva**, refused to work while they were in prison and were condemned to two years of solitary confinement. They were labeled the **Plantados** by their fellow political inmates, giving prestige and standing to the non-compliant attitude in prison. They were the first of a long list of **Plantados** on record.

(Continued)

Photos above, left to right:

José (Cheito) León (circled) at the Escambray Mountains in Cuba in 1963; a poster for the film *El Hombre de Maisinicú*; *Adolfo Rivero Caro*, a former Communist, founder in the 1970s of the *Comité Cubano de Derechos Humanos* with *Ricardo Bofill, Gustavo* and *Sebastián Arcos Bergnes, Jesús Yánez Pelletier* and *Elizardo Sánchez Santacruz*.

(Continuation)

- The year 1965 began in Miami with the assassination of **Juan José Peruyero**, a member of the *2506 Brigade*, and in Cuba with the arrest of **Polita** and **Ramón Grau**, leaders of the *Pedro Pan Operation* that facilitated sending 14,000 children to the US during 1961 and 1962, far from the Communist indoctrination in the Cuban schools.

- In July the police in New York seized a shipment of arms, munitions and heavy mortars destined to the fighters in Cuba; it was estimated to have a value of over $100,000.

- In a daring attack on November 13, ships under the command of **Tony Cuesta**, manned by men from **Comandos L, M-30-11 Movement** and **RECE** attacked the residence of Cuban President *Osvaldo Dorticós Torrado*, the *Octava Estación de Policía* and *Hotel Riviera*, residence of Soviet military trainers and technicians.

- A week later the Cuban government inaugurated the **Unidades Militares de Apoyo a la Producción (UMAP)**, where all young dissidents and opponents were sent without any legal accusations or process. The *UMAP* lasted until 1968.

- In March of 1966, for the first time, US coastguards began to actively seek and intercept exile incursions against Cuban territory. **Armando Fleites**, leader of two **Alpha 66** ships about to enter Cuban waters, was detained and transported to the US.

- In May, several boats from **Alpha 66** attacked for the third time the militia stronghold at *Playa Tarará*, a favorite vacation spot for the Cuban *nomenclatura*.

- In June, **Reynaldo Aquit Manrique**, dressed as a militia, escaped from the prison in Isla de Pinos in 1966. He wandered for four months and was recaptured after he asked the Mexican Ambassador **Gilberto Bosques** for help. Bosques had participated in the Mexican revolution in 1910 and had saved numerous Jews during WWII, but was a close friend of the Castros and Ernesto Guevara. He died in 1995, aged 103. Reynaldo Aquit remained in prison until 1974 and went into exile in Miami in 1980.

- US authorities arrested **Orlando Bosch** and five other leaders of MIRR, accused of attacking ships and sugar mills in Cuban territory.

(Continued)

Photos above, left to right:

Leopoldina (Polita) and **Ramón Grau**, founders and promoters of *Operación Pedro Pan*; a Havana newspaper extolling the benefits of the **Uniones Militares de Ayuda a la Producción (UMAP)**.

(Continuation)

- January of 1967 started with **Armando Fleites**, leader of an attack ship from the *Segundo Frente Nacional del Escambray (SFNE)*, engaging in combat with Cuban navy elements in Cuban territory.
- Also in January, **Gustavo Marín** and others organized and launched in the Woodstock Hotel in New York, just off Times Square, a new organization named **Abdala**, after the José Martí poem.
- In March the **DRE** accused Cuba for the extra-judicial use of firing squads before the *UN Commission on Human Rights in Ginebra*. The Cuban regime announces the closing of the *Cárcel Modelo de Isla de Pinos,* and, in New Jersey, Cuban exiles organize the *Movimiento Nacional Reformista* under the leadership of **Felipe Martínez**.
- A group of Cuban exile militants in **Alpha 66** land in Pinar del Rio, where the Cuban army is waiting for them. It was not clear who betrayed them.
- At the end of September, a group led by **Enrique Huertas**, President of the Cuban Medical Society, organized a march in Washington, D.C. to denounce the abuses in Cuba to the head of the **OEA** *José A. Mora*. It is estimated by the *Washington Post* that 12,000 Cuban exiles participated.
- In November, the *Representación Cubana del Exilio* (RECE) held its first national congress in Miami. Weeks later, the *Organización de Educadores Cubanos* is launched in Miami under the leadership of **Raúl Lastra**.
- During the entire year of 1967, Cuban exiles across the US and Europe continued to bring to the world news about the **hunger strikes** in almost every prison in Cuba, as well as the continuation of the **executions** and the **abuses** against opponents of the Cuban regime, particularly women.
- In July of 1968, the *Mikacesan Maru*, a Japanese ship doing business with Cuba, is attacked in the port of Galveston by members of **Poder Cubano**. In August, frogmen of **Poder Cubano** repit the operation against the British ship *Caribbean Ventura* and the Polish ship *Polanica* in the port of Miami. **Orlando Bosch** is arrested as the leader of these operations. He got a sentence of 10 years in a federal penitentiary.
- At the end of 1968, the *Coordinadora Nacional de Presos y Ex-Presos Políticos Cubanos* is launched in Miami to monitor prison conditions in Cuba and assist the families of prisoners in Cuba and in exile.
- In September of 1969, **José Elías de la Torriente** announces on an English TV station his *Plan Torriente for the liberation of Cuba*.

Photos below, left to right:

Enrique Huertas, President of the *Colegio Médico Cubano Libre*; **Armando Fleites**, leader of the *Segundo Frente Nacional del Escambray,* he joined the exiles in Miami in 1961, after the G2 entrapped and killed *William Morgan*; **José Elías de la Torriente**, author of the *Plan Torriente,* assassinated in 1974; **Abdala**, the dramatic poem by *José Martí* that gave its name to the **Grupo Abdala.** The poem was published by *Martí* and *Fermín Valdés Domínguez* in 1869 when they were both in their teens.

One of the most destructive and harmful consequences of the revolution of 1959 in Cuba was the division and disunion it brought within Cuban families. A case example —unfortunately typical for many families— was the dissention it created among the descendants of Antonio Maceo, and his brother José Maceo.

Antonio Maceo (el Titán de Bronce, 1845-1896) and **José Maceo (el León de Oriente, 1849-1896)** were both born from the union of Marcos Maceo and Mariana Grajales. Both joined the independence struggle in 1868 along with their father Marcos and their brothers Justo and Rafael. In 1878, during the 1877 *Mangos de Mejías combat*, José saved the life of his brother Antonio. The brothers were very close and both participated in 1875 during the events of *Lagunas de Varona*, in 1877 during the *Sedition of Santa Rita;* in 1878 they were together at the *Protest of Baraguá*. Unlike Antonio, who went abroad at the end of the war, José stayed in Cuba and was betrayed by Spanish General Camilo Polavieja who sent him to jail in Ceuta, after promising to allow him to go into exile. José escaped and joined Antonio in Central America.

Almost at the beginning of the War of 1895, José was killed at the **Battle of Loma del Gato**, near Santiago de Cuba on July 15, 1896 and Antonio died in the vicinity of **Punta Brava** on Decem-

After the advent of the 1959 revolution in Cuba the Maceo family, for the first time, experienced a schism. **Antonio Maceo's** grandson —also called Antonio— went into exile and became a member of the *Revolutionary Advisory Committee* with José Miró Cardona and Antonio de Varona. He had studied medicine in France, had been a surgery specialist at *Hospital de Emergencias* in Havana and had been a pioneer in public health in Republican Cuba. He died at age 89 and was buried in Miami.

José Maceo's grandson, who had fought against Batista in the 1950s, became a founder of *Cuba's Communist Party*, served 50 years in the Cuban military, was a national líder of the *Comités de Defensa de la Revolución* and was the lead person in the group that came to the US to secure the return of *Elián González* in 2000. He died in 2007 at age 88 and was burried in Havana.

Photos, left to right: **Antonio Maceo Grajales**, his grandson and namesake **Antonio** and his granduncle and Antonio's brother, **José Maceo Grajales**.

Castro makes an appearance at the
Ed Sulivan Show in 1959.

Stilstsville, the houses on sticks in the
middle of Biscayne Bay in 1959.

An Ad for
a ***Cuban Clinic***
in 1959, listing the
staff of Physicians
and the
monthly stipend
charged to its
members ($3.50).

One of the most intriguing figures of the early days of the Cuban revolution was **Carlos Franqui (1921-1910)**. He was born in Oriente, in a peasant family, and became a close friend of Castro and a writer who played an important role in the early days of the Cuban revolution. He ran the guerrilla's radio station, *Radio Rebelde*, from the *Sierra Maestra* in the late 1950s and in 1959 became the editor of *Revolución*, the official newspaper of the new Cuban regime. He was fired from this position in 1963 when he expressed his dissatisfaction with the pro-Russian bent in Castro's thinking and broke with the Cuban revolution in 1968, when Castro sided with the Soviets supporting the invasion of Czechoslovakia. After Franqui became an exile, *Revolución* was renamed *Granma* and turned into the official Cuban Communist party newspaper.

In 1984, Franqui published *Family Portrait With Fidel*, as well as several volumes combining poetry and graphic arts, in collaboration with Calder, Miró, Antoni Tàpies, and other well-known international artists. Throughout his life, however, many Cuban exiles rejected him for his active role in the early revolutionary days.

The Cuban revolution, before the advent of *PhotoShop* and other technical means of falsifying historical pictures, removed Franqui from one photo in which he appeared with Castro. It was a notorious deceit that Franqui exposed in the cover of his book. Many other deceptive manipulations of history took place during the initial

Photos above:
On the left, the cover of *Family Portrait With Fidel*, showing Franqui on the top picture between Castro and Almeida and in the picture on the center Castro and Almeida by themselves, with Franqui erased. Franqui's comment was «I have just discovered my photographic death». On the right, on top, one of the most published photos of Castro in the *Sierra Maestra*; on the bottom, the evidence that, for unknown reasons, the photo had been cropped. The original photo shows Castro with a peasant holding an image of the Virgin Mary.

Contrary to the way it was presented in the film *Godfather II*, Fulgencio Batista had a drink with his top military officers in the afternoon of December 31, 1958 and took the occasion to announce he was leaving Cuba for *"patriotic reasons."* Hours later his wife and children were waiting for him on a plane at the air field of Columbia Military Camp; the Batistas became the first exiles in 1959.

Photo al left: Batista at the final reception for his military cadres.

The main media support for the revolution of 1959 came from *Bohemia Magazine*. Contrary to most other newspapers and magazines, it flooded cities and towns in Cuba with revolutionary propaganda, creating myths and obscuring the inauspicious background of Castro. Its director, **Miguel Angel Quevedo**, would years later ask for the forgiveness of the Cuban people before committing suicide.

Photos: the myths of the successful invasion of Cuba by Castro's forces and the 20.000 murders under Batista. both created bv *Bohemia Maaazine*.

In the early hours of January 1, 1959, three Cuban military aircraft arrived in the United States; the first at West Palm Beach with 50 passengers, all friends and guests of Governor **Francisco R. (Panchín) Batista (1911-1970)**, the brother of the deposed President. He had been elected governor of Havana in 1948 and served in that post until his escape from Cuba on January 1st. Since 1933 he had been a close collaborator and apologist for his brother.

The second military aircraft landed in New Orleans at 5:00 AM carrying aboard Rubén Batista, the eldest son of the President, with some forty friends and family that included General **Francisco Tabernilla Dolz (1888-1972)**, his wife Pilar and his sons Francisco Tabernilla Palmero (aka *Silito*), Commander of the Cuban Army Tank Regiment and Batista's Chief Military Aid, and Carlos Tabernilla Palmeiro, Commander of the Cuban Army Air Force, The authorities in New Orleans were unprepared to receive so many immigrants, many of them without papers or baggage, and detained the entire group for close to ten hours while the presumed refugees were making frantic calls to the Cuban embassy in Washington and to their friends in other branches of the federal government.

Francisco Tabernilla had a long history in the Cuban army. In 1917 he graduated with the first class of the *Escuela de Cadetes*. During the 1933 revolt against Machado he had been the chief of operations at *La Cabaña* fortress, a position he resumed in 1952 after Batista's *coup d'état*. On January 1st 1959 he arrived in New Orleans late because in Havana he had gone through the formalities of accepting Batista's resignation as President. Years later Batista would denounce him as a traitor because of his secret conversations with Castro's followers on the eve of Batista's demise. According to his son Tabernilla «*died of sadness in exile*» at age 84.

Photos above: on the left, **Panchín Batista**, President Batista's brother and former governor of Havana with **Ernest Hemingway** in 1958. Hemingway was a *bon vivant* in Cuba, as comfortable with the dictator Batista as with Fidel Castro, a man he knew was destroying Cuba; on the right, General **Francisco Tabernilla Dolz**, at Columbia, hours before going into exile in 1959.

The third military aircraft left *Camp Columbia* at 2:00 AM on January 1st 1959. It was carrying President **Fulgencio Batista y Zaldivar (1901-1973)** and his immediate family into his second exile. Its destination was the Dominican Republic and the lateness of its departure was due to his wife Marta gathering family mementos from their home in *Kukine*, their countryside estate. Batista had concluded the travesty of a legal transfer of his presidential powers by 12:30 AM and anxiously waited at Columbia airfield while his wife attended to these family chores. Years later he would admit having some regrets about making no provisions for the hundreds of his followers that he left behind, exposed to the fury of the revolutionaries. At the time his main thoughts were to escape with his family, carrying several suitcases with enough funds to live through his first weeks in exile.

Photo below: the Jaragua Hotel in Santo Domingo, where Batista spent his first weeks in exile. For one entire floor his friend *Rafael Leonidas Trujillo*, the Dominican dictator at the time, was charging the Batistas $1,000,000 dollars monthly rent, which Marta found excessive.

Hotel Jaragua 1959

After becoming one of the first exiles in 1959, Batista left the Dominican Republic —too steep a rent— and moved to Madeira, then Estoril outside Lisbon. He was never admitted to the US as a resident, in spite of his first sojourn in Daytona in the 1940s. He died in Guadalmina, near Marbella, Spain, on August 6, 1973, almost 40 years to the date he had become Cuba's top man during the fall of Machado.

Photo left: **Batista** on the grounds of *Hotel Jaragua* in January 1959.

In the morning of January 1, 1959, once the people in Cuba found out that Batista had fled, chaos broke as his opponents took to the streets seeking revenge. They were joined by mobs of people taking advantage of a city with no credible authority; police, civil authorities, the military and the politicians, all had fled or remained inside their homes. After these demonstrations, many families, fearing things to come, decided to seek refuge abroad. The ranks of Miami political refugees began to swell unstoppably all through 1959.

Photos above: chaos in Havana on 1 January 1959.

For no reason, some Havana mobs began to destroy parking meters and vandalize city property on January 1, 1959.

Mob Scene in Havana After Dictator's Downfall

APOTEOSIS EN LA CAPITAL

The initial surge of exiles in Miami consisted of followers of Fulgencio Batista but there were also many Cubans that were afraid of the coming times of violence, uncertainty and instability and decided to take the road to exile. For completely opposite reasons many Batista exiles returned to Cuba to participate in what they believed was a resurgence of patriotism and a rebirth of the Cuban nation.

Prior to the Communists take over in Cuba in 1959 and the following years, the history of Communists' appeal and behavior in Cuba left a lot to be desired. During WWII their main concern was to support the USSR against *Nazi Germany* and, for as long as the US was partnering with the Russians to defeat Hitler, the **Partido Socialista Popular (PSP)** was acceptable and influential in the **Confederación de Trabajadores de Cuba (CTC)** and as members of Cuban government coalitions.

After the defeat of the Axis powers in 1945, Communists in Cuba were no longer tolerated and the **CTC**, under the leadership of General Secretary **Eusebio Mujal** began efforts to expurgate the Marxists from the top ranks. Mujal was a Communist militant prior to 1932 who in 1959 became the target of a failed assassination attempt by Castro's agents in Buenos Aires.

In 1947, Grau's Minister of Labor, **Carlos Prío Socarrás**, openly tilted the balance at the **CTC** with his support for Mujal. Only the *Sindicato de Estibadores* (Dockworker's Union) and the *Sindicato Tranviario* (Tram Drivers's Union) objected to Mujal's displacement of the Communists from the **CTC** leadership ranks. When it was needed, in fact, Communist labor leaders were murdered as it was the case with **Aracelio Iglesias** (from the Havana docks union), **Miguel Fernández Roig** (a cigar-makers leader) and **Jesús Menéndez** (leader among sugar workers).

After the 1948 elections, Prío became president and the **Communist-free CTC** began (without visible participation of the Marxists) an intensive campaign to defend worker's rights, particularly job security. The working classes reluctantly admitted such productivity measures as mechanization, wage freezing, longer hours and resorting to overtime rather than new hiring.

(Continued)

Photos below, left to right:

Aracelio Iglesias, Miguel Fernández Roig, Jesús Menéndez and **Eusebio Mujal.**

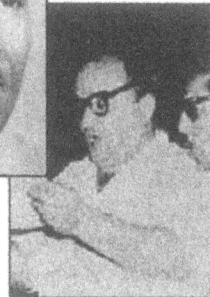

(Continuation)

The government position was that these measures were necessary to attract investment, promote diversification and eventually expand the economy and the labor force. By the time the 1952 elections came around there were only three candidates: **Fulgencio Batista**, a non-Communist that had a history of pacts with the PSP, **Carlos Hevia**, an avowed and honest anti-Communist, running with a heavy baggage of *Auténtico Party* corruption history, and **Roberto Agramonte**, from the anti-corruption, nationalistic and somewhat anti-imperialist but democratic *Orthodox Party*. The PSP could not collect enough signatures to participate as a party in the elections and had to remain as an observer.

After the 1952 *coup d'état* by Batista, the PSP continued to lose influence in Cuban affairs. Batista became fiercely anti-Communist and broke relations with the USSR, banned the PSP after the **26 de Julio** attack on the Moncada barracks, closed **HOY**, the Communist newspaper and deflected strikes in the banking sector, the railroads, the textile workers and the FNTA, the sugar unions. All of these failed strikes were organized by Mujal's CTC and not the PSP, who by then was not even having influence in their previous strong niche, the sugar labor organizations. The PSP began to characterize the other political parties as «*los partidos burgueses*», but whatever was left of its former popularity received a hard blow when they supported the crushing of the 1956 Hungarian uprising.

(Continued)

Photos below, top to bottom, left to right:
The celebration of the 70th birthday of **Joseph Stalin** by the Cuban PSP in 1949; **Blas Roca** at the PSP headquarters in 1950 and the old (top) and new (bottom) logos of the **Cuban Communist Party**.

When Cuban Communists joined the revolution on January 1, 1959, the popularity that the *Partido Socialista Popular* had in the 1930s had completely evaporated. Its leaders had included people like **Blas Roca Calderío**, *Secretario General*, **Jesús Menéndez**, (aka *El General de las Cañas*), **Carlos Rafael Rodríguez, Juan Marinello, Salvador García Agüero, Fabio Grobar**, **Lázaro Peña** (aka *El Capitán de la Clase Obrera*), **José Ramón Fernández, Flavio Bravo, Enrique Ovares, Alfredo Guevara, Severo Aguirre del Cristo, Osvaldo Sánchez, Joaquín Ordoqui, Jorge Risquet, Raúl Valdés Vivó, Teté Casuso, Romárico Cordero, Ursinio Rojas** and others whose names were hardly recognized by most Cubans.

The following two pages present some of the Communist card-carrying members that the Castro brothers forcibly injected into national positions, some of which later turned against him. They replaced hundreds of physicians, university professors, economists, businessmen, union leaders, journalists, artists, athletes, elected officials and many other Cubans who were taking the road to exile. By following this policy of *«loyalty trumping excellence»*, the Marxist government began to set back the development of Cuba in a tailspin that would inevitably and almost immediately result in ruin and despair.

(Continued)

Photos below, left to right:

José Ramón Fernández (left) and **Flavio Bravo** (right) with Castro; **Enrique Ovares Herrera** (left) and **Alfredo Guevara** (right) with Castro during the *Bogotazo*.

(Continuation)

José Ramón Fernández (aka *El Gallego*) was a graduate of Batista's *Cadet School* who was promoted to Captain by Castro in 1959; with those credentials and a secondary education diploma he eventually would be Professor Emeritus of the *Institute Enrique José Varona* in Havana.

Flavio Bravo, a former lottery street peddler, would be appointed during Castro's regime as *Chief of Operations of the Army* and President of the *Asamblea del Poder Popular*.

Enrique Ovares Herrera was in 1948 President of Cuba's *Federación de Estudiantes Universitarios (FEU)*. After graduating as an architect in 1951 he opposed Batista's and Castro's regimes and under Castro was in prison for 7 years before he went into exile in 1966. He designed many projects in Key Biscayne, Florida and died in 2006.

Alfredo Guevara, loyal Castro companion during the *Bogotazo* on April 9, 1948 (the massive riots after the murder of Liberal leader *Jorge Eliezer Gaitán*), became founder of the *Instituto Cubano de Arte e Industria Cinematográficos (ICAIC)* in 1959.

Photos below: **Fernández, Bravo, Ovares** and **Guevara** in the 1960s.

Joaquín Ordoqui was married to *Edith García Buchaca* (former wife of *Carlos Rafael Rodríguez*, an important PSP member); Joaquín and Edith were leaders of the PSP until they were accused to be CIA agents. Both served 10 years of house arrest. Their son sought asylum in Perú in 1987.

Osvaldo Sánchez Cabrera was a High School graduate and a member of the *Communist Party* since 1939. In 1956 he became the link between the PSP and Castro. After 1959 he served in the *Interior Ministry* in Havana.

Anibal Escalante was one of the founders of the *Partido Socialista Popular (PSP)* in Cuba in 1929 (with *Blas Roca, Fabio Grobar* and *Julio Antonio Mella*, among others). He supported dictators *Gerardo Machado* and *Fulgencio Batista* in 1931 and 1940; never got along with Castro, was implicated in a *de facto coup d'état* and served 15 years in prison.

Jorge Risquet Valdés was the leader of the Cuban forces in *Congo-Brazzaville* in 1965-67 and the organizer of the Cuban intervention in *Angola* in 1976-86. He served in Cuba's *Comité Central del Partido*.

Photos below: **Ordoqui, Sánchez, Escalante** and **Risquet** in the 1960s.

(Continuation)

Severo Aguirre del Cristo, a trade carpenter, joined in 1930 the *Liga de Juventudes Comunistas*, reaching the position of Secretary General by 1956. In 1959 he first became Vice Minister of the *Instituto Nacional de Reforma Agraria (INRA)* and later Dean of the *Facultad de Ciencias Agropecuarias* of the University of Havana. He never taught there. He presided the *Asamblea del Poder Popular* and was *Ambassador to Moscow*.

Raúl Valdés Vivó, joined the *Juventud Socialista* in 1946 as a writer for *Mella Magazine*. In 1959 he became subdirector of **HOY**, the Communist paper. In 1967 was appointed Ambassador to *Vietnam* and *Cambodia*. He was a prolific political author that claimed credentials as *Doctor en Ciencias Sociológicas, Ingeniero Economista, Profesor Titular de Historia y Filosofía*, yet there was no evidence that he obtained any such degrees anywhere.

Teté Casuso Morín was a student leader against the Machado regime in the 1930s when she married *Pablo de la Torriente Brau*; after he died during *Spain's Civil War* she became a revolutionary and had to flee to Mexico during the *Batista* regime in the 1950s. There he met Castro and helped him to prepare the *Granma* expedition. In 1959 she was appointed *Ambassador to Mexico*, Castro's press secretary and *Cuba's Delegate to the UN*. In October 1960, she resigned and denounced Castro. In exile in Miami she became editor of *Vanidades Magazine* and died of Alzheimer's.

Romárico Cordero Garcés was a worker at several sugar mills in Cuba when he became a Communist peasant leader in the 1920s. He was active in the struggles against *Machado* in the 1930s and *Batista* in the 1950s. As a **PSP** member, he represented the party in the *1940 Constitutional Assembly* and wrote in the newspaper **HOY**. It was said upon his death that Cordero «*had organized soviets in the Sierra Maestra years before Castro arrived and there was no poor family, hidden delinquent or marihuana farmer that was not loyal to Cordero*». Not 100% in tune with Castro's leadership, he was marginalized, although a revolutionary order and a medal to "*peasant revolutionary fervor*" was struck in his honor.

Ursinio Rojas Santiesteban was a labor leader and organizer of *soviets* (Communist action groups) in Cuba until 1948. After the assassination of *Jesús Menéndez*, he became *Secretario General* of the *Federación Nacional de Trabajadores Azucareros (FNTA)*. In 1959 he finished his High School and became a section manager at the *Instituto Nacional de Reforma Agraria (INRA)*. He was considered a key man in the movements of Castro's guerrillas into the western part of Cuba in 1959 and the man who "*bought*" the surrender of the City of Santa *Clara* in December of 1958. As *Romárico Cordero*, however, he was marginalized by Castro and his old **PSP** comrades, receiving honors but no real power and relevance in Cuba.

Photos below: **Severo Aguirre**, **Raúl Valdés**, **Teté Casuso**, **Romárico Cordero** and **Ursinio Rojas** in the 1960s.

On March 20, 1956, the Daytona Beach city fathers had proclaimed the 24th as "*Batista Day,*" in honor of the Cuban ex-president that left their shores in 1952 to overthrow the constitutional government of Cuba. Now, in 1959, they wanted no part of Batista and behind closed doors spoke badly of him, feeling no sympathy for the man that was imploring for a return to the US.

His followers, however, fared better. The first wave of post-Batista exodus was almost one hundred percent military and police officials and civil functionaries from the unseated Batista government. They ran at the Miami and Havana airports across pre-Castro exiles returning home. Quarrels and altercations broke out daily at both airports requiring local police forces to move to ensure a peaceful flow of passengers in both directions at the waiting areas by the gates. In Miami, a new exile leadership began to take place, as *batistianos* started to assume control of the institutions and habits of the returning-to-Cuba former exiles. Only business people, serious students, and the well-to-do leaving Cuba —the so called non-political upper class— walked quietly through the airport labyrinths without bothering the outbound returning exiles. During 1959 alone, close to 45,000 new exiles, most of them feeling they were going into an *extended vacation*, replaced 12,000 anti-Batista exiles and revolutionaries returning to Cuba.

As soon as Castro's rebels consolidated their hold on the Cuban government the execution of partisans from the Batista ranks got started. This sent chills among many Castro revolutionary followers who began to pressure the newly formed government to act more prudently and legally when it came to seeking retribution for possible malfeasance during Batista's tenure. The ranks of Miami Cuban refugees began to fill with people that had never sympathized with Batista but were worried by the cruelty of the revolutionaries they had supported with funding and arms.

Photos above, left to right: new Cuban exiles arriving at Miami airport in 1959; former exiles from the Batista regime arriving at the airport in Havana.

On January 13, 1959, barely a week after Castro and his troops arrived to Havana, **Manolo Fernandez (1922-1988)** *"el Caballero del Tango,"* left Cuba for the last time after obtaining political asylum in the US. He was taken to the *Martí Airport* in Havana by American Ambassador to Cuba **Earl T. Smith**, a friend of Manolo and his American wife Dolores.

Manolo Fernández became famous in Cuba with the popularity of the Tango in the 1940s and 1950s, after frequent visits by some of the best Tango interpreters in the world: Amanda Ledesma, Hugo del Carril, Libertad Lamarque, Mercedes Simoni, Astor Piazola, Enrique Santos Discépolo and many others. With Olga Chorens, Emilio Ramil and several others, Fernández became one of the best interpreters of Tangos in Cuba. They were frequent performers at the **Tango Club of Havana**, the cabarets **La Pampa** and **Rincón del Tango,** the **Museo del Tango** and many other venues. Manolo Fernández in particular was frequently doing his tangos at COCO Radio or at Radio Cadena Roja, injecting many interesting anecdotes and stories such as the long lasting friendship of **Eligio Sardiñas (Kid Chocolate, 1910-1988)** in Paris with **Carlos Gardel (1890-1935)**, who always was ready to sing *Cuesta Abajo* for the World Boxing Champ.

In 1959 Manolo Fernández, as President of the *Cuban Syndicate of Artists and Musicians,* organized a meeting of the syndicate to discuss the revolutionary takeover of the government in Cuba. He made the comment that «*the revolution was like a watermelon, green on the outside but red inside,*» adding «*Castro is not bringing the Revolution to Cuba; he is bringing Communism*». Tempers flared at the meeting and from that moment he was threatened, insulted and cursed. The meeting turned into a mob chanting *"Paredón."* An order to pick him up was issued by the police and he decided to be the first non-follower of Batista that requested asylum from political persecution. Within months he became as successful in the US and Puerto Rico as he had been in Cuba, and for many years he was an idol for all Cuban exiles.

Photos above:
Manolo Fernández and an **LP** published as a final tribute to him, showing an **sculpture in his honor** in Little Havana, Miami.

Left, **Father Agustín Roman** talks about **Father Varela;** *right,* Channel 4 **TV News Channel.**

Mail from **Radio Swam**, the clandestine Radio station used by Cuban Exiles to Communicate with their Sympathizers in Cuba.

Cuban exile journalists during the 1960s: Luis Felipe Marsans, Guillermo Martínez Márquez, José Ignacio Rivero, Floridano Feria, Ariel Remos, Roberto Pérez Fernández, Laurentino Rodríguez, Ramiro Boza, Armando Alejandre and Willy del Pino.

Photos above: All through the year 1959 there were Cubans returning to Cuba (*photo on top*) and others flying from the island (*photo at the bottom*); those leaving openly surpassed those that were returning from the exile during Batista's dictatorship; many were soon to depart once more.

Photo above: As reported by *LIFE Magazine*, within two months in 1959, exiles in Miami began to protest the initial violent actions of the Castro government, particularly the possibility of Soviet military equipment in Cuba and taking members of the Cuban Air Force and the Military to firing squads without the benefit of a proper judicial process.

Oscar Benjamin Cintas (1887-1957) was a very prominent Cuban railroad and sugar magnate as well as an important patron of the arts and culture of Cuba during the first half
of the XX century. He served as *Cuban Ambassador to the US*
from 1932 to 1934, when the Platt Amendment was abro-
gated; in the 1940s he created *Cuban Art Foundation*, trusting
its management to the *Chase Manhattan Bank* before his
death. Knowing that the final manuscript of **Lincoln's Get-
tysburg Address** (one of the most valuable documents in
Oscar Cintas' collection) was in Cuba at the advent of the revolution in 1959, the trustees of the *Chase*, in an almost *cloak-
and-dagger* operation, rescued this important historical document to present it to the *White House*, as had been the wish
of Oscar Cintas. This final manuscript of Lincoln's Gettys-burg
Address is now in the *Lincoln Room* of the White House.

As per the trustees' wishes, the **Cuban Art Foundation** became the **Cintas Foundation** in 1963; it has provided over
300 scholarships to Cuban artists, writers, filmmakers and
scholars since 1941. These awards have been limited to Cuban artists in exile, or living outside Cuba. The vast scope of
the collection reflects «*the heterogeneous nature of the artistic production of Cuban artists, spanning across various generations, and their significant aesthetic and historical contribution to modern and contemporary art*», according to its
statutes. The roster of **Cintas Fellows** is a testament to the
talent and creativity of the Cubans and their direct descendants who have lived outside the island since 1959. The **Cintas
Foundation** is the oldest entity in the United States dedicated to the support of artists of the Cuban Diaspora.

Photos above, left to right:
Oscar B. Cintas; one of the **Grecos** in the Cintas Collection; **Cintas**
(handling a book) at an art auction in **Parke-Bernet** in New York.

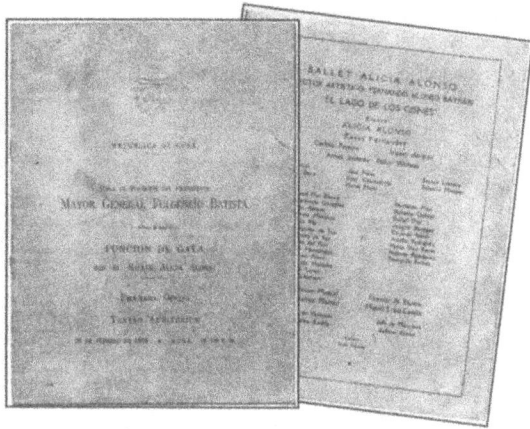

Very few Cuban exiles could understand, much less justify, the position of **Alicia Alonso** regarding the Castro regime in Cuba. Even after knowing her solid Communist past, it was difficult to explain her loyalty to Castro after thousands of families had been divided, hundreds of youngsters had been shot at **La Cabaña** fortress and Cubans were suffering a miserable lifestyle while the *Communist Nomenclatura* continued to live royally as owners of the entire economy of the island.

Alicia, an alumna from *Sociedad Pro-Arte Musical*, had made her debut in Broadway in 1938 and soon became part of what is today the *New York City Ballet*. After joining the *American Ballet Theater* she had the opportunity to work with Mijail Fokine, George Balanchine, Bronislava Nijinska, Antony Tudor, Jerome Robbins, Agnes de Mille, and most star ballet figures of the XX Century. In 1948 she founded in Havana the *Alicia Alonso Ballet* (today's *Ballet Nacional de Cuba*). Over the years she performed at the *Ballet de la Opera de Paris*, the *Opera de Vienna*, the *Ballet San Carlos* in Naples, the *Opera de Praga*, the *Scala de Milán, the Bolshoi,* and has been a *Ballerina Assoluta* in every important ballet venue.

Having been born in 1920, **Alicia Ernestina de la Caridad del Cobre Martínez del Hoyo** —her full name, became a living legend, more so since, already blind, her last performance was at age 75, guided by a hidden-from-view *partenaire*. Perhaps the best explanation for her devotion to Castro, rather than her long standing (70 years) Communist credentials, is hidden in a program for her performance on 25 February, 1955 at the *Teatro Auditorium* (today's Amadeo Roldán) in Havana. It was a **Gala Performance** in honor of **Fulgencio Batista**, on occasion of his swearing-in after his implausible and unconvincing election to the presidency of Cuba. Years later **Guillermo de Zéndegui**, as president of the *Instituto Nacional de Cultura*, stopped Cuba's subsidies to the *Alicia Alonso Ballet* because their performances were exclusively presented to «*la élite social*».

Photos above: **Alicia Alonso** as the Black Swan in *Swan Lake*; the Auditorium program for her Gala Performance **honoring Fulgencio Batista** as he assumed the presidency of Cuba in 1955.

The most consistent and all-time generous benefactor of Cuban exiles in Miami was **Coleman Francis Carroll (1905-1977)**, Archbishop of Miami from 1958 until his death. He was born in Pittsburgh, the second of three children from a very poor Irish family. His father was a railroad brakeman and patio clerk for *Carnegie Steel*, his mother a housekeeper. He was ordained priest in 1930 after graduating from *Duquesne University*; in 1958 became the first Bishop of the newly defined *Diocese of Miami*, comprising 200,000 Catholics and extending north to include half the state of Florida.

Carroll was swift, wholehearted and passionate in the way he received the Cuban exiles in the early 1960s. When Msgr. Bryan O. Walsh as head of *Catholic Charities* asked for his help to resettle about 200 Cuban refugee children —in the early days of the *Pedro Pan* operation— Carroll declared «We'll take all of the 7,000 estimated to come and even more, if there are more.» Carroll waited for many of them at the Miami airport and used his own funds and resources to feed them for more than a year, until the US began to support the operation.

Years later, at an event in the Miami Stadium where more than 15,000 Cuban refugees gathered to thank Carroll, the newspapers reported that at the moment Carroll began to speak...

«...the whole crowd, as one, when they realized that this foreign bishop in a foreign land was reaching out to them, began to scream, then they raised white handkerchiefs, and then they applauded louder than a 747 jet. They just could not stop, as Archbishop Carroll began to cry.»

Carroll died at age 72 and was buried in the priest's section of *Our Lady of Mercy Cemetery* in Miami.

Photos above:
Archbishop Carroll on the day of his designation as Bishop of Miami; on the right, cooking for a Cuban exile fundraising event.

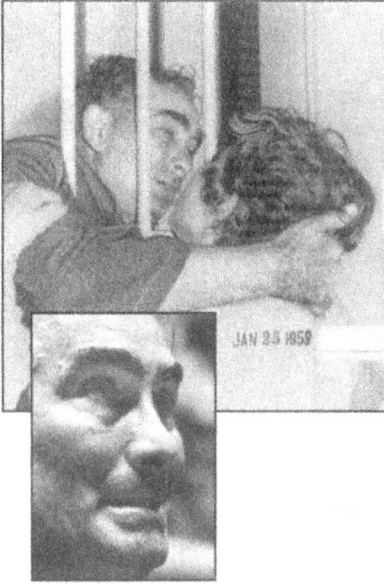

Regardless of what their feelings were with respect to the revolution, Cubans were horrified when this picture was shown on TV and the papers in Cuba. *On the left*, **Jesús Sosa Blanco** is reaching through his prison bars to grab and kiss his wife during her last visit to him. He was at *La Cabaña* prison and would be put to death the following day by a firing squad. The picture, by Delio Valdés, was first shown in the newspaper *El Crisol*. Cubans had never seen such cruelty from their government. *Below the photo, above*, the frightened face of Sosa Blanco. *On the right*, Sosa Blanco listening to his sentence in a circus-like atmosphere.

On the left, the poster for **Cuban Story**, a documentary film made by **Errol Flynn** during the first days of the Cuban revolution. Flynn happened to be in Havana on January 1, 1959 (he owned a movie theater in Cuba), and filmed the upheaval in the streets. Cuban exiles saw the film in Europe (it was shown at the *Moscow Film Festival* and a few other venues, but never in Cuba or the US). The film was then taken from circulation until 2002. Until he died in 1959, Flynn was a devoted fan of Castro, an accused statutory rapist, an alleged incestuous father, a Nazi sympathizer, leading the life of a freewheeling hedonist.

As the number of executions without trial of former military officers grew in Cuba, hundreds of young students and dissidents of the revolutionary movement began to be detained in the fortress of *La Cabaña* in Havana. Many would fall at the hands of **Ernesto (Ché) Guevara**.

The number of opponents taking asylum in foreign embassies also grew to unprecedented levels and they began to swell the ranks of exiles in Miami, the New York area and several South American capitals. It soon became the largest exodus in the history of any country in the New World.

Photos above: the inhumane execution of Santa Clara Police Captain ***Cornelio Rojas*** following a bogus trial and apparently specific orders to shoot at his face. Rojas had been a fighter for democracy in 1931. His father fought in the 1895 war of independence under Calixto García. There were many testimonies, however, that Rojas had abused opponents to Batista in the years preceding the dictator's fall;

Below, a *miliciano* stands guard above the prisoners at *La Cabaña* fortress. Few of them escaped death sentences imposed at daily midnight sessions of Guevara's phony revolutionary tribunals.

Castro's arbitrary revocation of the decision of a military tribunal that exonerated pilots and mechanics of the *Cuban Air Force* accused of bombing the rebels in the *Sierra Maestra,* was for many Cubans the last straw in their commitment to the revolution. The pilots were retried and found guilty. This intensified the stream of exiles seeking refuge in the US.

Photos above, top to bottom: Havana mobs asking for more executions; the trial of **Evelio Otero Montano**, executed February 10, 1959; Com. **Felix Lugerio Pena**, the man who presided the military tribunal that found the pilots innocent. He *"commited suicide"* four months later, in June of 1959; **Hernando Hernández**, Havana's former Chief of Police awaiting his turn; finally two photos of the group of pilots as shown in the newspapers.

For over half a century Cuban exiles have felt the effects of what historians have rightly called the **Cassandra Paradox**. In Greek mythology the prophetess *Cassandra* was doomed to both see the future and suffer the frustration of being ignored. As they looked to what was happening in Cuba, many Cuban exiles tried in vain to warn Cubans in the island that progress is never assured and civilizations and communities could easily retrogress and be far worse in the future than what they were in the past. The ruins of classical Greece offer a contemporary evidence that things could get worse rather than better with time; so do the ancient temples of the Maya, the streets of Detroit, the economy of Argentina or the current state of the city of Havana, to mention only a few examples.

In Cuba, the initial enthusiasm of the 1959 revolution proved to be a very thin and flimsy veneer that could not last more than a few weeks. It dissolved the moment Castro imposed a new trial to the 42 Cuban Air Force pilots accused of bombing the *Sierra Maestra* rebels, who were found innocent in March of 1959. They were taken to the *Boniato prison* instead of being freed after their initial acquittal. Few Cubans remember, after 50 years, that a second trial, lasting 8 hours, was organized in the absence of the accused; this trial did not rendered any decisions. The following day Castro appeared on TV and all radio stations and ordered 19 pilots to be sentenced to 30 years of forced labor, 9 gunners to 20 years and 14 mechanics to 2 years. This sentence —decreed by one man that had no legal authority to do so— was carried faithfully until completion.

For the next 50 years many Cubans, both in exile and in the island, appealed to the civilized world to stop the criminal, vicious and oppressive situation in Cuba. They could foresee what the revolution was leading to; yet very few people listened. As in the *Cassandra Paradox*, those that spoke because they could see the future were ignored.

Photos:
Left: the Tribunal (five commanders of the Rebel Army) that heard arguments (in the second trial) to impugn the absolution of the pilots and gunners during the first trial: Commanders **Belarmino Castilla**, **Carlos Iglesias Fonseca**, **Manuel Piñeiro Losada**, **Demetrio Montseny Villa** and **Pedro Luis Díaz**; right: **Lugerio Pena** during the first trial.

On October 12, 1960, at the *La Campana* farm, a few miles from the city of Santa Clara, in Cuba, **Plinio Prieto (1923-1960)**, an anti-Castro rebel fighting on the mountains of *El Escambray*, was executed with his friends Sinesio Walsch Rios, José Palomino Colon, Ángel Rodríguez del Sol and Porfirio Ramírez Ruiz. They did not have the benefit of a fair trial. At noon on that day, over 150 anti-Castro guerrillas were brought to the Officers Club of the *Santa Clara Barracks*. It was the *Causa No 829*. The revolutionary tribunal — all members of the PSP, the *Cuban Communist Party*—was presided by First Lieutenant Claudio López Cardet; the accusing officer was a Captain *Juan Escalona Reguera*. Both López and Escalona became famous for their many victims of mockup trials where the sentences were coming from Havana and preceded the trials.

Plinio had been a teacher at the *Escuela Superior # 3 Marta Abreu* in Marianao, Havana. He had been an organizer of the *Second Escambray Front* against Batista and returned to the mountains when he realized the revolution had acquired a Communist slant. He was betrayed by a spy —according to witnesses, a friend called Félix Hurtado— and made prisoner in the town of *Cumanayagua*, taken to the G2 prison in Havana and moved to Santa Clara for his sentencing; 106 of his followers —mostly workers, students and *campesinos*— were sentenced to 30 years.

By a strange coincidence, the place where Plinio and his friends were assassinated came to be where in January of 1998 *Pope Juan Pablo II* would offer his first mass in Cuban territory.

Photos above, *top to bottom*: the Castro propaganda machine justifying their executions and sentencing practices; *on the right*, **Plinio Prieto** at the time of his death.

Some of the first voices that opposed the takeover of Cuba by the Communists were the members of the *Movimiento Demócrata Cristiano (MDC)*: Luis Aguilar León, Jorge Mas Canosa, José Ignacio Rasco, Manuel Suárez Carreño, Valentín Arenas, Enrique Villareal, Jesús Angulo Clemente, Eddy Carreras Vallina, José Fernández Badué, Oscar Miñoso Bachiller, Ramón Galeano Arango, Enrique Ros, Segundo Miranda, Manuel Fernández Pérez and Heriberto Corona, to mention only a few. Several other organizations were also early contestants in the struggle against Communism, such as *Vanguardia Demócrata Cristiana*, an early movement with excellent leadership that broke with the MDC in 1961.

Photos above:
Featured articles about *Vanguardia Democrática Cristiana* in *Avance* and *Diario Las Americas* in September 1961; *Amalio Fiallo* and *Jesús Angulo* and a book by *Fermín Peinado,* years later, still in exile, after a lifetime dedication to the return of Cuba to a democratic path.

THE DISILLUSIONED, DESPERATE, DISGUSTED TRY TO GET AWAY

More Cubans began to flow into exile when Castro's followers began to ignore other organizations like the **Directorio** which had contributed significantly to the fall of Batista. The numbers grew as people were turned off by the public calls for "*Paredón*" by the followers of Castro and by the shootings without trials. An unprecedented abuse of power was the reversal of the acquittal of airmen of the regular Cuban Air Force by Castro. The burial of *Diario La Marina*, followed by other media (newspapers, radio and television) was a clear indication of the end of a free press. Homes, businesses and industries, domestic and foreign, were confiscated. Groups of *militia-mobs* replaced the regular army.

Disillusioned Cubans reacted in several ways in 1959: many decided to conspire against the regime, risking to be imprisoned and perhaps executed. Others sought refuge in an embassy, traveled abroad —mainly to the US— and joined the ranks of exiles. A large number remained in Cuba, unable to do anything because of the terror.

Photos above: a LIFE magazine report on the **disillusioned** in 1959; a 1959 protest by a group of exiles in New York City.

While the executions that started in the *Sierrra Maestra* were continued in the cities in Cuba during 1959, the lists of refugees began
to swell as many Cubans decided to abandon the island in search of
a safer environment. Few thought at the time that their exile would
be long-drawn and for many, a life-long exile.

Photos above: the rebels in the *Sierra Maestra* **executing dissidents**
among their ranks; early in 1959, a march of **revolutionary zealots** in Havana asking for execution of opponents to the revolution; in the meantime,
in Miami, hundreds of Cubans —*Batistianos* and former combatants against
Batista— were registering as exiles at what they called "*El Refugio*."

Among the most notable exiles in 1959 and subsequent years were the leaders and founders of the Radio and TV Media in Cuba. The role of Cubans in the development of TV in the Americas was nothing short of spectacular. Several "*media moguls*" began to leave the island, among them, Cuban-born **Diego Cisneros (1896-1980)** and his son **Gustavo Cisneros (1945-)** founders of Venezuela's network *Venevision*, and Cuban-born **Goar Mestre (1912-1994)** who, in conjunction with CBS and Dumont, launched *Channel 13* in Argentina) and **Gaspar Pumarejo (1913-1969)** who, in partnership with RCA, launched the first TV station in Cuba on October 24, 1950. In Cuba, in 1958, the country had 25 TV stations working in Havana, Matanzas, Santa Clara, Ciego de Avila, Camagüey, Holguín and Santiago de Cuba. With the Cisneros, the Mestres and Pumarejo, many relatively unknown Cuban exiles became instrumental in the inauguration of television and advertising in Argentina, Peru, Puerto Rico, Venezuela, and all across the US Spanish-language media market.

The TV personalities who stayed in Cuba had to work in the State-controlled broadcasting system and in the *Cuban Institute of Cinematographic Art and Industry*. Those who left became important figures in the development of broadcasting and advertising corporations in Buenos Aires, Caracas, Lima, Miami, New York City, Rio de Janeiro, and San Juan; many of these early Cuban exiles had a profound influence in the telenovelas produced years later in Mexico, Brazil, and Miami.

Photos: top, ***Romulo Betancourt***, ***Diego Cisneros*** and ***Carlos Andrés Pérez***; bottom, left to right, ***Goar Mestre***, ***Gustavo Cisneros*** and ***Gaspar Pumarejo***, the three great "TV Moguls" of the Americas.

As the year 1959 progressed, more and more talented people in Cuba began to leave the island disappointed with the dogmatic and undemocratic ideologies of the revolution. Two brilliant women artists joined the Cuban exile community in Paris in 1959.

Gina Pellón (1926-) had been a graduate from the Academy of San Alejandro in 1954, and a teacher at the *Vedado Institute*. In 1959, she earned a scholarship to the *Cité Universitaire* in Paris. Disillusioned with the happenings in Cuba she overstayed her visa, fleeing from the Cuban dictatorship of Fidel Castro, and in 1960 made her first solo exhibition in Luzern, Switzerland. She is known for her abstract expressive paintings in strong colors, usually depicting women. She has also written collections of poems.

Nivaria Tejera (1929-) was born to a Cuban mother and a Spanish father from the Canary Islands and moved with her parents to Tenerife at an early age, where her father was taken prisoner at the outbreak of the Spanish Civil War. She returned to Cuba when he was freed in 1944. Soon she began to write and publish poetry and in 1954 went to Paris as an exile from the Batista regime; she went back to Cuba in 1959 with great enthusiasm for the revolution. Soon, however, she broke her political ties to Cuba and returned to Paris, where she became internationally known for her poetry, her novels and her essays.

*Photos top to bottom: **Nivaria Tejera** in Paris with **Heberto Padilla** in 1959; **Gina Pellón** receiving from **Dr. Alberto Bustamante** the Herencia Cultural Cubana Award in 2010.*

A familiar experience that Cuban exiles never got to enjoy for much time were the baseball games at the *Bobby Maduro Stadium*, at 23rd Avenue and NW 10th Street, in Miami.

The *Bobby Maduro* was a stadium built to fulfill the dreams of a young Cuban millionaire, José Manuel Alemán, in the 1940s. He was the son of a hero of the Cuban Independence War of 1895 and at age 45 he owned *Cape Florida*, the *McAllister Hotel* and a magnificent home in the 4000 block of Pine Tree Drive. He believed he could lure a Major League Baseball Team to Miami by building a beautiful and comfortable stadium. His dream was billed at the time as «*a park only second to Yankee Stadium.*» After a 2.2 million investment, it was ready for playing ball on opening night, August 31, 1949. It was baptized the Miami Stadium.

In time, it attracted players like Ted Williams, Jackie Robinson, Mickey Mantle, Satchel Paige, Jim Palmer and Cal Ripken Jr. But it never attracted a Major League Team or enough fans among Miamians. The situation did not improve with the presence of thousands of fans among the Cuban exiles. It was said that on opening night in 1949, 13,000 tickets were sold, a record that would never be broken. José Manuel Alemán died of Hodgkin's disease in 1950; his son José Braulio sold the stadium to the City of Miami in 1958, and moved to Cuba in 1959. The stadium was rebaptized as *Bobby Maduro*. In the mean time, in Cuba, José Braulio lost all his fortune and returned to Miami as an impoverish refugee. A Sunday morning in July of 1983, living in a rundown home in Little Havana, he shot his entire family and took his own life. He was 51 years old.

Photos above: the stadium, **Boby Maduro** (for whom the Stadium was named, owner of the *Havana Sugar Kings*), and the Stadium front.

One of the first Castro revolutionaries that deserted and joined the exile ranks was Commander **Pedro Luis Díaz Lanz (1926-2008)**. He was a commercial pilot for *Aerovias Q,* a small carrier in Cuba when he began to smuggle weapons and supplies from Costa Rica, Venezuela and Florida to the *Sierra Maestra* rebels in 1958. Upon the triumph of the revolution he became Chief of the *Revolutionary Air Force* as well as Castro's personal pilot.

In February of 1959, as head of the Air Force, he promised many of the members of the pre-Castro Air Force to rejoin the service. Within weeks of following his advice, they were taken into custody, indicted and sentenced, without consulting Diaz Lanz. At that point he became vocal in his opposition to the communists and Castro deposed him on June 29, 1959. He sought asylum in Miami and on July 14 he gave a deposition to the US Senate Internal Security Subcommittee about the inroads of Communism in Cuba.

Later in 1959 he flew a twin-engine plane —reportedly a B-25— over Havana, dropping through the bomb hatch anticommunist leaflets with the help of his brother Marcos. It was said that he later joined the CIA in anti-Castro activities.

In 2008, after years of extreme poverty and profound depression because what he felt was a hopeless situation in Cuba, he took his own life in Miami with a gunshot to the chest. Lanz was the grandchild of a veteran of the 1895 Independence War and a great grandchild of one of José Marti's sisters.

Photos above: **Diaz Lanz** testifying in the US Congress
and a portrait dated 1959.

During most of 1959 Miami residents felt that it was interesting to watch the drama of the Cuban refugees in the evening news. By the end of the year, however, many had second thoughts about this uncontrollable Tsunami of people that could alter the very character of the city.

Indeed, the early arrivals had come with money and had family or friends in Miami. They were received by someone who knew in advance they were coming. By the end of 1959 the wealthy and well-connected were scarce; the prevalent exiles were desperate and penniless Cubans, educated and learned but also scared and ready to take any job, earn whatever money, sleep 10 or 12 to an apartment and saving all they could manage to bring others like them to the city. There was rarely a home that did not have more guests than family members and perhaps an actual wage earner for every four or five people looking for jobs.

The Catholic Church, with the help of the federal government, rushed to the scene to help accommodate the hordes of new refugees arriving every day in Miami. A similar situation was taking place in Union City, New Jersey and to a certain extent in New York, New Orleans and Chicago.

Photos above: many families, not having cars, had to rely for their daily sustenance on purchases of groceries at *La Vaquita* (the **Farm Stores** drive-in establishments, typically with prices of convenience stores); others would go to **Royal Castle** franchises, where you could get a hamburger and a cup of coffee for 25 cents, and all the catsup you could consume.

As more and more professionals, business people, lawyers, teachers and trade people were streaming into Miami, a very different inflow of immigrants was taking place in the Dominican Republic. The initial prevailing outpourings were sponsored and hired by the Dominican *Servicio de Inteligencia Militar (SIM)*; the exiled military men found ready positions serving the Trujillo regime.

Eleuterio Pedraza flew in with Batista; he had been Chief of the *National Police in Cuba* and in *Dominicana* he organized an anti-Castro conspiracy, planned to blow up a ship in Havana harbor and organized a squadron of airplanes to burn the Shell refinery and several sugar fields in Cuba. He knew he was "*fusilable*" in Cuba. **José María Salas Cañizares** had been known in Santiago de Cuba as "*Masacre Cañizares*." He also landed in *Dominicana* in early 1959. **Manuel Ugalde Carrillo** had been Chief of the SIM and was accused in Cuba as the master of death in the *Presidio Modelo* in Isla de Pinos. **Angel Sánchez Mosquera** was the Chief of Operations in *Sierra Maestra* where he earned a reputation as a ferocious criminal.

Also in Santo Domingo under the command of Trujillo for a while were **Conrado Carratalá Ugalde** and **Esteban Ventura Novo**, who eventually moved to Miami and stared *Ventura Detective and Protection Security Service* in Miami Beach. A late arrival was **Julio Laurent**, former Chief of the Naval Intelligence Service in Cuba, who presumably missed the escaping aircraft in Havana because of a drinking orgy he had on the 31st of December at *Tropicana* Night Club.

Photos above: a gallery of *rogues* that went to exile in the Dominican Republic following Fulgencio Batista. *Top row*: **Eleuterio Pedraza**, **José María Salas Cañizares** and **Manuel Ugalde Carrillo**.
Bottom row: **Julio Laurent, Conrado Carratalá** and **Esteban Ventura**.

M-9—The Mercy Hospital, Miami, Fla.

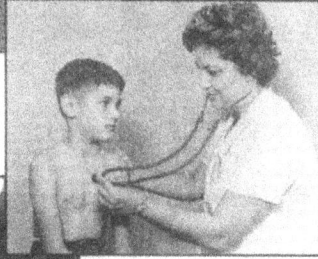

As more refugees poured into Miami and the New York area, practical solutions began to be found. The Diocese of Miami opened a **Refugee Center** at 130 NE 2nd Avenue where meals were served and a few dollars dispensed to help refugees to get a temporary refuge in one of downtown cheap traveling salesmen hotels. The Dioceses also began to place refugee children in non-existing openings in Catholic schools. The class size immediately jumped to 6o students in most schools. Since the bulk of refugees had no money and could not afford Blue Cross/Blue Shield medical insurance, the Church's **Mercy Hospital** in Coconut Grove was opened to take care of refugees free of charge. An appeal was made to the National Catholic Welfare Council, who began to solicit help from some fifty dioceses in two dozen states in the US East and Southwest. The bills to support the influx of refugees reached $150,000 a month by the end of 1959 and all Catholic parishes began to have a second collection at all Masses.

Photos above from top to bottom: **Mercy Hospital** in 1959; a nurse during a medical check-up; the **Refugee Center** lobby; **SPAM**, the canned meat distributed early in 1959 before the federal government program took over with the "*carne del refugio.*"

Without going through immigration, Cuban refugees descending from the planes that brought them from Havana were asked to submit to a quick physical examination. Most of them were given a bill of health, photographed, fingerprinted and introduced to the **Catholic Charities** staff. Few were sent to *Opalocka airport* for further questioning. Almost always they were not students on the way to College or wealthy would-be immigrants that had enough funds to settle themselves in comfort; they looked tired, decidedly middle class, many of them professionals seeking freedom from coercion, brainwashing and the efforts of the Castro regime to indoctrinate them into Marxism. As one prestigious lawyer from Cárdenas said years later *«I was ready and proud to work in a butcher shop, but I told my coworkers... if any of you ever takes these knives and murders anyone, I would be happy to help you as your lawyer.»*

In Havana, the Castro newspapers were presenting the Miami refugees as *«poorly dressed, fearful, mentally sick and depressed, uncouth, disoriented and unhappy.»* It was part of the effort of the revolutionaries to stem the flow of Cubans leaving the island. Nothing was further from the truth. The human capital that had made Cuba one of the most progressive countries in the Americas was rejecting socialism by walking away rather than simply complaining about it.

Photos above: the former building of the *Miami News* newspaper in the process of being converted to a **Cuban Refugee Center** by the federal government; *on the right*, a brochure sent to all points in the US in an effort to relocate refugees all across the US and alleviate the overcrowding in Miami.

The first foreign trip of Castro after January 1st 1959 was to Caracas, Venezuela on the 25th of January. There he spoke to the students at the *Universidad Central*, met with legislators and invited the Venezuelan revolutionaries to collaborate in the overthrow of Rafael Leónidas Trujillo in the Dominican Republic. While this was happening, hundreds of Cubans in Havana were desperately trying to get on one of Pan American flights to freedom in Miami.

Photos above top to bottom: Castro meeting with Rear Admiral **Wolfgang Larrazabal**, a military leader during the overthrow of dictator **Marcos Pérez Jiménez**; Castro arriving at *Maiquetía*, Caracas on June 23, 1959; Multitudes in Caracas welcoming Castro; on the very same day, hundreds of future Cuban refugees trying to board a Pan Am flight to Miami.

In 1959 Cuban exiles, on top of their efforts to secure a stable *modus vivendi* for themselves and their families, had to challenge the propaganda campaign initiated by the Cuban dictator. Castro went into a well financed campaign to earn the respect of the US and the world to his present and projected actions in Cuba. He visited US politicians, fraternized with American decision-makers and showed up at the United Nations, all within a few weeks and —contrary to the tradition of politicians from Cuba— without openly asking for foreign aid.

Photos above: On April 16, 1959, he had lunch with **Christian Herter,** US Under Secretary of State, at the Statler-Hilton in NY; a few days later he met with VP ***Richard Nixon*** since President Eisenhower declined to meet with him; he had met ***Philip Bonsal***, the last US Ambassador to Cuba in March 1959; At every event he met Cuban exiles protesting for his presence and his empty promises.

There has been a lot of controversy about Castro's visit to the US in 1959. Most historians feel that, after years pondering and day-dreaming about his future, he knew exactly what he wanted to happen in Cuba and what he wanted to do in the US. Some analysts, rather apologetically, talk about a Castro whose ego was bruised by Eisenhower's rebuff when he did not want to receive him in the White House. Nothing further from the truth.

Castro decided to play the populist and misbehave during his visit to New York. Claiming to be uncomfortable at a five star hotel in Manhattan he had his group pack up and move to the *Theresa Hotel* in Harlem. Even there, at the best black hotel in the city, he complained about the food and had his entourage buy ingredients to roast several chickens in their rooms for the entire 21 men Cuban delegation. As usual, a large group of Cuban refugees followed him everywhere he went during his visit to New York, protesting his one-man rule in Cuba.

Photos above: **Castro** greeting his followers across the street from the *Theresa Hotel*; Castro with **Khrushchev** at the *Theresa*.

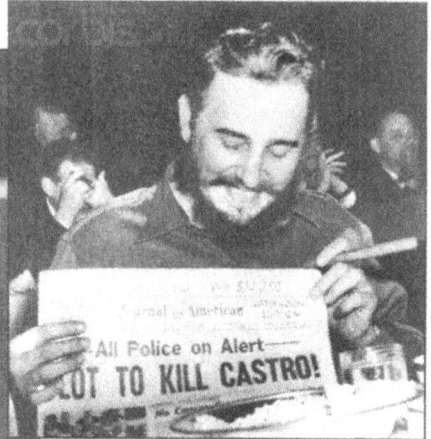

Photos above, top to bottom: Castro meeting with **Malcolm X** at the *Theresa Hotel*; meeting **Gamal Abdel Nasser**, the Egyptian dictator, on the street in front of the hotel; Castro *learning of a plot to kill him during his New York visit;* Castro *addressing the UN General Assembly* in 1959.

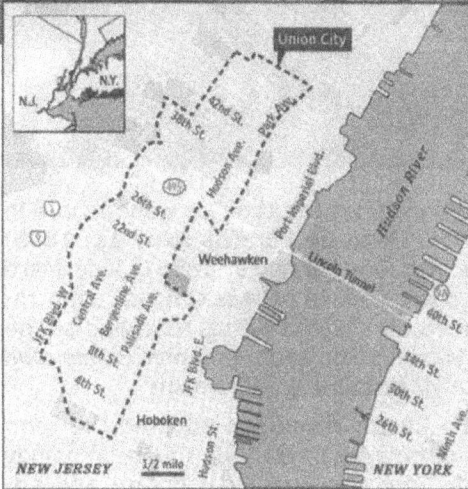

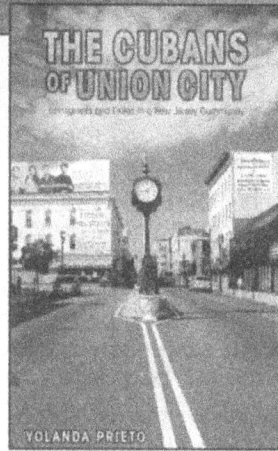

Starting in 1959, a strong flow of Cubans settled also in the area of *Union City*, searching for work in the city's embroidery factories. The flow lasted into the 2000s and, as a result, Union City to this day, has a significant Cuban population that includes the owners of most of the storefronts and restaurants along *Bergenline Avenue*, one of the main commercial streets in the city. As early as the 1960s, Union City —the merger of Union Hill and West Hoboken, became the largest Cuban populated city in the US after the Miami area.

Just like in Miami, Cubans took any available jobs when they arrived, as long as they could provide for their families. Soon they became self-employed and created an informal economy —with little initial capital— built on the principle of helping each other. It allowed them to develop a loyal customer base which became the secret of their success.

*Photos above, **Bergenline Avenue** in 1959; a city map of the times and the cover of the celebrated book by **Yolanda Prieto**.*

In his **War Diaries**—his writings from the time he went ashore in Cuba at *Playitas de Cajobabo*, cerca de Baracoa (May 11, 1895) to the day of his death in *Dos Rios* (May 29, 1895), José Martí wrote on May 4 about the court-martial of **Masabó**, a Cuban rebel who had raped and robbed. At the end of this trial, and as the death sentence was read, Máximo Gómez commented «*This man is not our comrade: he is a vil gusano, a vile worm*».

Based on this anecdote, the Castro revolution adopted the term **gusano** as the opposite of **comrade**, presenting this terminology as a coinage of José Martí. *Comrade* was an honorary and endearing term for those in favor of the revolution; **gusano** was an insulting and a contemptuous slur for those opposed to the revolutionary credo. Máximo Gómez use of the term "**gusano**" was intended for a vile and morally deprived person.

By the 1980s these denominations had completely lost popular support. Both the term **comrade** or **compañero**, and **gusano** or **contrarevolucionario** had lost their rhetorical intentions. The **gusanos** (worms) had blossomed into **mariposas** (butterflies). They came visiting from Miami with gifts and cash to help the stranded inhabitants of Cuba that had nothing to show for years of sacrifice for the revolution. Contrary to **Gregor Samsa** in Kafka's *Metamorphosis* (who waked up to find himself turned into an insect that was hated by his family), the **gusanos** lost their humanity in Cuba but did not turned around and died; they left for a land of opportunity and returned to their society happy and successful, probably too often and for trivial reasons.

Photos above: Long lines seeking visas at the *Office of US Interests in Havana*; successful **gusanos** arriving from the US at Havana's airport.

While Castro was calling the Cuban exiles "*gusanos*" (worms), and books, films, newspapers and magazines in the US were exalting the novelty and exoticism of the revolutionary narrative, the exiles were establishing a solid base for survival in their new environment. Many Cubans believed the exile was a temporary condition yet they did not waste time and began to absorb American values with the hope that, in the worst of cases, they would be able to live decently in the US and in the best of cases they could transport the fruits of their efforts to tomorrow's Cuba.

(Continued)

Photos above top to bottom: "***gusanos***," the negative epithet used by Castro that Cuban exiles adopted for themselves full of pride; TIME and LIFE, two of several US magazines that never understood the tragedy of Cuba.

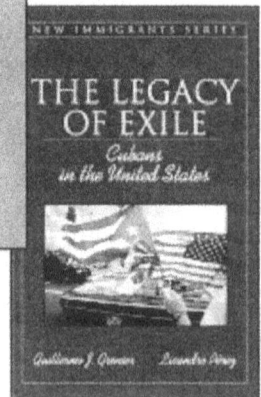

(Continuation)

Cuban exiles opened restaurants, bookstores, supermarkets, gas stations, record shops, hardware stores, appliance and furniture stores. Students hit the books hard to get credentials and develop skills useful in a future Cuba. Professionals revalidated or complemented their University titles to absorb the up-to-date knowledge and practices in their careers. Those inclined to business transactions began to secure contacts to continue or open businesses in Cuba. The rich Cuban exiles were opening banks, buying car dealerships, founding corporations and acquiring investment real estate. Cuba, however, was always present. The exile years were always seen as a transitional period to a future life in Cuba.

Photos above top to bottom: The story of the Cuban exile, its anguish, dedication and success has been told many times.

As the year 1959 advanced it was clear that not only the *Batistianos* were leaving Cuba but also many prestigious families that sensed the Castro government eventually would be coming after them. These were families of means, investors, entrepreneurs, and owners of businesses that were providing employment and producing exports that were contributing to the island economy. They were mostly descendants of men and women that had made fortunes in the island with their hard work and persistency, many of them denying themselves the fruits of their labor for many years in order to make a future for their children.

It was well known in Cuba that **no immigrants from Spain had brought fortunes to Cuba**. They had come to Cuba with only dreams and stoicism as their weapons. After years of hard work they had accumulated *know-how* and a good fortune that guaranteed the success of their heirs. The following pages illustrate the homes they built after they became an upper class that was, by and large, honest, conservative and with sound ethical principles. Their going into exile was an irreparable loss of talent to the young **Republic of Cuba**.

Photos: the homes of
Alfonso Gómez Mena and
Alfredo Hornedo
In Havana.

Photos above, top to bottom, left to right: the Havana homes of **Antonio Tarafa**, the **Marqueses de Avilés**, the **Condesa de Revilla de Camargo**, **Pablo González de Mendoza, Catalina Lasa / Juan Pedro Baro** and **Bernardo Solís.**

As the decade of the 1960s started it became clear that the issue of Cuba had an international dimension and was intermingled with the existing Cold War between the US and the Soviet Union. Hundreds of refugees in Eastern Europe were pouring under the Iron Curtain out of the Soviet sphere of influence. The US was presenting it as a tangible proof of the inadequacy of the communist way of life. Cuba became a parallel case in the Americas. The US decided to encourage Cubans to seek the exile route and Havana and Miami became a theater of operations in the Cold War. The failure of communism in Cuba would exemplify the perils of anti-Americanism and left-leaning political postures... more so than the amateurish US actions against *Jacobo Arbenz* in Guatemala in 1954.

Michigan **Senator Philip Hart (1912-1976)**, a D-Day veteran in 1944 for which the *Hart Senate Office Building* was named, held hearings in Miami in 1961 and concluded that «*a major refugee assistance program must be started in Miami in a way that reflects a conscious understanding that our action in this area bears directly on our foreign policy*».

Miami **Mayor Robert King High (1924-1967)**, who had led a delegation to Cuba that was snubbed by Castro, declared upon his return «*we can no longer treat the matter of Cuban refugees as a welfare problem. These people who gave up their homes, and in some instances their families because of their refusal to knuckle under to communist tyranny should be allowed to taste the fruits of freedom*».

H. Frank Williams (1921-1989), the Dean of the School of Arts and Sciences of the *University of Miami* added «*the refugee problem is something larger than a Miami community problem; we see Miami as the battle front of the Cold War. The United States is now a country of first asylum, and the way in which we handle these people who had chosen to leave a Communist area is important to the Cold War*».

*Photos above, left to right: **Senator Philip Hart, Miami Mayor Robert King** and **Dean Frank Williams**.*

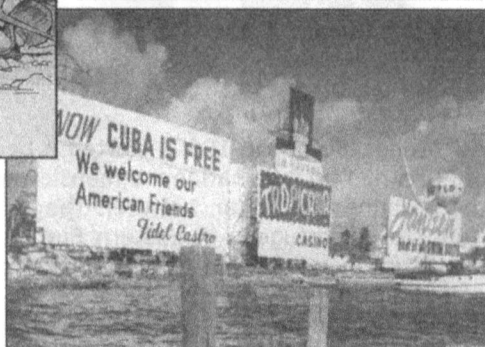

The Cuban refugee impetus in Miami began to transform the city. Small business began to appear all over a section of Miami that became known as *"Little Havana."* Ten small newspapers —the celebrated *periodiquitos*—began to be published, supported by ads from Cuban small businesses. On December 30, 1960 a Cuban theater opened at 313 West Flagler, featuring a somewhat risqué French film, "*Este Cuerpo Tan Deseado*". In December 1960 the former owner of the *La Gran Via* in Havana, opened in Miami Beach the first Cuban restaurant —of many to follow— in the Miami area.

At the corner of SW Eighth Street and 35th Avenue an entrepreneurial **Felipe Vals** was making arrangements to buy for $97K a lot that some friends claimed it was too far west from *"little Havana"*. It became first a neighborhood joint and within a few years made Felipe *"the Czar of Cuban Cuisine"* and his **Versalles** an international known eatery destination. At 223 N.W. 3rd Avenue Cuban exiles found a new employment agency fully staffed by Cubans. Along Biscayne boulevard you could not drive two blocks without been proposed **Cuban Liberty Bonds** by fellow exiles. All through Miami, small businesses owned and operated by Italian-Americans and Jewish proprietors began to change their names and ownership to names familiar to Cubans. All through the 1960s, the number of Cubans seeking admission into the US kept climbing at a brisk pace and Castro's propaganda and infiltration in Latin America continued unabated. Castro's effort even included billboards in the port of Miami.

Photos above: Castro's propaganda while
Cubans were seeking exile at the US embassy in Havana.

The numerous *"periodiquitos"* published by the Cuban exiles in Miami in the 1960s served five purposes: first, they established a historical record of the feelings and concerns of the exile community at different times. Second, they reached a wide audience at a time where there was no internet or any other way to call the attention of the exiles to many important events that could have an influence in their future. Third, they were an inexpensive means of advertising for new businesses in the community, as well as a good source of employment tips and opportunities. Fourth, they provided an easy and clear description of the mores, the expectations and the culture of the Americans, particularly for Cuban seniors and those who were not fluent in the English language. Fifth, they helped many exiles to overcome their isolation and preserve and maintain a sense of identity and community.

Photos below top to bottom: a selection of some of the local exile newspapers in the Cuban exile Miami community in the 1960s.

Some scenes from the life of Cuban exiles during 1959 and the early 1960s.

Photos below, top to bottom:
Cuban exiles receiving medical supplies at the **Jackson Memorial Hospital**; two young girls waiting for their parents *at Miami airport;* Refugees waiting to be processed at the **International Rescue Committee**; exiles at the **Cuban Refugee Center**.

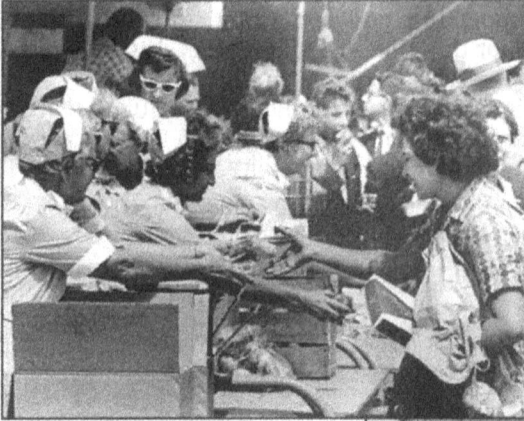

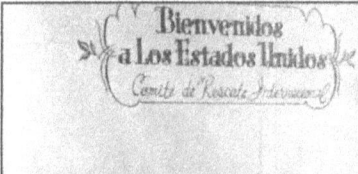

(Continued)

(Continuation)

(Continued)

Photos above:
Food distributed at the **Cuban Refugee Center** in Miami (today's *Freedom Tower*); an appeal for help to Cuban exiles from the **American community**;; a group of Cubans taking English classes at the **Lindsey-Hopkins Learning Center**; a meeting of Cuban exiles recently relocated to **West New York** and **Union City** in 1960.

The optimism of Cuban exiles during the first months of the revolution was evident by the humor of the cartoons in the Miami exile press during 1959 and 1960.

From top to bottom: the people ready to stand tall and defeat the Castro revolution; a **médico chino** stating that not even he could save the moribund revolution; the people kicking away Fidel, Raul, Ché and Khrushchev; finally the power pecking order in Cuba: Khrushchev, Castro and the Cuban people.

JURAN LA CONSTITUCION DE 1940

El domingo anterior unos ocho mil cubanos se congregaron en el Bayfront Park para prestar el juramento a la Carta Magna en un acto cívico emocionante al cual conreró el señor Norman Díaz. Representantes de todos los sectores, y de todos los grupos políticos, asistieron al patriótico acto en que se puso de manifiesto, además del acatamiento a la Constitución, se le en las instituciones democráticas y en la libertad. El señor Norman Díaz pronunció un bello discurso que fue coronado por el acto de jura de la Ley de Leyes, mientras los presentes agitaban pañuelos blancos. Las palabras del

CUBANOS EXILADOS EN MIAMI

señor Norman Díaz fueron premiadas por grandes aplausos, especialmente cuando subrayó que la Constitución de 1940 garantizaba el respeto a la libertad de todos los ciudadanos, los derechos humanos, la libre empresa, la libertad de expresión, la libertad de prensa, la libertad de palabra, las elecciones libres, la libertad de enseñanza, la libertad de adorar a Dios, todas las cuales ha conculcado el gobierno comunista que asoló el poder el primero de enero de 1959.

WMIE was a commercial station in Miami, broadcasting on 1140 AM, from its studies located on 36th Street, Northwest. It had 10,000 watts of power and it could be heard clearly in the central provinces of Cuba, and parts of Havana, Pinar del Rio and Camagüey. In the early 1960s, at the beginning of their exile, Cubans began to rent space in this station (it was originally transmitting in English only). One of the most popular rented spaces was **El Periódico del Aire** (Journal on the Air), by **Juan Amador Rodríguez (1920-2002).** Just as popular was the **Noticiero**, run by another Cuban exile, **Norman Díaz**. As more and more Cubans moved to Miami, more and more radio slots were rented until the entire transmission of WMIE was in Spanish. Several well known Cuban radio personalities had their first job in exile at WMIE: **Eduardo González Rubio, Aleida Leal and Carlos Acosta**, among others. The station eventually became **WQBA**, pronounced in Spanish as W-Cuba.

Photos above:
Norman Díaz had an extraordinary ability to organize political rallies such as the one presented in the two photos above: a gathering of over 8,000 Cuban exiles at *Bayfront Park* in Miami to pledge allegiance to the *1940 Cuban Constitution* that had been eliminated by the Castro regime.

Miami in the early 1960s

Miami Airport.

Belle Isle, Miami.

Le Jeune Avenue, Miami, looking towards *Hialeah*.

Two views of **Calle Ocho** before *Little Havana*.

Miami in the early 1960s

The **City of Hialeah** and the race track.

Burdine Stadium, later known as the **Orange Bowl**.

Area South of Bird Road and East of 117th Avenue (Where the Turnpike was later built), showing **Westwood Lake**.

I-95 under construction as it bridged over 72nd Street in the Northwest.

New York Times.

NEW YORK, TUESDAY, JANUARY 18, 1961.

KENNEDY TO MEET WITH EISENHOWER AGAIN ON JAN. 19

U. S. Helps Train an Anti-Castro Force At Secret Guatemalan Air-Ground Base

Clash With Cuba Feared — Installations Built With American Aid

By PAUL P. KENNEDY

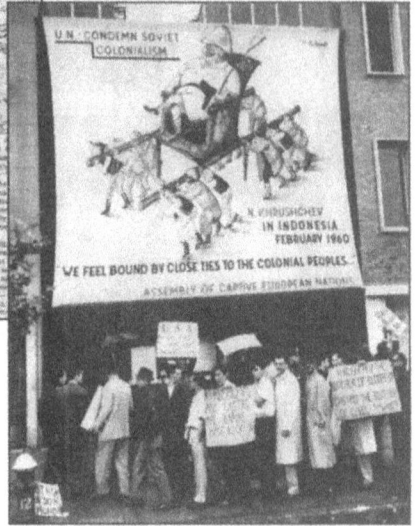

ANTI-CASTRO UNITS TRAINED TO FIGHT AT FLORIDA BASES

Force There and in Central America Is Reported to Total 5,000 to 6,000

By TAD SZULC

Special to The New York Times.

MIAMI, Fla., April 6—For nearly nine months Cuban exile military forces dedicated to the overthrow of Premier Fidel Castro have been training in the United States as well as in Central America.

An army of 5,000 to 6,000 men constitutes the external fighting arm of the anti-Castro Revolutionary Council, which was formed in the United States last month. Its purpose is the liberation of Cuba from what it

As the early 1960s progressed there were many indications that the US would help the Cuban refugees in Miami to invade Cuba and do away with the Castro regime.

Photos above top to bottom: in 1960, Cuban exiles in New York and Miami were preparing public opinion through public protests, while the papers were disclosing that the time for an invasion of Cuba by exiles was approaching.

The Miami Herald

Court Upholds Bible Reading in School

3 Other Usages Barred

Rebel Air Raids Panic Cubans;
Castro Demands U.N. 'Stop U.S.'

2 Bombers Put Down
In Florida After Raids

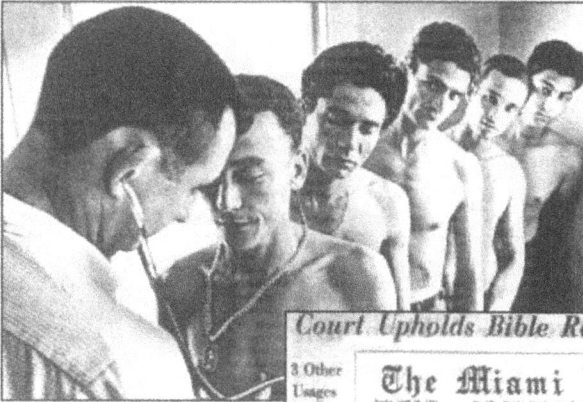

Cuban exiles in Miami began to be trained for a possible invasion of Cuba. It was to start with a concentrated bombardment of Castros's air bases across Cuba. Close to 2,000 exiles were recruited for the projected invasion and the US broke its diplomatic relations with Cuba ahead of the incursions.

Photos above top to bottom: Cuban exile recruits in Miami; the local papers provided news about the attacks on the Cuban air bases; a group of Cuban exiles trained for amphibious operations to assist in the beaches (for the man in the circle, see page 168); the word got out in Cuba that there were no diplomatic relationswith the US as of March of 1961.

The attention of the entire Miami exile community was focused on the news about **Brigade 2506** as soon as it became known that it had landed in Cuba. Very soon the radio waves were filled with bad news and an air of gloom and despair invaded the entire city.

Photos above top to bottom: the leaders of the Bay of Pigs invasion: **Manuel Artime, José Pérez San Román, Antonio Maceo** and **Antonio Varona**; The map of the theater of action; the sinking of the *Hudson*, the supply ship of the rebels; exiles were glued to the radio long after it was known that the invasion had not succeeded in establishing a beachhead.

CAPTURA DE LOS ESBIRROS

Photos above top to bottom: **Adlai Stevenson**, US representative in the United Nations, showing pictures of Cuban Air Force planes that had "deserted" to Florida; **Bohemia** magazine in Cuba reports of the *Bay of Pigs* fiasco; prisoners of the **Brigade 2506** in Cuba; General **Rafael del Pino** piloting a Lockheed T-33 jet. He downed several B-26's of the invading brigade and a few years later would seek asylum in Miami.

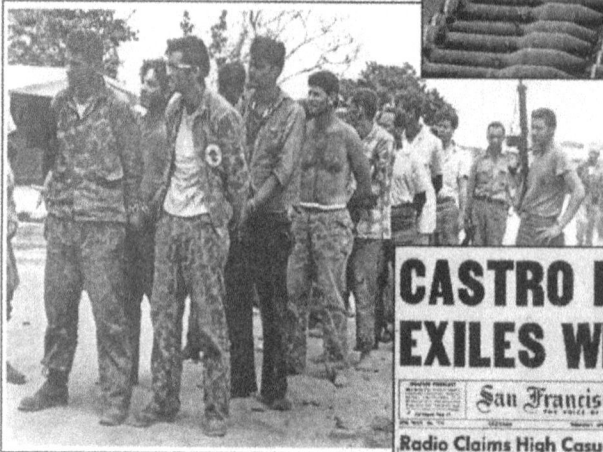

CASTRO REPORTS EXILES WIPED OUT

San Francisco Chronicle FINAL

Radio Claims High Casualties
Boats Sunk, Arms Seized

Photos above top to bottom: Castro's troops moving towards the beaches at **Playa Girón**; weapons confiscated to the defeated invaders of **Brigada 2506**; prisoners under custody at the beach; newspapers reports were given first page in the US press.

Photos above top to bottom: top two photos, captured members of the 2506 Brigade were assembled in Havana to «*receive some lessons*» from the revolutionary government. The Brigade members were received like heroes by Miami exiles; the **Kennedys** came to Miami not to deny that promises were broken but to apologize for their failure to support the invaders at critical moments. They made new promises of future support.

After the failure of the **Bay of Pigs** invasion, the CIA offered to the pilot-trained Cuban exiles the possibility of combating Communism in other venues such as the Congo, where Castro was assisting the leftist *"Simba"* warriors to take over the country.

The Congo crisis (1959-1965) started with the announced independence of the Congo from Belgium (June 30, 1960), its colonial master. During the ceremony of turning the reins of power to the Congolese, Prime Minister designate **Patrick Lumumba** insulted *King Baudoin I* of Belgium saying, among other things, «*Nous ne sommes plus vos singes*». (We are no longer your monkeys). A mutiny ensued and the Belgians had to re-take power. **Moise Tshombe** seized power in the province of *Katanga* and a secessionist war was declared on July 11, 1960, with the support of the Belgians, and under the leadership of Tshombe. The US and other western powers supported **Tshombe** and Leopoldville's Chief of the Army **Joseph Mobutu**, while the Soviet Union, China and Cuba supported the central government of **Joseph Kasa-Vubu**. Prime Minister **Lumumba** was assassinated and UN Secretary General **Hammarskjöld** died on a plane crash as he was trying to mediate. After the UN troops controlled *Katanga* the civil war was apparently at an end, but the rural insurgencies continued.

A group of rebels calling themselves *"**Simba**"* (Swahili for Lion) rebelled against the central government. **Tshombe** (the man who had seceded before) was appointed Prime Minister to lead the war against *Simba*. Castro sent Ché Guevara to help the *Simba* rebels and the US organized a group of Cuban exile pilots, calling themselves the *"**Makasi**"* (Swahili for strong and powerful), to fight the *Simba*. In six months, controlling the air, the **Cuban Makasi** defeated the Simba, attesting what could have happened in the **Bay of Pigs** if the *2506 Brigade* had had the same promised US support.

Photo below: The Cuban Exile pilots that as part of the **Makasi** defeated the Castro-suported **Simba** during the Congo Wars of the 1960s.

A Summary of the complex situation in the Congo, with the intervention of Cuba, the US, the USSR, China, Belgium, the Cuban exiles and many other countries could be summarized as follows:

- **Patrick Lumumba** was always considered the "**African Castro**" by the Western powers.
- **Moise Tshombe** was the vehicle to secede *Katanga*, the richest province of the Congo; Belgian troops returned to help him.
- The USSR aided **Lumumba**, even after he turned away from **Kasavubu**. The UN favored Kasavubu-Mobutu and not Lumumba.
- On January 17, 1961 Lumumba was **killed by Congolese enemies** and not by the CIA.
- **Mobutu's** government became increasingly corrupt and his army collapsed in June 1964, failing to fight the Simba.
- The US had no **Bureau of African Affairs** or any interest in Africa until 1958.
- Britain, France, Germany and Belgium refused to fight the **Simba**.
- The Simba grew in strength and **took Stanleyville** in 1964.
- In October 1964 the CIA-trained **Cuban Exiles** began to fight in Congo. The Cubans fought with C-130s, T-28s and B26s.
- Ché Guevara with a code name "**Talú**" (the Wandering King) became the main trainer of the Simba.
- Thanks to **Cuban Exiles** (the "**Makasi**") Stanleyville and all the hostages taken by the Simba and not yet murdered were **rescued**.
- The **Malasi** decisively defeated the **Simba** within six months.
- **Castro recalled Ché Guevara** from Congo and sent him to Bolivia.
- In the US **Malcolm X** was anti-Tshombe.
- **Tshombe** was overthrown by **Kasavubu**, who within a month was overthrown by **Mobutu**, who ruled the Congo for almost 30 years.

Photos, from top to bottom, left to right:
Ché Guevara in the Congo, **Moise Tshombe**,
Patrick Lumumba, **Mobutu Sese Seko** and **Joseph Kasavubu**.

Días del
DIARIO DE LA MARINA
EN EL EXILIO

Año CXXIX.—Número 17   Miami Beach, Sábado 29 de Abril de 1961   PRECIO 15 CENTAVOS

LOS MARTIRES DEL 17 DE ABRIL

Por primera vez en su larga historia como nación, Cuba se sintió sola en la trágica madrugada del 17 de Abril de 1961, día de la frustrada invasión. Solos, desasistidos de América, y del mundo, los cubanos se enfrentaron al más cruel de los imperialismos. Cuba creyó que tenía el respaldo del mundo libre en su lucha contra el comunismo, y sus hijos se lanzaron, impetuosamente, sin reservas, sin dudas, en el más audaz asalto que se ha realizado jamás contra ninguna fortaleza comunista. Sobre las calcinadas arenas de la playa de Girón, y en la ciénaga, y en los montes cercanos, estaba agazapada la tremenda verdad: Cuba estaba sola. Nadie la respaldaba. Nadie la seguía en su gigantesca lucha. De pronto, como en un estallido cegador, los cubanos comprendieron que habían llegado a la mayoría de edad. Tenían sobre sus hombros la responsabilidad enorme de libertar a su Patria, mientras los demás países —tan amenazados como Cuba— se cruzaban de brazos . . .

Allí, en la tarmpa de la ciénaga, los cubanos libraron la batalla más hermosa, porque lucharon, inútilmente, contra un enemigo cien veces más poderoso. Y más aun: sin esperanzas de vencer. Pero los cubanos lucharon y murieron. Y aquella oscura playa quedará ya, por siempre, como el primer sitio de América donde hombres de América se enfrentaron, por primera vez a los ejércitos rojos.

El 17 de abril es día de duelo. Pasarán muchos años, y el 17 de abril será siempre el día de los mártires, porque habrá pocos mártires de esta calidad superior. Son los primeros mártires de la larga lucha que se avecina en todo un Continente cegado por el miedo y el odio.

Toda la palabrería panamericanista que endulzó los oídos del hemisferio durante décadas, se hundió en el más absurdo de los ridículos. Playa Girón, con sus mártires, era un reto a la vacuidad de un sistema inoperante. Hace falta algo más que las palabras, hace falta algo más que las veladas untuosas de una diplomacia ineficaz. La lucha contra el comunismo es a muerte. América pone las palabras tan solo, y a Cuba le ha tocado el doloroso honor de poner los muertos.

Nuestro destino histórico nos ha colocado en la posición de ser la avanzada de las dos Américas en esta lucha. Cuba, martirizada, bañada en la sangre de sus hijos, está llamada a servir la causa de América en el altar de los sacrificios.

Los mártires del 17 de abril —a los que la propaganda canallesca de las hienas del fidelismo ha pretendido enlodar con algunas supuestas presencias indeseables— son mártires de América.

¡Qué importa que se rebusque ardorosamente en los antecedentes de algunos de los expedicionarios para cubrir de oprobio a los demás!... Cristo murió entre dos ladrones y no por eso su sacrificio supremo quedó empañado.

Más honrados quedan los mártires por este gesto de desinterés político. Ellos estaban conscientes de que la sangre que va al sacrificio no puede ser clasificada. Fueron, sencillamente, seres humanos, hombres de Cuba y de América, atraídos a la playa trágica por los secretos designios de la Providencia que quiso mezclar allí todas las sangres, todas las culpas, todas las inocencias, como si quisiera señalar con esto cuál ha de ser el nuevo destino de la nueva Cuba que ya se alza sobre el horizonte. O Cuba es un crisol donde se funden las conciencias de todos sus hijos o será por siempre un peñón de odio y resentimiento.

Para los cubanos no puede haber otra cosa que luto y meditación en los días por venir. El holocausto del 17 de abril nos señala un camino. Esa sangre nos impone deberes supremos porque es sangre nuestra, sangre de nuestros hijos, de nuestros padres, de nuestros hermanos, de nuestros compañeros. ¡Que nadie se sienta desligado del martirio, porque este martirio es de todos y todos hemos contribuido a él!

Una lección, una sola lección, se yergue de entre los escombros humeantes de Playa Girón: tenemos que ser mejores, tenemos que estar más unidos, tenemos que ser más fuertes que nunca, tenemos que desligarnos de las menudas ambiciones de poder, tenemos que ser humildes, tenemos que despojarnos de odios y pasiones bastardas.

Nuestro destino como nación no está, ya, en las manos de nadie, sino en las nuestras. No dependamos de nadie, sino de nosotros mismos. No podemos andar ya por la historia con andaderas sino con nuestros propios pies.

Y el que traicione esto, el que pretenda sobreponer su incapacidad a su soberbia a la voluntad de un pueblo que peregrina en busca de su mejor destino está traicionando la sangre de los mártires del 17 de abril.

Esa sangre dice que tenemos que seguir peleando, pero no al servicio de unos pocos, no en burdos trajines de politiquería, sino al servicio de la nación cubana y siempre con pasos firmes y seguros.

Nuestros hijos, no son mercenarios.

¡Nuestros hijos, son patriotas y mártires de la Libertad de América . . . !

Por Dios por Cuba: y por la Democracia

The reaction of the Cuban Exile press to the news of the defeat of the **Playa Girón** (Bay of Pigs) invasion force.

Operation Pedro Pan, was a mass exodus of over 14,000 unaccompanied Cuban Children to the US between 1960 and 1962; it impacted the life of these Cuban children and will forever be imprinted in the soul of the Cuban nation. This large transfer of children was organized by **Mons. Bryan O. Walsh** in the US and **James Baker**, director of *Ruston Academy* in Cuba, with the help of **Amador Odio, Sara del Toro, Ramón** and **Polita Grau, Olga Serra, Esther de la Portilla** and many other Cubans that risked their freedom and livelihoods to deliver Cuban children from the designs of the Communist government in Cuba intending to take possession of the *patria potestad* of their parents.

The children were temporarily sent to encampments in Florida located at **Kendall, Florida City, Matacumbe** and **Opa-Locka**, as well as institutions in Miami such as **St. Joseph Villa, St. Raphael's Hall**, the **Cuban Boy's Home**, the **Ferré House** and **Casa Carrión**; some went directly with their families or were sent to foster homes throughout the US.

The following photos illustrate some of these temporary quarters and the return visit, forty or fifty years later, of many of the children. Most of the children reunited with their families within months; others took a few more years and a small fraction never again reconnected with their parents.

(Continued)

Photos above, top to bottom: Young women at the **Florida City** Camp; Young men at the **Kendall Home** Camp.

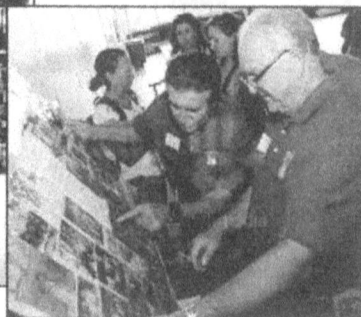

Photos above, top to bottom, left to right: Young women at the **Florida City Camp**; Young men at the **Opa-Locka** Camp; the dining room at **St. Raphael's Hall**; small children at **St. Joseph's Villa**; two photos 50 years later, as the "*kids*" returned to the camps and tried to remember names and places.

The US was clearly embarrassed on the world stage by the failure of the **Bay of Pigs** invasion in 1961, an operation planned by CIA Director Allan Dulles, crafted by the Eisenhower administration, approved and later abandoned by President John Kennedy. In the process, US Ambassador to the UN, Adlai Stevenson, had been caught in a lie as he showed evidence to the UN's Security Council that the US was not connected to the adventure. The truth was that the US had organized the invasion of Cuba, a sovereign nation, had supplied the equipment, trained the invaders, provided the rationale for conflict, promised assistance to a thousand proud and brave Cuban exiles, and at the critical moment abandoned them to failure, finally ending up denying involvement.

Emboldened by their **Bay of Pigs** victory, the Castro brothers decided to continue their fight against the US by joining the **Vietcong** troops fighting the South Vietnamese. It was well known at the time that the US had invited the US-trained Cuban pilots of the failed **Bay of Pigs** invasion to join the American armed forces; this was also seen by Castro as a good opportunity to once more fight the Cuban exiles. It became known in Castro's and CIA circles as the **Cuban Program**.

(Continued)

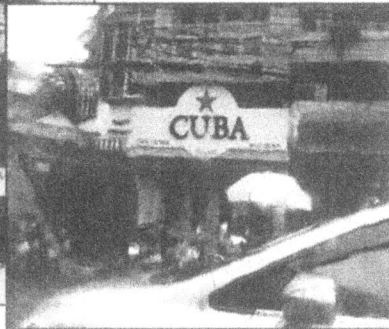

Photos above, left to right, top to bottom:
Vietnamese and Cuban stamps; **Ricardo Alarcón**, Cuban Foreign Minister with his Vietnamese counterpart **Nguyen Phu Trong**; the **Hanoi Hilton** (inside white line) and a bar named **Cuba** nearby, both in Hanoi.

(Continuation)

As soon as they reported for duty, Cuban officials in Hanoi began to brutally torture and kill American POWs, hoping there were Cuban exiles in their ranks; they beat them senseless in a program sanctioned and supported by the North Vietnamese. The Cuban Program was initiated around August 1967 at a **Cu Loc POW camp** known as *The Zoo*, a former French movie studio on the southwestern edge of Hanoi. The program was continued at secret bases at **Monkai** and **Laokai**, about 100 km from the Chinese border. CIA analysts identified two Cuban military attachés among the torturers: **Eduardo Morejón Estévez** and **Luis Pérez Jaén**; they were the men at the Hanoi Hilton that the POWs called *Fidel* and *Chico*. Other Cuban exile veterans identified **Dr. Miguel Angel Bustamante O'Leary**, President of the *Cuban Medical Association*, as *Fidel*, and **Major Fernando Vecino Alegret**, director of the *International Communist Youth Training Center*, southeast of Santiago de Cuba, as *Chico*.

CIA documents also revealed that as many as 17 POWs, Americans and Cuban-born pilots, were taken to Cuba in the mid 1960s and were kept at **Villa Marista** in Havana, a prison run by Castro's G2 (the intelligence and repressive service). This was confirmed by Dr. Miguel A. D'Estefano, director of the *Cuban Solidarity with Vietnam Committee* in the *El Mundo*, a Havana newspaper, in August 1968. The purpose of internment of US and Cuban exile pilots in Cuba was to obtain additional intelligence about US training and military tactics, as well as exile activities.

In 1977-78 **Morejón Estévez** served under diplomatic cover as a member of Cuba's delegation to the UN in New York; in the years since 1980, the other three Cuban officials named above have been reported to be *living in Miami as exiles*. No attempts have ever been made to either arrest or expel them from the US.

Photos below:
CIA composite drawings of the Cuban Agents that tortured POWs in North Vietnam (known to the POWs as **Fidel**, **Chico** and **García**).

ASESINOS

Composite drawing of "Fidel"   Composite drawing of "Chico"   Composite drawing of "García"

AGENTES DEL GOBIERNO COMUNISTA DE CUBA, MIEMBROS DEL EQUIPO DE EXPERTOS ENVIADOS POR FIDEL CASTRO A VIETNAM DEL NORTE CON EL OBJETIVO DE APLICAR TECNICAS DE TORTURA A PRISIONEROS DE GUERRA NORTEAMERICANOS.

Photos above top to bottom: the aftermath of the Bay of Pigs invasion. It meant a consolidation of the revolution in Cuba. This military fiasco empowered Castro, who felt he had vanquished the American-supported troops and had inflicted a decisive defeat to US imperialism. The entire world press tended to agree with him.

The first reaction of Cuban exiles after the failure of the Bay of Pigs was to confront the Castro sympathizers that still lived in Miami after their exile against Batista had ended. They were practically routed out of Miami, sometimes with excessive and objectionable violence. Such was the case with the bombing of **Paula's Restaurant** on 435 NE First Avenue, near the **Gesu Church** at 118 NE Second Street, a deed accomplished by **Rolando Masferrer**, who had never —before or after— received any support from law-abiding Cuban refugees.

Cuban exiles were so eager to fight Communism that a year later, they were easy to recruit by the CIA and the *Committee to Re-elect the President* [Nixon], for such activities as the Watergate break-ins in May and June of 1972.

Miami and Havana, two cities sharing a good part of their histories and development since the wars of Cuban independence and throughout 50 years thereafter, became in 1961 irreconcilable enemies as Miami became the forefront of the fight for Cuba's liberation from Communism and Castro continued to refer to the Cubans in Miami as the "*Miami mafia*".

Meantime, in Puerto Rico, 66 Cuban refugees got together and organized a group whose purpose was to continue the fight that had started in the *Bay of Pigs*, this time with no reliance whatsoever on the CIA or the US government. They gave their movement the name **Alpha 66**.

Photos above: the location of **Paula's Restaurant** in downtown Miami, no longer there after 1978 due to urban renewal; the five Watergate burglars in 1972. From left to right, **Bernard Baker, James W. McCord Jr., Frank Sturgis, Eugenio Martínez (Musculito)**, and **Virgilio González**. All but McCord were veteran anti-Castro exiles from Miami.

An emboldened Castro began in mid 1961 to take revenge on both Catholics and Protestants in Cuba. They were forbidden to run their schools and all religious learning institutions were confiscated. Bishops, priests and ministers were placed under house arrest. Christians were expelled from the *Communist Party* and denied government employment and university admissions. By the end of 1961 the government started a program of systematic expulsion of Catholic priests and Protestant ministers.

On September 17, 130 priests —including **Bishop Eduardo Boza**— were forced out of their churches and convents, taken to the port of Havana and forced to go into exile on board the *Covadonga*, a ship from *Transatlántica Española*. It was Castro's best solution to his inability to create a "*Cuban Catholic Church*" that would have responded to him. Other priests and nuns were given deadlines for abandoning the territory of Cuba. Of all priests forced to take asylum in Spain, close to 80% moved to Miami, Madrid and New York within two years, engrossing the multitude of new exiles that decided to leave Cuba when it became impossible to practice their faith.

Photos above top to bottom: the **Covadonga**; the reception of Cuban exiles in Madrid to the expelled priests and nuns; the entire Cuban community of **La Salle Brothers** as they arrived to the Miami airport.

A number of veterans from the Bay of Pigs were invited to join the regular US military forces, with the purpose of developing military and leadership skills suitable for a new effort to liberate Cuba.

Photos above, left to right: **Félix Rodríguez**, who would be one of the captors of Ché Guevara in the mountains of Bolivia; **Jorge Mas Canosa**, years later the founder of the *Fundación Nacional Cubano-Americana*; **Eneido Oliva**, future Deputy Commanding General of the *D.C. National Guard* and Major General in the *US Army Reserve*; **Luis Posada Carriles**, accused of being one of the most dangerous anti-Castro terrorists in recent history but who has never been found guilty of any charges in the US.

After the *Bay of Pigs*, Cuban exiles in Miami became regular listeners of very popular Miami radio stations.

Photos above top to bottom, left to right: some of the lead personalities of Cuban Miami radio; **Juan Amador Rodríguez, Rosendo Rosell, Manuel Reyes, Tomás García Fusté, Eduardo González Rubio** and **Arturo Artalejo.**

A large percentage of veterans from the **2506 Brigade** went on to develop their interrupted careers in the US. A noteworthy example was **Eduardo Zayas-Bazán**, a former frogman (see page 153) in the failed invasion who was wounded, captured and jailed for one year. He became Chairman of the Foreign Language Department at *East Tennessee State University* and authored two dozen books published by Prentice Hall and used in some 150 schools and universities across the US. *Photo at right:* the **Zayas-Bazán family**.

The late 1960s and the 1970s were years of almost uncontrolled terrorism within the Cuban exile communities. Just in Miami there were close to 100 terrorist incidents, two thirds of which involved explosives; the rest were armed attacks and assassination attempts. In Puerto Rico there were 47 bombings or attempted bombings for political reasons. In New York City 30 terrorist incidents were reported in the 1970s; 21 were reported in New Jersey, of which 13 were bombings.

Inexcusably, radical elements within the Cuban exile communities attributed their aggressiveness to their belief that the US was abandoning their support for all anti-Castro causes once the failed Bay of Pigs had occurred, and the Kennedy-Khrushchev pact had taken effect after the Missile Crisis of 1962. Several groups of Cubans decided to continue the series of violent actions that had been backed by the CIA (funding) and the FBI (intelligence) since 1960 against Castro. Mistakenly, they did not consider their actions to be a form of terrorism but a simple continuation of actions that were previously planned, funded and fully backed by the US. The Cuban exiles' all around war, now planned, funded and backed by Cuban exiles, was characterized by bombings of diplomatic facilities of Cuba and her allies worldwide, attacks on ships of Cuba and her trading partners, Cuban coastal facilities, communist sympathizers, and people and organizations, including law enforcement, that tried to stop their war tactics.

Photos below:
Some newspaper accounts of terrorist activities in the US where Cuban exiles were apparently involved;

Several egregious political shootings began to take place in Miami. In December, 1967, **Orlando Bosch Avila (1926-2011)**, a Cuban-born Miami pediatrician, organized a group called *Acción Cubana* (Cuban Action, also known as Cuban Power). This group began placing bombs at Post Offices in New Jersey and in New York City in December, 1967; in January, 1968, they planted a bomb aboard a B-25 cargo plane. The bomb exploded with the plane still on the ground; the rationale for this bombing was that it was carrying non-medical cargo to Mexico for reshipment to Cuba.

The group undertook three other bombings in Miami trying to stop the shipment of industrial supplies to Cuba. In February, 1968, it placed a high explosive bomb at the Russian Embassy in Washington, D.C. In total, the actions involved about 15 persons; they were responsible for over 50 bombings in the U.S. during 1968. Among those attacked were the British freighter *Cranwood* off Key West in May, 1968; the Japanese freighter *Asaka Maru* at Tampa, Florida, in May, 1968; the Japanese freighter *Mikagesan Maru* on June 1, 1968; the British freighter *Caribbean Venture* in August, 1968 and the Spanish ship *Coromoto* in September, 1968.

Photos above:
The of the most visible Cuban exiles with accusations of terrorism. They were trained by the CIA, accused before tribunals and exonerated, and finally admitted to live free in the US. *Top row:* **Orlando Bosch**, *on the bottom row,* **Luis Posada Carriles**; both at different stages of their lives.

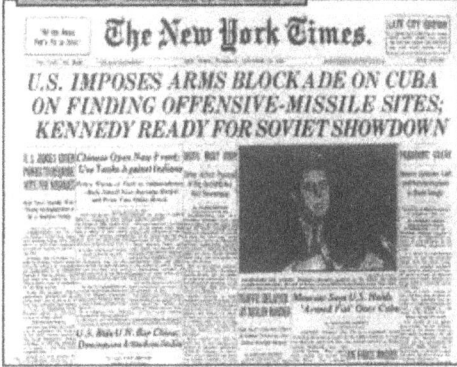

After the failure of the *Bay of Pigs*, the governments of Cuba and the Soviet Union began to build launching bases in Cuba for medium-range and intermediate-range ballistic nuclear missiles (MRBMs and IRBMs), all of which could reach the continental United States, Puerto Rico, the Panama Canal and most of the Caribbean islands. Cuban exiles in Miami were not surprised when the so called **Missile Crisis** occurred (October 1962). The introduction of Russian missiles in Cuba had been denounced on TV at "Meet the Press" by the DRE. Moscow and Washington controlled and resolved the crisis, in spite of efforts by the Castro's government to have a say in its management and final outcome.

Photos above top to bottom, left to right: Soviet ships disembarking **nuclear weapons** in the port of Mariel, Cuba; some of the sites armed with nuclear weapons in Pinar del Rio; some of the US press at the time.

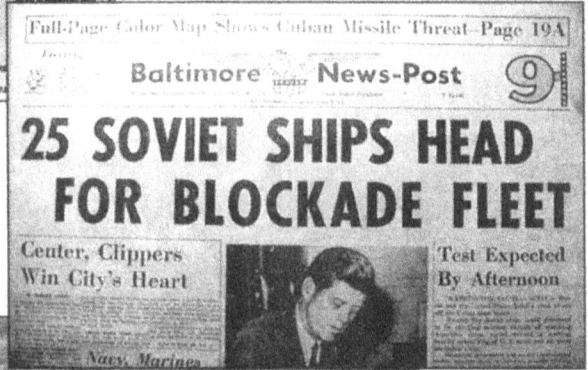

25 SOVIET SHIPS HEAD FOR BLOCKADE FLEET

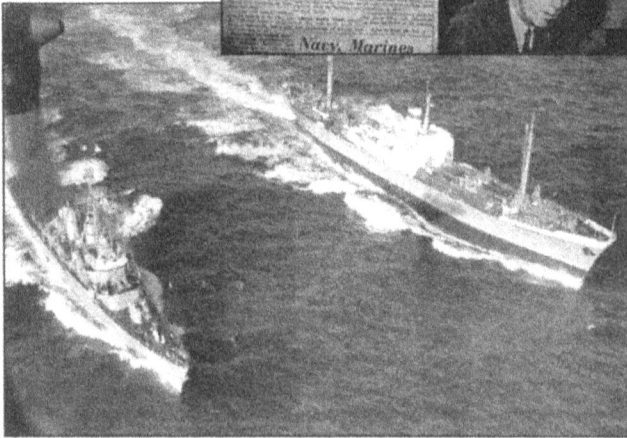

Finally, the Soviets blinked upon the persistent political and military pressure of the United States; they agreed to remove the Soviet Missiles from Cuba but at a severe cost to the freedom for which the Cuban exiles had been fighting for so long. It would be an event as disloyal to the Cuban exiles as the reluctance to support the men on the beaches of the *Bay of Pigs* with the promised or implied aerial coverage. This time, however, it had far longer reaching consequences. It sealed forever the stability of the Cuban government and precluded any effective support by the US for the Cuban exiles anti-Castro efforts. See next page.

Photos above: the US press followed the developments of the crisis on an hourly basis. *On the bottom photo,* the US Navy approaches a Soviet vessel and commands it to turn back or be ready to be boarded by US troops.

Why have we undertaken to render such military and economic aid to Cuba? The answer is: we have done so only out of humanitarian considerations. At one time our people accomplished its own revolution, when Russia was still a backward country. Then we were attacked. We were the target of attack by many countries. The United States took part in that affair. This has been documented by the participants in aggression against our country. An entire book has been written on this by General Graves, who commanded the American Expeditionary Force at that time. Graves entitled it American Adventure in Siberia.

We know how difficult it is to accomplish a revolution and how difficult it is to rebuild a country on new principles. We sincerely sympathize with Cuba and the Cuban people. But we do not interfere in questions of internal organization; we are not interfering in their affairs. The Soviet Union wants to help the Cubans build their life, as they themselves desire, so that others would leave them alone.

You said once that the United States is not preparing an invasion. But you have also declared that you sympathize with the Cuban counterrevolutionary emigrants, support them, and will help them in carrying out their plans against the present government of Cuba. Nor is it any secret to anyone that the constant threat of armed attack and aggression has hung and continues to hang over Cuba. It is only this that has prompted us to respond to the request of the Cuban Government to extend it our aid in strengthening the defense capability of that country.

If the President and Government of the United States would give their assurances that the United States would itself not take part in an attack upon Cuba and would restrain others from such action; if you recall your Navy--this would immediately change everything. I do not speak for Fidel Castro, but I think that he and the Government of Cuba would, probably, announce a demobilization and would call upon the people to commence peaceful work. Then the question of armaments would also be obviated, because when there is no threat, armaments are only a burden for any people. This

would

*Photo above: page 6 of the letter of **Khrushchev** to **Kennedy** on **October 26, 1962** asking assurances that the US would never help Cuban exiles to fight Castro.*

- -

THE WHITE HOUSE

TEXT OF A LETTER BY THE PRESIDENT
ADDRESSED TO THE CHAIRMAN OF THE
PRESIDIUM OF THE USSR SUPREME
SOVIET, NIKITA KHRUSHCHEV

October 27, 1962

Dear Mr. Chairman:

I have read your letter of October 26th with great care and welcomed
the statement of your desire to seek a prompt solution to the problem.
The first thing that needs to be done, however, is for work to cease
on offensive missile bases in Cuba and for all weapons systems in Cuba
capable of offensive use to be rendered inoperable, under effective
United Nations arrangements.

Assuming this is done promptly, I have given my representatives in
New York instructions that will permit them to work out this weekend
-- in cooperation with the Acting Secretary General and your representative -- an arrangement for a permanent solution to the Cuban problem
along the lines suggested in your letter of October 26th. As I read your
letter, the key elements of your proposals -- which seem generally acceptable as I understand them -- are as follows:

1) You would agree to remove these weapons systems from Cuba under
appropriate United Nations observation and supervision; and undertake,
with suitable safeguards, to halt the further introduction of such weapons
systems into Cuba.

2) We, on our part, would agree -- upon the establishment of adequate
arrangements through the United Nations to ensure the carrying out and
continuation of these commitments -- (a) to remove promptly the quaran-
tine measures now in effect and (b) to give assurances against an invasion of Cuba.   .... I am confident that other nations of the Western
Hemisphere would be prepared to do likewise.

If you will give your representative similar instructions, there is no
reason why we should not be able to complete these arrangements and
announce them to the world within a couple of days. The effect of such
a settlement or easing world tensions would enable us to work toward
a more general arrangement regarding "other armaments", as proposed
in your second letter which you made public. I would like to say again
that the United States is very much interested in reducing tensions and
halting the arms race; and if your letter signifies that you are prepared
to discuss a detente affecting NATO and the Warsaw Pact, we are quite
prepared to consider with our allies any useful proposals.

But the first ingredient, let me emphasize, is the cessation of work
on missile sites in Cuba and measures to render such weapons inoperable,
under effective international guarantees. The continuation of this threat,
or a prolonging of this discussion concerning Cuba by linking these problems to the broader questions of European and world security, would
surely lead to an intensification of the Cuban crisis and a grave risk to
the peace of the world. For this reason I hope we can quickly agree along
the lines outlined in this letter and in your letter of October 26th.

(s)   John F. Kennedy

# # # # #

Photo above: the **Kennedy-Khrushchev Pact** of **October 27, 1962** that sealed
indefinitely the fate of Cuba as a Communist country.

No matter how hard they tried, the Kennedys (**John**, the President and **Robert**, the Attorney General), could never redeem themselves from the actions they took during the **1961 Bay of Pigs** invasion and the **1962 Missile crisis**. In the minds of most Cuban exiles, during the **Bay of Pigs** they betrayed the men they sent to fight in Cuba; during the **Missile Crisis**, they fell into the trap set by Castro when he invited the Soviets to install missiles and atomic weapons in Cuba.

Photos above, left to right, top to bottom:

Jackie and **John Kennedy** welcoming the veterans of the *Bay of Pigs* invasion to an *Orange Bowl* rally in December 29, 1962; an excerpt of Kennedy's words at the rally; John Kennedy on C-SPAN TV describing the **failure of the invasion**; a belated memo from Robert Kennedy insinuating future help to the Cuban exiles. It never came.

The outcome of the Missile crisis created such gloom and devastation among Cuban exiles the world over, and such unhappiness in Cuba, that by the end of the decade an additional 150,000 refugees had left Cuba. The impact of this exodus can best be appreciated by the number of artists and musicians that abandoned Cuba over the next 5 years. The list would be too large to present but some representative names are worth mentioning:

Belisario López, Bobby Collazo, Zoraida Marrero, Julio Gutiérrez, Otto Sirgo, Manolo Torrente, Arsenio Rodríguez, José Fajardo, Roberto Ledesma, Guillermo Portabales, Estelita Santaló, Xonia Benguría, Alberto Garrido, Guillermo Alvarez Guedes, Orlando Vallejo, Ñico Membiela, Ernesto Lecuona, Maruja González, El Dúo Cabrisas-Farach, Fernando Albuerne, Blanca Rosa Gil, Flor de Loto y Marisela Verena, Carmita Jiménez, Olga y Tony, la India de Oriente, René Touzet, Osvaldo Farrés, Javier Dulzaides, Marta Pérez, Leopoldo Fernández, Celia Cruz, Olga Guillot, La Lupe, Rolando La Serie, la Sonora Matancera, Xiomara Alfaro, Dinorah Ayala, Juan Bruno Tarraza, Marta Casañas, Lilia Lazo, Rolando Ochoa, Pepa Berrio, Mimí Cal, Jorge Guerrero, Margarita Lecuona and Tito Hernández, among others. The photos of some of these are presented above.

*Photos above, top to bottom, left to right: **Alberto Garrido, Otto Sirgo, Ernesto Lecuona, Fernando Albuerne, Celia Cruz, Olga, Tony y Lissete, Guillermo Alvarez Guedes, Marta Pérez, Rolando Ochoa, Tito Hernández** and **Olga Guillot.***

After the failure of the **Bay of Pigs** invasion in 1961 and the en-snarement of Cuba as an inconsequential and disposable pawn in the Cold War after the **Missile Crisis** in 1962, the situation of the Cuban exiles around the world could best be summarized as follows:

- They understood that the US would cooperate in the struggle to save Cuba from the Communists only when and if it would serve the interests of the US.
- They knew the initial support and encouragement of the US to anti-Castro exiles during the Eisenhower administration —for which they were very grateful— was partly due to the need to show the world how miserable life was under Communism.
- The US had the right to act according to its best interests and could not be criticized when these did not coincide with those of a free Cuba and the objectives of the Cuban exiles.
- The same could be said of all the Latin American and other nations that had turned their faces *vis-à-vis* the Cuban drama, particularly **Spain** (la Madre Patria) and **Mexico** (the recipient of generous help from Cuba during its 1911 revolution).
- Faced with a similar situation after the fiasco of the *Fernandina Plan* (US confiscated the expeditionary ships bound for Cuba to launch the 1895 War of Independence), **José Martí** increased his effort to bring about the war in Cuba rather than abandon the struggle.

The Cuban exiles, particularly those in the US, began to be actively involved «*on their own terms*» in the infiltration of freedom fighters inside Cuba and the boycott of Castro's regime across the world.

Photos above: the March 13, 1962 **Lemnitzer's Letter** (Chairman of the US Joint Chiefs of Staff) setting up the objectives of the US *vis-à-vis* Cuba; the house in **Fernandina Beach**, Florida, from where in 1895 José Martí saw his invasion plans crumble.

Many examples of Cuban exiles risking their lives after infiltrating in Cuba followed the discouraging events of the **Missile Crisis**.

Cuban exiles had to close a guerrilla warfare training camp in **New Orleans** following instructions from the *Cuban Revolutionary Council,* headed by Dr. José Miró Cardona in Miami. The Council was discouraging training of anti-Castro forces in American territory. The exiles had obtained a track of land north of Lake Pontchartrain and had raised large sums of money and late model weapons. Plans were to train 50 to 75 exiles as guerrilla fighters every two months, as reported by the *Miami Herald* in July of 1962.

The *New York Times* reported on September of 1962 that a *"pirate vessel owned by* **Alpha 66**" had entered a harbor in north-central Cuba and fired more than sixty shots into the British freighters *Newlane* —loading sugar for Communist countries— and the *San Pascual*, a Cuban ship (carrying molasses) that was also boarded, dynamited and machine gunned. No casualties were reported.

In the Bahamas **Manuel Ray**, a former Minister of Public Works in Castro's revolutionary government and later head of the anti-Castro *Cuban Revolutionary Junta*, was captured at Anguila Key by a British destroyer decoy as he and other exiles were loading ammunition for the war in Cuba; newsman Andrew St. George, was part of the expedition. Taken to a magistrate of the British colony they were fined five pounds each and had their weapons confiscated.

Photos above, top to bottom: Anti-Castro guerrillas in the **Escambray Mountains**of Cuba. **Alpha 66** exiles in training in the camps of Miami listening to Nazario Sargén, at left; **Manuel Ray**, founder and President of the anti-Castro *Movimiento Revolucionario del Pueblo (MRP)* in May of 1960.

One of the groups of anti-Castro opponents that had more prestige and following among internal dissidents in Cuba and Cuban exiles abroad was the *Movimiento Revolucionario del Pueblo (MRP).* It was created late in 1960 by the merging of three other groups:

The *Movimiento 30 de Julio,* led by Manuel Ray, Felipe Pazos and other former members of the first revolutionary cabinet when Castro's *26 of July Movement* took over the reins of government in Cuba after January 1st 1959.

The second group was the *Movimiento Verde Olivo,* led by Rufo López Fresquet, Raúl Chibás and many of the old leaders of the *Partido Ortodoxo.*

The third group was *Acción Democrática Revolucionaria (ADR),* led by former members of the *Federación de Juventudes de Acción Católica Cubana (FJACC)* such as Antonio Fernández Nuevo (Toñito), Andrés Valdespino and Amalio Fiallo. This third group, based on an existing and powerful organization —the FJACC— that had chapters across the entire island, eventually became the controlling organization of the MRP.

Competing for popular acceptance with the *MRP* was the *Movimiento 30 de Noviembre (M-30-11)* —named after the 1956 uprising in Cuba led by Frank País. The *M-30-11* was a labor-based movement led in Cuba by David Salvador and, among exiles, by former labor leaders opposed to the forced replacement of Salvador as Secretary General of the CTC, the *Confederación de Trabajadores de Cuba.* At some point in time the M-30-11 was considered as the MRP labor affiliate.

Photos above, left to right: Felipe Pazos, former President of the Banco Nacional de Cuba in 1959, went into exile at the end of the year; Raúl Chibás, went to the Sierra Maestra in 1958 to support Castro and was in exile by 1960; Antonio Fernández Nuevo, President of Juventud Católica, went into exile in 1960; Frank País, organizer of the movement against Batista, whose antagonism with Fidel Castro was probably the cause of his death under strange circumstances.

In the end, the efforts of the Cuban exiles in supporting an anti-Castro front in the mountains of central Cuba failed. Leaders like Jesús Cabrera, William Morgan, Julio Emilio Carretero, Zoila Aguila (*la Niña de Placetas*) and José (*Cheito*) León were either captured and shot or died in battle.

Photos below, left to right: **William Morgan**, former *Comandante* in the Castro revolution, executed on March 11, 1961. His wife Olga was sentenced to 30 years; **José (Cheito) León Jiménez**, one of the last guerrilla chiefs, who captured and shot Alberto Delgado Delgado, a Castro agent who was later the subject of a propaganda film entitled *El Hombre de Maisinicú*; **Julio Emilio Carretero**, Chief of the Escambray rebels, executed at La Cabaña on March 9, 1964; **Zoila Aguila**, the only woman chief at the Escambray mountains. She was captured after fighting for four years and was sentenced to 30 years in solitary confinement. She became insane, was released after 15 years and sought refuge in Miami where she never recovered. Finally **Alberto Delgado Delgado**, the man who infiltrated the anti-Castro fighters and was portrayed as a hero in the Cuban revolutionary film *El Hombre de Maisinicú*.

After the resolution of the *Missile Crisis* at the end of 1962, the US rightfully felt it had won a serious psychological battle against the Soviets. Kennedy felt confident in the military superiority of the US after prevailing over the Soviet Union from a position of clear advantage. He also felt confident that this incident would serve as an inducement to Third World countries to recognize the hegemony of capitalism and reject Communism as a political, economic and social model. Unfortunately, more and more, he was getting the US involved in «*saving Vietnam from the Communist aggression,*» an effort at which the French had failed miserably and that was creating very negative press in Europe. It also made smaller countries believe that imperialist ambitions were consuming most US politicians.

The failure of the support given to Cuban exiles in Miami to infiltrate and launch a guerrilla war in the mountains of Escambray in Cuba was taken by Kennedy as proof that it was not realistic to expect a popular insurrection inside Cuba in the style of the rebellion Castro had launched from the *Sierra Maestra*. On the other hand, Kennedy suspected a split was forming between Cuba and the Soviets because the highhanded way the Missile Crisis had been resolved without Castro having anything to say.

Photo at left: **José Miró Cardona** leader of the *Consejo Revolucionario Cubano (CRC)*, in the front page of TIME magazine the week after the *Bay of Pigs* fiasco.

To Kennedy, the alternatives in the spring of 1963 seemed clear. The US could either «*continue helping the Miami exiles to harass and irritate the Castro government with hit-and-run attacks that would keep a climate of disorder and impotence in Cuba*» or the US could commit its army, once and for all, to seek a violent overthrow of the Cuban regime under the credible excuse that «*it would protect the rest of Latin American countries from the perils of Communism*».

The first alternative was chosen, as long as the exiles' actions were originating outside US territory. **José Miró Cardona (1902-1974)**, as head of the *Consejo Revolucionario Cubano (CRC)*, agreed to the plan even though the memories of the unfulfilled promises of *the Bay of Pigs* fiasco were still fresh in his memory. Soon, however, Miró disagreed with the increasingly rigid rules-of-engagement of Kennedy and the love affair with the US administration came to an end. Miró withdrew from the *Consejo Revolucionario Cubano*, the Kennedy administration suspended the monthly support to the CRC —that according to some sources amounted to $250,000 monthly— and the *Consejo* disbanded itself.

A large number of Cuban exiles in the late 1960s made Puerto Rico their home, particularly after the **Bay of Pigs** (1961) and the **Missile Crisis** (1962). For the adults in these families, the geography, climate, music, and many cultural traits of the island, as well as a fair amount of shared history, were a strong incentive to live in Puerto Rico. The young in the family, however, were often troubled by an existential question: **Am I Cuban or Puertorrican?**

In the 1960s native Puertorricans received Cuban exiles with open arms. Most Cubans brought to (mostly) San Juan a professional know-how and a determination to start a new life after the failure of the Republic of Cuba to protect their patrimony and their safety. Many became managers, teachers, TV personalities or technicians, sales-persons, builders and commercial agents and/or clerks. They protected and employed each other and became somewhat clannish, much like the Puertorricans themselves were. A small minority, however, became opportunistic, greedy, arrogant and unscrupulous, bringing about a backlash that was already noticeable in the 1980s.

What divided more Cubans from Puertorricans were, however, their political outlooks. Most Cubans declared themselves pro-Statehood (after all, Governor *Luis A. Ferré*, the patriarch of pro-statehood feelings was a well known descendant from Cubans). These Cubans quickly began to act politically their beliefs. Many Puertorricans, particularly the *pro-independentistas*, began to consider most Cubans as unwanted outsiders that were meddling in the island political status. It was far from the words of **Lola Rodríguez de Tió** who had said «*Cuba and Puerto Rico are two wings of the same bird*». The condition of **Cubanness**, if openly practiced in certain circles, became umpleasant for some Cuban exiles in the island.

Photos below, top to bottom, left to right:
Political leaders in Puerto Rico in the 1960s and 1970s. Pro-Commonwealth: **Luis Muñoz Marín, Jaime Benitez, Rafael Hernández Colón**; pro-Statehood, **Carlos Romero Barceló, Luis A. Ferré**; pro-Independence, **Pedro Albizu Campos, Juan Mari Brás** and **Rubén Berríos**.

The long strand of **Cuban-Puertorican** common history has always been a powerful incentive for Cuban exiles to seek refuge in Puerto Rico.

Photos, top to bottom, left to right:
A **War Bond** issued in 1870 pro-Independence of both Cuba and Puerto Rico; music from **Celia Cruz** (Cuba) and **Tito Puente** (Puerto Rico) in the 1950s; a cartoon showing the **Philippines**, **Cuba** and **Puerto Rico** pleading to Uncle Sam for their independence; **Gen. Juan Rius Rivera**, a Puertorrican hero of the *Cuban War of Independence*; **Cuban exiles** at a rally in San Juan in 1972.

Cuban Exiles in Puerto Rico

Photos, top to bottom, left to right:
one of the paintings in the series *"Los Combatientes"* by **Rolando López Dirube;** **Henry Gutiérrez**, one of the builders of modern Puerto Rico; **Felipe Jiménez**, Cuban painter; **Carlos Franqui**, former director of *"Revolución,"* the newspaper published in 1959 Cuba; **Blanca Rosa Gil**, a popular Cuban diva turned Church minister in Caguas, Puerto Rico; **Manuel Ray**, founder of the *Movimiento Revolucionario del Pueblo (MRP)*, **Leví Marrero**, one of Cuba's top historians and geographers and **Jorge Mañach**, the distinguished Cuban philosopher, who took refuge and died in Puerto Rico.

On September of 1963 the **American Legion** —at its convention in Miami— asked President Kennedy to "*proceed boldly alone*" to end Communist rule in Cuba even if other nations of the hemisphere would not join in such an effort. President Kennedy responded that he did not favor military action against Cuba, adding that «*it is quite obvious that Cuba is a Soviet satellite, and that Premier Castro was serving the Soviet Union, but military action would not be in the best interests of the United States and could bring grief to the people of Western Europe*». The President also suggested that «*the United States had taken every step short of military action against the Communist regime of Premier Fidel Castro,*» a statement that was promptly disputed by Cuban exiles in Miami.

Photos above: the American Legion Memorial in Miami; the coat of Arms of the American Legion.

On November 23 1963, however, **President Kennedy** was assassinated in Dallas, Texas.

Photo above: the New York Times front page on the day of President Kennedy's assassination.

The assassination of **John F. Kennedy (1917-1963)** moved the US like no other event had done since World War II. Because of his almost obsessive determination to make amends for his indecisiveness during the *Bay of Pigs* fiasco, there were immediate rumors that either Cubans from the island or Cuban exiles, or both, were implicated. His killer, **Lee Harvey Oswald (1939-1963)**, for instance, had been distributing propaganda for Castro's *Fair Play for Cuba Committee* in New Orleans in 1963. Also **David William Ferrie (1918-1967)**, a known activist member of the anti-Castro *Cuban Democratic Revolutionary Front*, also from New Orleans, had made a speech in which he mentioned that «*Kennedy ought to be shot for his betrayal of the Bay of Pigs combatants*». He had been photographed with Oswald in 1962. (*Photo above*, Ferrie circled on the left, Oswald circled on the right).

The issue of Cubans from the island or Cuban exiles from Miami *viv-à-vis* the assassination of President Kennedy had an additional intriguing dimension. Since 1959 an atmosphere of conspiracy surrounded the relations between the US, the Miami Cuban exiles and the revolutionary government of Cuba. The following story is intriguing.

In 1957, US professional diplomat **Earl Edward Tailer Smith (1903-1991)** was appointed Ambassador Extraordinary and Plenipotentiary to Cuba by President Dwight Eisenhower. Smith's wife since 1947 had been a New York socialite named **Florence Pritchett (1920-1965)**. She accompanied him to Cuba. Mrs. Smith, as per reliable sources, had been having an affair with then Senator John F. Kennedy since 1944. According to FBI files from 1957 to early 1960, when he assumed the presidency of the US, Kennedy had secretly visited Florence in Cuba more than a dozen times. They also met in Miami, as the Kennedys and the Smiths had contiguous summer houses in Palm Beach, Florida.

Earl T. Smith became a bitter opponent of Kennedy when he found out his long lasting relationship with his wife; his dislike of Kennedy became an obsession after the fiasco of the *Bay of Pigs* (which he rightly attributed to Kennedy's indecision during the 1961 invasion). Smith lost a substantial amount of money when an empowered Castro nationalized the *US Sugar Corporation*, of which Smith was a major investor; he blamed Kennedy for his losses.

In 1965, a very reputable Hearst Papers news reporter, **Dorothy Killgallen (1913-1965)**, interviewed Jack Ruby, Lee Harvey Oswald's killer, out of earshot of sheriffs' deputies. Afraid for her life she never published the interview but gave her notes to her closest friend, Florence Smith (Pritchett). It seemingly implicated her husband, Earl T. Smith, as the man who had financed the Kennedy murder. On November 8, 1965 Mrs. Killgallen was found dead in her 16-room apartment at 630 Park Avenue, New York. Florence Smith (Pritchett) died two days later at her Palm Beach estate.

Photos above, from left to right: US Ambassador to Cuba *Earl T. Smith* in 1959; Mrs. Smith (née *Florence Pritchett*); Hearst newswoman and Pulitzer Price Nominee *Dorothy Killgallen*.

Efforts to renew the war in Cuba continued after Kennedy's death. On May 20, 1964, the *New York Times* newsman **Tad Szulc** reported that **Manuel Ray**, the leader of *Cuba's Revolutionary Junta*, was preparing to land secretly in Cuba to start «*a long and pain-staking process of hammering together an effective underground organization.*» He added that «*the Revolutionary Junta has never contemplated the formation of guerrilla combat groups in the Cuban mountains since the regime's powerful military apparatus would make the odds against the success of such an operation overwhelming.*»

Szulc expressed the view that if Manuel Ray succeeded in landing in Cuba and eluded the Castro security forces for at least two weeks, his chances of building an underground organization would have grown immeasurably, and that Havana's decision to order a military "*high alert*" was indeed motivated more by concern with Mr. Ray than with the expected repetition of coastal raids by other groups.

Castro, however, was successful in his efforts to stop Manuel Ray and to eliminate all fighters from the mountains of Escambray — most of them former 1959 anti-Batista guerrillas that turned against Castro as they became disenchanted with the revolution.

Cubans living in Miami waiting for Escambray missions, in the meantime, were arrested systematically by federal US authorities because their actions violated the secret US-Soviet agreements between Kennedy and Khrushchev. They nevertheless continued trying to move public opinion in the US towards a more favorable position of the US government towards the removal of the Communist regime in Havana. All along, several embassies in Havana continued to provide sanctuary to an unending procession of new exiles.

Photos below: the precarious conditions at the *Embassy of Ecuador* in Havana, with hundreds of exiles living in shacks built in the gardens and the patio; in 1963 a group of exiles interrupted a baseball game in *Yankee Stadium* to embrace **Camilo Pascual**, calling attention to the suffering in Cuba.

Jack Kofoed

Miami Already Has Too Many Refugees

If Lyndon B. Johnson had stuck to Bobby Baker, his Texas oil depletion friends, the Johnson family fortune and steers on the ranch, we wouldn't have so many cold sweats when waking up in the middle of the night. What will happen to the United States of America after LBJ gets through with us, God alone knows!

The scary thing is that we used to have checks and balances, but the President has Congress so cowed they come nuzzling up to his knees like pooches looking for a new kind of TV dog food.

We're up to our armpits with Cuban refugees. Many have become good, solid members of the community, but others have been a drag, and a number have added to the criminal problem. As a whole, they imposed burdens, financial and otherwise. The problem has been partially resolved. Now comes another one even more difficult to handle.

Right out of the bright blue yonder the great revolutionist barbudo Castro made an announcement. He said he was tired of having his gun slingers shoot down citizens who wanted to flee to the Yankee Paradise. Now any Cubano who didn't like the sweet communism of Cuba could take off for the U.S. As a matter of fact, he'd fly two free plane loads a day if the U.S. would pick up the tab for maintenance.

In short, he wanted to get rid of the old and sick, the ones who don't like him. With a mob like that, Fidel could slide in spies and saboteurs in the best Communist tradition. He didn't mention thousands of political prisoners on the Isle of Pines, but they may be included. In short, Castro's going to get rid of an enormous number of people who contribute nothing to the revolutionary regime, or are actively opposed to it.

Mr. Johnson grabbed the bait like a hungry snook. Bring 'em all in, he said. If Castro doesn't want them, that's recommendation enough. What's to be done with them? How can they be absorbed? They will add to the unemployment and welfare problems. And, how the importation of thousands of unhappy, unsettled people, most of whom can't speak the language, will be a blow against Communism in Cuba I am at complete loss to understand.

And what happens to the supposed "underground?" Castro can't be deposed by town meetings and endless arguments among Cubans here. Vietnamese refugees are in worse plight than these people. Will Mr. Johnson next suggest that in the war against poverty and communism, what the hell, let's bring the Vietnamese in, too? Alice, in her dizziest days in Wonderland, never saw anything like what's happening here under the God-complex of Lyndon B. Johnson.

Congress has become only a muted echo of thunder from the White House. Even Republicans seem to have shrunk into the shadows, afraid to do more than squeak their dislike of what's going on. That once august body even agreed that should President Johnson decide there might be a possible Communist takeover in a South American country, he'd be justified in sending Marines or paratroopers there to keep things in hand until a government that suited him was in power.

We have no more right to dictate how any country shall run its internal affairs than that nation has to move bayonetted brigades into Washington and tell us what political pattern we must follow.

For years Central and South American countries regarded us as "the Colossus of the North" and equated all the United States as an American fruit company, with countless Marines to enforce their demands. Our Dominican adventure convinced many we had not changed. That congressional statement makes a lousy Hallowe'en joke of the "Good Neighbor Policy."

Not everyone in Miami was happy or at minimum discreetly annoyed by the presence of Cuban refugees. Since 1959 *John C. (Jack) Kofoed (1923-2008)*, a Miami Herald veteran reporter with 44 consecutive years of service to the paper, became the nemesis of all Cuban refugees by his frequent and aggressive articles against them.

(Continued)

*Photos above: a **Kofoed** article, October 5, 1965; a photo of **Jack Kofoed**.*

THE MIAMI NEWS

Established in 1896

James M. Cox, Jr.   Daniel J. Mahoney   William C. Baggs
   President   *Publisher*   *Editor*

   Jack Tarver   John L. Fey   James Bellows
Executive Vice-President   *General Manager*   *Managing Editor*

4B   Sunday, January 18, 1959   61st Year, No. 246

Fidel Castro's Strength Is From The People

**We Have No Right To Meddle
In Cuba's Internal Affairs**

(Continued)

Jack Kofoed was a well known author and journalist. In the 1960s he published such articles in the Herald as *"Miami Already Has Too Many Refugees*," Miami Herald, Oct. 5, 1965; "*Cubans' Manners Irk Their U.S. Hosts*," Nov. 10, 1965; years later he would author "*Who'll Help the Refugees? Americans, That's Who!*," May 7, 1975; "*Is Marisela Cuban or Is She American?*," December 1,1975; "*Cubans Should Pledge Allegiance, and Mean It*," January 3, 1976.

Over the years other reporters and executives of the *Miami Herald* were equally impatient and ungracious about Cuban refugees. Thirty years later, for instance, **Tom Fiedler**, the *Miami Herald* editor, would respond to readers complaining about his recurrent criticism of Cuban refugees by stating «*the 22 people who listened to Cuban radio are stirred up by little Chihuahuas nipping at our heels*," referring to the radio newsmen's displeasure with the *Herald's* repeated criticisms about Cuban refugees.

Carl Hiassen, a *Miami Herald* general assignment reporter with a very peculiar humor, would also be regularly critical of anything Cuban from his opinions and editorial columns in the *Herald*.

Photos above: a 1959 *Miami News* pro-Castro note; **Tom Fiedler**, Miami Herald's editor; **Carl Hiassen**, the novelist-reporter from the *Herald*.

Nunca podré morirme,
mi corazón no lo tengo aquí.
Alguien me está esperando,
me está aguardando que vuelva aquí.

Cuando salí de Cuba,
dejé mi vida dejé mi amor.
Cuando salí de Cuba,
dejé enterrado mi corazón.

Late y sigue latiendo
porque la tierra vida le da,
pero llegará un día
en que mi mano te alcanzará.

Cuando...

Una triste tormenta
te está azotando sin descansar
pero el sol de tus hijos
pronto la calma te hará alcanzar
Cuando...
Cuando...
Deje enterrado mi corazón,
mi corazón, mi corazón.

Life in Miami, Union City, New York, Paris, and other centers that had attracted exiles continued to witnesses the adaptation of Cubans to the cultural models of their new environments. **Luis Aguilé (1936-2009)**, an Argentine singer and composer with more than 700 titles to his credit wrote and sang *Cuando Salí de Cuba*, a hit song that became the unofficial hymn of Exiled Cuba.

Photos above: the **Luis Aguilé** Long Playing that brought tears to every Cuban exile in the 1960s; the lyrics of **Cuando Salí de Cuba**. Luis Aguilé in Madrid a few years before his death in 2009; some of the many records and films inspired by the song.

The world around Cuban exiles in the 1960s

Photos below: Mons. Agustín Román during the construction of the *Ermita de la Caridad* in the late 1960s; the *Drive-In* on Bird Road, on the west side of the Palmetto (the road was not yet fully operational); the monument erected in honor of José Martí in *West New York* in January of 1968; the expansion of the *Versalles Restaurant* in Miami, late in the 1960s.

The world around Cuban exiles in the 1960s (continued)

Photos above, top to bottom: in an effort incorporate the masses to his revolutionary vision, Castro created the *milicias* and got women to enlist on these *shock troops*; in Miami the men of *Alpha 66* continued to train for their anti-Castro activities; a group of pro-Castro activists is formed in the midst of the exiles: the *Brigada Antonio Maceo*, organized by a man named *Andrés Gómez* (circled) and financed by the Castro regime; many political prisoners in the jails in Cuba refused to be indoctrinated and were forced to spend years in their underwear. They were called the *"plantados."* In the photo *Ernesto Díaz Rodríguez*, of *Alpha 66*, who served 22 years in prison.

The world around Cuban exiles in the 1960s (continued)

Photos above, top to bottom: in 1965 the Miami exiles see their numbers increased substantially by the *Camarioca exodus*, which brings 80,000 additional refugees to the US; Castro organizes the *Tricontinental* meeting in Havana, an opportunity to embrace such well-known friends as *Yasser Arafat*; in the US east coast several Cuban students decide to bring attention to the situation in Cuba by *pulling a car* from Connecticut to Washington, DC; in the US the works of Cuban architects in exile began to be noticed, as in the Bacardí building in Miami, designed by *Henry Gutiérrez.*

The world around Cuban exiles in the 1960s (continued)

Photos above, top to bottom: Cuban exiles in Miami demonstrate in front of the *Miami Beach Convention Center* on occasion of the 1968 **Republican Convention**; Spain continues to help the Castro government, this time shipping —on credit— a lot of 40 **Pegaso Trucks** on February 16, 1964; some national TV networks began to be sensitized to the truth about the totalitarian regime in Cuba in December of 1966; on May 27, 1964, a five man board of Cuban exiles lobbies the **Organization of American States** in Washington, D.C., to take actions against the Communist government of Cuba.

In the last photo, left to right **Jorge Mas Canosa**, 24, **Vicente Rubiera**, 51, **Aurelio Fernández Díaz**, 43, **Ernesto Freire**, 53 and **Erneido Oliva**, 31. They were the founders of the *Representación Cubana del Exilio (RECE)*, an organization promoted by *Bacardí's* president **Pepín Bosch**.

Aurelio de la Vega (1925-), born in Havana, Cuba, became a musical power in the US since the early 1960s. He had been, among many other distinctions, Dean of the School of Music of the *University of Oriente*, VP of the *Havana Philharmonic Orchestra* and a musical lecturer in the US since the early 1950s. After leaving Cuba in the early 1960s he continued to receive numerous honors, such as, Past-President of the Los Angeles Chapter of the *National Association of Composers, U.S.A.*, 1964-1968, Visiting Professor of Music at the *University of Rio de Janeiro* (Fulbright Research Award, Washington-Rio de Janeiro), Professor of Music and Director of the Electronic Music Studio at *California State University*, Northridge. In 1971 he was awarded the Outstanding Professor Award of the entire *California State University System*. He has refused twice the *Friedheim Award* of the *Kennedy Center for the Performing Arts*.

De la Vega has lectured widely in the United States, Canada, Mexico, Puerto Rico, Venezuela, Argentina, Brazil, Spain, Chile and, of course, Cuba. His main areas of interest have always been contemporary music, electronic music and the musical arts of Latin America. His compositions have been published and commercially recorded; almost all have been commissioned works. They include solo piano, symphonic pieces, chamber music, solo instruments, vocal music, solo guitar, ballet music and electronic music works. His works have been played by great orchestras, ensembles, important instrumentalists and singers in four continents and have been recorded by Panart, Orion, Avant, Crystal, Opus One, Vienna Modern Masters and Centaur, among other prestigious studios.

He has been an example of Cuban depth and creativity and has honored Cuba and its exiles with a relentless productivity and musical mastery.

Mons Eduardo Boza Masvidal (1915-2003), as Auxiliary Bishop of the Archdiocese of Havana, was expelled from Cuba by the Communists in September of 1962, together with 130 other priests and nuns in what was the first purge of religious ministers by the Castro regime. He was accused of having engaged in counter-revolutionary activities. He was arrested by members of the *Committee for the Defense of the Revolution*, a government organization that assigned followers to hunt dissidents in their area.

He had been born in Camagüey and was ordained on February 28, 1944 by Manuel Cardenal Arteaga, the first Cuban Cardinal. In the late 1940s he was a professor at the *San Carlos and San Ambrosio Seminary* in Havana and Chaplain of the *Colegio del Sagrado Corazón*. His last assignments in Cuba were as pastor of *Our Lady of Charity Church* in Havana, prosecutor in the *Cuban Ecclesiastical Tribunal* and Rector of the *Catholic University of Villanueva*.

He was chosen by Pope John XXIII as Bishop of Vinda in 1960 and participated as part of the Cuban Church in the *Second Vatican Council* (1962-1965). Once in exile he founded the *Unión de Cubanos en el Exilio (UCE)*, with chapters in most important cities in the US, South America and Europe. He died on March 16, 2003 from pneumonia while serving as *Vicario General* in Los Teques, Venezuela.

Photos above: **Mons. Boza** at the time he went into exile in 1962 and a few weeks before his death in 2003 with **Fr. Francisco Villaverde O.P.** on his side.

Castro was extremely irritated and had not forgotten Eisenhower's disdain for him; Ike had sent and unfriendly VP Richard Nixon to met him in 1959. He was also upset by the bilateral Soviet-US agreement to remove the missiles from Cuba. He felt a need to have tanks, planes, missiles and other armaments for Cuba's "*defense*."

In 1963, after the Soviets had also dissed him, a Cuban government delegation led by him showed up in Moscow. This time the Russians agreed to bring him into their tent. He was even kissed in the cheek by Brezhnev; it was said that Castro repeatedly cleaned his face with the cuffs of his sleeve all the way home. This time there were no Cuban refugees witnessing the event or complaining publicly.

Photos above, top to bottom: **Castro** met **Nixon** in 1959 as **Ike** refused to give him an audience; Castro couldn't believe **Brezhnev** was really going to kiss him; Castro and the Soviet leaders in 1963.

While all these events of serious international impact were occurring, the Cuban refugees in Miami were trying to survive in a new environment that they had not anticipated would last more than a few months.

Physicians began to study for the *ECFMG* certification (*Educational Commission for Foreign Medical Graduates*) in order to obtain an unrestricted license to practice medicine. The success rate among Cuban trained physicians was 79.5% while only 57.2 of worldwide candidates were achieving certification.

Cuban exile lawyers, teachers, architects, accountants, nurses, engineers and other professionals began to update their skills in light of the US practices at the *University of Miami* and other institutions of higher learning across the US. While they waited to obtain the corresponding licenses, they distributed newspapers house-to-house, painted buildings, pumped gas in gas stations, mowed lawns, worked in supermarkets and construction projects and did whatever jobs they could in order to support their families. Skilled workers (masons, woodworkers, upholsterers, mechanics, and others) began to find jobs in the cities where they resided. Most Cuban exiles were happy when they could finally drop the government subsidies and were capable of providing for themselves.

Photos below, top to bottom: the coveted **ECFMG** certificate for Cuban exiled physicians; the "**tomateras**" in Southern Florida, where many Cuban ladies worked to help sustain their families in the early days of exile.

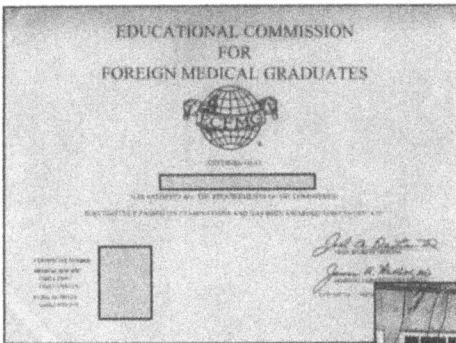

As the 1960s were coming to an end the world continued to generate unexpected events that impacted the lives of the thousands of refugees that had left Cuba. Some of these events are presented in this and the following page.

*Photos above: **Martin Luther King** speech at the Washington Mall and news of his assassination late in 1968; the organization of the **Comités de Defensa de la Revolución** in Cuba; training of urban citizens in Cuba to turn them into self-sufficient farmers in the agricultural belt around the Capital; finally, the continued **anti-Castro marches**, this time in the streets of Manhattan in 1967.*

Considering the importance that Cubans have always given to the education of their children, it was not long before private schools in Miami were flooded with the children of Cuban refugees.

Photos above, top to bottom: **Carrollton School of the Sacred Heart**; **La Salle High School**; **Lincoln-Marti** Academies; **Conchita Espinosa** Academy; **Columbus High School**; **Belen Preparatory School**.

Juan Manuel Salvat (1940-) was in 1959 Vice Secretary General of the School of Social Sciences of the *Federación Estudiantil Universitaria (FEU)* of the *University of Havana*. As one of the most active student leaders in Cuba he was one of the organizers, in February of 1960, of a ceremony at the statue of José Martí in Havana's *Central Park* to redress the desecration of the statue committed by Soviet Minister **Anastas Mikoyan (1895-1978)** when he placed a flower arrangement with the hammer and sickle at the foot of the monument. He was arrested and expelled from the University in May of 1960 at the behest of Castro. He took refuge at the Brazilian Embassy and joined the Cuban exiles in Miami in August of 1960. He secretly returned to Cuba in December of the same year and helped reorganize the *Directorio Revolucionario Estudiantil*, returning to Miami in 1961, after the failed *Bay of Pigs* invasion.

After other guerrilla campaigns in Cuba, in 1965 he founded **Ediciones Universal** in Miami, a great cultural effort that has been operating since 1975 from its own building at 31st Avenue and Calle Ocho in Miami. He has been a leader in the publication and distribution of books dealing with Hispanic culture, particularly those referring to Cuba. By 2012 his *Ediciones Universal* had published over 1600 titles and had reached all corners of the Spanish reading world.

Salvat is a founding member of the *Latin Chamber of Commerce (Camacol)*, a member of the Board of Directors of *Editorial Cubana*, a former board member of the *Cuban Museum of Arts and Culture*, a member of the *Agrupación Católica Universitaria (ACU)*, the Hispanic Committee of the *Miami Book Fair International* and other organizations related to the world of books and culture.

Photos above, top to bottom: Salvat during his days of struggle against Castro and Communism in Cuba. With him, **José A. Lanuza**, **José (Gugú) Basulto** and **Alberto Muller**; **Salvat** during a book presentation at *Casa Bacardí* and, finally, in his office at *Ediciones Universal*.

Scenes from the 1960 confrontation of the students from the *University of Havana* and **Anastas Mikoyan** in Havana's *Central Park*, when the students attempted to remove the flowers that Mikoyan had deposited in the statue of **José Martí**.

Photos above, top to bottom:
Anastas Mikoyan with journalist **Elsa Guillén** and a group of Cuban Communist sympathizers; before the ceremony was over a group of students approached the statue, protesting the presence of Mikoyan and his tribute to the Apóstol José Martí; Castro's security forces fired in the air to disperse the protesters; Martí's monument and Mikoyan with Castro and Guevara.

Elsa Guillén eventually sought refuge in the US and for many years lived in the Bronx, NY. Most of the student protesters also became exiles. **Mikoyan**, who continued his stay in Cuba after finding out his wife *Ashkhen* had died the day he arrived in Havana, opposed the placing of missiles in Cuba in 1961 and got in the wrong side of Castro. A soviet official once said of Mikoyan: «*The rascal was able to walk through Red Square on a rainy day without an umbrella* [and] *without getting wet*».

Some events of Cuban exiles in the 1960s.

Photos below:

April 19, 1961, Cuban exiles at a demonstration in front of the *USSR delegation to the UN* on Park Avenue, New York; ***December 15, 1961***, Cuban exiles lining President Kennedy's parade route in *San Juan, PR*, asking for guns to battle Castro in Cuba; ***April 5, 1963***, Exiles in training at *No Name Key* in Florida, as shown in CBS News with Walter Cronkite.

Aside from all patriotic or civic considerations, it has often been said that two things have always tied Cuban exiles to their island: *Cuban food* and *La Guantanamera.*

More than *Siboney* and *El Manisero*, *La Guantanamera* has been the most national and international song that Cuba has ever given to the world. Its author was **Joseíto Fernández (1908-1979)**, a humble shoe shiner and newspaper boy, born in an unpretentious dilapidated house in *Los Sitios*, one of the poorest Havana neighborhoods. He ventured into the musical world joining trios, sextets and orchestras until he joined first **Radio Lavín** and later **CMQ Radio** in Havana with **Orquesta Típica**, his own band. At noon time CMQ had a program called **El Suceso del Día** (the daily incident), at the end of which he began to sing a melody (a *guajira-song*) he had been interpreting for several years: **La Guantanamera**. *Coralia Fernández* would sing lyrics composed by *Chanito Isidrón* wrapping up the lessons to learn from the [mostly police] incidents presented in the program. The **Suceso del Día** remained 14 years in the air, during which time his contract prohibited him to interpret the song anywhere else. The song was so tied to unfortunate events that Virgilio Piñera incorporated it, with his own lyrics, in his opening of **Electra Garrigó**, his pioneering theater of the absurd play.

(Continued)

Photos below, left to right, top to bottom:

Joseito Fernández; the program for the premier of **Electra Garrigó** and the music sheet of *Guantanamera.*

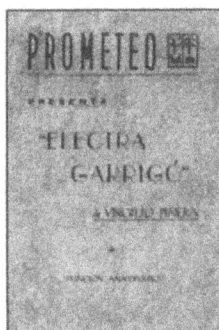

(Continuation)

The first interpreter that brought together the verses of José Martí and the rhythm of Guantanamera was **Julián Orbón (1925-1991)**, an Asturian whose name was given to the *Oviedo Conservatory School* in Spain. Orbón was a member of *Orígenes*, the celebrated magazine ran by *Lezama Lima* in Havana. One of Orbón's friends in *Orígenes* was **Hector Angulo (1932-)**, who became an instructor in a summer camp in the US in 1962; there he met **Pete Seeger (1919-)**; Angulo sang for the camp boys **La Guantanamera**, with the Martí lyrics, and taught it to Seeger. Seeger incorporated the song to his repertoire and presented it on June 8, 1963 at **Carnegie Hall**. In the audience at *Carnegie Hall* was Jim Brady of the group **The Sandpipers**, who learned the song from Seeger. Both recorded the song and **La Guantanamera** broke high into the *Hit Parade* in New York and London in 1964. It was almost immediately recorded by *Joan Báez, Libertad Lamarque, Los Cinco Latinos, Marco Antonio Muñiz, Joe Dassin* (French), *Jimmy Fontana* (Italian), *Karel Gott* (Czech) and *Edjean Kluger* (Dutch), to mention just a few. The name **Joseito Fernández**, however, never appeared in the recordings; only Pete Seeger's. Joseito never received a penny for it.

It has been said that in Cuba, and among Cuban exiles, «*hasta los perros sabían ladrar La Guantanamera*» (Even the dogs knew how to howl *La Guantanamera*). Both in the island and in exile, almost a century after *El Suceso del Día,* Cubans continue to say «*le cantó una Guantanamera*» (he protested vociferously), and «*se armó la Guantanamera*», (there was a major quarrel).

Photos below:

Top left, **Julian Orbón**; on the rest of the page, **Pete Seeger**, the **Sandpipers** and some of the hundreds of recordings of Guantanamera.

By the end of the 1960s the number of Cuban intellectuals and writers that had taken the road to exile had already made a dent in the quality of educational and creative quests in the island. The exodus of creative literary, artistic and scientific minds continued into the decades of the 1970s and 1980s. Among the first to go were *Enrique Labrador Ruiz, Eugenio Florit, Severo Sarduy, Guillermo Cabrera Infante, Matías Montes Huidobro, Lino Novás y Calvo, Eduardo Manet* and *Lydia Cabrera;* they were followed by *Belkis Cuza Malé, Heberto Padilla, Carlos Victoria, Ana María Simó, Ricardo Pau-Llosa, Reinaldo Arenas, Andrés Reynaldo, Gustavo Pérez-Firmat, Jorge Castellanos, José Sánchez Boudy, Iván Acosta, Manuel Serpa* and many others too numerous to list. Most stayed in Miami; some began to explore other important cultural centers, far from the political confrontations and obsessions of Miami: they were found in New York, Paris, London, Madrid, Stockholm and Barcelona.

Opening new territories to their works in a cultural environment that did not necessarily know their names and achievements, well known Cuban talents like *Lydia Cabrera* had to begin to validate their erudition and scholarship through self-publishing. Painters and sculptors, like *Cundo Bermúdez*, not having a friendly government promoting their works, began to sell their productions from their homes while anticipating that sooner or later the support of galleries and art critics would be there. In the end, not one writer, plastic artist, poet, teacher, musician, entertainer or scientist in exile could conclude that he or she had been more successful in Cuba than abroad. They all preserved their *cubanismo* while widening their fame and scope in the broader and more demanding scenario of the US, Europe and the rest of the world.

Photos below, top to bottom, left to right:

Lydia Cabrera, Enrique Labrador Ruiz, Cundo Bermudez,
Belkis Cuza Malé, Jorge Castellanos, Ricardo Pau-Llosa,
Matías Montes Huidobro, Lino Novás y Calvo, Gustavo Pérez-Firmat
and *José Sánchez Boudy.*

III

The Decade of the 1970s

Cuba is forsaken and victimized by the Cold War

CUBANS LEAVING THE ISLAND in the first years of the decade of the 1960s were viewed by the US (and by themselves) as temporary exiles that would return to Cuba after toppling Castro's regime. As such, they were welcomed with open arms. From the perspective of the US, they were providing evidence that common citizens in the Americas would reject radical leftist political credos. Moreover, as tensions between the Cuban regime and the US intensified, the flow of Cuban exiles contributed to the isolation of the Cuban Communist regime.

The circumstances were dramatically changed after the *Bay of Pigs* fiasco. It was a watershed for the Cuban exiles, for Castro, for Kennedy and for the US. After the Bay of Pigs, many exiles gave up hopes for a quick resolution of the Cuban problem and began to consider the certainty of a long absence from

Cuba and the need for family reunification in the safety of the US. Just before and after the Bay of Pigs, two events took some of the shine from the empowered Communists in Cuba: the French ship *La Coubre* exploded in Havana harbor on March of 1960 and the USSR was caught *in fraganti* placing missiles with nuclear heads in Cuba's countryside in October of 1962.

After the Bay of Pigs, the Missile Crisis.

This time Kennedy seemed to act decisively and, whether it really happened or not, he claimed he had averted a world nuclear conflagration, forcing the Soviets to remove the missiles and the nuclear armaments from Cuba. Cuban exiles suspected but had no proof that Kennedy and Khruschev had made a pact after the 1962 Missile Crisis that precluded any further US efforts to intervene militarily in Cuba on the side of freedom. As a palliative for that pact (openly disclosed many years later), the US discontinued all attempts to deport illegal arrivals of Cuban exiles, expanded its *visa waiver* program and began to grant *extended voluntary departure* status to all Cuban refugees. In many ways it was recognition of the failure of the US executive to act decisively in *Playa Girón*, as well as a concession to the long lasting status of Cuba as the *"best buen vecino"* of the US.

From there on the US would limit its defense of democracy in Cuba to the diplomatic (resolutions at the Organization of American States meetings, for instance), economic (an ineffective embargo backed by the *Trading with the Enemy Act* in 1963) and public relations fronts (the endless lines of Cubans *"voting with their feet"* were presented as clear proof of a definitive rejection of Castro).

Cuba responded by closing its doors in early 1970 (the end of the freedom flights in 1973); a seven-year period of limited migration to the US began. Only a few thousand political prisoners and family members seeking reunions were crossing the Florida straits or reaching Europe in the late 1970s.

The *Vuelos de la Libertad*.

Prior to that, in spite of its difficulties and procedural slowdowns in Cuba, over 250,000 exiles had boarded the 45 minute charter flights separating Varadero and Miami, twice every weekday from 1965 through 1973. They arrived penniless, with a prescribed maximum of three changes of clothing and no other valuables (everything was routinely confiscated at the Havana airport: jewelry, photos, books, family heirlooms, letters, cash and even pens). These *Vuelos de la Libertad* (Freedom Flights) were authorized by US President Lyndon Johnson after a short lived but dangerous escape route through the port of *Camarioca* was started by Miami exiles trying to rescue family members (3 to 5,000 or so made it) in rented boats out of Key West and Coconut Grove. As they left, they were called *"gusanos"* and their passports were stamped *"NULO."* Most arrived in Miami dazzled but also sad, afraid and stupefied, without funds for even a simple meal or to pay for lodging, without knowing anyone and not having any addresses or phones to call.

By the end of the *Vuelos de la Libertad*, 510,000 Cuban exiles had settled in the Miami area and 120,000 elsewhere in the US and Europe. The most visible evidence of this mass migration was *"Little Havana,"* which by the end of the 1970s had been transformed into a lively and busy Cuban enclave. A July 1973 article entitled *"Cuba's Exiles Bring New Life to Miami"* in the *National Geographic* magazine (which had characterized Cuban refugees as the «golden exiles» in 1967), stated «*There are so many Cubans living in Miami that at times it feels like another country had sprouted up within the city limits . . . exiles have left their indelible mark on Miami. By any indicator, their impact has been, to say the least, profound...*»

Cuba looses to the priorities of the Cold War.

During a good part of the 1970s, the Cuban issue became fully immersed in the politics of the Cold War. The US, after the assassination of President Kennedy, became more and more invested in the Vietnam War. Ngô Dinh Dièm, President of South Vietnam (the *"Churchill of Asia,"* according to Lyndon Johnson) had been overthrown, shot and killed in 1963, together with his brother Nhu, all with the tacit approval of President Kennedy. The *Tonkin Resolution* had been approved by Congress in 1964 (authorizing President Johnson to take all necessary measures to repeal attacks against US forces) and the US began to send thousands of its troops through the *Danang* airfield to wage war against North Vietnam (500,000 by one account). Teach-ins began to be held at many American Universities and by 1968 the Vietcong had threatened Saigon in the celebrated *Tet Offensive*, a military defeat but a political victory for the Communists. Finally, the *My Lai* massacre of March 16, 1968, was instrumental in the stunning announcement of President Johnson that he would not be a candidate for re-election. By then Nixon, aided by Kissinger, had assured his first election as President, had promised to end the Vietnam War and had initiated the peace talks in Paris. By the second half of the 1970s Saigon fell to the Communists, all American troops evacuated the city, and Hanoi was declared the capital of a unified Vietnam. The world leadership of the US had never been so widely challenged and its prestige had never been so low.

As these momentous events were happening, Cuba was more and more perceived as just a deserved nuisance to the US rather than a threat to world peace. No countries in the continent or the world were willing to cooperate with the US in the containment or isolation of Communism in Cuba. Henry Kissinger, as the arbiter of American foreign policy, was more interested in a *détente* with the Soviet Union and China than in a moral debate centered on Cuba. The Europeans were eager to sell goods to Cuba; Spain was ready to open hotels in the island; the Canadians were enjoying cut rate beach deals four hours from home; the Latin nations were simply glad that someone was sticking it to the US. The *New York Times* kept hammering a single narrative that had started in 1971 in its editorial policy: relations with Cuba «*needed to be normalized.*»

From the standpoint of Nixon or Kissinger, any mention of Castro, Communism or Democracy and Civil Rights in Cuba was sure to jeopardize arms control negotiations with the Soviets and be a slap in the face of the Chinese, at the time the most totalitarian regime in the world. The only ripples in those years of *laissez-faire* towards Cuba were the increasing military involvement of Castro's Cuba in the *Angolan War*. In late 1975 Castro had sent 4,000 choice troops, with Soviet funding and firepower, to support the *Popular Movement for the Liberation of Angola -MPLA* , against South Africa and the US supported Jonas Savimbi's *UNITA* movement. Cuba was also supporting Puerto Rico's independence in the UN. Other than small indications of US displeasure with Cuba's Angola and Puerto Rico advocacies, the US official positions of Presidents Ford and Carter were limited to boring cold war refugee-pleasing (and South Florida vote-getting) rhetoric.

Cubans in exile at the end of the 1970s.

As the decade of the 1970 was reaching its end, the US Bureau of the Census found in 1980 [1] a total of 803,234 persons of Cuban origin (700,000 Cuban-born and the balance their children and dependants), a number that would increase substantially after the so called *"Mariel Boatlift"* from April to September of that year (about 125,000 additional souls). This was contrasted to the estimate in 1958 (based on projections from the 1950 Census) of less than 75,000 persons born in Cuba or descendant of Cubans living in the US, a number that included Cuban students at American Universities.

In 1980, even though it was estimated that only 7 percent of Cuban refugees had been born or had lived in the countryside, in small rural towns or in fishing hamlets, more than 97% had settled in large metropolitan areas in the US, mostly the Miami-Fort Lauderdale, New York-New Jersey and the Greater Los Angeles areas. Moreover, the trends also indicated that those initially living in other cities within the US had begun a slow and unstoppable migration to Miami, sardonically known among exiles as their own *"cementerio de elefantes,"* or final

---

[1] The demographic characteristics of Cuban exiles in 1980 were:

- *median age: 37.7 years; seniors: 12%; seniors living with their children: 30.7%;*
- *seniors living in institutions: 1.3% (among American-born seniors it was 5.9%);*
- *male to female ratio in the 25-39 age bracket: 1.22;*
- *average number of children in families with parents in the 35-44 age bracket: 2.04;*
- *median family annual income: $18,245 (average for the entire US: $19,917);*
- *families annual income above $50,000: 5.2% (average for the entire US: 5.6%);*
- *working women above 16 of age: 55.4% (average for the entire US: 49.9%);*
- *adults with College Degrees: 16.6% (average for the entire US: 16.2%).*

"*resting*" place; this flow has never abated from 1959 to recent times.

Experts began to predict in 1980 that most Cuban enclaves —with the exception of New York and the Greater Miami area— were bound to disappear; that second-generation Cubans would be more-often-than-not bilingual and would fully integrate into the American melting pot; and that the stream of political exiles would increasingly turn into a typical outflow of people seeking economic opportunities not likely to be found in a socialist environment. No one disputed the fact that the 1970s saw the consolidation of the revolution in Cuba and the assimilation of Cuban exiles in the US and Europe.

Cubans in Cuba at the end of the 1970s.

The idealism and hopeful patience shown by many Cubans during the first decade of revolution collapsed into a cynical accommodation and a expedient compromise of the leaders with the masses during the second decade.

Greater productivity was beyond anybody's reach (as demonstrated by the plummeting production results of the sugar industry); self-sufficiency in foodstuffs was no longer presented as an attainable goal but as a proof of the Spartan nature of the revolutionary ideals; government supporters (inside and outside Cuba) were asked to blame cyclical scarcity of normal societal needs to the US embargo (blockade in their terminology). Moral incentives, however, were de-emphasized and central planning encouraged as the final solution to the poverty and dearth of articles and facilities that existed in other poor countries. Young children were placed in Day Care centers, presumably to allow both parents to work but in reality to instill loyalty to the revolution. The faltering revolutionary masses were falsely elated with visits to Cuba (starting in 1977) of miniscule groups of exile leftist radicals such as the *Brigadas Antonio Maceo*. The government in Cuba redoubled its efforts and its social pressures to make all people join the *Comités de Defensa de la Revolución, CDR,* (Committees for the Defense of the Revolution), making those who did not join to be considered suspect because of their attitude toward the government and the community. Homosexuality was no longer considered a product of decadence, yet all homosexuals were removed from the field of education and many were sent to rehabilitation camps.

Yet the most scandalous and scurrilous move of the Communist leaders took place when the government that had most divided the Cuban family welcomed a group of exile *Dialogueros* to Havana, under the guise of promoting the reunification of Cuban families from both sides of the Florida straits. All of a sudden the *"gusanos"* became respectful members of the Cuban community abroad.

In spite of the high-road simulated by the revolutionary leaders, discontent continued to be prevalent in Cuba. It eventually resulted (Spring of 1980) in the largest disorganized flotilla of disgruntled, disillusioned and irritated Cubans arriving at US shores. Most of them came to Florida in boats provided by the Miami exiles. As it was said at the time, «...*many of them left Cuba; others were sent from Cuba*».

EDUCACION Y SALUD EN CUBA
by Garrinche

The
1970s

- In January of 1971, a group of pro-Castro Cuban activists attacked the offices of **Alpha 66** in Miami.
- On March, 16 Cuban exiles, members of **Operación Abdala,** took control of the *UN building* in New York for a few hours to bring attention to the tragic situation in Cuba.
- Many literary and academic Cuban exile personalities protested for the detention in Cuba of **Heberto Padilla** and his wife **Belkis Cuza Malé**.
- **Lorenzo del Toro** founded in Miami the magazine *Ideal* to bring a Christian perspective to the plight of Cuban exiles.
- In October of 1971, at a military garrison in Samá, north of Banes, several commandos exchanged fire with the Cuban military in what was the first engagement of the **Plan Torriente**.
- Cuban exiles with no affiliation attacked the offices of the *Delegación Cubana a las Naciones Unidas* and the *Oficina de Asuntos Comerciales de Cuba* in Montreal.
- In April 1972, **Amalio Fiallo, Silva Meso** and **Pbro. Reinerio Lebroc** organized in Caracas a *Festival de Arte Cubano*, committed to reaffirm the Cuban roots of the exiles. The festival ran for the next ten years.
- On May 24, **Pedro Luis Boitel** died in *El Principe* prison in Havana.
- On May 28, 14 Cuban exiles, members of **Operación Abdala,** took control of the *Statue of Liberty* in the port of New York for a few hours to bring, attention to the death of **Pedro Luis Boitel** in Cuba.
- The merchant ships *Aguja* and *Plataforma* were attacked by members of the **FLNC** and sank in international waters.
- Unknown and unaffiliated Cuban exiles presumably placed bombs on the same day at the offices of the Cuban Travel Agency **Va-Cuba** in New York, Montreal, Miami and Mexico City.
- **Orlando Bosch**, once freed from prison, started in Miami the organization *Acción Cubana*. He had pledged not to use again the name **MIRR**.
- Unknown groups of Cuban exiles attacked the *Office of Commertial Affairs of Cuba* in Santiago de Chile, as well as the residence of its manager.

(Continued)

Photos above, left to right:

Lorenzo del Toro, in 2011, 40 years after the publication of the first issue of *Revista Ideal*; **Heberto Padilla** and **Belkis Cuza Malé** at the time of the Padilla Affair and the support they received by Cuban exiles; **Andrés Nazario Sargén** addressing the *Alpha 66* commandos in their camp.

(Continuation)

- After 272 days of experimentations by Cuban penitentiary authorities (irregular feeding hours, isolation in dark cells, nakedness, sudden changes in temperature, scarcity of space, lack of water, deceitful clocks, strong air streams, invasions of rodents, etc.) political prisoner **Enrique García Cuevas** died at a prison in Santa Clara, Las Villas on June 23, 1973.

- In August, 28 year old **Juan Felipe de la Cruz**, a member of *Acción Cubana,* died at a hotel in Avrainville, east of Paris, as he was preparing an explosive device to take the life of Cuban Minister *Ramiro Valdés.*

- In October of 1973, **Guillermo Martínez Márquez** denounced the abuses and murders of the Cuban regime before the *Sociedad Interamericana de Prensa (SIP).* The organization vigorously condemned Cuba.

- Naval commands from the **Frente Cubano de Liberación Nacional (FCLN)** intensified its attacks against Cuban fishing and merchant ships from the Caribbean, down the Pacific Coast and up the Eastern US waters.

- At a meeting in Irazú, Costa Rica, **Manolo Ray**, **Tony Santiago**, **Mario Rivadulla** and **Charles** and **Roberto Simeon** organized the *Partido Revolucionario del Pueblo (PRP);* Tony Santiago became its first president.

- In April of 1974, unknown assassins took the life of **José Elías de la Torriente** in his own home. Since he had been involved in the development of the Westchester area in Miami and was in litigation, it was never clear if his death was a business or a political retaliation.

- As the 1970s progressed, Cuban exiles lost a lot of credibility due to the excessive violence of the commandos as they attacked Cuban and Soviet diplomatic missions in Mexico, Panamá, Lima, San Juan, Buenos Aires, Madrid, Paris, Kingston, London, Mérida, Caracas, Lisbon, Trinidad, Barbados, Bogotá, San José and Quito. Most Cuban exiles began to disassociate themselves from these actions and to stop their support.

- In August the **Frente Nacional Cubano (FNC**), a political and financial group, was created at the conclusion of a Congress organized by **Organización Abdala**.

(Continued)

Photos below, left to right:

Enrique García Cuevas, one of the many political prisoners in Cuba who died without receiving medical attention; the **Manacas Prison** where *Enrique García Cuevas* was tortured until he died; **Guillermo Martínez Márquez** and the logotype of the **Interamerican Press Association.**

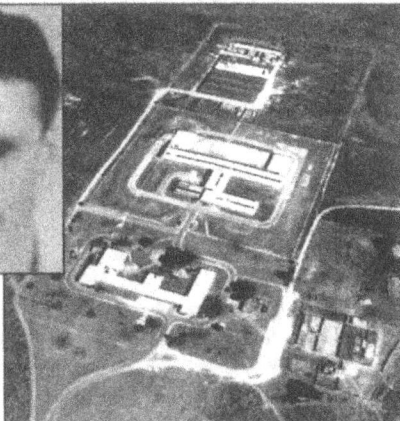

(Continuation)

- In January of 1976 **Ricardo Bofill** launched in Havana the *Comité Cubano Pro Derechos Humanos* an organization that began to present and defend in Cuba the 30 articles of the *Universal Declaration of Human Rights*.
- On April 5, 1976, **Humberto Medrano**, the last director of the confiscated Havana newspaper *Prensa Libre*, suggested to declare April 5 *Día del Preso Político Cubano*.
- In July, **Orlando Bosch** set up the *Coordinadora de Organizaciones Revolucionarias Unidas (CORU)* in Banao, Dominican Republic. It brought together a dozen anti-Castro revolutionary organizations.
- On October 25, 1976, **Aldo Vera**, a former commander of the Cuban rebel army and the founder of the anti-Castro organization **La Cuarta República** is assassinated in San Juan by pro-Castro activists.
- In mid 1977, the **Amadeo Roldán Theater** (formerly the *Auditorium*) is bombed in Havana by a group with headquarters in Miami.
- **Teo Carrasco** finished a mural he had designed and painted at the *Ermita de la Caridad* in Miami.
- Cubans in exile lamented the assassination (by the Cuban military?) in the *Combinado del Este* prison in Cuba, of **Rafael del Pino**, a WWII veteran, friend and companion of Castro during the *Bogotazo* (massive 10 hour riot in Bogotá, Colombia, after the assassination of *Jorge Eliézer Gaitán* on April 9, 1948, which caused 5,000 deaths). Del Pino helped organize the 1956 expedition of the *Granma* from Mexico to Oriente, Cuba, but disagreed with the Communist tilt of the revolution and was condemned to 30 years, of which he had already served 17.

(Continued)

Photos above, left to right:

Top row: **Adolfo Rivero Caro** and **Ricardo Bofill**, defenders of Human Rights in Cuba*; Rafael del Pino Siero*. He opposed his friend Fidel Castro, was made prisoner in 1959, served 18 years and died in prison.
Bottom row: **Humberto Medrano**, last director of *Prensa Libre, a* prestigious newspaper during the republic; **Aldo Vera**, old member of the *Movimiento 26 de Julio* in Havana, appointed *Chief of Police* of the Capital in 1959, exiled in 1960, allegedly murdered in Puerto Rico by *Tony de la Guardia. On his left in the* photo is **Armando Hart**, future *Minister of Education*;

(Continuation)

- At the end of 1978, Cuban exiles in Caracas, under the leadership of **Mons. Eduardo Boza Masvidal**, organized the *Fundación de Ayuda a los Cubanos en el Exilio*. Its purpose was to coordinate activities that would facilitate the adaptation to Venezuela of Cubans seeking refuge there and to obtain visas for former political prisoners after they were freed.
- In the same vein, the Miami organization **Facts About Cuban Exiles (FACE)**, signed an agreement with **Simón Alberto Consalvi** (Foreign Minister of Venezuela during the presidency of **Carlos Andrés Pérez**), to guarantee the logistics, reception, housing, media attention, feeding and employment of former political prisoners that had finished their sentences and were seeking a place to live outside Cuba.
- As a result of the FACE-Venezuela agreement, several **Hogar Cubano Residences** were established in Venezuela. This agreement lasted until 1987, when the visas were discontinued by President *Jaime Lusinchi*. **Carlos Andrés Pérez** had received asylum and shelter in Cuba after the 1948 *Coup d'état* of *Carlos Delgado Chalbaud* against duly elected *Romulo Gallegos*.
- During September 7, 8 and 9 of 1979, Miami received more than 1200 delegates from over 40 Cuban exile organizations to attend the first **Congreso Mundial por la Libertad y la Democracia**. The preparatory sessions had taken place in California, Chicago, New Jersey, New York, Caracas and Puerto Rico. The main organizer and moderator was **Manuel Antonio de Varona**. During the second *Congreso* (24, 25, 26 April, 1981), the delegates agreed to found the *Junta Patriótica Cubana*, again with Varona as the president. The third *Congreso* (11, 12, 13 November, 2011) expanded its name to *Congreso Mundial por la Libertad, la Democracia y la Soberanía de Cuba*.
- In October of 1979, a group of Cuban writers, artists and intellectuals began to organize a **Congress of Cuban Intellectuals**, to be held in Paris in 1986, with **Armando Valladares** as its Honorary President.

Photos below, left to right:

The presidency of the **Third World Congress for the Liberty, Democracy and Sovereignty of Cuba; Carlos Andrés Pérez,** President of *Venezuela;* **Manuel Antonio de Varona,** president for 12 years of the **Junta** ~~Patriótica Cubana~~

Hijackers land in Algiers with ransom from Miami

On July 31, 1972, **Delta Flight 841**, en route from Detroit to Miami, was hijacked by a man called **George Wright**, accompanied by four other adults and three small children. It was one more aircraft sequestered by radical leftists or insane people since 1958, when the first airliner was hijacked and taken to *Nipe Bay* in Cuba. Upon landing in Miami, Wright, a known killer and prison escapee, demanded $1 million, gasoline and a change of pilots. He asked to be taken to Boston, and at his arrival he instructed the pilot to fly to Argelia, where he sought and obtained asylum. The money and the plane were eventually returned to the US by the Algerian government. Wright and his companions were released by the Algerians after only a few hours of detention.

In 2011, 39 years after this incident, George Wright was *arrested* at *Kennedy airport* as he attempted to enter the US surreptitiously.

Aircraft hijacking incidents **between the US and Cuba** reached their peak in 1969 but went on until the year 2000, when they reached 118 incidents. Currently, pilots and flight attendants are trained to comply with the hijackers' demands, get the plane to land safely, let the security ground forces handle the situation and advise passengers to sit quietly and not make any "*heroic*" moves that could endanger themselves or other people.

Photos above, top to bottom:

The **Delta Flight 841** in Miami, as an FBI agent (in shorts, as requested by the hijackers) delivered the ransom money.

The 1970s were years of violence and ideological confusion among many radical Cuban exiles. In desperation for the long term prospects of the Castro regime in Cuba, several groups of exiles began to take justice in their own hands and soiled —forever— the respectable image that Cuban exiles had so carefully and honestly crafted in the US and the world. With their contemptible behavior they made the rest of the exiles look primitive, barbaric and uncivilized.

What follows is a summary of some of their violent deeds.

1968 From MacArthur Causeway, pediatrician **Orlando Bosch** fired a *bazooka* at a Polish freighter. Incredibly, the city of Miami later declared an "*Orlando Bosch Day*." Federal agents would jail him in 1988.

1972 *Julio Iglesias*, performing at a local nightclub, said he wouldn't mind «*singing in front of Cubans.*» Audience erupted in anger. Singer required police escort. Most radio stations dropped Iglesias from playlists. One that did not, *Radio Alegre*, received bomb threats.

1974 Exile leader **José Elias de la Torriente** was murdered in his Coral Gables home after failing to carry out a planned invasion of Cuba.

1974 Bomb blast gutted the office of Spanish-language Magazine **Réplica**.

1974 Several small Cuban businesses, citing threats, stopped selling **Réplica**.

1974 Three bombs exploded near a **Spanish-language** Radio station.

1974 **Héctor Diaz Limonta** and **Arturo Rodríguez Vives** were murdered in an internal exile power struggle.

1975 **Luciano Nieves** was murdered after advocating peaceful coexistence with Cuba.

1975 Another bomb damaged **Réplica**'s office.

1976 **Rolando Masferrer** and **Ramon Donéstevez** were murdered in an internal exile power struggle.

1976 Car bomb blowed off the legs of *WQBA-AM News* director **Emilio Milián** after he publicly condemned exile violence.

1977 *Juan José Peruyero* was murdered in an internal exile power struggle.

1979 The Cuban film **Memories of Underdevelopment** was interrupted by gunfire and physical violence instigated by two exile groups.

1979 A bomb was discovered at **Padrón Cigars**, whose owner was part of a group traveling to Cuba to talk to Castro.

1979 A bomb exploded at **Padrón Cigars**.

Cuban Newsman Is Maimed As Bomb Explodes in Car

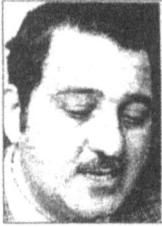

By EDNA BUCHANAN
And DOROTHY GAITER
Herald Staff Writers

A bomb planted under the hood of his station wagon shattered the legs of the news director of Spanish-language radio station in Little Havana Friday.

Emilio Milian, 45, who railsted against terrorist violence in Miami, stepped into his station after a show, got into his WQBA car, turned on the ignition and the device detonated at 11 p.m.

Late Friday doctors at Memorial Hospital amputated both of Milian's legs below the knee and at 2 a.m. today his surgery, the hospital said his condition was described as critical but stable.

Moments before the

Milian has been approached in the parking lot by Rosa Delgado and three friends who had found a little lost boy. Miss Delgado, who attended Garces Commercial College on the first floor of the concrete-

Emilio Milian
...critical

Jury Selection to Resume In Bookstore Bomb Trial

By JOE CRANKSHAW

Selection of a jury for the trial of three men charged with the May 8 attempted bombing of a Little Havana adult bookstore continues this morning before Dade Circuit Judge Ellen Morphonios.

Five jurors tentatively were selected for the panel Monday even though defense attorneys for Antonio Rafael de la Cova, Max Maria Cortes and Gary E. Latham had claimed impaneled jurors would not be found in Miami.

Attorneys on both sides provided two surprise after it became apparent that no jury acquisitions were going to develop.

ASSISTANT STATE Attorney Hank Adorno revealed that Miguel Angel Peraza, a confidential FBI informant who was with the three defendants at the time of the alleged attempt, would not be called as a main witness in the case.

Adorno did not provide any information as to why Peraza would not be called, and attorney Alfonso Sepe said he expects that Peraza may be called as a witness by the defense.

Sepe also added a surprise by announcing that his client, Latham,

PERAZA   SEPE

will withdraw a guilty plea he entered in U.S. District Court to charges related to the bombing attempt.

Latham, De la Cova and three are scheduled to go on trial on the federal charges Aug. 2, before U.S. District Judge C. Clyde Atkins.

Sepe, Assistant Public Defender Mel Black, representing De la Cova, and attorney Nathan Kurta representing Cortes, spent Monday morning putting motions before Judge Morphonios.

THE ATTORNEYS individually and collectively asked the judge to delay the case to allow more time for preparation of their defenses, and for a change of venue to move

the trial out of Dade County.

The attorneys also asked that the judge compel the prosecution to provide them with all statements made by their clients or any time and on any subject.

Adorno argued that the state had released all statements pertinent to the trial and that the other documents still held dealt with other crimes, including homicides, now under investigation by the Metro Public Safety Department.

"They are entitled to all statements made by their clients," ruled Judge Morphonios, giving the defense one of the two favorable rulings it received during the morning.

THE OTHER favorable ruling came when Judge Morphonios said she would reserve judgment on charging the size of the trial until it could be determined if selection of a jury would be tenable.

Defense attorneys had argued that pretrial publicity, which they said included 45 articles in a three-month period plus numerous radio and television broadcasts, had "poisoned the mind of the community" and also provided inaccurate information.

Turn to Page 2D Col. 4

All through the 1970s several groups of anti-Castro exiles tormented Miami residents with their radicalism and violent reactions to each other, as well as to exiles that were not actively involved in the struggle to overthrow Castro. Some of these groups were:

- *Movimiento Insurreccional Martiano,* headed by Ramón Sanchez and Luis Crespo.
- *Movimiento Nacionalista Cubano,* headed by Guillermo Novo-Sampol.
- *Abdala,* headed by Gustavo Marin-Duarte.
- *Omega 7,* headed by Eduardo Arocena.
- *Acción Cubana,* headed by Orlando Bosch Avila.
- *Alpha 66,* headed by Eloy Gutiérrez Menoyo and other leaders of the former *Segundo Frente del Escambray.*

These groups tried —without success— to operate under the umbrella of the *Coordinación de Organizaciones Revolucionarias.*

In the 1970s they were responsible for close to 45 terrorist related bombings in Dade County alone. When the tacit approval of radical Cubans began to diminish, the groups began to target businesses and individuals that were trying to normalize relations with Cuba or to make family reunifications possible. Individuals like **Rolando Masferrer** (director of a Miami's *Replica Magazine*), **Emilio Milián** (a popular radio commentator) and **Ramón Donéstevez Domínguez** (publisher of *Verde Olivo* magazine) were murdered. Businesses like *Padrón Cigars* and *Continental Bank* were bombed.

These incidents were repudiated by most Cuban exiles as offensive anti-social acts of aggression perpetrated by bands of thugs that had gotten out of control. The same Cuban exiles which had previously viewed with sympathy such actions against Castro began to condemn the radical actions of those «uncontrolled scoundrels.»

On page 5 of the *Miami News* of April 16, 1976, the following news was reported as a follow up to a report on the murder of **Ramón Donéstevez Domínguez**:

«Metro police say slain Cuban exile leader Ramón Donestevez bilked 72 Cubans out of thousands of dollars late last year when he accepted the money for a promised trip to Cuba that never occurred. As they sift the many possible motives for the killing, police are trying to determine if an enraged victim pulled the trigger that ended Donestevez' stormy life Tuesday inside his Perrine boat-building factory office. The police informed that evidence showed that Donestevez had taken between $400 and $2,000 from each of 70 persons, and in two instances accepted $4,000 for the longed-for trip back to the exiles' homeland. Donestevez never returned the money after an attempt to make the trip failed in December when his boat with 72 passengers and a crew of five became disabled in rough seas and had to be towed back to Miami Beach.»

It would have been a violation of Donestevez' parole for him to go to Cuba. At the time of his death, Donestevez was on probation for extorting money for what prosecutors said was an earlier planned trip to Cuba. He had pleaded guilty to the charge in a separate case in 1973.

According to Miami County Medical Examiner, on April 13, 1976, **Ramón Donestevez** was found by a co-worker, slumped on his desk at his place of business, victim of a shot fired by a high power rifle, most likely a 30-6, with a soft point bullet.

Photos above: on the left, **Emilio Milián**, news director of WQBA, lays on the ground, severely injured, after a car bomb exploded beneath him; **Ramón Donestevez** in his office at *Piranha Diesel Corporation* in Miami, with his Verde Olivo newspaper.

Among Cuban exiles, many of the most fervent critics of the Cuban revolution were at one time the most active spokespersons for the regime that destroyed the Republic. After their self imposed exile, however, only a few of the former advocates limited themselves to a post-disappointment grieving or gloomy silence; most became eloquent denouncers of the ideologues-tyrants-gangsters that took over in Cuba.

The picture above, taken by Pedro Yanes, was published in the 1970s by Vicente Echerri, one of the best Cuban journalists and writers in exile. It was taken at the Connecticut home of **Dr. Alexander Coleman** (second from right), professor of Latin American literature at the University of New York.

The first man on the left, reading a paper, is **Raúl Chibás (1916-2002)**, brother of Eduardo Chibás, the founder of the *Ortodoxo Party* and a political mentor of Castro. Raúl was a convinced anti-Communist but had climbed the *Sierra Maestra* in 1957 in support of Castro's revolution; he descended with the rank of Commander. In 1960 he became an exile, and died years later in Miami.

The second man from the left, wearing a loose tie and a sweater, is **Carlos Franqui (1921-2010)**; he was a former head and director of *Radio Rebelde* during the *Sierra Maestra's* days and the editor of *Revolución*, the first Castro newspaper, after the triumph of the revolution. His paper orchestrated the intervention and burial of the *Diario de la Marina*, the dean of the Cuban press prior to 1959. Franqui was proud of his peasant past, was disappointed with the Communists before joining Castro (he had been a proofreader in **Hoy**, the Cuban Communist newspaper in the 1940s) and was unjustly accused by his exiled enemies as the *Goebbels* of the Castro regime. Other exiles have defended him claiming he was the leader of the *Girondins* within the Cuban revolution. He became an exile in 1968 and died in Puerto Rico at age 89.

(Continued)

(Continuation)

The third man from the left, in the corner, is **Guillermo Cabrera Infante (1929-2005)**. He was raised inside a Communist family in the town of Gibara, near Castro's birthplace. As a film critic and novelist in the 1950s he was acclaimed as a weaver of sublime and ravishing wordplays. He was ostracized in Cuba after his magazine *Lunes de Revolución* was closed; he ended up in Belgium as cultural attaché from 1962 to 1965. Once he became an exile in London in 1965 (not Miami, New York, Madrid or Paris), he entered, with his novel *Tres Tristes Tigres,* in the immortal rank of James Joyce's *Ulysses* and Mark Twain's *Huckleberry Finn.* In 1997 he received the *Premio Cervantes* from King Juan Carlos of Spain. He died in London at age 76.

Finally, the man on the extreme right is **Heberto Padilla (1932-2000)**, dressed with a sport's jersey that highlights his mental independence and his disregard for authority. He originally applauded the revolution but eventually exposed its totalitarian asphyxiation and enslavement of the mind. As a man of revolutionary instincts he felt entitled to criticize and denounce the course of a revolution when fierce loyalty trumped truth and common sense. He believed in his right to immunity as a writer but unknowingly went beyond the limits acceptable to the revolutionaries. His 1971 persecution, arrest, and mock trial (when he was forced to recant on TV his ideas and all his work), marked a pivotal point in the literary and political narrative of the revolution. He went into exile in 1980 and settled in *Princeton*, New Jersey. He died while teaching as a visiting professor at *Auburn University*, at age 68.

Photos below, left to right:

Raúl Chibás on the day he returned from the *Sierra Maestra;*
Carlos Franqui as director of the newspaper *Revolución;*
Guillermo Cabrera Infante in his days as director of *Lunes;*
Heberto Padilla, during his trials for disloyalty in 1971.

The story and fate of many Cuban exiles was dramatically typified in the early 1960s by the inevitable doom surrounding the future of **Armando Valladares (1937-)**, a bestselling author, poet, painter and eventual US diplomat.

Valladares was a student at the *School of Visual Arts* in Pinar del Rio in 1960 when he was arrested for his disapproval of strategies to implant Communism in Cuba. Among his alleged crimes was his refusal to display a poster promoting Communism in Cuba during his employment at the *Cuban Postal Bank*. With no other reason than his opposition to the Castro regime he was sentenced to 30 years in prison. He added to his troubles a refusal to be "*rehabilitated*" and was subject to torture, periods of solitary confinement and total isolation from the rest of the incarcerated political prisoners.

Without access to writing materials he began to scribe poetry with his own blood in cigarette papers and succeeded in smuggling his work to Paris, where the *PEN Club* honored him with the *Freedom Prize* for writers in prison. *Amnesty International* took his case and lobbied French President *François Mitterrand* to seek his release from Castro's jails, which occurred in 1982, some 22 years after his incarceration.

After his release, his book **Against All Hope** was published in 18 languages and President Reagan presented him with the *Presidential Citizen's Medal*; he also appointed Valladares as *US Ambassador to the United Nations Human Rights Commission*, where Cuba was condemned as a systematic violator of Human Rights. Since his release from prison Valladares has been an indefatigable denouncer of the Cuban Communist regime. As late as 2004, the government of Cuba has accused him of criminal sabotage and as a member of a terrorist cell that includes, among other Cuban exiles, the writer and international political analyst Carlos Alberto Montaner.

Photos above:
Armando Valladares as a young man, at the time of the
publication of *Against All Hope* and in his mature years.

The Washington Post

Nixon Says He Won't Resign

Rhodes Will Vote To Impeach; House To Curtail Debate

Feels Such a Step Would Be 'Outside The Constitution'

Resignation Urged By GOP Senators

The New York Times

NIXON RESIGNS

HE URGES A TIME OF 'HEALING'; FORD WILL TAKE OFFICE TODAY

'Sacrifice' Is Praised; Kissinger to Remain

The 37th President Is First to Quit Post

Cuban exiles were witness in 1974 of a one-in-a-lifetime episode of American history: the resignation of the 37th President of the United States, **Richard Milhouse Nixon (1913-1994)** on August 9, 1974. He was engulfed in a series of clandestine and illegal activities (the *dirty tricks*) undertaken by a team of political burglars, several of which had close connections with Miami exiles: Bernard Barker, Eugenio Martinez, Virgilio Gonzalez, Frank Sturgis, Felipe De Diego and Reinaldo Pico were all from Miami.

Photos above: newspapers in the US at the early stages and at the end of the Watergate affair; bottom photo, **President Nixon** in his office, on a rare photograph with some of the Watergate burglars. These men were members of the "**Plumbers**," a group of anti-Castro Cuban refugees, former FBI agents and former CIA agents, among others.

Another event of the 1970s that gave some hope to the Cuban exiles worldwide was the death of **Dictator Francisco Franco**, an unseemly sympathizer of the Cuban dictator.

«*Españoles: Franco ha muerto*.» (Spaniards: Franco is dead). With those words, on November 20, 1975, forty years of Franco dictatorship ended. He left no other dictator to replace him. ***Carlos Arias Navarro***, president of the government at the time, gave the message to the people on all radio stations. There were many doubts about the future of Spain after the head of the government was no longer the *Generalissimo*. After his death, a political testament was read in which Franco had proclaimed ***Juan Carlos de Borbón y Borbón (1938-)*** as head of state, thus establishing a parliamentary monarchy. Days later the coronation took place; the young grandchild of the previous King became King Juan Carlos I of Spain.

On July 3, 1976, King Juan Carlos named ***Adolfo Suárez*** as his Prime Minister. Following the resignation of Suárez, ***Leopoldo Calvo Sotelo*** came to power; during his inauguration session, at a crucial moment of transition, a *coup* was attempted by sectors close to a Franco follower, ***Colonel Antonio Tejero***. The coup failed and Tejero was made prisoner. The following year the Socialists came to power, with ***Felipe González*** as the new president. He openly continued the inexplicable 15 year support of Communism in Cuba that Franco had established. After numerous scandals of corruption and economic crisis, ***José María Aznar***, from the Conservative Party, came to power. Cuban exiles were confident that the support of Castro as dictator in Cuba had come to an end with Aznar, and they were not disappointed.

Photos above: newspapers with the news of Franco's death;
Colonel Antonio Tejero as he irrupted into the *Chamber of Deputies*
with 200 of his men to announce a *coup d'état* on February 23, 1981.

Cuban exiles could never comprehend the strange relations of Spain with Castro and Cuban Communism, in spite of which — probably because the strong ties of Cubans to Spain as their motherland— many Cubans fled to Spain in the uncertain and turbulent years after 1959.

During the 15 years between the takeover of Cuba by the Communists (1959) and the death of Franco (1975), the relations of Spain and Cuba were nothing short of untypical and paradoxical.

Franco was perhaps the epitome of anticommunism, having defeated barely 20 years earlier (1939) the Communist leaning government of the *Republic of Spain*, after a war that had consumed almost a million victims and had ruined Spain for one full generation. Franco had been trying to portray himself since 1953 as a friend of the US, had authorized American military bases in Spanish territory and had expressed publicly that Cuba was a victim of the expansionistic ambitions of the Soviet Union. Yet he was the main defender of Castro's Cuba as an innocent casualty of the colonialist abuses of the US and went as far as recommending the Cuban regime to not waste *"even a penny"* compensating the US for the revolutionary expropriations of their Cuban investments. There was a precedent to this, of course: his frequent mention of *Ho-Chi-Minh* as a patriot resisting the colonial ambitions of France (the refuge of thousands of Republicans after the Spanish Civil War) and the US (the country that in 1898 put an end to the dreams of Spain as a world power in little more than 15 days).

(Continued)

Photos above: **Francisco Franco** at his meeting in Hendaya, French Pyrenees, in 1940 with **Adolph Hitler**; on the right Franco embracing **Ike** in December of 1959 at Franco's Palace of *El Pardo*.

(Continuation)

How could you explain Franco's support of Communist Cuba between 1959 and 1975, the year of his death?

- Could it be that Franco felt a communion with Castro's ancestors from Galicia?
- Was Franco ignorant of Castro's insults to Spain in *Telemundo* (January 20, 1960) that caused **Juan Pablo de Lojendio**, the *Marquis of Vellisca* (Spain's Ambassador to Cuba) to confront the Cuban dictator in front of the TV Cameras?
- Why was it that Franco never commended the *Marquis* for his gallant defense of Spain *vis-á-vis* the accusations of Castro?
- Who can explain Spain's support of the Cuban revolution and its anti-Americanism after Castro had denounced President Eisenhower for «*embracing Franco the butcher?*
- Why didn't Franco even protest for the expropriation of property to more than 3,200 Spaniards living in Cuba?
- Why did Franco open Communist Cuba to receive millions of dollars of investments in hotels from *Sol Meliá Properties* and other Spanish companies after none of the Spanish residents in Cuba in 1959 received any compensation for their expropriated businesses?

Photo above: the **Marquis of Vellisca** defending the honor of Spain after Castro's insulted his country. He was expelled from Cuba on the spot; *on the right*, one of 22 hotels that the **Sol Meliá Hotel Chain** has built in Cuba.

An event in September of 1973 in faraway Santiago de Chile also had a profound impact in the minds of those Cuban exiles that were actively trying to isolate Castro's Cuba from the rest of the continent: the Communists lost their grip on the traditionally democratic *Republic of Chile* when the presidency of Salvador Allende was interrupted by a *coup d'état* engineered by General of the Army Augusto Pinochet.

Salvador Allende (1908-1973) was generally considered the first elected Marxist head-of-state of a country in the Americas. As a member of the *Socialist Party*, he was a senator, deputy and cabinet minister. He unsuccessfully ran for the presidency in the 1952, 1958, and 1964 elections. In 1970, he allegedly won the presidency in a close three-way race. His family belonged to the Chilean upper-class and had a long tradition of political involvement in *"progressive"* causes. His grandfather founded one of the first secular schools in Chile. Allende had graduated with a medical degree in 1926 at the University of Chile. As a teenager, his main intellectual and political influence came from the shoemaker *Juan De Marchi*, an Italian-born anarchist.

Allende had won the 1970 Chilean presidential election as leader of the *Unidad Popular* ("Popular Unity") coalition. On September 4, 1970, he obtained a narrow plurality of 36.2 percent to 34.9 percent over *Jorge Alessandri*, a former president, with 27.8 percent going to a third candidate, *Rodomiro Tomic*, of the *Christian Democratic Party (PDC)*, whose electoral platform was similar to Allende's.

Photos above: the September 11, 1973 attack on the **Palacio de la Moneda**, the seat of Government, in Santiago de Chile, on the day the Chilean army executed a *coup d'état* against President Allende, who died in the effort; a photo of Allende and General Augusto Pinochet, the leader of the coup.

Cuban exiles were of two minds with respect to the ascent to power in Chile of **General Augusto Pinochet (1915-2006)**. On one hand they considered him one more military man in Latin America that had reached the presidency through a military *coup d'état*. On the other hand, he was justifying the *coup* as «*a fight against Communism that would ensure economic freedom.*» This sounded good, even though it had a counterpart on Castro's claim that his revolution had the purpose of «*fighting imperialism and ensuring social rights.*»

Both dictators shared the same tools of repression yet Pinochet's ultra-conservative ideology could never match the popularity among the "*democratic global community*" of Castro's left fascist and undemocratic totalitarianism.

The facts were clear, however: Cubans were leaving their country at the risk of their lives, preferring freedom and uncertainty rather than the siren songs of a Communist revolution; people emigrating from Latin America or anywhere else in the planet, on the other hand, were choosing the US rather than Cuba as the place where they wanted to reside. It was therefore an inexplicable "*Ideological Blindness*" to attack the US and worship Castro; it eloquently demonstrated how poorly democratic values were understood throughout the world.

Photos Above: three pictures of **Castro** with **Pinochet** during a visit of the Cuban dictator to his Chilean counterpart in the 1970s.

Abel Pérez, director of the weekly *20 de Mayo* in Los Angeles, in the 1970's.

Mons. Agustín Román during the construction of the *Ermita de la Caridad* in Miami, 1970s.

The **Castro** family in Lugo, Galicia. Neither Fidel, nor anyone in his family, were ever in the same photo as **Francisco Franco**, his Galician mentor.

The Board of **Municipios de Cuba en el Exilio** in the 1970s.

In 1975 a small artistic group in Miami, the *Miami Latin Boys*, made a major musical impact when its keyboard player-director, *Emilio Estefan Jr.*, invited a guest vocalist, *Gloria Fajardo*, to join the group and renamed it the **Miami Sound Machine**. By September 1979, Emilio and Gloria were married and the group was on its way to international fame.

The **Miami Sound Machine**, with **Gloria Estefan** as a soloist, began recording and releasing albums, 45s, and 12"s on the *Audiofon Records* label in Miami. Soon they grew in popularity in both the United States and around the world. By 2001 they had sold 100 million albums worldwide, one third of them in the US. Gloria went on to win numerous Grammy Awards and became the most successful crossover (Spanish to English fans) female singer of all times in Latin music.

The **Miami Sound Machine** and Gloria were at the peak of their fame when a truck slammed into the back of their bus while they were on tour in March of 1990. It forced Gloria to retire for a year as her back had to be repaired with two titanium rods permanently placed along her spine, and her wounds secured with 400 stitches. Her comeback album, **Mi Tierra**, received a Grammy award as "*best tropical Latin album of 1993.*" Both Gloria and Emilio have continued to be successful and generous with the Cuban Miami community for many years.

Photos above: the original **Miami Latin Boys** and **Gloria Estefan** with the **Miami Sound Machine**.

The history of Cuban music extends beyond the well known *Afro-Cuban* rhythms, the *zarzuelas* of the first 50 years of the republic, the big *popular orchestras* and the *boleros* of the 1940s and 1950s and the *guaguancos* —recently and unnecessarily rebaptized as *salsa*— into the *trova*, the *protest songs* that denounced the genocide of revolutionary Cuba and the *nostalgic songs* of exile in the second half of the XX century.

The nostalgic songs include popular melodies such as *He perdido una Perla* by Rosendo Rosell, *Yo Regresaré* by Luis Demetrio, *Si no Regreso a Cuba* by Chucho Navarro, *Por si acaso no Regreso* by Angie Chirino, made famous by Celia Cruz, *Nosotros los Cubanos* by Marisela Verena, and many others. Among all of these, *El Son se fue de Cuba* by Luis Frometa (Billo) became a hymn for the Cuban exiles:

El son se fue de Cuba	Guajiro de mi tierra,
mataron su alegría,	si pasas por La Habana,
sus notas están llenas	no oirás risa cubana
de una cruel melancolía.	porque el son se fue de allá.

Of equal importance was *Cuando Salí de Cuba* by Luis Aguilé:

Cuando salí de Cuba,	Una triste tormenta
dejé mi vida dejé mi amor.	te está azotando sin descansar
Cuando salí de Cuba,	pero el sol de tus hijos
dejé enterrado mi corazón.	pronto la calma te hará alcanzar.

And in recent times *Ya Viene Llegando* by Willy Chirino:

Apenas siendo un niño allá en la Antilla	Ahí empezó la dura realidad, ¡Ay Dios!
Mi padre me vistió de marinero	de todo el que se tira la maroma
tuve que navegar 90 millas	de sobrevivir fuera de su idioma
y comenzar mi vida de extranjero	de sus costumbres y su identidad

Photos: *El Son se Fue de Cuba, Cuando Salí de Cuba, Willy Chirino* and *Nosotros los Cubanos.*

ASSASSINATION ON EMBASSY ROW

BY JOHN DINGES & SAUL LANDAU

On September 21,1976, a booby-trapped car exploded on Washington's Embassy Row, killing two of its three occupants, Orlando Letelier, former Chilean ambassador, and 25-year-old Ronni Moffitt. The FBI crowned a slow-moving investigation with the uncovering of Michael Townley, expatriate American born in Waterloo, Iowa, professional assassin for Chile's secret police. Townley turned star witness for the prosecution. Two Cuban exiles were convicted for the murders. The head and two officials of Chile's secret police were indicted but not extradited to stand trial. The author-investigators present a stunningly authentic and spellbinding reconstruction of the sinister chain of events that allowed a "friendly" foreign government to stage an unparalleled act of *(continued on this flap)*

The violence that was engulfing Miami in the mid 1970s was also taking place in other places around the Americas. **Marcos Orlando Letelier Solar (1932-1976)**, a Chilean economist and diplomat during *Salvador Allende's* presidency, was killed by a car bomb on September 21, 1976, in *Sheridan Circle*, Washington, DC. He had been serving as Senior Fellow of the *Institute for Policy Studies* and was teaching at *American University*. He had become a leading voice against Augusto Pinochet's regime in Chile. Pinochet was implicated in the death of Letelier.

The FBI investigated the killing of Letelier and obtained the conviction of *Michael Townley*, who confessed he had hired five anti-Castro exiles, led by **Luis Posada Carriles** and **Orlando Bosch**, to booby-trap Letelier's car. Years later, in 1995, Letelier's son, **Juan Pablo Letelier**, affirmed in an article published in *El Mercurio* de Chile, that neither Pinochet nor the Cubans had anything to do with his father's murder.

Resorting to violence was not exclusive to some radicals among Miami exiles; it happened in other Cuban exile communities and was forcefully disapproved by all Cuban exiles across the world. A case in point was the rejection of such radical activism in the New York, New Jersey and the eastern seaboard areas, where lots of Cuban refugees had found safe harbor.

On September 21, 1976, **Orlando Letelier**, a member of the Marxist Chilean government of *Salvador Allende,* was blown up in his car in Washington, D.C.; a few months later **Eulalio Negrín**, exiled since 1962, director of Social Services in Union City, New Jersey, began to receive death threats for having recently visited Havana and for having passionately defended the *Castro-Exiles diálogo*. In March of 1977, his office was finally demolished by a bomb. At the end of 1979 he was assassinated. Almost at the same time **Carlos Muñiz**, owner of a travel agency in San Juan with special permission to schedule visits to Cuba was shot and killed while driving his car in the city. Credit for these uncivilized acts was claimed by several groups: the *Cuban Nationalist Movement*, *Omega 7* and *Group Zero*; federal officials believed all three to be one and the same.

Not content to distress and afflict Miami with violence, this group or groups began in the late 1970s to become active along the *Union City-Weehawken-West New York* corridor. In October of 1975, according to FBI records, they shot **Bernardo Leigh**ton, the leader in exile of the *Chilean Christian Democratic Party*, in Rome (he survived); they also reportedly attacked a Russian ship docked in Elizabeth, New Jersey in September 1976 (minor damage), shot a bazooka at the United Nations building during a visit by Ché Guevara (no casualties), placed a bomb at the *Academy of Music* on 14th Street in Manhattan to disrupt a pro-Castro rally in 1976 (the bomb did not explode), and heckled *Fr. Andres Reyes* at the *Holy Family Church* in Elizabeth because he had recently visited Cuba (services were interrupted).

Photos below, on the left, **Orlando Letelier**, Chilean economist, socialist politician and diplomat, with Castro on a visit to Cuba; On the right, reportage on the death of **Eulalio Negrín** in Union City. Negrín was later eulogized in *Cuba* and buried with honors.

Cuban Refugee Leader Slain in Union City

¿QUIEN QUISO MATAR A LEIGHTON?

Bergenline Avenue is a narrow, 40 block-long street of mom-and-pop businesses, *bodegas* and *fondas* (small eateries) in the *Union City-Weehawken-West New York* corridor. It fully belongs to the history of Cuban exiles in the North East of the US; it is a sort of linear *Little Havana* rather than the dispersed *Little Havana* of Miami. For a time it hosted 120,000 Cubans and proudly boasted signs that said "*La Lucha Sigue,*" (the struggle continues), "*Cuba SI, Castro NO,*" and "*Ché Asesino.*"

Most Cubans in *Bergenline* and *New York Avenues* in Union City were Catholics, at least in name. They did not like having their Masses interrupted; they were also middle class and blue collar, hard working members of a community that abhorred violence and bad manners. They disliked the pressures of the groups that occasionally came around asking for the proprietors to close their business in protest for trivial conflicts, or collecting donations for mundane causes. To many of them, the aggressive group tactics felt like mafia enforcements. On March 25, 1976, for instance, a bomb exploded in a Weehawken street, another in a pharmacy in Union City and a third one on a bag just about to be loaded on a TWA jet destined for the West Coast. The pharmacy, *El Español*, was guilty of selling medicines to Cubans traveling to Cuba; it was the result of a mafia-style edict: «*Any Cubans, Americans or Puerto Ricans traveling to Cuba will be dealt with without pity, regardless of motive*».

It would be a distortion of facts to assume that Cuban exiles in New York and other areas of the Eastern seaboard protected or tolerated the actions of these radical zealots or had any relationship with them except their common national origin; like in Miami, they detested to be seen as accomplices of America's enemies or ungrateful malevolents giving quarter to terrorists.

Photos above, left: **Carlos Muñiz Varela**, leader of the pro-Castro *Brigada Antonio Maceo*, murdered in Puerto Rico in 1979; *On the right*, **Bernardo Leighton Guzmán**, leader of the *Christian Democrats* in Chile and former VP during the presidency of Eduardo Frei.

In 1978 a group of Cuban exiles returned to Cuba and met with Fidel Castro to open the possibility of an agreement between Cuban exiles and the Cuban government, as well as to negotiate the release of political prisoners.

The so-called *"diálogo"* became one of the most controversial and divisive moments of the Cuban exile history since 1959.

The activists traveling to Havana favored granting Castro the elimination of the *"embargo"* that was preventing Cuba from doing business *"on credit,"* with US guarantees backed by American Banks in the form of lines of credit. They were mostly members or future members of Departments of Humanities and Political Sciences at several American Universities.

Among the most vocal among participants of the *"diálogo"* were:

Wayne S. Smith, former *Chief of the U.S. Interests Section in Havana from 1979-82* and future professor at *Johns Hopkins University;* **Robert A. Pastor**, who would become a Professor at the *School of International Service* at *American University* in Washington and Director of its *Center for North American Studies;* **Louis A. Pérez** soon to be editor of the journal *Cuban Studies* and the J. Carlyle Sitterson Professor of History at the *University of North Carolina* at Chapel Hill; **Miguel González-Pando** a participant in the *Bay of Pigs* invasion. On his return he was expelled from *Brigade 2506,* the association of *Bay of Pigs Veterans;* **María Cristina Herrera**, founder of the *Instituto de Estudios Cubanos (IEC)* at *Florida International University* in 1969; **Félix Masud-Piloto** future professor at *De Paul University,* in Chicago. Other exiles flying to Havana included María de los Angeles Torres, Damián J. Fernández, Jane Franklin, Lourdes Casal, Guillermo Grenier and Max J. Castro, all favoring the breaking of the US *"embargo"* to Cuba.

Photos above, left to right: **Wayne Smith,**
Robert Pastor, Luis A. Pérez, María Cristina Herrera
and **Félix Massud-Piloto**

54 exiles begin 'dialogue' with Castro

Miami banker Bernardo Benes and 53 other Cuban exiles were to meet today with President Fidel Castro in the first two-day dialogue conference in Havana to discuss the release of political prisoners.

Details of the meeting were announced by Cuba's Foreign Ministry after it released the names of the 14 political prisoners freed last week in Cuba. Those 14 men are expected to enter the United States soon.

A spokesman for the foreign ministry said the 14 have been freed "as a gesture of goodwill." But he would not say if the prisoners and their relatives would be allowed to leave with the commission members after the meeting.

"That depends on the U.S. screening committee that arrived here last week and how fast they move," he said.

The political prisoners are screened by a special U.S. Justice Department task force to make sure spies or criminals are not allowed to enter the country.

The 54 exile representatives were invited to Havana by the Cuban government after Castro suggested discussions with the exile community during a press conference Sept. 6.

Today's conference at the Palace of the Revolution in Havana was to be open to the press for the opening ceremonies but delegates did not know if reporters would be allowed to attend the actual negotiations with Castro, his cabinet ministers and Cuban legislators.

A spokesman the Cuban Foreign Relations Ministry said discussions will center on the political prisoner release, the reunion of Cuban families and possible visits to the island by exiles.

Also to be heard, he added, are topics which have been presented to the government by individual members of the delegation.

Those issues include: the right of exiles to vote in Cuban elections; dual citizenship problems; possession of a Cuban identification card; participation in Cuban mass organizations; constitutional problems involved in preserving the right of Cuban citizenship; possibilities of university-level studies and academic research in Cuba.

The leading figure among the 54 representatives is Benes, who led secret negotiations for 15 months with the Cuban government — with the knowledge of U.S. government officials. Benes also headed a six-member delegation that picked up 46 former political prisoners in last month's first direct flight to Miami.

Benes presented an agenda to Castro dealing exclusively with the questions of release of political prisoners and procedures and priorities for the reunion of Cuban families.

Others in the delegation include several Catholic priests, Bay of Pigs veterans and members of the Antonio Maceo Brigade, a group of 53 young Cuban exiles which went to Cuba in December 1977 to visit the island and to do volunteer work.

The 14 prisoners released last week and free to travel to the U.S. were identified as:

Alfredo Izelaya Valera, Gabriel Orozco Alcover, Augusto Jose Andion Garcia, Marcelino Leal Rodriguez, Bernardo Flores Bien, Arnoldo Hernandez Luejes, Felipe Sanchez Olivera, Elio Leal Sanchez, Emilio Victor Liufrio Bofill, Celestino Suarez Rodriguez, Manuel del Valle Caral, Jose Domingo Paz Lama, Luis M. Lebredo Jorge and Richardo Leal Sanchez.

Further participants of the "*diálogo*" were, among others: **Ramón Agüero Grau**, nephew of Polita Grau Alsina, the key person in the *Pedro Pan* exodus of young children; **Bernardo Benes**, VP of the *Banco Continental de Miami*; **Lourdes Casals Valdés**, psychologist and member of the board of *Areito Magazine*; **Manuel De Dios Unaue**, newspaperman from *El Diario La Prensa* of New York; **Vicente Dopico**, member of the staff of *Areito*; **Manuel Espinosa**, Pastor of the *Iglesia Cristiana Evangélica Reformada* de Hialeah; **Francisco González Aruca**, owner of *Marazul Travel*; **Francisco González Muñiz** and **Napoleón Vilaboa**, members of the *2506 Bay of Pigs Brigade*; **Enrique Oslé**, Jesuit priest; **Marifeli Pérez-Stable**, member of the *Brigada Antonio Maceo*; **Dolores Prida**, a NY newswoman and **Andrés Reyes**, a NY Catholic priest.

*Photos above, left to right: **Bernardo Benes, Reverendo Manuel Espinosa, Francisco González Aruca** and **Marifeli Pérez-Stable**.*

nación
y emigración

KARTEL
Areíto Comunista

YA ESTA PASANDO de castaño oscuro lo de la revista Areíto. Desde sus madrigueras de New York, los acólitos de Fidel Castro que la editan han trasladado su cuartel general para Miami. Estos pillos intelectualoides comenzaron por el ya famoso camino de la apertura, continuaron por el archiconocido y hediondo de la coexistencia y ya están de lleno en el del colaboracionismo, que en términos de política y de guerra significa traición. Y eso es lo que son. Una cáfila de audaces a quienes les falta inteligencia para comprender que su propósito es vano en medio de este ghetto, que, mayoritariamente, si puede ser acusado de indiferente, no quiere saber nada de teorías marxistoides ni de fidelismos disfrazados.

En el último número de la revista, los amiguitos del Kremlin se fueron bien lejos. Ya no es sólo crítica literaria para realzar los valores de la otra orilla, ni ensayos sobre economía que envuelven una admiración más que adicta hacia las barbaridades que se han llevado a cabo en Cuba por la pandilla castrista. Ahora publicaron la constitución que el genio ratonero de Blas Roca escribió, bajo el dictado de Fidel, para institucionalizar la satrapía. Y remachan el clavo con una entrevista hecha a McGovern, el agente publicitario del barbudo en tierras del Tío Sam.

* * *

The *"diálogo"* with Castro was part of a concerted effort by some sectors of the Cubans in the Miami community to seek a solution to their exile and possibly return to or at least have personal and free access to Cuba. Three groups were heavily involved in this project. The **Areíto Magazine**, the **Brigadas Antonio Maceo** and some of the members of the **Cuban Research Institute** of *Florida International University*. Their position was heavily criticized by a large segment of the Cuban exiles since the early 1970s.

Photos above, top to bottom: logotype of the **Nación y Emigración** meetings; a hard critical article about **Areíto**; two photos of volunteers of the **Brigadas Antonio Maceo** in Cuba.

UNETE AL CONTINGENTE
de la
BRIGADA ANTONIO MACEO

Cuba
en solidaridad con Centro
América y el Caribe.

- Opongámonos al bloqueo contra Cuba
- Apoyemos la normalización de relaciones entre EE.UU. y Cuba

Cubanos
Residentes
en el Exterior
Contra el Bloqueo
y el Terrorismo

In its relentless effort to infiltrate the exile community all across the globe, the Cuban government next step was to create **Cubanos Residentes en el Exterior (CRE)** (Association of Cubans residing outside the island), a "*non-political*" group better suited to attract the help of Cuban natives living abroad, particularly those that had been taken overseas by their parents at an early age. Some of the same individuals that were responsible for *Areito*, the *Antonio Maceo Brigades* and the *Dialogues* with the Cuban regime began to organize the periodic visits and meetings of this new group in Cuba.

Photos above, left to right: **Arlenz Abram**, from the *Asociación José Martí* in Brussels; **Vivian López**, from the *Asociación José Martí* in Mexico; **Max Lesnik**, from the *Alianza Martiana* in Miami and **Andrés Gómez** from the *Brigada Antonio Maceo* in New York.

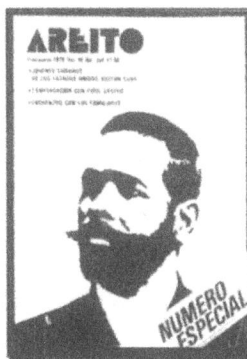

LA BRIGADA ANTONIO MACEO ESTÁ COMPUESTA POR JÓVENES QUE RESIDEN FUERA DE CUBA.
ANSIOSOS POR PALPAR LA REALIDAD CUBANA, UN CONTINGENTE DE LA BRIGADA VIAJÓ A
CUBA EL INVIERNO PASADO, CAUSANDO GRAN IMPACTO EN SUS INTEGRANTES Y EL PUEBLO
CUBANO.
AL COMPARTIR NUESTRAS EXPERIENCIAS DEL VIAJE CON OTROS JÓVENES QUE RESIDEN FUERA
DE LA ISLA, HEMOS CONFIRMADO NUESTRA OPINIÓN QUE LA MAYORÍA DE LA JUVENTUD CUBAN
EMIGRADA TIENE GRAN INTERÉS POR REENCONTRARSE CON CUBA Y CONOCER SOBRE ELLA. ES
ES UNA DE LAS RAZONES PRINCIPALES DEL POR QUE HEMOS DECIDIDO ORGANIZAR UN SEGUND
CONTINGENTE QUE VIAJARÁ A CUBA EL PRÓXIMO VERANO.   TE INVITAMOS A QUE SOLICITES
PARA PARTICIPAR EN ESTA EXPERIENCIA CON NOSOTROS.

NOS UNE:
-EL APOYO A LA NORMALIZACIÓN DE RELACIONES
 ENTRE ESTADOS UNIDOS Y CUBA.
-EL APOYO AL LEVANTAMIENTO DEL BLOQUEO
 ECONÓMICO DE CUBA IMPUESTO POR EEUU.
-EL APOYO AL CESE DE HOSTILIDADES HACIA
 CUBA POR ESTADOS UNIDOS Y ORGANIZACIONES
 FUERA DE CUBA.

PUEDEN SER MIEMBROS:
-LOS QUE HAYAN SALIDO DE CUBA POR
 DECISION DE SUS PADRES.
-LOS QUE NO HAYAN PARTICIPADO EN
 ACTIVIDADES CONTRARREVOLUCIONARIA
-LOS QUE ESTÉN DE ACUERDO CON LOS
 TRES PUNTOS DE UNIDAD MENCIONADOS
 AQUÍ.

Photos above, top to bottom: **Felipe Pérez Roque**, Communist Cuba's Foreign Minister, addressing a meeting of *Cubanos Residentes en el Exterior (CRE)*; an **Areito** special issue where the recruitment of young exiles for the "*Maceitos*" was presented; the Areito appeal to Cuban exiles to join in the "*contingents*" that would go to Cuba to train as propagandists of the Cuban revolution in their own exile communities; **Ricardo Alarcón**, Presidente de la *Asamblea del Poder Popular* de Cuba addressing the visiting CRE participants.

In 1977 the first bilingual situation comedy in the US was produced by PBS in Miami, Florida, under the name of *¿Qué Pasa USA?* It was aired across the United States and for the first time it gave faces to the Cuban exiles. The comedy explored the tribulations and hard work of the *Peña* family as they struggled to adapt to a new country and a new language. It was created by *Luis Santeiro*, a long time playwright and writer for *Sesame Street* and a winner of 16 Emmy Awards

In the series, the grandparents, Adela (*Velia Martínez*) and Antonio (*Luis Oquendo*) wanted to maintain Cuban values and traditions. They never tried to learn to speak English. The teenage children, Carmen (*Ana Margarita Méndez*) and Joe (*Steven Bauer*) spoke good but somewhat accented English. Their parents, Juana (*Ana Margarita Martínez Casado*) and Pepe (*Manolo Villaverde*) spoke heavily accented English but could alternate between the two languages. Pepe and Juana and her parents Adela and Antonio were born in Guanabacoa. Joe was born in Cuba, Carmen in Miami; both were raised in Miami.

The entire series (39 episodes) was taped before a live studio audience in Miami. The series received six *Emmys* and ended in 1980. Andy García was a guest teen-aged friend on several episodes. *¿Qué Pasa USA?* is considered an American sitcom classic. It was budgeted at $300,000 a year, an amazing feat considering the extraordinary high quality of the show. It was broadcast across the US and has run in syndication for over 30 years.

Both *Velia Martínez* and *Luis Oquendo* died in the early 1990s; *Ana Margarita Martínez Casado* went on to a theater career in New York; *Manolo Villaverde* became a successful insurance agent; *Steven Bauer* married and later divorced Melanie Griffith and became a Hollywood star; *Ana Margarita Méndez* became an executive at a Lasik company called *MedEye*.

As more and more Cuban refugees arrived to Miami all through the 1970s, they began to adapt to Miami and Miami began to adapt to them.

*Photos above, top to bottom: a **new refugee** kisses the Miami ground in gratitude for having arrived safely; the **Máximo Gómez Park** on Calle Ocho, a favorite meeting place for senior Cubans; the downtown of Miami became a **bilingual commercial area** in the 1960s and 1970s; hundreds of **fondas** (popular eateries) began to open across the city, offering café, guarapo (sugar cane juice), Cuban sandwiches and most of the delicacies Cubans were accustomed to eat.*

In the 1970s many international artists that had been popular in Cuba during the time of the Republic began to visit and perform for their now exiled public in the city of Miami. They continued their regular visits until they retired, never agreeing to take their art to a captive audience in Cuba. Some of them were **Lucho Gatica**, **Sarita Montiel**, **Libertad Lamarque** and **Marco Antonio Muñiz**.

The **Calle Ocho Festival** became an annual March event started by Cuban refugees in Miami in 1978 and open to people of all ethnic backgrounds and age groups; it runs across some 24 city blocks of Calle Ocho in Little Havana. The festival is sponsored every year by the Kiwanis Club of Miami, following a tradition started by Cuban-born **Leslie Pantín Jr.** and **Willy Bermello**, who wanted to have a street party that would display the Cuban and Latin-American lifestyle for their American neighbors.

The festival became in 2001 the largest street festival held yearly in the United States, far larger than anything organized in New York, New Orleans, Chicago or Los Angeles. Thousands of people —some years estimated as many as 1.2 million— attend the event for the dancing, eating, and getting to know everyone and everything that is part of Miami, and specifically Little Havana and the Cuban exiles.

The festival has received performers such as Willy Chirino, Oscar de León, El Gran Combo, Celia Cruz, The Barrio Boys, and the Miami Sound Machine. All sorts of Latin music can he heard at the festival: Cha-cha-cha, Conga, Merengue, Cumbia, Guaguancó, Salsa, while the public tries the foods of Cuba and the Americas: Mediasnoches, Sandwiches Cubanos, Yuca con Mojo, Tostones, Arepas, Pan con Chorizo, Churrasco, Chicharrones and Lechón Asado. The **Calle Ocho Festival** is a Cuban and Latin blend of Mardi Gras, the New York City Saint Patrick Day Parade plus the Havana and the Rio Carnivals.

The **Scull sisters** (Haydee and Sahara) were born and reared in pre-Communist Cuba and studied painting and sculpture at the *Escuela de Bellas Artes de San Alejandro* in Havana. Their joint art can be best described as a three dimensional, facetiously capricious and impulsive portrait of typical Cuban characters doing all sorts of activities, first in Cuba and later in Miami. They were both born in the *Cayo Hueso* neighborhood of Havana, one of the poorest areas of the Cuban capital. **Haydee** settled in Miami in 1969 while **Sahara** left Cuba in 1973. Since the early 1970s they began to produce paintings using their own techniques. Their works reflect their keen eyes, their razor-sharp wit and a very personal and subtle Cuban humor. They have been for 50 years the most genuine interpreters of Cuban folklore, bringing to artworks the typical characters and happenings of the everyday life of Cuba and Miami, full of humor, color and flavor.

Haydee Scull passed away on October 23, 2007, at their home in the trendy Art Deco district of Miami Beach. Two months later **Sahara's** health began to fail and she passed away at Mount Sinai Hospital on Saturday, May 31, 2008. They never revealed their birthdates or their weights to anyone and both died of the same disease, an excessive calcification of their arteries.

The photos present the two sisters, in Cuba as minors, and in the US as adults, as well as some samples of their art.

Some aspects of the exile's interests and disillusions in the Cuban and Miami scenarios in the 1970s.

Photos Above: Cuban National Poet **Agustín Acosta (1886-1979)** went into exile in Miami in 1972; the **Catholic Church** in Cuba met in 1973 with Castro and his UN delegate Raúl Roa. The Church got no concessions from the government; **George McGovern**, presidential candidate in 1972 visited Cuba and socialized with government authorities. He lost to incumbent **Richard Nixon** in one of the largest landslides in American history.

In 1975, Castro surprised the civilized world when he decided to send 30,000 Cuban troops to intervene in the Angola civil conflict. He shocked and stunned both Washington and the Cuban refugees by sending thousands of soldiers into a conflict that had no direct impact on the interests of his "*revolution*." His actions, he claimed, were in response to the South African invasion of Angola. He declared that the US State Department knew of South Africa's intentions beforehand, although Secretary of State Kissinger made declarations to the contrary in the US Congress. Castro also proclaimed that he had made the decision to deploy troops without informing the Soviets, a fact that few people believed.

It was not the first international conflict embraced by Castro. In 1961 he had assisted the *Algerian rebels* in their fight against France's colonial power, and in 1964 he had committed Cuban troops to *Guinea-Bissau's* Independence War from the Portuguese.

Photos *above*: the newspaper accounts of twelve Sudafrican and 300 Cuban casualties at an encounter in Angola;
General Rafael del Pino, Castro's proclaimed "*Hero of Playa Girón*," greeting **Agostinho Neto** (1922-1979), President of Angola and Secretary General of the *Angolan Communist Party*, in 1976.

Victory is Certain!

The 25 year old Angola Civil War began immediately after Angola became independent of Portugal in November of 1975. It started as an internal conflict between the *Peoples Movement for the Liberation of Angola* (MPLA) (led by **Agostinho Neto** and supported by the Soviet Union and Cuba) and the *National Union for the Total Liberation of Angola* (UNITA), founded by **Jonas Savimbi** and supported by the US and South Africa. The MPLA achieved final victory in 2002, after 1,500,000 people had been killed and Angola's infra-structure had been devastated. The war had displaced more than 4 million from their hometowns, fully one third of Angola's population. By 2002 more than 15 million landmines had been laid by both sides. More than 6,000 children had been forced to fight in the war.

JONAS SAVIMBI A KEY TO AFRICA

Jacobo Machover (1954-) is a long-term Paris based Cuban-born journalist and literary critic for various media, including *Magazine Littéraire*, Libération, Clarín, and *Revista Hispano Cubana*; he *has been a correspondent in Paris of Diario 16 and Exchange* 16. In 1970 he visited Cuba and as he left he became a political exile and no longer an émigré in the French capital. Machover has since written numerous books demystifying the revolution. He is currently a professor of Romance languages, Hispanic literature and civilization at the *Universities of Avignon* and *Paris XII*, and also teaches at the *Graduate School of Management* in Paris.

Machover is the author of numerous novels and essays: *Memorias de Dos Siglos, El Heraldo de las Malas Noticias, Guillermo Cabrera Infante, Ensayo a Dos Voces, El Año que viene en... La Habana, La Memoria Frente al Poder, Memorias Colectivas La Habana, El Final de un Mundo y La Cara Oculta del Che*, among others.

Eduardo Manet (1931-) is a Cuban-born writer living in Paris since 1968, after a brief visit to Cuba in 1959. He studied Philosophy, letters and civil law in his native Cuba and by 1950 he had published three plays. From 1951 to 1959, he went to Europe and studied literature in Perugia, Etruscology in Rome, as well as theater in London (Old Vics' studio). In 1959 he returned to Cuba, working as a screenwriter and film director in the ICAIC. In 1968, disillusioned about the Cuban revolution, he returned to France to never return to Cuba. His novels —most of them dealing with Cuba— have won many literary prizes: *The Mauresque, L'ile du Lézard Vert, Habanera, Rhapsodie Cubain, D'amour et d'exil, La Sagesse du Singe, Maestro, Mes années Cuba, Ma vie de Jesus, La Conquistadora, Un Français au coueur de l'Ouragan Cubain, Marranos, Las Monjas* and quite a few others.

Photos above, left to right:
Jacobo Machover and **Eduardo Manet**.

Zoé Valdés (1959-) an exile in Paris since the 1990s is by all accounts one of Cuba's most original and imaginative writers. She has become one of France's most prestigious best-sellers. She has been widely translated into French, German, English and many other languages. Her works usually tell of woman's spiritual and sexual awakening; most often she castigates severely the spiritually devastating Castro regime. It has been said that she is «*a master at spinning a steady tale of passion while pulling beauty out of a world full of detestable, horrendous, execrable and abominable realities.*»

In her narrative Zoé often employs different inanimate objects, animals and spirits to convey the story to the readers; suitcases, trees, manatees, or *Mandinga* entities. In her mind, they skillfully move the action better than a human story-teller could do. Her work is a continuous homage to Cuba, a tribute to the integrity and suffering of her besieged and tormented native land. Daily life in the big cities and the deprived countryside of her island, their old and the new dramas, are always rendered in a way that reminds the reader of both the necessity of love and the ever present fear of getting lost.

She is a regular collaborator with *El País, ELLE, Vogue, El Mundo, El Semanal* and *Qué Leer* in Spain, as well as *Le Monde, Libération, Le Nouvel Observateur,* and *Beaux Arts* in Paris. Among her recent best-seller books are *La Nada Cotidiana, En Fin el Mar, Te di la Vida Entera, Café Nostalgia, Los Aretes de la Luna, Querido Primer Novio, La Ficción Fidel, El Pie de mi Padre* and *El Todo Cotidiano*.

Prominent Cuban exile intellectual

Luis Enrique Aguilar Leon, J.D., Ph.D. (1926-2008), was a Cuban journalist and historian; a professor to Bill Clinton at *Georgetown University* and a classmate (Class of 1944) of *Fidel Castro* at a Jesuit school in Havana. He was a political writer for the newspaper *Prensa Libre* and the magazines *Bohemia* and *Carteles*, as well as the director of *Universidad del Aire* (University of the Air) on the Cuban radio network CMQ in the late 1950s. He went into exile in 1960 and became a professor, first at *Columbia University*, then at *Cornell University* and finally, for over 30 years, at *Georgetown University*. After his retirement he moved to South Florida and taught at the *University of Miami* until 2002. Aguilar struggled the last years of his life on a futile fight with Alzheimer's disease. He died on January 5, 2008.

Lundy Aguilar, like his friends used to call him, had written two of the most popular articles read by Cuban exiles in his 50 years of absence from Cuba. The first one was *La Hora de la Unanimidad* (1960), the closing column published in *Prensa Libre,* the last free paper left in Cuba after the advent of the Communist regime. In that article he gave a dramatic warning about the horrors of a totalitarian government like the one seizing Cuba. The second article was published in exile, *El Profeta habla de los Cubanos* (1986), a narrative in the style of *Khalil Gibran*, describing the most outstanding qualities and peculiar transgressions of the Cuban character.

It is interesting that Bill Clinton included Lundy Aguilar as one of his memorable teachers in his biography *My Life* but Lundy Aguilar — as he told his friends many times— could not remember when he had young Clinton in his *European History* class at *Georgetown*.

Huber Matos (1918-) was a Commandant of the Cuban Revolution sentenced by Castro to 20 years in prison for *"acts of sedition and treason"* in October of 1959, nine months after the success of the revolution. He had been a teacher and rice grower in Manzanillo, a member of the *Partido Ortodoxo* and an active participant against the Batista dictatorship. Matos' *"sedition"* was to oppose the growing influence of Communists in the government established by the revolution in 1959. During Castro's stay in *Sierra Maestra*, Matos had been the main supplier of weapons to the rebels with the help of **José Figueres**, president of Costa Rica.

On December 11, 1959 Matos was tried in a sort of *court martial* and condemned to 20 years in prison, which he served in its entirety. Years later, after leaving Cuba, he declared: «*I spent a total of sixteen years in solitary confinement, constantly being told that I was never going to get out alive, that I had been sentenced to die in prison. They were very cruel, to the fullest extent of the word... I was tortured many times; I was subjected to all kinds of horrors, all kinds, including the puncturing of my genitals*».

Years later, in June 2007, after an active, worldwide and continuous participation in the struggle of Cuban exiles to overthrow Castro, he wrote an open letter to his former comrades in arms of the *Cuban Revolutionary Army* inviting them to join in the re-start of the Republic of Cuba by breaking their loyalty with the Castro brothers and revolting against Communism.

Photos below: **Huber Matos** in a statement to the press describing the message sent to Fidel Castro from his prison jail; The cover of his 2004 book ***Como Llegó la Noche***.

Cuban Journalists in exile in the 1970s

Cubans have always been enthusiastic readers of newspapers (in 1958 Havana had 16 papers published daily, from early morning to late afternoon) and Cuban exiles, of course, were always supporters of the press and the journalists that brought to them news about Cuba, their guest countries and the world in general. It would be very lengthy to outline all the journalists that have been keeping Cuban exiles informed during fifty years of absence but a few representative members of the exile press follows.

Agustin Tamargo (1925-2007) was an important journalist both in print and on radio. He was born in Puerto Padre, Oriente, and moved to Havana in 1944. During Batista's dictatorship he lived as an exile in New York City. Upon returning to Cuba he supported Castro but in 1959 he became disillusioned as Cuba turned Communist. He first moved to Caracas and later to Argentina and New York, where he became head editor *of El Diario/La Prensa*. He began to collaborate wit*h Radio Mambí* in 1980.

Guillermo Martínez Márquez (1900-) was an exceptional journalist in Cuba, the founder of the *Juventud* Magazine in 1915 and later a writer for the newspapers *El Heraldo de Cuba, La Libertad, El Sol, El Mundo, Ahora, El Repórter,* as well as the magazines *Bohemia* and *Carteles.* He directed *El País* and presided over the *Sociedad Interamericana de Prensa* before leaving Cuba. In exile he wrote mostly for *Diario las Americas* in Miami.

Guillermo I. Martínez (1944-). The son of Guillermo Martínez Márquez is an internationally recognized journalist and radio and TV personality, winner of the *Daily Gleaner Award* for editorial commentary and twice nominated for the *Pulitzer* Prize. His career extends from Miami (Senior Editor of *The Miami Herald* and Senior VP of news to *Univision*) to Washington, D.C., Los Angeles, Argentina, Chile, Perú, Ecuador, Venezuela and Puerto Rico. He has written for the *Sun-Sentinel, El Sentinel, Diario Las Américas* (Miami), *El Diario La Prensa* (New York), *and La Opinión* (Los Angeles); he has also provided político, social and economic commentary for *Radio Caracol* in Miami and New York.

(Continued)

Photos above:
Agustín Tamargo, Guillermo Martínez Márquez
and **Guillermo I. Martínez.**

(Continuation)

Horacio Aguirre Baca (1932-) was born in New Orleans and raised in Nicaragua; he finished his law degree in Panamá and in 1953 founded **Diario las Américas** in Miami with his brother Francisco. Aguirre has distinguished himself for his support to the arts, children's issues, freedom of the press and the needs of seniors. He was President of the *Sociedad Interamericana de Prensa (SIP)* and has been honored by the Vatican and several Latin American countries. In the words of Nestor Carbonell «*cuando otros le niegan apoyo al exilio, Horacio exalta sus virtudes; en momentos desoladores, él es el puntal más sólido que han tenido los exiliados Cubanos.*»

Other prestigious **journalists** in exile with numerous readers among Cubans were *Luis Aguilar León, Pablo M. Alfonso, Armando Alvarez Bravo, Dora Amador, Martín Añorga, Liz Balmaseda, Ramón and Rolando Bonachea, Eduardo Boza Masvidal, Nestor Carbonell Cortina, Juan M. Clark, Luis Conte Aguero, Angel Cuadra, Jorge Domínguez, Enrique G. Encinosa, Manuel Fernández, José Manuel Cortina, Orestes Ferrara, Roberto Luque Escalona, Carlos Márquez Sterling, Humberto Medrano, Carlos Alberto Montaner, Luis de la Paz, Armando Pérez Roura, Marcos Antonio Ramos, José Ignacio Rasco, Ariel Remos, Nicolás Rivero, Rafael Rojas, Enrique Ros and Eduardo Suárez Rivas,* some of which are shown above.

Photos, top to bottom, left to right:
Horacio Aguirre, Liz Balmaseda, Angel Cuadra, Luis de la Paz, Pablo Alfonso, Carlos Alberto Montaner, Juan Clark, Armando Alvarez Bravo, Humberto Medrano, Marcos Antonio Ramos, Rev. Martín Añorga, Ariel Remos, Armando Pérez Roura, Roberto Luque Escalona and **José Ignacio Rasco**.

IV

«Before boarding the boats, we were sorted into categories
and sent into empty warehouses: one for the insane,
one for murderers and hard-core criminals, another for prostitutes
and homosexuals, and one for the young men who were
undercover agents of State Security to be infiltrated in the United States.»

REINALDO ARENAS IN *BEFORE NIGHT FALLS*.

«To witness this half century long phenomenon 90 miles from America
begs the question: If America can emancipate Afghanistan
from totalitarianism and talk about emancipating Iraq
from totalitarianism, why don't Cubans deserve emancipation?»

MYLES KANTOR, *LUDWIG VON MISES INSTITUTE* WRITER.

Unrelenting Abuses in the 1980s

A World that no longer cared for Freedom in Cuba

OF ALL POLITICAL MIGRATIONS that took place during
the Cold War (such as Hungarians, Czechs and Berliners from
Eastern Europe, Vietnamese and Laotians from Southeast Asia,
Argentineans, Mexicans, Salvadorians and Nicaraguans from
South and Central America), none was more mediatic and
symbolic than the migration of Cuban exiles. The US and the
Soviet Union were competing for the superiority of their political and economic systems and Cubans in America became living evidence of unsurpassed success after their flight to freedom to the US.

The motivations for seeking political (rather than economic)
refuge cannot be separated from the notion of *thrusting* or *forc-*

ing. There is always a human reluctance to uproot oneself from the native land to settle in an unfamiliar place; individuals only do that when compelled, coerced or forcibly *pushed* to do it. The motivations for economic refugees, on the other hand, are rather different. They are attracted to opportunities that are not available to them or are inferior in their environment and are thus *drawn*, tugged-in, teased, challenged or lured into making a move. Whether you have been *pushed* or *pulled* into leaving your country of origin makes a big difference in attitudes, perceptions, resolve, permanency, disposition, contentment and many other feelings that affect the elusive and indefinable condition of personal happiness.

In 1980 a large number of Cubans (over 125,000 people, aboard 1,700 vessels in about 27 weeks) left the port of Mariel and moved to the US. Many were forced by their opposition to dramatic changes in the political conditions of Cuba[2]; some also feared for their lives if they made public their discontent. It is hard to say how many, but they were probably the vast majority. Many others, however, were probably happy to compromise with these changes, but were lured by their families in the US or simply by the many stories of a very pleasant future waiting for them in the land of plenty. A third group, as mentioned before, were spies, moles, snoops and Castro's undercover agents, as well as delinquents, derelicts, tramps and vagrants (Castro called them *antisocial scum elements*) that came among the Cubans arriving in boats to the US. By all accounts they were easily recognizable and most were sooner or later returned to their lair before they could infiltrate, sabotage and foster internal conflicts among the Cuban exile communities.

At the time of this massive and confusing influx of Cubans into the US (it was President Carter, who invited them proclaiming «*the US would welcome the Cubans with an open heart and open arms*»), it was not clear what legal document would be the basis for bringing the process under control, the *Cuban Refugee*

---

[2] By most accounts, the revolution in Cuba moved quickly through numerous identities: democracy, humanism, nationalism, socialism, Marxist-Leninism, Castroism, and finally a cleptocracy and raw Fascist gangsterism.

Adjustment Act of 1966, or the new *Refugee Act of 1980*. Four years later, in December of 1984, the *Immigration and Naturalization Service (INS)* began to process the *Marielitos* under the *Cuban Refugee Adjustment Act*.

Those initial days were followed by a US-Cuba agreement that returned to Cuba 2,746 Cubans not eligible for admission into the US because of medical or criminal backgrounds. Such agreement was broken by Castro after the US began to broadcast *Radio Martí* to Cuba on May 20 of 1983. *Radio Martí* broke the silence and the isolation from information imposed by the Castros, and fostered anti-revolutionary commentaries, editorials by independent and underground journalists in Cuba, Cuban-life-in-America stories and old fashioned radio dramas. All this without Castro's political indoctrination and without his twisted, slanted quotations from the Cuban patriot José Martí. It was said at the time that the one thing driving Castro nuts about *Radio Martí* was the name of the station.

The *1980 Mariel Flotilla of Chaos* arriving in the US from Cuba (the passengers median age was 31 years old; only 10% were older than 45) lasted from April 15 to October 31. Cuba was in the midst of one of its terrible economic downturns and the socio-economic pressure mounted when more than 10,000 disaffected citizens burst into the Peruvian Embassy in Havana.[3] At the time, Jimmy Carter was President of the US and was naively trying to establish improved relations with Castro.

Most Cuban exiles and Americans did not see the ensuing immigration wave with good eyes. The exiles, because they did not see in the new arrivals the political determination, sacrifice and endurance that they were accustomed to seeing in other exiles; they were fearful of what those new refugees would do to their image of success. The Americans, because the large number of new Cubans was a threat to an already declining

---

[3] A man named *Héctor Sanyustiz* used a bus as a battering ram and drove it through a fence of Havana's Peruvian Embassy on March 28, 1980. *Ernesto Pinto Bazurco*, the diplomat in charge, granted political asylum to him and his three friends. In a few hours, 10,800 other Cubans forcibly entered the crowded embassy grounds.

economy in the Florida area. The press made matters worse by highlighting the large number of blacks (40%), the preponderance of lower socio-economic classes (over 70% were blue collar workers) and the presence of delinquents and prior offenders among those forced into the boats by Cuban authorities (15% to 25% of the *émigrés* were petty thieves, black marketers, small drug dealers, vagrants and army deserters, but *"only"* 2% were serious criminals and were denied citizenship).

In spite of a fairly tepid reception (compared with the years 1959 through 1979), more than 50% of the Mariel expatriates decided to remain in Miami. Unemployment in Miami rose in the first six months of 1980 from 5% to over 7% (following US trends in other regions) but the generosity of the established exiles made it easy to accommodate the new Miami arrivals. They had, after all, rented and bought small boats and showed up in Mariel harbor to pick up entire families. Initially the new refugees were placed in special camps (*Fort Indiantown Gap*, Pennsylvania; *Fort McCoy*, Wisconsin; *Camp Santiago*, Puerto Rico, and *Fort Chaffee*, Arkansas). The only camp experiencing any serious disturbances was *Fort Chaffee*. They were resolved by two Cuban leaders imported from Miami: Mons. Agustín Román, Auxiliary Bishop of Miami and César Odio, Miami City Manager. Milder and less important riots occurred in Oakdale, California and Atlanta, Georgia.

No other US city had ever adapted so fast to such a drastic influx of labor (20% increase of the labor force in 26 weeks) as Miami did. The salaries and levels of employment of non-Cuban Whites, Blacks, Cubans and other Hispanics remained stable through the assimilation of the new Cuban expatriates.

During the Mariel Boatlift, in spite of that orderly absorption of new Cubans by already established Cubans, some traditional Miamians objected strenuously to the influx of more immigrants in what they called «*a bizarre and massively sea lift across the Cuba-to-Key West Silk Road*,» a veiled reference to drug and arms trafficking from Pakistan to the US through the ancient 4,000 miles *Great Silk Road* that linked Europe with China during the Han Dynasty.

Opinion polls in May of 1980 indicated that 57% of voting adults in Miami felt *Marielitos* should not be accepted in the US and should be returned to Cuba; 75% opined that President Carter had shown to be spineless when he approved their admission to the US; 64% expressed that Castro had made a fool of Carter.

Journalists began to write against the new wave of immigrants and published articles in which they openly declared that Miami was providing cover to «*billion-dollar drug-smuggling Latin-American millionaires that had turned Miami into the Hong Kong and the murder capital of the Western World.*» They complained about «*huge caravans of destitute refugees in busloads with blacked-out windows headed north; with the south-bound lanes jammed with Cuban Americans towing a strange armada of fiberglass speedboats, cabin cruisers, and ungainly fishing boats towards Key West, a once-lazy backwater fishing resort that has now been transmogrified, overnight, into a seething fortress of thieves, smugglers, and criminally insane Cuban refugees ...*»

An issue that complicated the disposition of the cases dealing with the new Cuban arrivals was the simultaneous occurrence of a large interdiction of Haitian nationals in high seas by the US Coast Guard. Close to 24,000 were intercepted in the decade of the 1980s. Their eligibility to land in the US was determined on board the Coast Guard boats. During the decade, only 11 were allowed entry in American territory and were allowed to apply for political asylum. Cubans justified the numbers by arguing that Haiti had not suffered a *Bay of Pigs* fiasco, hence the US owed them nothing. Early in 1991 the number of additional Haitians landing in Miami after a perilous ocean trip reached 35,000 in nine weeks (a wave of protesters after the September 1991 military coup that deposed Jean-Bertrand Aristide, President of Haiti). They were also threatened with deportation. A case for discrimination (*Haitian Refugee Center, Inc. v. Baker* 953 F.2d 1498, at the 11th Circuit Court in 1992) reached all the way to the US Supreme Court, which upheld the legality of the intersection and repatriation of this new wave of Haitians.

Looking back, the most significant difference between the 1959-1979 Cuban exiles and the exiles that came during and after the 1980 Mariel exodus was the nature of the Cuba they would remember after they left.

Until the *Mariel exodus*, Cuban exiles leaving for the US had in their minds the country they knew in their infancy, adolescence and mature years. You could say that the Cuba they would forever remember (as *Republican Cuba*), was an imperfect society, ran occasionally by corrupt politicians, with many economic ups-and-downs, but a society with predominant periods of freedom of expression, assembly, education, movement, prosperity and association. Without any reservations, a flourishing and promising society.

Once Cuba began to evolve into a Marxist country, loyalty to an ideology prevailed over honesty, dedication, capabilities and individual merits. That was the Cuba the 1980 *Marielitos* and after-1980 expatriates were escaping; a Cuba that they would remember as a land of nightmares, oppression, favoritism, scarcity, and total control of education, press, employment, advance opportunities and family unity. In no other place in the continent but Cuba, since 1959, the desire to move to another country was judged anti-patriotic. In no other country citizens were dispossessed of all their belongings and forbidden to ever return if they changed their minds. That has been, in general terms (and there are always exceptions) the fundamental difference between the historical Cuban exiles (1959-1979) and the post-Mariel expatriates (1980-present).

Everything else was collateral: pre-1980 Cuban exiles had a passion for baseball and would always remember the *Cuban Baseball League* as Havana, Almendares, Cienfuegos, and Marianao. Post-1980 expatriates, on the other hand, will always remember Cuban baseball as the *Cuban National League of* Industriales, Henequeneros, Vegueros, Citricultores and Azucareros. A small detail that made all the difference in the world.

The 1980s

- The second **Congress of Cuban Intellectuals** took place in New York in October of 1980 with **Jorge Vals Arango** as its Honorary President.
- Also in October of 1980 a large conference took place in Caracas where **Huber Matos** launched the organization **Cuba Independiente y Democrática (CID)**. Matos had been in political prison in Cuba for 20 years. CID started to publish its newsmagazine in December of that year and began to broadcast its **short-wave radio programs**, directed to Cuba, in July of 1981.
- In December a group of opponents to the regime in Cuba took over the offices of the **Vatican State** in Havana. All clergy abandoned the building and a group of special security troops entered the site at the request of the *Nuncio Apostólico*. The government troops made eight arrests.
- In July of 1981 a new organization started in Miami: the **Fundación Nacional Cubano-Americana**, under the leadership of **Jorge Mas Canosa**. Its approach was to lobby the executive and legislative branches of the US government for a more assertive action seeking the freedom of Cuba.
- On August 18, the second Congress of **Cuba Independiente y Democrática** took place in Miami. In Caracas Cuban exiles under the leadership of **Marta Moré de Fiallo** founded the *Instituto de Promoción Cultural Cubano*, to preserve the cultural values of the exiles and promote cultural freedom in Cuba.
- The third **Congreso de Intelectuales Cubanos** took place in Washington in October of 1982 at the same time as the third **Congress of Cuba Independiente y Democrática** took place in New York.

(Continued)

Photos below, left to right:

Cuban poet **Jorge Vals Arango**, was 20 years in prison before he reached Miami; Commander **Huber Matos**, also having served 20 years in prison, embracing Mons. Enrique Pérez Serantes, Archbishop of *Santiago de Cuba*; the logotype of the **Cuban-American National Foundation** and its founder **Jorge Mas Canosa**.

(Continuation)

- In Valencia, Venezuela, a group of former Cuban political prisoners orga-nized the **Asociación de Ex-Presos Políticos Cubanos**, under the leader-ship of **Gustavo Rodríguez Pulido**. Days later, in Caracas, a group of young Cuban exiles founded the **Fraternidad de Jóvenes Cubanos Libres**, a study group committed to expand the knowledge about Cuban history among young Cubans in Venezuela.
- Under the leadership of **María Valdés Rosado**, the **Movimiento Demócrata Cristiano** opens a chapter in Havana with the purpose of help-ing former political prisoners and promote political change in Cuba.
- In April of 1983, a group of Cuban intellectuals that had left the island as part of the *Mariel Exodus* starts publishing the magazine **Mariel** under the direction of **Reynaldo Arenas**.
- Cuban exiles began to help a large number of political prisoners organize the **Nuevo Presidio Político Cubano Plantado** at the *Combinado del Este* prison in Havana. The *Plantados* refused to be integrated with the common delinquents and to dress like them in the prisons in Cuba.

On August 20, **Cuba Independiente y Democrática** held its fourth Con-gress in Los Angeles, California and its fifth Congress, for the second time, in Miami.

(Continued)

Photos above, left to right:

Reynaldo Arenas; the **Revista Mariel** published 8 issues between 1983 and 1985, under the direction of **Reynaldo Arenas** and **Carlos Victoria** with the support of **Lydia Cabrera**. Both Arenas and Victoria committed suicide a few years later; **Carlos Victoria**; the logotypes of **Cuba Independiente y Democrática** and the **Unión de Ex-Presos Políticos Cubanos**.

(Continuation)

- On May 20, 1985, **Radio Martí** began its transmissions to Cuba as the result of an effective lobbying effort by the **Fundación Nacional Cubano-Americana**.

- **Cuba Independiente y Democrática** had its sixth Congress in Caracas, Venezuela, on September 12 and on September 26, in Miami, the **Partido Nacional Democrático** was organized.

- On October 19, 1985, **Casa Cuba** was opened in Caracas, Venezuela, by a combined effort of the **Fundación de Ayuda a Cubanos del Exilio**, the **Unión de Ex-Presos Políticos Cubanos**, **Solidaridad de Trabajadores Cubanos** and the **Instituto de Promoción Cultural**. Its purpose was to have a central place to develop activities favoring the freedom in Cuba and to provide a place for temporary stay to the increasing number of Cuban exiles relocating in Caracas. During the 1960s there had been other temporary shelters for Cuban exiles such as **Quinta Hogareña**, **Quinta Micar**, **Quinta Antillana**, **Casa José Martí** and **Hogar Cubano**.

- On June of 1986, the news magazine **Disidente Universal** began publication in San Juan, Puerto Rico under the direction of **Angel W. Padilla**. The magazine was smuggled into Cuba every month; its publication was possible by a grant from the *National Endowment for Democracy (NED)*.

- **Cuba Independiente y Democrática** had its seventh Congress in Philadelphia on August 31st. The following week in San Antonio de los Altos, Venezuela, the **IV Congress of the Solidarity of Cuban Workers** took place. A month later, in Madrid, **the IV Congress of Cuban Intellectuals** took place, with **Eloy Gutiérrez Menoyo** as the new President.

(Continued)

Photos below, left to right, top to bottom:

The logotype of **Radio Martí; Jorge Luis Pérez García (Antúnez)**, a well known dissident in Cuba, reading an issue of **Disidente Universal** in Havana; **Eloy Gutierrez Menoyo**, former revolutionary and political prisoner, a controversial exile figure; the **Casa Cuba** in Caracas on a festive day.

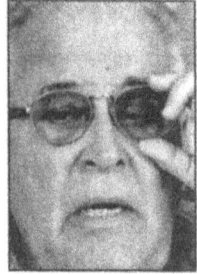

(Continuation)

- In Miami, on November 27th of 1986, a group of former Cuban political exiles launched the **Club de Ex-Presos Políticos Cubanos y de Combatientes**, the **EXCLUB**; among its members were **Angel de Fana, Angel Cuadra** and many other former fighters for freedom in Cuba. Its first activity was a Cultural and Patriotic event at the **Koubek Center** of the University of Miami in February of 1987.
- Also in November of 1986, **Ramón Saúl Sánchez** organized the **Comisión Nacional Cubana**.
- In mid May, Cuban exiles in Madrid organized the **Asociación Cubano-Española** under the leadership of **Ernesto Vandama Puente**.
- In July, the **Museo Cubano de Arte y Cultura** organized an exposition and sale of works of art made by Cuban exiles during their prison terms in Cuba.
- In Caracas, on September 3, Cuban exiles from all corners of the world met in the fifth **Congreso de Intelectuales Cubanos** and designated **Ernesto Díaz Rodríguez** as their President. The organizing committee included **Pedro Corzo, Martha Moré de Fiallo, Andrés Trujillo Carbonell** and **Silvia Meso**, among others.
- Commemorating the *Grito de Yara* in Cuba, the **Comisión Cubana de Derechos Humanos y Reconciliación Nacional** was organized in Havana on October 10, under the leadership of **Elizardo** and **Gerardo Sánchez Santa Cruz**.
- On December 10, the *International Human Rights Day*, **Radio Martí**, from its studios in Miami, broadcasted to Cuba the first session of an activity recorded in Havana and sent clandestinely to the US.

(Continued)

Photos above, left to right, top to bottom:

Angel de Fana, leader of the *Plantados*; **Angel Cuadra**, President of the *PEN Club*, **Ramón Saúl Sánchez**, leader of *Movimiento Democracia*; **Pedro Corzo**, promotor del *Instituto de la Memoria Histórica Cubana contra el Totalitarismo*; the logotypes of the **Museo Cubano de Arte y Cultura** and of the **PEN Club de Escritores Cubanos en el Exilio**; **Elizardo Sánchez Santa Cruz**, leader of the *Comisión Cubana de Derechos Humanos*.

(Continuation)

- During the first months of 1988, two chapters of the **Comité Cubano Pro Derechos Humanos** were organized: in Caracas, on February 24th, under the leadership of **Silvia Meso**, and in Puerto Rico on March 4th, under the leadership of **Father Miguel Angel Loredo** and **Kemel Jamis**.

- On April 10th, based on information provided by people in Cuba, **Armando Valladares**, former political prisoner and in 1988 US Ambassador to the *Comisión de Derechos Humanos de las Naciones Unidas*, denounced the violations in the island and got the Commission to assign a member to investigate the situation in Cuba.

- On September 5th, the *relator* of the UN, *Ambassador Alioune Sene* from Senegal, received in Havana a 500 page document entitled **Informe Acusatorio al Régimen Estalinista de Cuba**, presenting 350 specific violations of *Human Rights* in the island. Over 1600 Cuban citizens were present at a meeting in the *Comodoro Hotel* in Havana with Mr. Sene, including **Sebastian Arcos Bergnes**, a former assailant of the *Moncada Barracks* in 1953, appointed Vice Minister in 1959, who joined the opposition while in jail for having tried to leave Cuba with his family. He was the first prisoner in Cuba that decided to remain a prisoner rather than be forced to leave the island.

- **Sebastian** and his brother **Gustavo Arcos Bergnes**, had also been at the *Moncada Barracks*, had been appointed Ambassador to Belgium in 1959, had turned against the Castros and had been sentenced to 10 years in prison. The two brothers were subjected to the worst case of *"repudiation"* by angry mobs led and organized by Castro's political police. They both led the **Human Rights Movement** in Cuba and eventually went into exile. Sebastian died in Miami in 1997 and Gustavo in 2006.

- In January of 1989 Castro finalizes his plans to visit Venezuela and the **Fundación Cubano-Venezolana**, the **Comité Pro Monumento a José Martí** and the **Comité Cubano Pro Derechos Humanos** in Caracas organized an informative nation-wide campaign to inform citizens of Venezuela about the realities in Cuba. **Roberto Fontanilla**, **Pedro Corzo** and **Silvia Meso** were the main organizers.

(Continued)

Photos below, left to right, top to bottom:

Silvia Meso and **Roberto Fontanilla Roig**, important leaders of Cuban exiles in Venezuela; **Father Miguel Angel Loredo**, alumnus of *La Salle* in Cuba, pastor of *San Francisco Church* in Havana, jailed for 10 years in several Castro prisons, expelled from Cuba in 1984, witness to the situation in Cuba in Nestor Almendros' and Jorge Ulla's film **Nadie Escuchaba**; **Sebastian** and **Gustavo Arcos Bergnes**. With their brother **Luis** of the *26 of July Movement*, they were leaders in Cuba's *Human Rights causes*.

(Continuation)

- In a surprise move, in February 21, 1989, the Bulgarian Ambassador to the **Comisión de Derechos Humanos de las Naciones Unidas (UNHRC)**, meeting in Geneva for its 45th session, voted to condemn Cuba for its violations of Human Rights. A 400 page report, the most detailed ever presented at the *UNHRC*, had been prepared by the **Comité Cubano Pro Derechos Humanos.**

- In Roma, the Italian section of the *Internationale Gesellschaft für Menschenrechte (IGFM)*, a world-wide organization in defense of Human Rights, organized an international congress with the theme **A Perestroika for Cuba.** It took place at the headquarters of *Mondoperaio Magazine* with the participation of writer **Reynaldo Arenas**, film director **Orlando Jiménez**, professor and writer **Jacobo Machover** and actress **Miriam Acevedo**, all Cuban exiles.

- Starting in the 1980s and for several years thereafter, the **Comité Cubano Pro Derechos Humanos (CCPDH)** presented a request (with the corresponding documentation) to the *Consejo Económico y Social de Naciones Unidas (ECOSOC)* to be recognized as a *Non Governmental Organization (NGO)*. The **ECOSOC**, yielding to pressure from Cuba and other nations that very often violated Human Rights themselves, never accredited the **CCPDH** or gave it the right to speak at their meetings.

- Late in the 1980s, three Cuban Bishops in exile, **Eduardo Boza Masvidal** (Caracas, VEN), **Agustín Román** (Miami, USA) and **Enrique San Pedro** (Brownsville, TX), began to formulate plans to organize in Miami the **Comunidad de Reflexión Cubana en la Diáspora (CRECED)**, to help sustain Cuban ideals among exiles.

Photos below, left to right, top to bottom:
The Building of the **Comisión de Derechos Humanos de las Naciones Unidas (UNHRC)**, in Geneva and the logo of the organization; Cuban **Bishop Enrique San Pedro**; writer and Human Rights activist **Jacobo Machover** and actress **Miriam Acevedo**, all Cuban exiles and very strong and tireless defenders of Human Rights in Cuba.

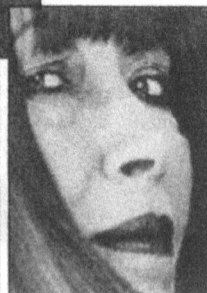

The Peruvian Embassy Episode in 1980

In 1980, an amazing history of escape from Communism took place when 120,000 Cubans went into exile in the now notorious **Mariel Exodus**.

The antecedents of the Mariel can be traced to a few years earlier, when many *gusanos* (worms) started to visit Cuba after the Castro-Carter agreement that allowed visits to Cuba after the opening of quasi-diplomatic relations. Hundreds of exiles went to Cuba with gifts, perfumes, small appliances and other eye-opening examples of the good life in capitalist USA.

At the end of 1979, a Cuban policeman named Angel Gálvez, with the help of one of the guards at the *Peruvian Embassy* (at Fifth Avenue and 72nd Street in Miramar, Havana), jumped the fence with his uniform and his weapon and sought asylum. The feat became widely known in Cuba although nothing was published in the official press. On January 17, 1980, at 8:30 PM, a *Leyland* public bus (route 79) slammed the fence with 12 passengers (four men, three women, five children) and entered the Embassy grounds. The news spread throughout Havana like wildfire. This time the Castro regime asked the Peruvian Ambassador to return the 12 persons seeking asylum.

The Peruvian Ambassador, **Edgardo de Habish Rospigliosi (1930-1999)**, agreed and five days later the gates of the Embassy were opened for half a dozen of Cuban soldiers to enter the premises and arrest the persons seeking refuge at the Embassy.

The President of Perú, **Fernando Belaunde Terry (1912-2002)**, proceeded to fire the Ambassador and requested from the Cuban government the return of all the would-be exiles to the Embassy, a demand that was satisfied in a few hours.

(Continued)

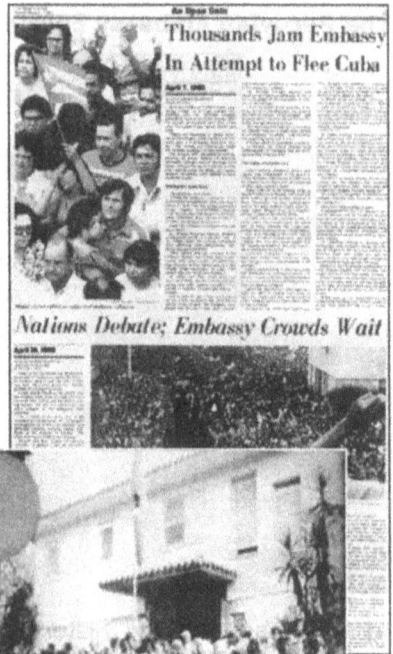

Thousands Jam Embassy In Attempt to Flee Cuba

Nations Debate; Embassy Crowds Wait

(Continuation)

By mid February, three other Cubans had entered the Embassy asking for the right of asylum. In March, another vehicle with three persons on board succeeded to make its way into the Embassy. Finally, on April 1st, 1980, a much greater escape took place. An unemployed 31-year old bus driver, **Hector Sanyústiz**, together with another bus driver friend, **Francisco Diaz Molina**, and other friends and family, took another bus from the same line (route 79, bus 5054) and made a run into the Embassy. The guards opened fire and one bullet ricocheted and killed Pedro Ortiz Cabrera, a 27 year old policeman from the *Department of the Interior*. After the Peruvian Ambassador refused to return the asylum seekers, the government of Cuba retired the guards from the Embassy.

News of the Peruvian Embassy without custody was almost immediately known in Havana. By noon the following day, 300 other Cubans had entered the territory of the Embassy. The following day (Easter Sunday), over 7,000 had sought asylum and were asking for help from the Peruvian government to leave the island.

Over the next few days, Castro, impotent before this public relations nightmare, announced he was opening the port of Mariel for all the Cubans that wanted to emigrate.

(Continued)

(Continuation)

While Cubans continued to enter the Peruvian Embassy, hundreds of government mobs began to harass and physically attack them screaming *"escoria"* (dregs) and throwing tomatoes and stones. It was alleged in Cuba that several TV personalities joined the accusing crowd, including **Carlos Otero**, who was imputed, falsely or not, to show up at the Mariel port with several threatening dogs. Otero would later become the main attraction of such Cuban TV programs as *Para Bailar*, *Sabadazo*, and *Carlos y Punto*; he was widely accused of being an agent of the Cuban security apparatus. In 2007 he joined the exile in Miami and within days was hired by TV 41, *América TV*, declaring that

«*in Cuba, everyone has collaborated with the dictatorship.*»

Under continuous harassment, the total number of asylum seekers reached 10,000 by Wednesday of the week after Easter. The government newspaper *Verde Olivo* had a headline «*Let them all leave, except those in the Bus,*» referring to Sanyústiz and his bus passengers. everyone

(Continued)

Photos above: **Carlos Otero** and the mobs recruited by the Castro regime to harass and punish anyone getting close to the Peruvian Embassy in 1980.

Photos below: the **Cubans inside the Embassy** expressing that they did not want food, but an exit visa to leave Cuba. The gallant President of Perú **Fernando Belaunde Terry** in 1980

(Continuation)

It had not been easy to do what the asylum-seekers at the Peruvian Embassy had accomplished. It was almost impossible in 1980 to obtain a visa to leave Cuba. There were only three options: try a dangerous crossing of the Florida Straits, escaping through the heavily guarded North coast of Cuba; seek asylum in an embassy of any of the Castro-friendly Latin American countries; or crash the gates of a heavily guarded and unfriendly Latin American Embassy.

In 1980 the repressive powers of the Cuban government were at their peak. The regime was emboldened by the economic, military and political support of the Soviets. There were two laws in the books, the **Ley de Peligrosidad** (Law of Dangerousness) and the **Ley de Vagancia** (Law of Vagrancy) that allowed the government to arrest men who did not cut their hair to the length considered "*manly*" by Castro; such violations could get people ten years.

The 10,000 would-be refugees in the gardens of the Embassy were visited from the streets by *Fidel Castro* and *Ramiro Valdés*, the *Minister of the Interior*. From the distance they were figuring out how to resolve the logistics and the terrible public relations quandry that the invaders of the Embassy were presenting. They both were on the phone constantly with the head of the Cuban Army Raúl Castro. In the meantime, people inside the Embassy were listening to *La Voz de las Américas*, the US international radio station. It gave solace to the Cubans in the Embassy that the entire world was being informed of the events in Havana.

As days went by, 3,000 people from the Embassy gave up their intentions and left the grounds because of hunger, thirst, congestion and poor hygiene. The promise to bring food and water from the government of Cuba was rescinded after several government truck drivers had left their vehicles after unloading the food and water and had taken asylum in the Embassy.

Photos below: the *salvoconducto* (pass) for those who could not tolerate the conditions and left the Embassy. The draconian Minister of Interior **Ramiro Valdés**.

Castro finally declared the port of **Mariel** as a free zone opened to anyone wishing to leave Cuba; they had to have someone to pick them up. Nothing was reported in the press in Cuba. Cuban exiles in the United States, however, hurried to Miami and Key West to rent, borrow or buy boats to bring their families to the United States under the code name **Operation Mariel Boatlift**. The US dispatched the **USS Saipan** to assist Cubans in their deliverance and rescue mission. It provided such things as gas, food, medical attention, water and navigation instructions. Above the sea, several **US Air Force F-4s** began to look out for Cuban vessels in distress. In Key West and Miami the **American Red Cross** was waiting for them.

Operation Mariel Boatlift: a Summary.

- The boatlift took place from April 15 to October 31, 1980.
- Jimmy Carter was at the time the President of the United States.
- 10,800 Cubans had invaded the Peruvian Embassy in Miramar during the first two weeks of April, 1980.
- Over the next few weeks 125,000 Cubans (60% men, 20% women, 20% children) left Cuba in more than 1,700 boats of all kinds, most of them coming from Miami.
- 70% of the "*Marielitos*" left Cuba during the month of May.
- During the entire month of May, the *USS Saipan* (a US Navy ship) was stationed between Mariel and Key West to rescue exiles and refuel private vessels bringing refugees to the US.
- The US also placed several F-4s from bases in Florida and the Carolinas to "*provide air* cover" like *Brothers to the Rescue* would do months later.
- Close to 30 "*Marielitos*" died at sea.
- Close to 2,000 criminal "*Marielitos*" were jailed right away in federal prisons. The rest went to refugee camps, notably *Fort Indiantown* in Pennsylvania, *Fort Chaffee* in Arkansas and *Fort McCoy* in Wisconsin.
- The federal government spent close to $1 Billion in this operation.
- The "*Marielitos*" increased by 7% the Cuban population of Miami.
- The Castro regime forced the exiles' boats to take to Miami 12,500 "undesirables."
- On May 11, 1980, the *New York Times* falsely reported that most of the 125,000 "*Marielitos*" were criminals, homosexuals and mentally ill.
- It was proven later that only 2,800 were hard core criminals from the jails in Cuba.
- Close to 2,500 were inmates taken from mental health facilities directly to the port of Mariel by Castro's soldiers.
- The US government had to deport all of them back to Cuba.
- Half the "*Marielitos*" had members of their families in Miami.
- Castro immediately characterized the "*Marielitos*" as the "*escoria*" (dregs) of Cuban society.

Scenes of **Operation Mariel Boatlift** from April to October 1980.

Photos Above: the refugees in transit through the perilous waters of the **Florida straits**; the reception and registration at **Key West**; the tent camps under **US-95** and the **Miami Stadium** after the refugees arrived.

The Miami News — Tuesday

Carter calls for calm in Miami, orders probe of McDuffie case

PARADISE LOST?

Just as Miami was adapting to the new arrivals from the Mariel Exodus in Dec. 1980, Miamians experienced one of the most difficult times in the city: the **McDuffie Riots** (Dec. 17, 1980).

Arthur Lee McDuffie, 33, a Black insurance executive, was spotted by police doing daredevil stunts with his motorcycle. After a high speed chase he was caught, beaten and arrested by a dozen policemen. Four days later, he was dead after falling into a coma. The police department attributed his wounds to hitting a curb and going out of control on his bike. His skull was cracked by the force of a heavy blow by a policeman, some cops reported. Six officers stood trial in Tampa after a change of venue from Miami.

One of the accused policemen —allegedly the author of the killing blow to McDuffie's head— was a Cuban refugee, **Alex Marrero**, 25; he was charged with second-degree murder. The exile community immediately started a collection for his defense.

(Continued)

In 1980 Dade County had a population mix of Whites (70%), Blacks (15%) and Hispanics (15%, mostly Cuban refugees). Dade County was at the time a very Southern community. Until 1965, for instance, Blacks had to carry ID cards to get into Miami Beach and file a report of the reasons for their visit (usually for a day's work). In fact, 200 Black applicants to the Police Force had been turned down between 1970 and 1980. The Dade County Police Benevolent Association offered each policeman under indictment in the McDuffie case to pay their legal fees up to $2,000.

When the six-member all-male White Tampa jury found all the policemen —at 2:30 PM, May 17th, after a 2 hour deliberation— not guilty, riots broke in Miami. By 10 PM the city was in flames. In impoverished heavily-Black *Liberty City* and *Overtown*, six miles north of downtown, fires were set, stores vandalized, people were beaten, houses were looted and set on fire, windows were smashed all over the neighborhood, police cars were spray painted with the words "*looter*" or "*whitey.*" In *Liberty City* a White man that got lost in the city was pulled out of his car, beaten, stabbed, shot and run over. Altogether, after three days of rioting, eighteen persons had died and over 1,000 had been arrested. Governor Graham sent in 3,000 guardsmen until the violence finally subsided. Liberty City suffered close to $100 Million in damages.

(Continued)

(Continuation)

In the aftermath, Cuban refugees were accused of wielding money and power to control de city and wishing to displace Blacks. The six weeks of the McDuffie trial coincided with the first phase of the Mariel Boatlift. The McDuffie family sued *Dade County* and received a $1.1 Million settlement. From there on, for a long time, racial tension was a daily life happening in Southern Florida.

For the Cuban refugees in Miami, the arrival of the **Marielitos** and the **McDuffie riots** were a wake-up call. Evidently, their stay in Miami was no longer a temporary proposition; on the other hand, by virtue of the struggles to control local politics, Cubans decided to become American citizens *en masse,* to best claim political control of the city for themselves.

The Mariel exodus brought to Cubans in exile the sad realization that the mood of the opposition in Cuba was to emigrate rather than rebel and fight. Evidently, those already in exile could not ask those emigrating in the 1980s to do what they themselves had not done months or years earlier. The Miami exiles, therefore, almost unanimously worked hard to accommodate and help the new exiles even though, in a few cases, they showed a different driving force and goals that those of the exiles of the 1960s and 1970s.

A sign of hope for the future fight in Cuba, however, was the election of **Ronald Reagan (1911-2004)** to the presidency of the US in November, 1980. Reagan was a political conservative and a forceful anti-Communist. Cuban-Americans gave him 90% of their vote in 1980 and 1984. He had come to Miami and —in fairly clear Spanish— had greeted Cuban exiles with rallying cries of «¡Viva Cuba Libre! »

During his eight year presidency, however, he could not do much for the return of the exiles to a free Cuba, although he supported the "*Contras*" in Nicaragua and ousted the Cuban Communists from their priced possession of **Grenada**, the tiny Caribbean island where the Castro regime had established a beachhead. Cuban exiles, however, always believed that Cuba would not have been prey to the Communists had Ronald Reagan and not Kennedy been president of the US in 1960.

Photos Above: ***Ronald Reagan*** (1911-2004); the reception that Reagan received in Little Havana.

Cuban exiles have always known of pro-Castro activists and spies among their ranks. The intelligene services of the US have estimated that after 1970, at one time or another, the number of Castro's undercover agents among the exiles around the world has fluctuated between 2,000 and 3,000. In the years between 1970 and 2000, aside from the men infiltrated in *Hermanos al Rescate*, the most celebrated Castro's snoops in contact with Cuban exiles were **Carlos Manuel Serpa Maceita** (*agente Emilio*) and **Moisés Rodríguez Quesada** (*agente Vladimir*), two men that had been infiltrated during 15 and 20 years, respectively.

Serpa Maceira started his spying activities in 1975; without leaving Havana he was a frequent reporter for *Radio Martí*, *Radio Mambí* and the digital page *Cubanet*. He reached the position of spokesperson for the *Damas de Blanco* and was director of the *Unión de Periodistas Libres de Cuba (UPLC)*. He collaborated with *Radio República*, a station ran by the *Directorio Democrático Cubano (DDC)* in Miami. He became a friend of Michael Parmly, chief of Havana's *US Interest Section (SINA)*, and collaborated with educational activities at the SINA, sponsored by *Florida International University*. He failed to gain the trust of Nancy Pérez Crespo, founder of the *Nueva Prensa Cubana*, and Carlos Santana, a veteran *Radio Mambi* reporter in Miami, as well as Enrique Blanco, a well known Cuban blogger living in Puerto Rico.

Moisés Rodríguez Quesada worked for the Castro regime as an undercover agent since 1970. He was stationed at the Customs Office of *Martí International Airport*. For ten years he was infiltrated in the *Comisión Cubana de Derechos Humanos y Reconciliación Nacional (CCDHRN)*, the human rights organization presided by *Elizardo Sánchez Santa Cruz*, who never trusted him completely. His mission was to document the relations between the *SINA* and the Cuban dissidents; his house in Havana was the venue for coordinating meetings and, on one occasion, *Vicky Huddleston*, a State Department official and Principal Officer of Havana's *US Interest Section*, visited there to organize the support of the Cuban dissidents to the *Torricelli Act*. The *SINA* once funded one of his trips to Miami.

Photos above, left to right: **Carlos Manuel Serpa Maceira** *and* **Moisés Rodríguez Quesada***; Serpa interviewing* **Laura Pollán** *for Radio Martí.*

Christo surrounded 11 Biscayne Bay small islands with $3.1 million square feet of shiny pink fabric skirts in 1983.

The **Metrorail** was inaugurated in Miami in 1984.

Dan Marino and **Don Schula**, the best *Quarterback* and *Coach* in the NFL in the 1980s, were always the favorites of Cuban exiles.

Cubans in Toronto protesting the influx of **Canadian tourists** to Cuba.

On May 20, 1985, **Radio Martí** began broadcasting to Cuba. It was a station affiliated with the official international communication system of the American government, with the mission of conveying to Cuba the truth about the system that the Communists had installed in the island. Radio Martí was a product of the efforts and skills of **Jorge Mas Canosa (1939-1997)**, a *Bay of Pigs* veteran and one of the most effective leaders of the Cuban exile, with other prominent Cuban businessmen. In 1981 they launched the *Cuban American National Foundation (FNCA)*.

At first, the Cuban exiles in Miami were not very receptive to the Foundation; there were even car bumper stickers that read «Fidel and Mas Canosa, the same thing,» but with time the Foundation became an important organization in exile until Mas died in November, 1997.

Photos below: **Jorge Mas Canosa** as a member of the US army after *Playa Girón*, as an exile leader in 1964 and after the founding of the *FNCA* in the 1980s, some 20 years before his death; on the bottom the logos of **Radio** and **TV Martí** and the **FNCA**.

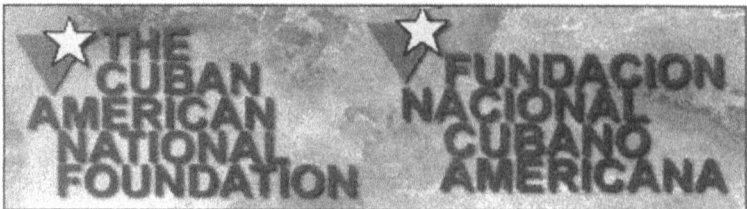

Not all the activities of Cuban exiles around the world were a source of pride for the community. There were, like in every society, a group of maladjusted individuals that proceeded in unseemly ways and brought embarrassment and disgrace to their friends; a relatively small number of Cubans, mostly immigrants from the late waves of arrivals after 1990, incurred in serious acts of dishonor, or even criminal behavior that injured the reputation of the exiles as a group. In an honest account of the Cuban exodus since 1959, they cannot be ignored.

The scammers to the US Federal Government were the most visible of swindlers among the exiles; since the 1990s they were all captured and jailed in the US, escaped to Cuba or sought sanctuary in other countries, mostly in Latin America or Spain. So many found *shelter in Cuba* that it was widely speculated that Cuba had trained them and was taking a cut of their bounty once they were given safe cover in the island.

Between the years 2008 and 2011 it was estimated that $545 million had been chiseled from the **US Medicare** program (the federal subsidized service of public health for people over 65 who reside legally in the U.S.) and close to 150 of the offenders had sought refuge in Cuba. The US government was only able to prosecute 16, most of them having arrived in Florida after 1990. The total booty of these 16 was estimated at $83 million. At a hearing in Congress, Senator Charles Grassley (R-Iowa) disclosed that 7 of the 10 most *active transgressors* were Cubans from Miami. The *Cuban Interest Section* in Washington never responded to any inquires from the FBI over these matters. In general, the fraud to Medicare was organized as a family business: parents hired their children, uncles, cousins and grandparents and everyone benefited from the schemes.

Some of the most offensive cases follow:

- In 1987 **Miguel G. Recarey Jr.** was found guilty in the largest Medicare fraud in history with his *International Medical Centers, Inc.* in Miami; The Company was put out of business by the courts after its gigantic medical fraud was discovered. It was alleged that the medical company was financed by the Miami mafia don *Santo Trafficante*.

Photo on the right:
Miguel Recarey in front of his Clinic, *International Medical Center*, in Miami.

(Continuation)

- In October, 1987, **Mr. Recarey** fled the United States, beginning an international fugitive investigative effort covering at least 3 continents and 11 countries. That same year, Recarey's *Miami-based International Medical Centers* collapsed, leaving an estimated $230 million in unpaid claims for its 200,000 elderly Florida members. In February 1988, Recarey was indicted *in absentia* on charges of conspiracy to defraud the US by fraud and misapplying U.S. government funds, wire fraud and false statements concerning *Medicare* payments received by his Company. Recarey had left the country for safe haven in Madrid, the same day he received an expedited $2.2 million income tax refund from the IRS. Recarey moved to Caracas for several years and used his influence with some Venezuelan government officials to avoid detention and to mislead U.S. law enforcement officials in their pursuit. It has been reported that Recarey alternates between his Madrid residency and his Cuban mansion in Havana.

- In 2007 **Eduardo Moreno**, accused of stealing $2 million in false claims to *Medicare*, escaped to Cuba after posting a $450,000 bond. Among the properties he left behind in Miami was a $200,000 black Rolls-Royce Phantom. He is known to own a company providing DJs to clubs in Havana.

- In 2007 **Fermín Rey**, fled from Miami to Ecuador after stealing $2.8 million from *Medicare* and posting a bond of $100,000 in Federal Court. He was captured by Mexican authorities, returned to Ecuador and recaptured there by the FBI. He received a 10 year sentence in the US.

- In 2008 **José, Luis** and **Carlos Benítez**, proprietors of a chain of clinics in Miami-Dade, milked Medicare for $84 Million and fled to the Dominican Republic from where they were successfully deported to Cuba. They had invested millions of dollars in the Dominican Republic in homes, motels, apartments, land, ships, horses, a helicopter, a Coca-Cola distribution plant and seaside hotels in Punta Cana, Bávaro, Higüey and the capital Santo Domingo.

- In 2009 **Michel de Jesús Huarte** pleaded guilty to a Medicare fraud and was condemned to 22 years in jail. His cohorts **Orlín Tamayo Quiñónez, Juan Carralero** and **Madelín Bárbara Machado** were able to escape to Cuba.

(Continued)

Photos below: Federal agents take into custody **Caridad Guilarte**, accused of illegally stealing funds from *Medicare* in Miami.

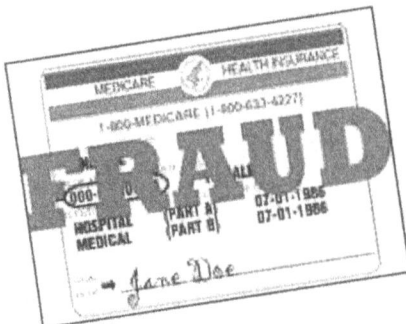

A sample gallery of Cuban-born indicted scammers to Medicare. All arrived in Miami after 1994, as part of President Clinton's *Cuban Adjustment Law.*

Photos above: top Row:

Abel Carranza, born in 1954; stole $2.1 million; now in Mexico.
Aiza Yudith Rodríguez, born in 1975; stole $9 million; on the lam.
Armando Fuentes Díaz, born in 1972; stole $786,000; on the lam.
Armando Zamora (sic), born in 1960; stole $500,000; now in Mexico.

Middle Row:

Eduardo Moreno, born in 1969; stole $2 million; now in Cuba.
Bárbaro Ortega, born 1962; stole $972,000; now in Cuba.
Carmen González, born in 1974; stole $8.2 million; now in Cuba.
Cesar L. Cordiví, born in 1974; stole $171,000; now in Cuba.

Bottom Row:

Esnardo Cabrera Hernández, born in 1967; $456,000; now in Cuba.
Luis A. Fuentes, born in 1949; stole $3.7 million; now in Cuba.
Magda Luz Lavín, born in 1958; stole $5 million; now in Colombia.
Vladimir Boroto Montenegro, born in 1963; stole $3.1 million; on the lam.

(Continued)

Among other maladjusted Cubans in the US that brought embarrassment to Cuban exiles were a few individuals involved in *Ponzi schemes*. A Ponzi scheme is a fraudulent investment operation that pays handsomely to old investors with monies contributed by new investors and not from revenues from any real business. As soon as new investors are not available, as it happens sooner or later, the entire operation collapses and everyone loses their money except those who were the first to invest.

Ponzi schemes were erroneously named after **Charles Ponzi (1882-1949)**, who offered 50% returns every 45 days in the 1920s, presumably dealing with international postage stamp coupons. He bilked hundreds of customers before his scheme was revealed by **Clarence Barron (1855-1928)**, the owner of the Wall Street Journal.

The first practitioner of Ponzi schemes, however, was **Baldomera Larra (1833-1901)**, daughter of the Spanish writer Mariano José de Larra; her pyramidal investments started to attract customers in the 1870s, fully 50 years before Ponzi; she promised to pay them 30% a month, which she did until her empire collapsed and she escaped to France and then Cuba —with 22 million reales— in 1876, ruining over 5,000 investors, many of them sophisticated Parisians.

Among the most notable Cuban-born Ponzi (or Larra) practitioners in Miami were **Gastón** and **Teresita Cantens**, the founders of *Royal West Properties, Inc.*, a company that lured investors with annual returns of 15%, presumably to be invested in the acquisition of speculative real estate properties in Florida's West coast. The Cantens swindled $135 million from their investors before they declared bankruptcy in 2011. As with Bernard Madoff among the Jewish rich, the victims of the Cantens were their friends within the close-knit Cuban exile community in Miami.

*Photos above: **Charles Ponzi** in 1920, **Baldomera Larra** in 1876, **Gastón** and **Teresita Cantens** in Miami in 2010, and their company logo.*

In the last years of the 1980s, two very famous Cubans died: **Desi Arnaz (1917-1989)** and **Dámaso Pérez Prado (1916-1989).** They were not political exiles since they had been living outside Cuba since the 1940s, but both supported the Cuban exiles and identified with their struggles. They had both expressed their reluctance to visit Cuba until the Communist regime in the island disappeared.

Desi Arnaz had gained fame in the US with his orchestra when he married Lucille Ball in 1940 and started the TV series *I Love Lucy*, where he played the role of Ricky Ricardo. He was born in Santiago de Cuba and became a celebrity in the US for his outstanding role in the *United Service Organization (USO)* enter-taining troops during WWII. He died of lung cancer at age 69. He is immortalized by two stars (one for films and one for TV) on the *Hollywood Walk of Fame*, at 6327 and 6220 Hollywood Boulevard.

Pérez Prado was an accomplished bandleader, musician, pianist and composer, known the world over as "*el Rey del Mambo*" (the King of Mambo). He was born in Matanzas, Cuba and in the 1940s was the piano arranger for the *Sonora Matancera*, a famous Cuban orchestra. In 1948 he moved to Mexico and created the Mambo, his own version of a fast Cuban *danzón*. He immediately became famous for his grunts during his performances (he was actually saying **¡Dilo!**). He was revered as a musical genius, the author of *Cherry Pink and Apple Blossom White* and *Patricia*. In 1959 the Castro government banned his music from Cuban radio.

Photos Above: **Pérez Prado** and his orchestra in the 1960s; **Desi Arnaz** with **Luci** in the late 1950s and **Desi** before his death in 1986.

Following a very old Marxist principle, the Castro regime in Cuba began in 1959 to erase from the memory of the nation the names of politicians, artists, writers, journalists, professors and any and all public figures that had taken the road to exile. In the process they unsuccessfully attempted to eliminate from Cuban history the contributions of hundreds of distinguished personalities that had placed the name of Cuba in a place of honor. A list of those whose names were buried in Cuba is difficult to compile. It includes among many others:

Alvaro de Villa, Celia Cruz, Luis Echegoyen, Gastón Baquero, Orestes Miñoso, Gerardo Gonzalez (Kid Gavilán), Minín Bujones, Velia Martínez, Ramiro Gómez-Kemp, Guillermo Alvarez Guedes, Lilia Lazo, Marina Rodríguez, Mary Munné, Julita Muñoz, Charito Sirgo, Dalia Iñiguez, Yolanda Fabián, Otto Sirgo, Blanquita Amaro, Alberto González Rubio, Juan Lado, Armando Osorio, Enrique Alzugaray, Carlos Badías, Ernesto Galindo, Luisa María Güell, Meme Solís, Santiago García Ortega, Jorge Félix, Paul Díaz, Olga Guillot, Tony Alvarez, Olga Chorens, Osvaldo Calvo, Manolo Urquiza, Albertico Insua, Guillermo de Cum, Manolo Coego, Sergio Doré, Jesús Alvariño, Normita Suárez, Gaspar Pumarejo, Alberto Garrido, Federico Piñeiro, Leopoldo Fernández, Aníbal De Mar, Mimí Cal, Luis Echegoyen, Manela Bustamante (Cachucha), Rafael Correa, Tito Hernández, Goar Mestre, Violeta Jiménez, Armando Roblán, Teté Machado, Teresa María Rojas, Armando Couto, Nestor Cabell, Flor de Loto, Miriam Acevedo, Julio Capote, Ada Béjar, Mario Martín, Norma Zúñiga, Teté Blanco, Rolando Barral, Martha Picanes, Griselda Nogueras, Aleida Leal, Maucha Gutiérrez, Roberto & Modesto Vázquez, Fernando Penabad, Marta Flores, and Salvador Lew, to mention a few.

Photos Above, left to right, top to bottom:

Ernesto Lecuona, Alberto Garrido and Federico Piñeiro (Chicharito y Sopeira), Enrique Alzugaray, Minín Bujones, Jesús Alvariño, Manela Bustamante e Idalberto Delgado (Cachucha y Ramón), Alberto González Rubio and Albertico Insua.

New generations of Cubans that were born or matured in exile and were also distinguishing themselves in the arts, literature, politics and the sciences were also condemned to be ignored in Cuba, even though they achieved the applause and the attention of many around the world through their talents. It is also difficult to produce an all inclusive list of names; many of them worked with talented individuals that had made a name for themselves in Cuba. It is difficult to distinguish between the two groups; both were firm in the decision to condemn the Communist government for their abuses and their tyrannical principles. Some of the classics and some of the new are presented here.

Carlos Oliva y los Sobrinos del Juez, Willy Chirino, Emilio y Gloria Estefan, Hansel y Raúl, Elsa Baeza, Franco Iglesias, Suzy Lemán, Marisela Verena, Rey Casas, Hilda Luisa Díaz Perera, Alma, Olga Díaz, Pili de la Rosa, Demetrio Pérez, Marta Pérez, Mario Fernández Porta, Rosendo Rosell, Lissette Alvarez, Marcia Morgado, Alina Interián, Lourdes Mensí, Christy Sánchez, Marilín Romero, Julie De Grandy, Gonzalo Rodríguez, María Madruga, María Meilán, Margarita and Manolo Coego Jr., Sergio Doré Jr., Adrián Mesa, Leticia Callava, Bernardette Pardo, José Alfonso Almora, Alina Mayo, Frank Cairo, Iván Acosta, León Ichaso, Mari Rodríguez Ichaso, Luis Santeiro, Pepe Bahamonde, Matías Montes Huidobro, José Corrales, Raúl de Cárdenas, José Triana, José Ignacio Cabrera, René Alomá, Dolores Prida, Fermín Borges, René Ariza y José Abreu Felipe, among others.

Photos below top to bottom, left to right: **Carlos Oliva, Leticia Callava and Celia Cruz, Pili de la Rosa, Marisela Verena, Mari Rodríguez Ichaso, Gloria Estefan** and **Willy Chirino.**

It was Cuba's loss to ignore for half a century the many accomplishments of some of its most talented artists, writers, musicians, and painters, simply because they went into exile:

Reinaldo Arenas, Juan Abreu, Nicolás Abreu, José Abreu Felipe, Carlos Victoria, Daniel Fernández, René Cifuentes, Roberto Valero, Miguel Correa, Andrés Reynaldo, Luis de la Paz, Reinaldo García Ramos, Carlos Alfonzo, Juan Boza, Gilberto Ruiz, Miguel Ordoqui, Laura Luna, Agustín Gaínza, Víctor Gómez, Eduardo Michaelson, Andrés Valerio, Luis Vega, Pedro Damián, Julio Venegas, Nelson Franco, Félix González, Gilberto Marino, Julio Hernández Rojo, Orestes Miqueli, Cundo Bermúdez, Manuel Mijares, María de los Angeles Montoya, Yolanda Cuellar, Rafael Díaz Palet, Julián Izquierdo, Tatiana Vecino, Adela Serra, Carlos Bermúdez, Rey Batista, Frank Falcón, Grisel González, Germán Barrios, Gonzalo Fontana, Cary Roque, Pepe and Carucha Camejo, Pepe Carril, Alberto Zarraín, Salvador Blanco, Pedro Tamayo, Marcos Miranda, Karla Barro, Armando Pico, Ciralina Quijano, Adolfo Fernández, Teresita Diego, Jesús García, Alexander Domínguez, Doris de Goya, Roberto Marín, Ignacio Berroa, Paquito De Rivera...

... Ricardo Eddy Martínez, Mike Porcel, Manolo Blanco, Rudy Pérez, Marlén Urbay, Raúl Gómez, Leonor Zamora, Malena Burke, Bobby Jiménez, Wilfredo Méndi, Martha Strada, Maggie Carlés, Luis Nodal, Annia Linares, Mirtha Medina, Delia Díaz de Villegas, Miguel Chávez, Osvaldo Rodríguez, Isaac Delgado, Juan Pablo Torres, Julito Martínez, Ramón Veloz, Reinaldo Miravalles, Miguel Gutiérrez, Gerardo Riverón, Arturo Sandoval, Albita Rodríguez, Zoé Valdés, Eliseo Alberto, Daína Chaviano, Antonio Orla, Luis Boffil, Manolo Feral, Armando Casín, Magaly Agüero, Lili Rentería, Alis García, Rodolfo Valdés Sigler, Cristina Rebull, Sonia Calero, Alberto Alonso, Rosario (Charín) Suárez, Camilo Egaña, Mario Vallejo, Edmundo García, Omar Moynelo, Jorge Hernández, Lázaro Horta, Amaury Gutiérrez, Roberto Ledesma, Jorge Bauer, René Barrios, Vicky Roig, Gonzalo Fontana, Blanca Rosa Gil, Xiomara Alfaro, Néstor Cabell, Norma Zúñiga, Marta Jorge, Chamaco García, Manolo Torrente, Alfredo Munar, Bebo Valdés, Ana Margarita Martínez Casado, Miguel de Grandi Jr., Bertha Sandoval, Roberto Torres, Concha Valdés Miranda, Ela O'Farrill, Zenaida Manfugás, José Le Matt, among others.

Photos Above: Four masters of the Arts in Cuba, **Cundo Bermúdez**, **Arturo Sandoval, Reinaldo Arenas** and **Sonia Calero.**

Many other Cuban artists, intelectuals, promoters, directors, producers and international figures went into exile. For two generations Cuba was for all practical purposes left without high caliber interpreters, seasoned drama artists, big-name plastic artists and top notch journalists. Gone at one time or another were:

Celia Cruz, Fernando Albuerne, La Lupe, Zoraida Marrero, Miguel De Grandi, Ernesto Lecuona, Margarita Lecuona, René Touzet, Mario Fernández Porta, Juan Bruno Tarraza, Osvaldo Farrés, Facundo Rivero, Guillermo Cabrera Infante, Zoraida Marrero, Julio Gutiérrez, Rolando Laserie, Bobby Collazo, Luis García, Francisco "Panchito" Risset, Nelo Sosa, Miguelito Valdés, Ñico Membiela, Arsenio Rodríguez, Alberto y José Fajardo, Israel (Cachao) López, Haydée Portuondo, María Luisa Chorens, Manolo Alvarez Mera, Tony Alvarez, Celio González, La India de Oriente, Orlando Vallejo, Orlando Contreras, Freddy, América Crespo, Servando Díaz, Manolo Fernández, René Cabell, Vicentico Valdés, Olga Chaviano, Wilfredo Fernández, Israel Kantor, Guillermo Portabales, Patato Valdés, Generoso Jiménez, Maruja González, and many others.

*Photos above, left to right, top to bottom: **Guillermo Cabrera Infante, Israel López (Cachao), Julio Gutiérrez, Manolo Alvarez Mera, Miguelito Valdés, Matías Montes Huidobro, René Touzet, Zoraida Marrero, Ñico Membiela, Xiomara Alfaro, Leopoldo Fernández** and **Ariel Remos**.*

One of the outstanding figures among American business leaders in the 1980s was a Cuban refugee, **Roberto Críspulo Goizueta (1931-1997)**, Chairman, Director and CEO of *The Coca-Cola Company* from August of 1980 until his death due to causes related to heavy smoking and lung cancer in 1997.

Goizueta was born in Havana, graduated from High School at *Colegio de Belén* and came to the US afterwards to improve his English skills at *Cheshire Academy* in Connecticut; he obtained a BS in Chemical Engineering at *Yale University* in 1953, and then returned to Cuba to join **Co-ca-Cola**. After a few years working for Coca-Cola in Cuba he was promoted to *Chief Technical Director* of five of its bottling plants in the island. In 1960 his family decided to go into exile after Castro rose to power in Cuba and began to transform the island into a Soviet outpost. Within four years Goizueta became —at age 35— *Vice President of Technical Research and Development* at Coca-Cola. In 1979 he was appointed *President* of the Company and in 1981 *Chairman of the Board*.

During Goizueta's 16 years of tenure at the helm of Coca-Cola, the brand became the best soft drink seller in the world. He launched *Diet Coke* and the *New Coke* (a marketing gimmick with which he secured Coke's position as a top seller among all soft drinks, beating its archrival *Pepsi*). In 1992 he started the *Goizueta Foundation*; it supported many cultural, educational and charitable institutions, among them *Emory University, Georgia Tech, University of Miami* and the *Colegio de Belén* in Miami.

Photos above, **Roberto Goizueta** *in the 1980s;*
*his book **I'd Like the World to Buy a Coke**;*
*a 1940s picture with his college sweetheart since their days in Cuba, **Olga Casteleiro**.*

Lo tirotean terroristas cubanos

Omega 7 leader gets life
for bombings, 2 murders

During the 1980s the Miami area was the site of over 25 bombings or attempted bombings to businesses or persons with alleged complicity or sympathies with the Communist government of Cuba. Since 1959 in fact, there had been an almost constant anti-Castro violence in Miami; most of it was disliked and regarded with aversion by the majority of the Cuban exile population. Some of the organizations responsible for these activities were the *Alliance of Cuban Intransigence (AIC)*, the *Revolutionary Recovery Insurrection Movement (MIRR)*, *Cuban Power*, *Omega 7*, *Movimiento Insurreccional Martiano*, *Comando Coro* and several others.

The perceived propensity of Miami to tolerate these aggressive activities was the basis for a legendary TV series called **Miami Vice**. The series starred *Don Johnson* and *Philip Michael Thomas* as two Miami detectives working undercover fighting crime, particularly drug trafficking. It ran from 1984 to 1990 on NBC. Most episodes were filmed in *South Beach* and the series was credited with launching the wave of admiration for *Art Deco architecture* and popularizing the *"T-shirt under an Armani jacket"* men's fashion, the *Ferrari Testarossa* and the $120,000 *Endeavour* speedboat.

Photos above: Pediatrician **Orlando Bosch** as he was taken prisoner by the FBI; a reportage of the bomb that killed the President of *Viajes Varadero* in San Juan, PR; **Eduardo Arocena** found guilty for his *Omega 7* violence; and an Ad for the popular 1980s TV program *Miami Vice*.

TERR☢RISM

By and large the Cuban exile communities condemned all acts of terrorism purported to be done on their behalf. The anti-Castro violence in Miami made it easy for the Cuban government to claim that the United States harbored, or at least tolerated, anti-Cuba terrorists. Many of these attacks on sympathizers of the Castro regime involved the use of pipe bombs, which occasionally failed to detonate. During the late 1980s, for instance, some of these attacks were:

- May 1, 1987, a pipe bombing at **Cubanacán** in Miami;
- May 2, 1987, a pipe bombing at **Almacén El Español** in Hialeah, Florida;
- May 25, 1987, a pipe bombing at **Cuba Envíos** in Miami;
- July 30, 1987, a pipe bombing at **Machi Community Services** in Miami;
- August 27, 1987, a pipe bombing at **Va Cuba** in Hialeah;
- January 2, 1988, a pipe bombing at **Miami-Cuban** in Miami;
- May 3, 1988, a pipe bombing at the **Cuban Museum of Arts and Culture** in Miami;
- May 26, 1988, a bombing at the residence of the executive director for the **Institute of Cuban Studies** in Coral Gables, Florida, claimed by the AIC;
- September 5, 1988, a pipe bombing at **Bella Cuba** in Miami;
- September 18, 1988, a bombing intended for a leader of the **Reunión Flotilla**, a Miami group which advocated that all persons should be able to enter or leave Cuba as they pleased;
- February 24, 1989, an attempted pipe bombing at **Almacén El Español** in Miami;
- March 26, 1989, a bombing at **Marazul Charters** in Miami;
- September 10, 1989, a bomb at **Super Optical** in Hialeah.

Most of these actions were carried out by Cubans originally trained by the CIA as members of *Commandos L* and the *Movimiento de Recuperación Revolucionaria (MRR)*, and had participated in maritime commando raids along the coasts of Cuba.

Although some of the bombings had specifically targeted residences, there were no deaths or injuries as a result. In the end, such bombings did not accomplish anything other than giving Castro excuses to infiltrate more and more agents among the Cuban exiles in Miami, New York, Union City, Paris, Madrid and everywhere. It was estimated at the end of the 1980s that over 3,000 "*moles*" were introduced by Castro among the Cuban exile communities.

12201 Southwest 82nd Avenue, Pinecrest

No other violent act in Miami can be compared with what happened on April 11, 1986 near Kendall in the south of Miami. It came to be known all across the world as the "**FBI Miami Firefight**." It falsely reinforced the notion (promulgated by Castro) that Miami was a violent town controlled by a *Cuban Mafia*. No Cuban exiles were even remotely involved in these events.

On that day, two armored-car and bank stick-up artists, **Michael Lee Platt (1954-1986)**, a former Airborne Ranger, and **William Russell Matix (1951-1986)**, a former Marine, confronted the FBI in a gun battle that felt and looked like the 1881 shootout at the *OK Corral*.

Acting on information provided by an ordinary citizen, the FBI deployed 14 men along the US-1 highway south of Miami, looking for a 1979 Chevrolet Monte Carlo in which two white males, aged 32 and 35, were travelling. They knew that Platt and Matix were armed with a shotgun, a Roger Mini-14 .223 caliber carbine and magnum revolvers. The bandits realized they had been sighted and were followed when they made the classic counter-surveillance tactic of making three consecutive right turns and the cars suspected of following them repeated the same maneuver. Instead of making a run and escape, Platt and Matix challenged the FBI to a slow speed light chase.

The bandits made a stand at the *Dixie Belle Shopping Center* at 12201 SW 82nd Avenue and as soon as they stepped out of their car they began to shoot at the FBI agents. Some 150 rounds were heard by frightened neighbors and shoppers. FBI agents **Ben Grogan** and **Jerry Dove** were killed by Platt at close range with his Mini-14, while Special Agent **Edmundo Mireles** killed both Platt and Matix with his .357 Magnum revolver after recovering from a Ruger Mini-14 .223 Remington round that had unutilized his left arm. In all, two FBI agents were killed and five were wounded.

No man infected more the social environment in Miami in the 1980s than **Pablo Escobar Gaviria (1949-1993),** the feared drug lord and capo of the *Medellin Cartel.* He singlehandedly controlled the world trade in cocaine through the 1980s and early 1990s. He mercilessly eliminated anyone who stood his way in Colombia or in Miami.

He had been born in Rionegro, Colombia; his first cocaine deal was made when he was 26 years old. In a few days his arresting officer was found dead, the 9 judges who would see his case received threatening notes and the evidence against him disappeared. Once free, he killed **Fabio Restrepo**, the head of the Medellín Crime Cartel and took his place. Soon he was making $2.8 billion a year —the most successful criminal in history— and was supplying 80% of the cocaine consumed in the US. In 1989 he entered politics, offering the nation of Colombia to pay its entire foreign debt, which amounted to $10 billion. During his unsuccessful campaign he assassinated three of his five opponents to the presidency of Colombia because they favored his extradition to the US.

His days of fame and fortune came to an end when a group called **Los Pepes** —mostly former aides that he had betrayed— began to kill anyone who had connections with him. The government, with the cooperation of the US, set up a team to search for him —dead or alive. He was finally caught and killed at one of his *"safe houses"* in Medellín, Colombia, on December 2, 1993, at age 44. By the time of his death his Cartel was producing 15 tons of cocaine a day and his monthly bill for rubber bands to wrap the stacks of cash was $2,500.

Photos Above: **Pablo Escobar** alive and dead.

The eighties were also known for the impunity with which Miami's *cocaine cowboys* did their business; they would murder a rival dealer in the middle of downtown or inside a shopping mall. Occasionally they would assault a competitor in a residential neighborhood, as it once happened in West Kendall when one of the cowboys executed an entire family including small children. The dealers were mostly Colombian drug traffickers who wanted to have the exclusive of the narcotics market in South Florida; at times they were assisted by some Cuban exiles who eventually ended up in federal jails serving long sentences.

A South Florida prominent Cuban drug trafficker, for instance, could be someone like **José Medardo Alvaro Cruz**, who called himself "*the godfather*;" he usually rode a Rolls-Royce with several bodyguards and was the absentee owner of several businesses in Miami. Alvaro was a 42 year old marihuana and cocaine smuggler that was known to ship 100 tons of drugs yearly into the US via Cuban waters. He boasted Passport number 247, dated 1976, issued by the Cuban Embassy in Madrid. During an undercover operation he was arrested by federal agents for delivering 200 pounds of cocaine to a presumed client. When witnesses refused to confront him he was convicted of tax evasion, in much the same way as Al Capone had been. He was condemned to 22 years in federal prison in Charlotte, South Carolina.

Photos Above: **José Medardo Alvaro Cruz**; *two scenes from real life and from re-enactments of the cocaine Cowboys' modus operandi: DEA agents in custody of a seized shipment and smugglers in their base of operations.*

Some of the news that Cuban exiles in Miami could read on the newspapers during the *Cocaine Wars* in the 1980s were:

- **Dadeland Mall** was the venue of the first shots in the *Cocaine Wars*. On July 11, 1979, two men emerged from a party supplies panel truck at the Mall's parking lot, casually walked over to the *Crown Liquors* store, removed two submachine guns from a paper bag, and killed a Colombian drug trafficker and his bodyguard.

- A man named **Harold Ackerman**, the Cali cartel's man in Miami, did $56 million in business in Miami in the ten months before his arrest in the early 1990s. He lived in a North Miami Beach home.

- Attorney **Juan Acosta**, whose clients included Augusto Falcón and Sal Magluta, was gunned down by a Colombian hit squad in his Miami office two days after receiving a subpoena to testify about his clients.

- The elegant and opulent **Brickell Avenue** became the banking center of the Miami's cocaine gangs. In 1982, 44 American banks were licensed to make international transactions and 36 foreign banks opened local branches with Brickell addresses.

- **Don Aronow (1927-1987)**, owner of the *Cigarette Racing Team Manufacturing Company*, was murdered on NE 188th Street in North Miami Beach, when he began to sell his famed Cigarette go-fast boats to the Coast Guard.

- The posh bayside Coral Gables neighborhood of **Cocoplum** was home to several high-profile traffickers, including Colombian kingpin *Hernán Arboleda*, who in May, 1996, fled his waterfront mansion at 286 Costanera Rd., leaving behind more than three million dollars in art, jewelry, and furnishings. His abrupt departure came just hours before federal drug agents were scheduled to search his opulent home.

(Continued)

Photos: **Don Aronow**, the designer, builder and racer of the *Cigarette* speed boats; the exclusive **Cocoplum** neighborhood in Coral Gables.

(Continuation)

- Don Johnson, the actor playing **Sonny Crockett** in the TV series *Miami Vice*, drove a *Ferrari*, wore *Versace* suits, and lived on a *sailboat* with his pet alligator Elvis. During *Miami Vice*'s run, Crockett's vessel was docked at the Miami Beach Marina (300 Alton Rd.) and the Bayside Marina (401 Biscayne Blvd.) Neither *Crockett* nor *Don Johnson* were ever involved in any illegal deal.

- **Dean Investments International** was a fake corporation set up by the FBI and DEA agents in a *Miami Lakes* shopping center as part of *Operation Swordfish*. As an investment, firm it laundered about $19 million for various drug dealers. This money-laundering sting led to the indictment of 61 drug dealers.

- The company **843 Auto Sales** was a car dealership at 843 NW 27th Ave. that provided *Miami River Cops* with vehicles.

- *Armando "Mandy" Fernández*, owner of the prized luxury-car dealership **The Collection** in Coral Gables, was indicted on drug-trafficking charges in 1993. Federal agents seized the business after the indictment of the former speedboat champ. Fernández was sentenced to eighteen years in prison after pleading guilty. Thanks to his ex-business partner, developer *Ugo Colombo* (an honest man), *The Collection* still continues doing business at 200 Bird Rd. in Coral Gables.

- **Rafael** and **Ray Corona**, father and son, were convicted in 1987 of racketeering. The feds busted them using a marihuana smuggler's money to buy South Miami based *Sunshine State Bank*. In a 1991 sworn affidavit, Ray Corona admitted to laundering tens of millions of dollars for convicted drug dealers Augusto Falcón and Sal Magluta.

(Continued)

*Photos: **Sonny Crockett**, the pretend-cop from Miami Vice; **Sal Magluta**, a real life Miami drug-dealer; and the poster for a celebrated documentary of the times.*

(Continuation)

- An apparently solid Miami financial institution, **Great American Bank of Dade County**, had the distinction of being the first to go down as part of *Operation Greenback* in 1982. Four bank officials were charged with laundering some $96 million in drug proceeds.

- The waterfront condominium complex **Harbour House** was the site where cocaine smugglers *Jon Roberts* and *Mickey Munday* posted girls in upper-floor apartments to serve as lookouts, watching for law-enforcement officials patrolling *Haulover Cut* in search of drug boats.

- Brian De Palma filmed the gruesome chainsaw scene in the Al Pacino's movie *Scarface*, at **Johnny Rockets**, a well known restaurant at 728 Ocean Dr., on the *Sun Ray Apartments*.

- *Jones Boat Yard*, at 3399 NW South River Drive, was a repair yard on the Miami River where corrupt Miami cops raided a fishing boat docked there and ripped off some 400 kilos of coke as the crewmen jumped into the river. Three non-swimming low level mobsters drowned, triggering the **Miami River Cops scandal**.

(Continued)

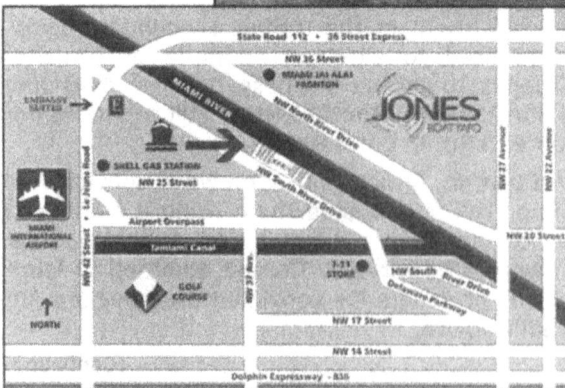

Photos: the water-front condominium from where drug lords in Miami kept glamorous girls as lookouts on **Haulover Cut** to warn of unusual activities by the feds; **Jones Boat Yard** on the Miami River.

(Continuation)

- **Severo Escobar**, a local operative for Colombian trafficker *José "Pepe" Cabrera Sarmiento*, was charged in 1992 with distributing some 15,000 pounds of cocaine. Feds grabbed a luxury Brickell condo, an expensive condo in Key Biscayne, a six bedroom home in Miami, and several properties in Hialeah.

- The **Federal Bureau of Investigations** had a payroll of over 700 special agents and support personnel to combat federal violators from Florida to Chile. Its North Miami Beach office was located at 16320 NW 2nd Avenue.

- A speed race took place in **Florida's Turnpike** in April 1979 between Colombian hit man *Conrado "El Loco" Valencia Zalgado* and rival drug runners who were trying to evade him. Valencia opened fire with his MAC-10; after the shootout, authorities found a handcuffed corpse in *El Loco's* abandoned car.

- A Miami county commissioner, **Joe Gersten**, reported on the morning of April 30, 1992, that his *Mercedes* had been stolen from his Coral Gables home. A small-time drug dealer and a hooker told police they robbed Gersten at knifepoint while he was smoking a rock with another prostitute in a dope house on NE 31st Street, just east of Biscayne Boulevard. Gersten fled to Australia rather than face prosecution; never returned to Miami.

Photos: **Severo Escobar IV**, son of *Severo Escobar III*, both notorious Miami drug smugglers. Severo IV was the nephew of **Pablo Escobar Gaviria**, *Il Capo de Medellín*; **Joe Guesten**, the infamous Dade County Commissioner, dressed here as an Australian Barrister. He moved to Sydney after being implicated in a drug-prostitution case in the 1990s; finally, the filming of the chain-saw scene in **Scarface** at Ocean Drive in Miami Beach.

Radio Martí 1180
Marathon Key, FL

RADIO Marti

The first U.S. broadcast to Cuba, as early as 1960, was **Radio Swan**, a station launched to support the Bay of Pigs invasion in 1961; it eventually led to **Radio Martí** and **La Voz de Fundación**. Jorge Mas Canosa was involved in all three operations, first as a former broadcaster with *Radio Swan*, later as president of the *Cuban American National Foundation* (which ran *La Voz de la Fundación*), and finally as the head of *Radio Martí's* Advisory Board.

Radio Martí's history began with a speech in 1981 by US President Reagan, where he declared that it was his intention to open a *Radio Free Cuba*, similar to *Radio Free Europe*. On October 4, 1983, Ronald Reagan signed the **Radio Broadcasting to Cuba Act, Public Law 98-111**. Unlike *Radio Free Europe*, *Radio Martí* was to be managed by *Voice of America*. Fidel Castro and liberal members of the U.S. Congress, complained and Cuba threatened to broadcast Cuban stations on frequencies interfering with commercial U.S. stations. The US ignored such threats and *Radio Martí* transmissions began on May 20, 1985 (1160 kHz) with 14 1/2 hours of programming using existing transmitters in Marathon Key, Florida (*shown above*). **Radio Martí** began to monitor Cuban radio, review Cuban publications, interview Cuban immigrants, defectors and visitors; they aimed to supplement what domestic broadcasts in Cuba were not presenting to the general public in the island. Within months, programming hours increased and included such items as news, entertainment, soap operas and messages by Miami's Cuban-Americans to their relatives on the island.

After its first transmissions from *Marathon Key*, the *New York Times*, in March of 1986, editorialized that contrary to their previous statements, *Radio Martí* was indeed filling a void in Cubans' desires to receive news, adding that *Radio Martí* was not simply broadcasting anti-Castro propaganda but rather supplementing the doctored news that Cuban audiences were getting from their government. The *NYTimes* even admitted that *Radio Martí* was the most-listened-to radio station in the island, that its ratings were always beating those of the official stations broadcasting in the island, and that it was an alternative to the monologue Fidel Castro had sustained with the Cuban people for decades.

On October 1985, **Amancio Suárez**, a Cuban exile entrepreneur, started **Radio Mambí, WAQI- 710 AM**, under the direction of **Armando Pérez Roura**, with the cooperation of **Agustín Tamargo, Juan Amador Rodríguez** and **Tomás Regalado**. It soon became the most popular radio station in Miami and South Florida. At the time **Salvador Lew** (future director of *Radio Marti*) was managing *WRHC Cadena Azul* and **Tomás García Fusté**, was the director of *WQBA, La Cubanísima*. Some radio personalities are shown below.

Photos, top to bottom, left to right.
First Row: **Salvador Lew, Tomás García Fusté, Agustín Tamargo, Armando Pérez Roura;** *Second Row:* **Enrique Encinosa, Ninoska Pérez Castellón, Felo Ramirez, Bernadette Pardo;** *Third Row:* **Oscar Haza, Marta Flores, Lourdes D'Kendall** and **Agustin Acosta.**

Delia Fiallo (1918-), born in Cuba, started writing novels in Havana in 1949 and wrote her first TV soap opera in 1957. She finished a doctorate in *Filosofía y Letras* at the *University of Havana* and in 1948 received the *Hernández Catá* prize for her novel "*El Otro.*" In 1951, she began to write for Cuban radio and later for Cuban TV.

Since those days, more than 1.6 billion people worldwide have seen her TV novels, starting with "*Lucecita*" (1967), "*La Señorita Elena*" (1968), "*Rosario,*" "*Esmeralda*" and "*Lisa, Mi Amor*" (1969), "*Peregrina*" (1973), "*La Zulianita*" and "*Rafaela*" (1975), "*Maria del Mar*" (1979), "*Emilia*" (1980), "*Leonela*" (1983), "*Topacio*" (1984), "*Cristal*" (1985) and "*Fabiola*" (1989). It has been said about her that «*nobody like Delia Fiallo has been better at developing scenes and techniques that maintain the suspense of its viewers from day to day.*»

With a remarkable discipline she became so popular throughout the Hispanic world that often she hardly had time to formalize her ideas on paper and had to dictate entire chapters of her scripts over the phone. Her greatest success occurred in Caracas after she went into exile in the 1960s. Her novels have been translated into eight languages and her TV soaps have been best sellers in many countries thanks to these translations. She most often included valuable information for everyday life in her novels. "*La Zulianita,*" for instance, contains a lesson in family planning; "*Crystal*" (1985) was the novel that won for her the European market. It called attention to women listeners about the importance of annual mammograms; "*Leonela*" —probably her more successful TV Series— had a message about adoption and abortion, as well as the consequences of alcohol dependency; "*Esmeralda*" (1970) was the first soap opera to hit the export market in Latin America. It was written in Venezuela; "*Lucecita*" (1967), the first novel she wrote when she went into exile in 1966, has always been her favorite. Since she left, she has never been back to Cuba.

Driven by frustration and impotence, Cuban exiles in the late 1980s were protagonists of two incidents that exacerbated the divisions and distrust among those who were relentless opponents to anything coming from Cubans in Cuba and those who felt that not everything originating in Cuba was tainted by a loyalty to the Cuban Communist regime.

The first incident was the 1986 selection of **Dolores Prida's** play **Coser y Cantar** for Miami's *First Annual Festival of Hispanic Theater*. Prida was a supporter of the revolution and had participated in the 1987 **diálogo**. The opposition of Cuban exiles to Prida's involvement provided an excuse for **Carl Hiassen**, the re-current *Miami Herald* offender of Cubans, to call Prida's opponents «*the always present Cuban drooling zealots*». More than anything else, Cuban exiles were indignant by the inclusion of Prida in the same stage where a work by **René Ariza**, a victim of Castro's prisons, would also be presented. In the end, Prida was asked to retire her play to another venue in Miami.

The second incident was the 1988 auction sale of four paintings by Cuban artists living in Cuba who supported Castro's revolution: Manuel Mendive, Mariano Rodríguez, Raúl Martínez and Carmelo González. The auction was organized as a fund raiser by the **Cuban Museum of Art and Culture** of Little Havana. During the auction, **José Juara**, a Cuban exile veteran of the **2506 Brigade**, bought a Mendive painting for $400 and burned it on the Museum entrance. The incident resulted in numerous headaches for the auction organizer **Ramón Cernuda**, the almost eviction of the Museum from city-owned property, the erosion of the Museum's financial support and its eventual closing for lack of funds.

Photos, top to bottom, left to right:
Manuel Mendive; poster for **Coser y Cantar**; the **Cuban Museum of Art and Culture**; the painting **El Pavo Real** by Manuel Mendive.

Esperanza Bravo de Varona is a Professor and Director of *the Cuban Heritage Collection* at the *University of Miami. She* graduated from the *University of Havana* with a degree in the liberal arts and a degree in *Library Sciences*. After coming into exile in 1965, she received a Master's Degree in *Library Sciences* from *Florida State University*.

The *Cuban Heritage Collection* comprises thousands of documents, books, periodicals and other valuable archival materials that span across 400 years of the history of Cuba. Many of its materials have been digitized and are available online, particularly photographs and historical documents. In 2009, the **Roberto C. Goizueta Foundation** granted the collection a $2.5 Million donation to sustain and increase the reach of its collection.

Esperanza de Varona, joined the faculty of the *University of Miami* as a newly arrived political exile. She has worked tirelessly to preserve and expand the collection and promote the history of Cuba, its culture and the accomplishments of Cubans of all times, including old and new Cuban exiles. Other extraordinary pioneering scholars and researchers at the *Cuban Heritage Collection* include **Rosa Abella, Ana Rosa Núñez** and **Lesbia O. de Varona**.

The Cuban Heritage Collection's extensive holdings include not only some 100,000 issues of those "little newspapers (*periodiquitos*) in exile," but also close to 45,000 rare and contemporary books; periodicals published in Cuba since the Colonial period to the present; and archival materials that include manuscripts, maps, photographs, illustrations, postcards, posters, audio and video tapes, and memorabilia.

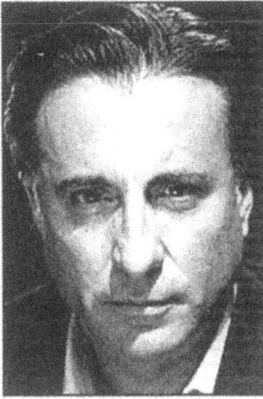

Andy García Menéndez (1956-) is a clear example of the opportunities offered to Cuban exiles in the US. He was born in Havana; his father René was an attorney and farmer and his mother Amelia an English teacher. When he was five years old his family went into exile in Miami after the failure of the *Bay of Pigs* invasion. He attended *Miami Beach Senior High* and played basketball and baseball, while his family developed a million dollar perfume business. He began his acting career while a High School senior and continued it at *Florida International University* in Miami, working with such novel actors as *Brett Ratner, Mickey Rourke* and *Luther Campbell*. He is one of Hollywood's most successful leading men and is admired as a friendly, immensely talented, down-to-earth and all-around good guy.

After graduation he went to Hollywood where he debuted with two small roles: in *Murder she Wrote* and in the first episode of *Hill Street Blues*, where he played a gang member. His career began to emerge as he was cast by Brian de Palma (in **The Untouchables** as George Stone, the Italian G-Man working with Elliot Ness) and Francis Ford Copola (in **Godfather III**, as *Vincent Mancini*, the illegitimate son of Sonny Corleone). For that role he competed, and won, over *Val Kilmer, Alec Baldwin, Vincent Spano, Charlie Sheen,* and *Robert De Niro.* The part won him an **Oscar** as *Best Supporting Actor* and catapulted him into international stardom.

In 2005 he co-wrote, directed and starred in **The Lost City** (titled **Adieu Cuba** in the French version), an anti-Castro film he had dreamed of putting together for 16 years. Altogether, he has acted in 66 films and TV series, produced 14 movies and directed 7 films. He owns 25 conga drums; was the sweetheart of *Carmen* in *Qué pasa, USA?* He has been invited to the *Havana Film Festivals* several times but has always declined because of his opposition to the regime.

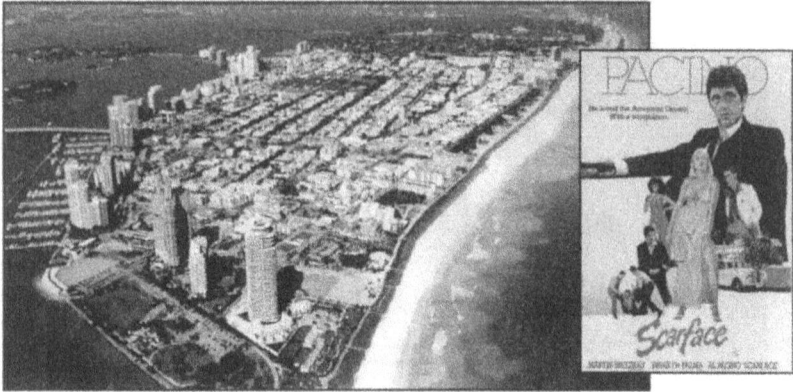

The area of Miami that was most affected by both the influx of **Marielitos** and the activities of the **Cocaine Cowboys** was *South Beach*. It is an area south of *Indian Creek Road,* occupying the 23 southernmost blocks of Miami Beach. In the 1890 it was a huge co-conut plantation; in the 1910s it became urbanized by the construc-tion of the *Collins Bridge* by **John Collins** and **Carl Fisher** (later called the *Venetian Causeway)* in the 1920s and the *MacArthur Causeway* in the 1940s. Given the mild weather and fabulous beaches, the best lots of South Beach were soon grabbed by people like *Harvey Firestone, J.C. Penney, Albert Champion* and *Rockwell La Gorce.* Black people —African Americans that had helped build many of the original *Art Deco* buildings— were not permitted to live anywhere near the private residencies of the richest families in the US. Jewish people were also subjected to Jim Crow laws and were not allowed to live north of Fifth Street, although later many Syna-gogues and Yiddish Theatres were built in the area South of Fifth.

Following Pearl Harbor, *South Beach* was invaded by the *Army Air Corps* and after the war it became a retirement community with most of its ocean-front hotels and apartment buildings filled with elderly people living on small, fixed incomes. In the 1980s both the **Marielitos** and the **Cocaine Cowboys** found the natural beauty and low prices of the area and moved in. South Beach became a peculiar mix of drug mobsters, Cuban *Marielitos* and little old ladies. Yet in the late 1980s, the *beautiful* people began to move in.

In a few years, a true demographic renaissance began with an in-flux of photography and apparel trade industry professionals and real estate moguls. *South Beach* became a fashion and a gay Mec-ca; as always, it continued to be one part drifter grounds and one part fantasyland, a destination for persuasive con-men and una-bashed tricksters and deceivers. As some of the best citizens of *South Beach* used to say «*if you have not been indicted you're not invited.*» *South Beach*, to this day, is *a* surreal combination of Hol-lywood and Vegas, a place of wealth but also of desperation, an is-land of broken illusions that casts an irresistible allure.

Photos: the **South Beach** area in the 1980s and the poster
for Al Pacino's **Scarface**, a tale of *Marielitos* in South Beach.

V

«Rhetoric is a poor substitute for action, and we are trusting
only to rhetoric. If we are really to be a great nation,
we must not merely talk; we must act big.»

THEODORE ROOSEVELT, 1858 – 1919, US PRESIDENT
AT THE TIME OF CUBAN INDEPENDENCE.

«Marxism has been tremendously fashionable in our time,
so it has infected a very large number of major institutions
in many countries of the world. I suppose that we shouldn't be
too surprised that it should infect the Church as well.»

JEANE KIRKPATRICK, FORMER US SECRETARY OF STATE.

A Long Awaited Vulnerability
Castro Survived Chaos after the fall of the Soviets

«*IF THE SOVIETS WITHDRAW their support from Cuba to-morrow, the Cuban problem will be solved in 48 hours,*» were the words of Jorge Mas Canosa, head of the Cuban American National Foundation, at a conference organized by the University of Miami in May of 1990, a few days before a scheduled Washington meeting between US President George H. Bush and Soviet President Mikhail Gorbachev. The response by Georgii Arbatov, a close adviser to Gorbachev was «*Cuba remains our friend. We offer no hope that assistance to Cuba would end any time soon.*»

There were clearly neither *Perestroika* [4] nor *Glasnost* [5] oppor-

---

[4] The program of economic and political reform, reconstruction and reorganization in the Soviet Union initiated by Mikhail Gorbachev in 1986-87.

[5] Policy permitting open discussion of political and social issues and freer dissemination of news and information, also started by Gorbachev in 1995.

tunities in Cuba; no opportunity for self-determination; no intention on the part of the Soviets to influence or interfere in Cuba's internal affairs; no will on the part of the Castros to make changes from inside as was happening in the Soviet Union. These events were not surprising to anyone following the deteriorating Cuba-USSR relations since the 1980s. Outwardly the Soviets were supporting Castro. Internally they were not. During the presidency of Gorbachev the Soviet leaders began to question the basic tenets of the Marxist-Leninist credos; slowly, they began to transform economic structures and political alliances and even started to seek an amicable accommodation with the US. Castro was caught by surprise since his survival was based on a fierce ideological divide between the US and the USSR. He took the side of those organizing an abortive coup against Gorbachev and his reformers, and very late realized he had taken the wrong side. To spank Castro and show him who was the boss, Gorbachev announced a symbolic unilateral withdrawal of a training brigade of nearly 3,000 Soviet troops from Cuba. It was followed by a substantive reduction of military supplies and funds for training programs; from there on such services had to be paid; they were no longer gifted. Cuba saw its military defenses vulnerable and imperiled. Eventually it was a much wider phenomenon that Castro had visualized and he was caught, perhaps for the first time, "sleeping at the wheel."

Cuba at the end of the Cold War

The early 1990s were witness to a drastic alteration of world politics. The Cold War (a term coined by George Orwell in 1945) was coming to an end. The period of peace without military action but with fear (because a mutual assured destruction between the US and the USSR or between NATO and the COMECON), was brought to completion. No more proxy wars, military coalitions, strategic conventional force deployments, arms races or even rivalry at sporting events. Also, presumably, no more assistance to Communist revolutions, threats of nuclear warfare, ethnic or revolutionary wars, refugee and displaced person crises, political intimidations or subversions.

Interestingly, historians, political scientists and journalists have never been in agreement as to who started the Cold War. Some attribute guilt to the Soviet Union for having unilaterally expanded its sphere of influence into Eastern Europe after WWII. Others blame the US for its efforts to isolate and condemn the Soviet Union ideologically even before the end of WWII. What has been shown to be evident, however, is that Marxist leaning dictators outside the Soviet Union (in Cuba, Nicaragua and later Venezuela) completely ignored the demise and rejection of Marxism by the Soviets and made sure their power grab would continue, not with ideological and material inspiration from Mother Russia but, if need be, as pauper and indigent free lancers of revolution and chaos.

The end of the Cold War brought no changes in Cuba and therefore no changes in the US policy towards the Cuban revolution. Cuba became a pariah in the eyes of its former socialist partners. The Hungarians, the Polish, the Czechs and the Russians left her to rot and try to survive on its own. Within Cuba, however, a power struggle was inevitable. Castro reacted to the end of Soviet magnanimity by imposing a harsher rationing system. Factories were told to reduce working hours or close. *Bona fide* economists were startled by the absurd solutions the *máximo líder* had found, yet they were used to similar stupidities like *Café Caturla* planted in city patios, *midget cows* growing in chests of drawers, tasteless *microjet bananas*, 10-Million-Tons *sugar crops*, the sexual exploitation of *Ubre Blanca*, the *bionic super-cow*, the dehydration of the *Zapata Swamp*, and others).

To make matters worse, oil prices at the end of the Cold War were climbing and sugar prices decreasing. No Soviet subsidies were promised anymore (only comforting words but no cash), no ideological support, no funds for international adventures like in the early 1980s; it suggested the inevitability of a Cuban economic collapse. In fact, with the severe shortage of gasoline, diesel, foodstuffs and cash (due to the implosion of the oil-rich Soviet Union and the end of its favorable provisions of fuels — below market— and foreign exchange to Cuba), began years of run-away deprivations in the island during what was called the *"período especial"* that included, on August 5, 1994, a brief uprising known as the *"maleconazo."*

The old Soviet bloc had accounted for 85% of trade in Cuba; most of the trade had been barters (oil, raw materials and spare parts for sugar, fruits and the like). The situation became desperate in Cuba when commercial relations with the Soviet bloc and oil shipments were reduced by 90%, from $9 Billion in 1989 to less than $650 million in 1994. The dislocation of industrial and basic supplies was worse than those experienced in 1960 when Castro confiscated all American investments in Cuba.

Some enlightened Marxist economists inside Cuba urged Castro to either start heavy investments in tourism, facilitate visits and remittances from the *"US Cuban community,"* or normalize relations with the US government; these were seen as the only three viable sources of cash and survival. The orthodox and Marxist purists objected; the pragmatists pushed for any or all of these solutions.

Cuban exiles and the ethics of re-engagement with Castro

Within the exile ranks, similar power struggles took place. Jorge Mas Santos, son of Jorge Mas Canosa (strong anti-Castro leader, deceased in 1997), and heir apparent to the Presidency of the Cuban American National Foundation (CANF) began a quiet campaign for reconciliation and compromise with Castro's Cuba, even if CANF had to use the *Antonio Maceo Brigade* leaders to vouch for their good intentions. Most historical exiles (1959-1979), including Armando Valladares and several hundred political prisoners already in Miami, were opposed to any agreements with the Cuban authorities. The *post-1980 expatriates*, almost in unison, favored the talks with the Cuban regime.

Re-engagement with Cuba was also a subject of conversation in Washington. Reagan and Bush 41, as well as most Republicans, were *hawks* (militant anti-Castro) while most Democrats and many members of Congress from agricultural states were *doves* (pro-Castro or ready to talk to Castro). In the meantime, some tentative steps were taken by the US Congress. *Radio Martí* doubled-up as *Radio and TV Martí*, in spite of serious doubts that the TV signals could be easily intercepted by Castro. Congress passed an amendment to the *Trading with the Enemy Act*, lifting the ban on interchange of informational materials to and from Cuba, as well as the *Torricelli Act*, prohibiting any exports to Cuba except for humanitarian reasons.

Desperate Cubans began to take to the high seas and show up in Miami, one balsa at a time rather than in flotillas. It was estimated that 30% of them died in the effort. The Cuban government began to prosecute anyone trying to escape through that route. Cubans with proper tourist papers began to overstay their legal visits in the US and then seek exile status. Those exiting Cuba in the direction of Mexico had an advantage: they had no need to declare an anti-Castro position. Mexico welcomed them without requiring to denounce Marxism. More than 5,000 Cubans moved semi-permanently to Mexico (they could return to Cuba any time they wanted, no questions asked). Most of them were writers, artists, poets, professors, musicians and *"creative intellectuals."* Many exiles called them the *"cuerdaflojistas."*

Many academics in Cuba began to study the craving of Cubans in the island to go into exile or simply their yearning to reach Miami; these scholars became known as the *"gusanólogos."* Many academic scholars in Miami became their superior and senior counterparts; for many years they had been known as the *"cubanólogos,"* US scholars studying Cuban events from the shores of Miami.

Under the influence of the *gusanólogos* the Cuban government made a move and relaxed the regulations for Cubans in the island to visit the US, and Miami became their magnet. People applying for a permit to go to the US no longer had to fear to be fired from their jobs; their children were no longer removed from good school programs, the *Comités de Defensa* in their neighborhoods did not accuse them as *escoria* (dregs) or harass them as traitors.

Cuban residents began to visit Miami (all documents, transportation and fees paid by Cubans in the US), met their families and friends, enjoyed real *picadillo* and other meats, drank Scotch, visited air-conditioned supermarkets and department stores, took rides in new cars, watched non-proselytizing TV, and then overstayed their visas or returned to the island. Everybody knew that the *Department of the Americas* of the *Central Committee of the Cuban Communist Party* had everything well planned and under control. *Granma* and *Juventud Rebelde*, the two only island-wide newspapers published by the Cuban *Politburó*, began to drop the term *"Miami Mafia"* and began to refer to Cubans in Miami as the «*Cuban Community living abroad.*»

A new breed of Cuban residents in Miami began to emerge while in the island the repression of dissidents and members of the opposition continued unabated. Financial charts in the *Department of the Americas* were showing how much hard currency would flow to Cuba if Cubans in Miami were enticed to visit the island. For that to happen, the Miami ranks had to be enlivened with pro-Castro sympathizers extolling and exalting visits to Cuba. The entire bureaucratic procedure of securing a re-entry visa in Cuba was simplified; those who wanted to visit the US and return to Cuba would surely come back with goods and favors that would alleviate the scarcities in the island (Castro was even promoting collective kitchens to save fuel); those who decided to stay in Miami would be the best sloganeers for the right of Cubans in the US to visit their families in Cuba. For Castro it was a win-win proposition and the two-way flow Miami-Cuba began to save Castro from the consequences of the Soviet devastating collapse. Miami became (competing with Canada) the main source of tourists travelling to Cuba; it remained so, well into the XXI century.

A Generational change of mind?

As the 1990s were coming to a close, the issue of *Diálogo* or *No-Diálogo* with the Cuban government remained unresolved. Something became evident forty years after the start of the revolutionary government in Cuba:

A generational change was occurring in the exile community. Old leaders were dying or were becoming too old, frail or disenchanted after so many years of an unproductive quest. They had little objection to the raising of new voices in their midst. They had neither the power nor the inclination to prevent or purge anyone because they lived and shared a free society. While things were getting tighter in Cuba, Miami was ceasing to be a center of political extremism; by the 1990s, a multitude of voices could be heard.

There was no generational change in Cuba, however. All attempts to bring it about never survived the rapacity of the original revolutionaries. The 1959 generation, particularly those who had earned their badges in the *Sierra Maestra*, would not open a space to younger revolutionaries having their own perceptions of what had to be done to keep the revolution alive and functional. New voices, after any conceptual disagreement with the old comrades, were silenced and condemned to meaningless responsibilities, low level work in the party or a future limited to mindless chores in the countryside. To many of them it was a *de-facto* social and economic ostracism.

Under those circumstances, most historical exiles agreed that Cuba's future was dependent on events that had to happen in Cuba but were not happening. No intervention by the US, Europe or any other powers, would dislodge the old Marxists from the helm. The future had to be defined by Cubans in Cuba, perhaps with moral and economic support from Cubans abroad, yet there were no voices that could be heard other than those that had been in charge for half a century; those with blood in their hands. There were no *new* leaders with whom to talk or dialogue.

Cuba remained impervious to what had happened across the world when the Eastern European countries began to liberate themselves from Marxism. After the loss of support by the Soviets, it began to seek a new magnanimous partner that could sustain its outdated political model. It would find it at the end of the 1990s in Hugo Chávez. Marxism continued to prevail in Cuba. To many Americans, Castro looked like one of those swamp mutants in the horror movies that are killed a thousand times but always reappears aggressively from under the waters; to Cuban exiles, Castro became a real life reminder of the truth in the old Spanish saying that goes «*Bicho malo nunca muere.*»

The
1990s

- On February 22, 1990, the **Fundación Nacional Cubano-Americana** announced it had provided grants to the *University of Miami* to start a **Fondo de Estudios Cubanos**, dedicated to research and information about the Cuban reality.
- On February 24, the **Unión de Ex-Presos Políticos Cubanos** and the **Comité Cubano de Derechos Humanos** in Caracas organized an international network based in Miami, which included numerous countries in the Americas, with the purpose of making known the Cuban tragedy.
- In March, the Venezuelan National **Chamber of Deputies** and several legislative Assemblies around the country condemned the Cuban government for its violations of Human Rights.
- In August of 1990, the **Plataforma Democrática Cubana** was founded in Madrid to coordinate the efforts of several exile organizations. A document was produced and signed by **Emilio Martínez Venegas**, **Roberto Fontanilla**, **Miguel González Pando**, **Ricardo Bofill**, **Carlos Alberto Montaner** and other exile leaders.
- Almost simultaneously, in Miami, a group of Cuban exiles launched the **Coordinadora Social Demócrata Cubana**, with leaders **Enrique Baloyra**, **Lino Bernabé Fernández** and others.
- Cubans in Caracas welcomed on September 5th the leader of the **Movimiento Solidaridad** de Polonia **Lech Walesa** to their **Quinto Congreso de Solidaridad de Trabajadores Cubanos.**
- In October, the **Movimiento de Canarias por la Libertad y Democracia en Cuba** turned itself into a chapter of **Cuba Independiente y Democrática** with **Francisco Benitez Pérez** as its leader.
- At the closing of the year 1990, **Andrés Vargas Gómez** founded in Miami the organization **Custodios de Nuestros Símbolos**, dedicated to honor and conserve the Cuban heritage in exile.

(Continued)

Photos above, on the left, top to bottom: **Ricardo Bofill**; **Carlos Alberto Montaner**; **Enrique Baloyra** and **Lech Walesa**. *On the right, members of the* **Comité Cubano Pro Derechos Humanos.** *Ricardo Bofill is the fourth person from the left.*

(Continuation)

- In January of 1991, the **Fundación Nacional Cubano-Americana** displayed in Miami an exhibition of "**Cárceles de Cuba**". The exhibition later traveled to Madrid, Paris and many other capitals around the world.
- At the end of January the VI Congreso de la **Federación Mundial de Presos Políticos Cubanos** took place in Union City, New Jersey. In Miami over 100,000 Cuban exiles participated in the **Marcha del Pueblo Unido** through the streets of the city. It was organized by a group of organizations under the umbrella name the **Gran Cumbre Patriótica**.
- In March, the **Comité Italiano por los Derechos Humanos en Cuba** published the document **Cuba 1990**, denouncing the systematic oppression by the Castro government. It was edited by **Laura González del Castillo**.
- On the 96th anniversary of the *Manifiesto de Montecristi*, in the Dominican Republic, the **Solidaridad de Trabajadores Cubanos** and the **Central Latinoamericana del Trabajo (CLAT)** organized in Caracas a street protest for the repression in Cuba.
- On April 16th, 1991, once more, the **Comisión de Derechos Humanos de las Naciones Unidas** condemned the Cuban regime for its anti-human record.
- The **Partido Demócrata Cristiano** held its first congress in Miami on May 5th, 1991.
- José Basulto, a **2506 Brigade** veteran, launched **Hermanos al Rescate** in Miami.
- In August of 1991, the **Federación Mundial de Presos Políticos** had its Congress in Los Angeles and in September **Cuba Independiente y Democrática** had its Annual Convention in Miami. **Andrés Vargas Gómez** launches **Unidad Cubana** in Miami, joining many Cuban exile organizations in a common front.

(Continued)

Photos below, left to right:

The **1991 Marcha del Pueblo** through the streets of Miami; the rally in Barcelona, showing a reproduction of an isolation cell in Cuban prisons.

(Continuation)

- On September 30th, over 300 **Cuban political prisoners** worked to re-build a house in Miami to make it their museum and meeting place.
- On October 25, 1991, activists from the **Directorio Revolucionario Democrático Cubano** chained themselves at the gate of **Cuba's Inter-est Section** in Washington, D.C., an action that would be repeated in 2003 in Paris by members of **Reporters Sans Frontières** and a large group of Cuban exiles in that city.
- In January of 1992 Cubans affiliated to a socialist non-totalitarian credo met in Miami in the first **Congreso Socialista Democrático en el Exilio**, electing **Manuel Fernández** as their president.
- In March, the **Comisión de Derechos Humanos de las Naciones Unidas** condemned again the Cuban regime for its anti-human record.
- In April, Cuban exiles in Moscow organized an international conference under the theme **Del Totalitarismo a la Democracia: la nueva Rusia y la Oposición Cubana**, with large attendance from Eastern Europeans.
- **Tony Cuesta**, leader of **Comandos L**, died in Miami on December 2. He had risked his life in over 30 raids and actions against the Cuban regime.

(Continued)

Photos above, top to bottom, left to right:

Robert Menard, president of **Reporters Sans Frontières**, chained to the gate of the Cuban Embassy in Paris in protest for the lack of freedom of the press in Cuba, April 3, 2003. It was a demonstration organized by Cuban exiles in Paris; **Casa del Preso in Havana**, Calle 275 No. 16024 entre 160 y Final, Rio Verde, La Habana; **Casa del Preso en Miami**, 1140 SW 13th Avenue; **Tony Cuesta**, leader of **Comandos L,** died in Miami at age 66.

(Continuation)

- In January of 1993, **Eloy Gutiérrez Menoyo**, ex-Commander of the rebel army in Cuba, organizes **Cambio Cubano**, an organization seeking a dialogue with Castro. Menoyo eventually moves to Havana but claims he continued to oppose Castro.

- The **Asociación por la Paz Continental (ASOPAZCO)** and other exile organizations mounted an exhibition in Rome entitled **Prisión y Balsas**, showing actual homemade rafts, photos, documents and scale models of jails in Cuba. **Roberto Jiménez**, **Juan Clark**, **Angel Cuadra** and other Cuban political prisoners traveled to Rome for the exhibition.

- On March 10, the **Comisión de Derechos Humanos de las Naciones Unidas**, once more, was informed that Cuba rejected the visit of Colombia's **Rafael Rivas Posada** and Sweden's **Carl Johns Groth** as investigators of violations of human rights in Cuba.

- The **Bureau de Prensa Independiente de Cuba** was organized in Havana with the support of Miami's Cuban exiles. **José Manuel Brito López** became its first director.

- In June of 1993, **Luis Zúñiga** was appointed director of Miami's **Fundación para los Derechos Humanos en Cuba**, an organization that in time would have 13 chapters around the world.

- In Miami, on September of 1993, **Rolando Borges** was elected General Secretary of the **Coordinadora Internacional de Ex Presos Políticos Cubanos**.

- In Miami the **Círculo de Periodistas Cubanos** replaced the defunct **Asociación de Reporteros Cubanos** that had been founded at the advent of the Republic. **José Carreño**, former political prisoner, is elected as president.

(Continued)

Photos below, top to bottom, left to right:

Maripaz Martínez Nieto, presidente de **ASOPAZCO,** at the presentation of the book **En La Pupila del Kremlin** by **Alvaro Alba**; **Luis Zúñiga,** Executive Director of the **Consejo por la Libertad de Cuba** and a member of the US delegation to the **UN Human Rights Commission**; a historical photo of journalists and *políticos* in the 1970s: **Horacio Aguirre, Maurice Ferré, Fausto Lavilla and Guillermo Martínez.**

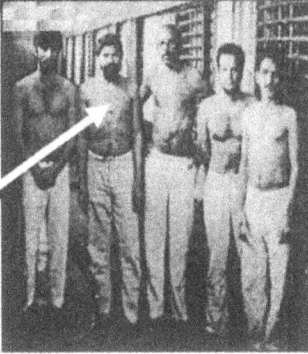

(Continuation)

- In 1994, in Stockholm, Sweden, Cuban exiles organize the **Unión de Cubanos en Suecia**.
- In Caracas, in April of 1994, hundreds of Cuban exiles honored **Mons. Eduardo Boza Masvidal** on the 50th anniversary of his ordination. Days later Cuban exile **Eduardo García Moure**, General Secretary of the **Central Latinoamericana de Trabajadores (CLAT)** presided the publication of the first issue of **Desafío**, a magazine for the working classes.
- On May 27th, **Rodolfo Frómeta** organized in Miami the **Comandos F-4**, a new organization seeking to overthrow the Cuban government.
- On July 13th 1994, in the northern coast of Cuba, the old tug boat **13 de Marzo**, with about 30 people on board, was attacked and sunk by four fast boats manned by Castro supporters. 41 persons died, including 10 children. Cuban exiles all around the world denounced this savage act.
- On August 5th, hundreds of residents of Havana rioted at the *malecón* seafront boulevard in what became known as the **maleconazo**. The exiles denounced the strong tactics of the secret police squelching the protest.
- The organization **Agenda Cuba** was launched in Miami by former members of **Organización Abdala**. Their purpose was to establish closer relations between the opposition in Cuba and the Cuban exiles.
- On August 30, several militants of the **Movimiento 30 de Noviembre** chained themselves to the entrance of the *Cuban delegation to the United Nations*. A violent reaction by the Cuban diplomats ensued.

(Continued)

Photos above, top to bottom, left to right:

Eduardo García Moure, world renown Cuban-born labor leader in Latin America; the logo of **Agenda Cuba;** a photo of **Rodolfo Frómeta** as a **Plantado** in a prison in Cuba (second from left, with an arrow); the entrance of the **Cuban Delegation to the UN**, with the glass door reflecting Cuban exiles picketing across the street. A police car is parked on the right.

(Continuation)

- In October of 1994 the **Comisión Interamericana de Derechos Humanos**, an organ of the **Organization of American States (OAS)** whose mission is to promote and protect human rights in the American hemisphere, denounced the deterioration of human rights in Cuba.
- Also in October, **Unidad Cubana**, as an umbrella organization, called for a demonstration in Miami calling it **La Marcha por la Libertad**. Hundreds of Cuban exiles participated in the march during the month of December.
- At the end of 1994 **CubaNet** was founded in Miami as a non-profit organization dedicated to the promotion of a free press in Cuba.
- On April 18th 1995 **Sergio Perodín** and his son, two survivors of the **Tugboat 13 de Marzo** massacre, presented a description of the incident at two different sessions of the **Congreso de la República de Venezuela**; the Senate on July 26 and the Chamber of Deputies on June 21.
- On July 13th of 1995, the first **Flotilla Democracia**, organized by the **Comisión Nacional Cubana** in Miami, was attacked in Cuban territorial waters by the Cuban Coast Guard. **Ramón Saúl Sánchez**, the group leader, announced on the high seas that the organization would continue to harass the Cuban government during future expeditions.
- On August 11, **Václav Havel**, president of the Czech Republic, issued a document entitled **S.O.S. from Cuba**, condemning the abuses in Cuba.

(Continued)

Photos below, top to bottom, left to right:

The **Marcha por la Libertad** organized by **Unidad Cubana** in Miami; the **CubaNet** logo; protests in Madrid for the massacre of the tug boat **13 de Marzo**; a poster announcing the trip in front of Cuban waters by **Movimiento Democracia**; **Václav Havel**, good friend of Cuban exiles and Cuba's freedom.

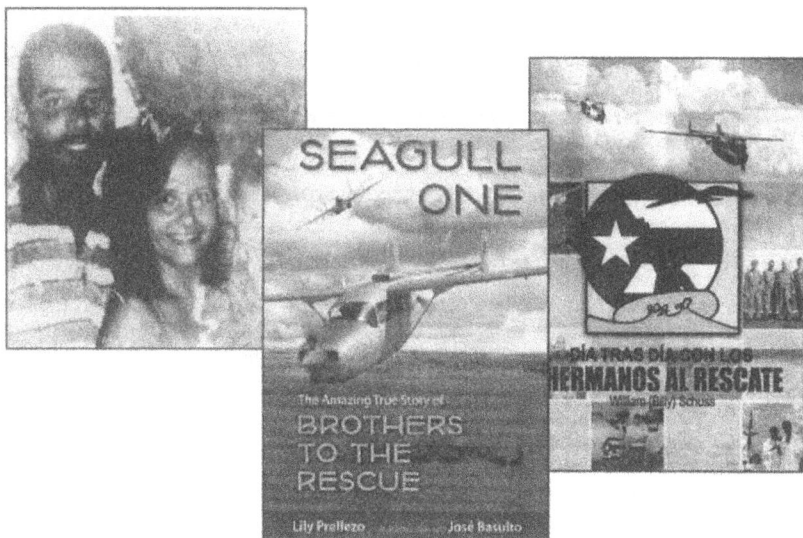

(Continuation)

- On September 2, 1995, **Ramón Saúl Sánchez** left Key West in the second **Flotilla Democracia** towards the waters in front of Havana. The flotilla had to return due to bad weather after the ship *Sundown II* shipwrecked causing the death of **Lázaro Gutiérrez** a *Democracia* activist.

- On October 10th, several exile organizations with followers in Cuba joined efforts under the name **Concilio Cubano**. It brought together professional, political, labor-oriented and human rights organizations of Cubans in Cuba and Cuban exiles across the US, Europe and Latin America. Together they supported a peaceful transition in Cuba. The Steering Committee included 11 mayor organizations and had plans to hold a general meeting in early 1996. In February of 1996, the Cuban political police arrested **Leonel Morejón Almagro**, founder of **Concilio Cubano** in Cuba, and impeded the realization of the general meeting in Habana.

- At the end of October, Castro visited New York to participate in the **General Assembly of the United Nations** and was received with multiple demonstrations by Cuban exiles.

- Throughout 1995 several exile organizations from the **Comité Unido del Exilio Cubano** organized numerous civil disobedience marches in Miami that interrupted traffic and were not well received by Miamians.

- On February 24, 1996, several MIGS M-29 from Cuba shot down two unarmed Cessna Skymaster 337 planes of **Hermanos al Rescate**, causing the deaths of pilots **Armando Alejandre Jr**, **Mario de la Peña**, **Carlos Costa** and **Pablo Morales**.

- The Venezuela chapter of the **Comité Cubano pro Derechos Humanos** obtained from the Venezuelan Senate a resolution condemning the shooting of the **Hermanos al Rescate** planes and the oppression in Cuba that prevented the meetings of **Concilio Cubano**.

(Continued)

Photos above, left to right:

Leonel Morejón Almagro and his family, a champion of non-violent means of change who had promoted many *Peace Congresses* within Cuba and was the coordinator of *Concilio Cubano* in the island; two books published after the MIG attacks on *Hermanos al Rescate*: **Seagull One** and **Día tras Día.**

(Continuation)

- In April of 1996, over 70,000 Cuban exiles met at the **Orange Bowl Stadium** in Miami in a public act honoring the memories of the dead pilots of *Hermanos al Rescate*, **Armando Alejandre Jr**, **Mario de la Peña**, **Carlos Costa** and **Pablo Morales**. **Sylvia Iriondo**, President of *Mar por Cuba* and one of the survivors of the attacks on the Cessnas, and **Madeleine Albright**, former US Secretary of State, were speakers.

- The **Federación Internacional de Editores de Diarios**, representing more than 15,000 newspapers in over 100 countries, recognized the work of Cuban exile **Indamiro Restano** and gave him its **1996 Pluma de Oro de la Prensa** for his struggles in favor of a free press in Cuba. Because of his legendary leftist past, his unconventional demeanor and outlandish comments, **Restano** never gained the support of Cuban exiles in Miami.

- In Paris, **Laurent Muller** organized the **Association Européenne Cuba Libre** and began to denounce the persistent assaults of the Cuban regime on human rights and freedom of the press. In time the association would be joined by many Cuban exiles and would set up weekly protests in front of the Cuban embassy in Paris. They were always joined by **Françoise Hostelier**, former member of Chirac's cabinet, and many other important French political leaders. The association began to publish the magazine **Nouvelles de Cuba** on September 15, 1996.

- Numerous groups of Cuban exiles disseminated across their communities in the US, Europe and Latin America, the document **La Patria es de Todos**, issued in Cuba on June 27, 1997 by opponents **Marhta Beatriz Roque Cabello**, **Félix Bonne Carcasses**, **René Gómez Manzano** and **Vladimiro Roca**.

(Continued)

Photos below, top to bottom:

Madeleine Albright's book **Madam Secretary; Indamiro Restano**, founder of **Armonía**, a Catholic non-violent Christian Democrat opposition group in Cuba. He was sentenced in May 1992 to 10 years in prison, founded the **Asociación de Periodistas Independientes de Cuba** and went into exile in 1995; the four authors of **La Patria es de Todos**, **Gómez Manzano, Bonne Carcasses, Roque Cabello** and **Vladimiro Roca**; **Laurent Muller**, relentless defender of Cuban freedom in Paris.

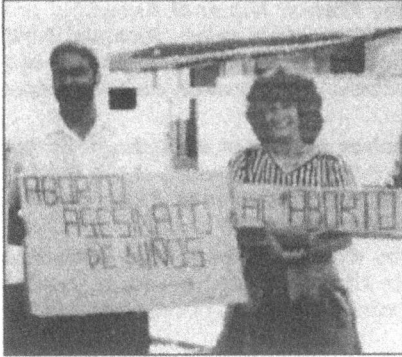

(Continuation)

- In October of 1997, as the **Asociación de Ex-Presos Politicos Cubanos** organized a massive concentration at the **José Martí Park** in Miami, the US Coast Guard intercepted a luxury yacht full of weapons trying to reach the **Isla Margarita** in the coast of Venezuela, where Castro was participating at a meeting of the **Cumbre Iberoamericana**.

- On December 7 of that year **Angel de Fana, José Pujals, Mario Chanes de Armas** and other former Cuban political prisoners launched **Plantados hasta la Libertad de Cuba** at a meeting in Miami. Most members of this new organization had completed 20 years of incarceration in Castro prisons.

- In 1997 Oscar Elías Biscet founded in Havana the **Fundación Lawton de Derechos Humanos**. It immediately was fully and enthusiastically supported by Cuban exiles around the world.

- In Paris, French President Jacques Chirac bestowed upon **Elizardo Sánchez Santa Cruz** the **French Prize for Human Rights**.

- **Pope John Paul II** visited Havana late in January of 1998. Hundreds of youngsters received him at the entrance steps of the *University of Havana*. Hundreds also marched from the *Cathedral of Havana* up to the *Plaza Cívica* (or Plaza de la Revolución) with an image of the *Virgin of Charity*, patroness of Cuba. At the Plaza, **Karla Pérez de Zambrano**, an activist for **Liga Cívica Martiana**, raised a sign reading **Abajo la Dictadura de los Hermanos Castro**. She was immediately detained.

(Continued)

Photos above, top to bottom, left to right:
The poster for the **VII meeting of the Cumbre Iberoamericana**, in *Isla Margarita* on October of 1997; The founders of **Plantados hasta la Libertad y la Democracia en Cuba**: standing, **Mario Chanes, Ernesto Díaz Rodríguez** and **Julio Ruiz Pitaluga**. Sitting, **Eusebio Peñalver** and **Angel De Fana**. Missing, **José L. Pujals Mederos**; Dr. **Oscar Elías Biscet** and his wife **Elsa Morejón** denouncing abortion in Cuba. Both were fired from the *Sistema Nacional de Salud* for their work for human rights in Cuba.

(Continuation)

- In March of 1998, the **Movimiento Cristiano de Liberación**, under the leadership of **Osvaldo Payá**, announced it was in the process of obtaining 10,000 signatures to demand from the **Asamblea Nacional del Poder Popular** a referendum to update the laws and treatment of Cubans in the island. The project became known as **Proyecto Varela**. (Ed. See page 528)
- On April 1, in Paris, the **Asociación Europea Cuba Libre (AECL)** published a 125-page report on human rights in Cuba. It was widely distributed to the press, all members of the **French National Assembly** and the members of the **UN Human Rights Commission**. **Ricardo Bofill** and **Rolando Borges** joined **Laurent Muller**, president of the **AECL**, at a press conference presenting this document in the **Maison de l'Amerique Latine** in Paris.
- The **Comité Italiano por los Derechos Humanos en Cuba**, with **Pax Christi** and a large number of Cuban exiles held a meeting at the *European Parliament* in Brussels with the theme **Inversiones Extranjeras y Derechos de los Trabajadores en Cuba**.
- In Caracas, on March 18, 1999, the **Comité Cubano Pro Derechos Humanos** obtained from the *Senate of the Rep*ublic a vote to request from the government in Cuba the release from prison of the signers of the document **La Patria es de Todos**.
- **Václav Havel**, as President of the Czech Republic, secured a condemning declaration for abuses in Cuba from the **UN Human Rights Commission**.
- On September 24 the **School of Journalism of Columbia University** awarded **Raúl Rivero** its *María Moors Cabot Prize* for his defense of freedom of the press in Cuba.
- On October 15, Cuban exiles in Ontario, Canada, launched the **Fundación Cubano-Canadiense** to provide information to Canadians about human rights in Cuba, particularly to those who were planning to travel there.
- Anticipating the **IX Latin American Summit** in Havana, several organizations defending human rights in Cuba held a press conference in Havana, at Dr. Biscet's home, to denounce the abuses in Cuba.

Photos below, left to right:
Osvaldo Payá in front of the entrance to the **Asamblea Nacional del Poder Popular**, on the day he submitted 10,000 signatures backing the **Proyecto Varela**; the **Maison de l'Amerique Latine** in Paris, where many activities demanding Cuba's freedom began to take place in the 1990s.

Cuban exiles had a difficult time understanding how educated and well meaning people could continue to favor the Communist regime in Cuba a year or two after it assumed dictatorial powers. A case in point was the devotion to the Castro government of someone like **Feliciana Menocal —Fichú** to her friends.

She was the daughter of *Chana Villalón Wilson* and *Juan Manuel Menocal Barreras*, both descendants of prosperous and prestigious Cuban families (properly listed in the *History of Cuban Families* by the Count of Santa Cruz). Feliciana had five siblings, Josefina, Juan Manuel and Enrique (twins), Alberto and Jorge. All left Cuba upon the advent of Communism but Feliciana stayed, living in the same house the family had built in 1909 in *El Vedado* and spending some months every year in the family's *Varadero* summer home.

Feliciana was not a stranger to the $50,000 parties that well-to-do families had frequently organized during the years of her youth, in the 1940s and 1950s. She had been educated to speak flawless English and perfect French. She dressed for parties with designs from Paris couturiers; French pastries were brought from Paris for her wedding. When she married, her house had been redecorated to show her wedding gifts. According to her, «*we had a silver room, a coral room, a golden room and so on*».

In a 1991 interview with Irish newswoman Lynn Geldof, however, Feliciana, then 58 years old, made the following statements:

- Fidel Castro is a **political genius**.
- The Cuban revolution is second only to the **French revolution**.
- We have become a **society without classes**.
- We all **dress the same**; we all have the **same habits**.

(Continued)

Photos above: the statue of **Alma Mater** at the main entrance of the University of Havana. *Mario Joseph Korbel (1882-1956)* was the sculptor. The model for the face was **Chana Villalón**, mother of **Feliciana Menocal Villalón (Fishú)**, the main character in this story; Chana was the niece of **Mario García Menocal**, third President of Cuba (1912-1920).

(Continuation)

- This society may have its defects but it is a much **fairer** society.
- Maybe we need just **a little bit more** of consumer goods.
- Cubans have never been **politically persecuted** [*by the revolution*].
- In 1969, when my mother in law died, she had a **chauffeur**, a **cook**, a personal **helper** and three **live-in maids** (sic).
- I agree with Ché's thoughts in his farewell letter: «*I leave nothing to my children because **the state will take care** of them*».
- We have been **attacked mercilessly** by other countries.
- People that had left the island —just like my brothers and sister— loved **their way of life** more than their country.
- I don't even throw away the bottles because **everything is useful**.
- Our schools for the children are so **luxurious**, it's incredible.
- The investors in Cuba lost some properties. I believe it's fair that they lost them. I don't think **compensation** was needed.

It escaped Feliciana's attention and intellect that in Cuba:

- Hundreds of people opposed to the regime had been **executed**.
- All **private schools** had been seized and closed.
- All independent (private) **newspapers** were made to stop publication.
- All **TV and radio stations** began to be operated and heavily censored by the government.
- All **businesses** were confiscated.
- No Cubans of military age **could leave the island**.
- All legally obtained **private property** had been confiscated.
- **Phone communications** with family living abroad was first monitored and then discontinued.
- Most of the **religious orders** were forced to leave Cuba.
- A system of **citizen spies** (the *Committees for the Defense of the Revolution*) was organized to keep everybody under strict, absolute and continuous surveillance.
- All **civil organizations** were made illegal and disbanded.
- The government organized *Brigades of Quick Response* to **disperse** and **attack if necessary** any group of citizens meeting for any purpose other than what the government dictated.
- *Labor Unions* and *Student Associations* were placed **under the control** of the *Communist Party*.
- Citizens **could not live anywhere** they wanted but had to follow government orders as to where they were most useful.
- An **Apartheid** system was established by which not all citizens had the right to use all recreational facilities and spaces; most were reserved for tourists and high government officials.
- Top government officials were granted **exclusive use** of the best facilities in the island (housing, restaurants, etc.)

Photos at right:
The most visible hypocrisy of the Cuban revolutionary government after half a century of Communism was the creation of luxury establishments for the **nomenclatura** and wealthy tourists in a presumed "*classless society*;" lavish resorts were open only to the *new classes*, which no longer included people like **Feliciana Menocal**.

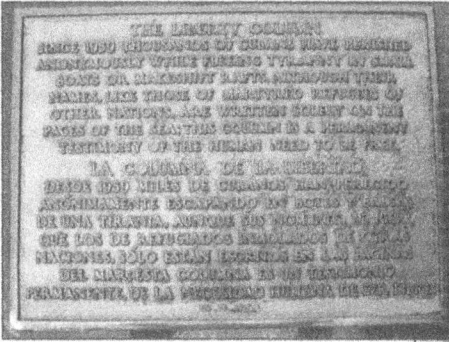

Liberty Column in downtown Miami, at *Bayfront Park*, with an inscription that reads: «*Since 1959 thousands of Cubans have perished anonymously while fleeing tyranny in small boats or makeshift rafts, although their names, like those of martyred refugees of other nations, are written solely on the pages of the sea; this column is a permanent testimony of the human need to be free*». Inaugurated on December 7, 1994.

Monument to **Father Félix Varela** on the site of the **Ermita de la Caridad** in Miami.

PADRE
FELIX VARELA
1788 - 1853

Jorge Mas Canosa in New York, campaigning for the release of the family of Cuban pilot **Orestes Lorenzo** in 1992. Lorenzo ended up landing a small plane in traffic along a Cuban coastal highway and quickly picked up his wife and two sons from the roadside before turning back to Florida.

Two Cuban exile brothers, heroes in the late 1990s in Mayor League Baseball in the US: *Orlando (el Duque)* and *Liván Hernández*.

The *Miami Hurricanes*, the football team that Cuban exiles loved.

The *Homestead-Miami Speedway* racetrack was started as an idea to help Dade County recover after Hurricane Andrew in 1992. *Ralph Sánchez*, a *Cuban Pedro Pan* exile and longtime motorsports promoter in South Florida, built the track in 1995 and ran it for several years.

Two events that consumed the interests of Miami's Cuban exiles in 1990 were: the outcome of the trial of Colombian-born **William Lozano**, the 30 year old police officer who had shot a Black man — 32 year old Clement Lloyd— as his motorcycle threatened to run over him, and the visit to the Miami area of **Nelson Mandela**, the hero of the anti-Apartheid movement in South Africa.

The shooting of Lloyd by Lozano had occurred at 6:04 PM on January 16, 1989, as a police car was chasing Lloyd for speeding and not coming to full stop at a stop sign. As the motorcycle approached Lozano, who was standing on the street and felt threatened by the speeding cycle, he fired a single shot that instantly killed Lloyd. A passenger in the motorcycle, 24 year old *Allan Blanchard*, was thrown violently as the motorcycle ran without control; Blanchard died of injuries as he crashed against a wall. The case went to criminal trial; Lozano was charged by the prosecution as a trigger-happy cop that failed to act prudently. His defense characterized him as a man acting in self-defense in the face of an eminent threat.

The jury convicted Lozano of manslaughter in the deaths of two Black men on December 10, 1998. The seven week trial had been broadcast live on local TV and radio. Many Cuban refugees rallied to Lozano's defense and raised funds for his appeal. The incident had provoked three days of inner-city rioting, leaving one man dead and $1 Million in damage. Lozano's defense claimed that the *Dade County Circuit Court*'s decision was influenced by fear of another riot. A very similar incident had happened in 1984 when **Luis Alvarez**, a Cuban exile, had been accused of manslaughter in the shooting of *Nevell Johnson*, a man that had threatened Alvarez with a hidden .22 caliber handgun. Alvarez was acquitted in that case.

Lozano was defended by famed defense attorney **Roy Black**, the lawyer that would go on to defend and acquit *William Kennedy Smith* of sexual assault in 1991 and *Salvador Magluta*, the power boat racer accused of smuggling 75 tons of cocaine, in 1996. Black lost the case for Lozano, successfully appealed and won acquittal in a retrial.

Photos above: **William Lozano** (circled) with his attorney **Roy Black** (at right, with glasses); the Miami 1998 Black riots in Overtown.

The **Nelson Mandela** affair took place in June of 1990. Mandela had brought his anti-Apartheid message to South Florida; his visit had been welcomed until in a national televised interview he defended his support for Fidel Castro, Yasser Arafat and Muammar Gadhafi expressing they had «*supported the African National Congress in its early struggles against Apartheid.*» Several elected mayors in the Miami area objected to those expressions of support, among them, *Xavier Suárez* of Miami, *Raúl Martínez* of Hialeah, *Pedro Reboredo* of West Miami, *José Rivero* of Sweetwater, *Gilda Oliveros* of Hialeah Gardens (all Cubans) and *Alex Daoud* of Miami Beach (the only non-Cuban). They issued a declaration that stated: «*We find it beyond a reasonable comprehension that Mr. Nelson Mandela, a victim of oppression by his own government, not only fails to condemn the Cuban government for its human rights violations, but rather praises the virtues of the tyrannical Castro regime.*»

The city of *Opa-locka*, a suburb to the north of Miami, declared the day of Mandela's arrival as *Nelson Mandela Day*. At the *Miami Beach Convention Center* Mandela spoke to 6,000 union members of the *American Federation of State, County and Municipal Employees (AFSCME)*, and received $274,500 for the *African National Congress*. Cuban exiles responded with a half page ad in the papers urging Mr. Mandela, who was imprisoned by 27 years, to «*help free the longest-held political prisoners in the world.*»

In the end, a Black boycott was announced for July 17, 1990 when the mayors refused to apologize to Mandela. Altogether it cost Miami $27 million. Boycott leaders approached *Major League* baseball owners in an effort to dissuade them from locating a *National League* team in Miami. The *Baseball Ownership Committee* approved a Miami team nevertheless. A final comment by a Committee of Cuban exiles was «*We don't have anything against Mr. Mandela. We only object to his support of Castro. For 31 years Castro has been doing the same thing to Cubans as the South African Government has done to blacks, including Mr. Mandela.*»

An event unrecorded by history on March 2, 1931, brought hopes to hundreds of thousands of Cuban exiles in the summer of 1991. In Privole, Stacropol kray, Southwestern Russia, a man named **Mikhail Sergeyevich Gorbachev** was born. From 1985 to 1991 he would be General Secretary of the *Soviet Union's Communist Party* and from 1990 to 1991 President of the *USSR*. His efforts to democratize the Soviet Union (through a policy of **glasnost**, i.e., openness) and decentralize its economy (through a policy of **perestroika**, i.e., restructuring) brought down Communism and broke the Soviet empire into its former constituent states. As a result of his efforts, the USSR ceased to exist on December 31, 1991; and on that day, unexpectedly, the **Cold War** was also over.

Given the fact that the USSR was no longer existent, Cuban exiles were hopeful that the years of Soviet domination in Cuba would soon be over. Most Cuban exiles, with reason, felt that the future in Cuba was jeopardized by the **US-USSR Cold War**. The War had turned hot on the Korean peninsula in 1950, when North Korean troops, supported by the Soviets, crossed the 38th parallel. It became a matter of pride when on October 4, 1957, the Soviets launched *Sputniks 1 and 2*, and placed a dog named *Laika* into space. Five years later, Kennedy and Khrushchev signed a pact for the US not to invade Cuba after the missile crisis; it sealed the victory of Communism in Cuba and the fate of the island.

By 1975, Castro had intervened in Angola with 36,000 troops, fighting a proxy war for the USSR. Later, in 1979, the Soviets invaded Afghanistan, and the US fought a proxy war, backing the *Mujahideen* against the URSS. Given the end of the Soviet Union, Cuban exiles, mistakenly, felt that the liberation of Cuba, now without the yearly $6 billion support from the Soviets, was a done deal. It was a major disappointment when Castro's government became the only Communist state that survived *glasnost* and *perestroika*.

(Continued)

Photos, left to right:
Mikhail Gorbachev (1931-); **Boris Yeltsin (1931-2007)**, on August 18, 1991, atop the turret of a USSR tank onto which he had climbed to make a memorable speech to abort a coup against **Mikhail Gorbachov**, Secretary General of the Soviet Communist Party.

(Continuation)

With the removal of the Berlin Wall, the Castro regime in Cuba began to descend into a final societal, ideological and economic collapse. Castro's nation-destroying policies were only viable with the benefit of Moscow's magnanimity. All the Kremlin's efforts, however, had not produced in Cuba a sustainable society; when Boris Yeltsin dismantled the Soviet empire, Cuba was left to fend for itself.

At first, Castro decided to try a closer state control of the economy; it worsened the island economic situation. He then opened the island for a sort of limited well-controlled capitalistic-inspired entrepreneurship; it was an attempt to see if Cubans, by themselves, could rescue the regime from its traumatic and chaotic economic disorder.

(Continued)

Photos above, top to bottom, left to right:
The ***construction*** of the Berlín Wall, 1962;
Castro's first visit to the ***Berlin Wall***, June 13, 1972;
Castro will Work for Dollars, from Chicago's ***Reason Magazine,*** 1994;
The ***London Herald*** on November 9, 1989.

(Continuation)

By then, Cuba was a beggar-state; it had suffered for many years from the doctrine of loyalty-above-capacity in its leadership. Its bureaucrats were happy to live well and ignore the need to problem-solve. From the bottom up all civil servants were habituated to disdain any admonitions of revolutionary duty. Non-compliance, obliviousness and nonchalance began to be the response of many Cubans to the requests for efficiency, honesty and dedication by the revolution. Cuba had become a country of overwhelming bureaucratic mediocrity.

In a country already hardened by improvisations and social experimentation, the Castro brothers extolled and promulgated a *special period*, a new appellative for widespread scarcity of meat, soap, shampoo, toothpaste, pencils, vitamins and other superfluous luxuries of the capitalistic middle class.

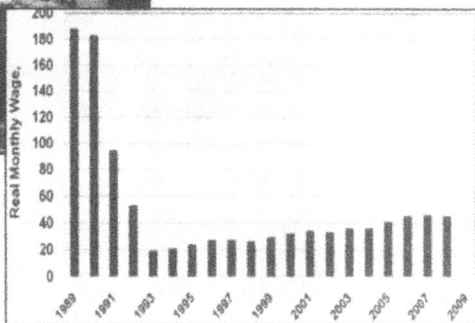

Photos above, top to bottom, left to right:
Empty **food markets** in Havana; the **propaganda** of the official government newspaper in Cuba; An empty **store** in Santiago de Cuba; the monstrous **drop in Cuban monthly wages** after the fall of the Soviet Union in 1991.

On May 27, 1990, *Georgii Arbatov*, a close adviser to Soviet President *Mikhail Gorbachev* and a member of the *Supreme Soviet*, participated in a two-day conference on **Soviet Policy towards Cuba** organized by the **University of Miami**. The conference was a sort of warm-up for the following week's meeting between President George Bush and Mikhail Gorbachev in the White House. Several important US State Department officials and some Miami's Cuban exiles were invited.

During the first morning session of the conference **Jorge Mas Canosa** declared, «If the Soviets withdraw their support from Cuba tomorrow, the Cuban problem will be solved in 48 hours. Everybody knows that.»

Bernard Aronson, US Assistant Secretary of State for Inter-American Affairs added, «There is neither perestroika nor glasnost in Cuba... We don`t wish violent change for Cuba. All we wish is self-determination for the Cuban people. They have waited 31 years and I believe they are tired of waiting».

Arbatov deputy, **Yuri Pavlov**, responded to Mas Canosa and Aronson in the following terms: «When changes come, they should come from inside the country as they are doing in the Soviet Union».

Pavlov words were very important since he had become the Soviet leader in charge of deciding the nature of the Soviet-Cuba relationship. He had been a Soviet diplomat since 1954 and his first serious task had come during the October 1962 Missile Crisis. Later he had spent several years in London and Australia; in 1982 had been sent to Costa Rica; in 1990 to Chile and after 1990, to the US.

Photos, top to bottom, left to right:
Georgii Arbatov, member of the staff of the *Central Committee of the Soviet Communist Party*; **Yuri Pavlov**, head of the Latin American division of the Soviet Foreign office; **Jorge Mas Canosa**, **Bernard Aronson** and **Mikhail Gorbachev**.

(Continued)

In an interview after the *University of Miami* conference **Pavlov** revealed that:

- The Cominterm's policy had been to **foster local revolutions** everywhere in the Americas.
- Latin America was regarded a superb **source of raw materials and food** products for the Soviet Union.
- The Soviets preferred to make gains in Latin America through the economy and **not through armed struggle**, like Castro wanted; the USSR never approved Castro's adventures in Latin America.
- Soviet Missiles in Cuba, under the direction of General Kliev, Commander in Chief of the Soviet troops in Cuba, were indeed **pointed towards American cities**.
- Khrushchev never knew of the **17:1 advantage of the US** in the number of nuclear warheads and he reprimanded Soviet leaders for keeping him in the dark.
- Castro did not know that the Soviets **would not have** sacrificed their own safety in order to save the Cuban revolution.
- The Soviets were never informed about what **Ché Guevara was attempting to accomplish** in Latin America.
- Castro obtained from the Soviets an enormous plant to produce **Kalashnikovs** (sub machine guns) as well as its ammunition.
- Despite Castro's recommendation, the Soviets were **never ready to support Allende** in Chile.
- The Soviets did agree to supply weapons and economic assistance to Nicaragua, in spite of **not liking Daniel Ortega**. They gave him *MIG Fighters* when they actually needed helicopters.
- Weapons given to the Sandinistas and to the Salvadorian guerrillas were **American weapons** captured in Vietnam, never Soviet made weapons.
- Foreign Minister **Shevernadze** opposed to give aid to Noriega so as not to antagonize the US.
- Shevernadze and US Secretary of State Baker agreed to a **Quid pro Quo** «*if you accept our formula on Central America, we (the US) will accept your (the USSR) formula on Afghanistan.*»
- «*The Cuban drain was one* **of the major factors** *which bled the Soviet economy, although not probably the main one. The main one was the*

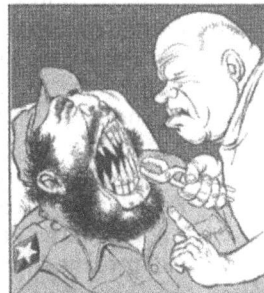

Photos above, left to right: **Mikhail Kalashnikov**, the famous weapon designer holding an AK-47 (Автомат Калашникова-47); **Eduard Shevardnadze**, the man responsible for many top decisions on Soviet foreign policy in the *Gorbachev Era*; a Russian cartoon showing **Khrushchev** extracting missiles from Castro while saying
«*This is going to hurt me more than you.*»

The decade of the 1990s was witness to the death of several leaders of the Cuban exile community who had been exceptionally dedicated to the Republic they left behind. One of these men was *Carlos Márquez Sterling (1898-1991)*.

Marquez Sterling was an attorney and professor of the University of Havana, a former president of the Cuban House of Representatives and a former Minister of Education and Labor, as well as President of the Constitutional Assembly in 1940. He was a nephew of *Manuel Márquez Sterling* (brother to his mother), the former ambassador to Mexico that had so valiantly tried to save the life of President Francisco Madero during the Mexican Revolution. He had been placed under house arrest in 1959 and went immediately into exile. He taught in the 1950s at *Columbia University* and in 1979 moved to Miami to teach at *Biscayne College* and at *Florida International University*. During his exile he wrote some 20 books and numerous articles for *Diario las Américas*.

Another of these distinguished men was *Antonio (Tony) de Varona y Loredo (1909-1992)*, Prime Minister of the last constitutionally elected government of Cuba.

Varona was born in Camagüey and graduated from the School of Law at the *University of Havana*. He was a founder of the *Directorio Estudiantil Universitario (DEU)* that participated in the overthown of the dictatorship of Gerardo Machado in 1933. As a founding member of the *Partido Revolucionario Cubano*, he became a member of the *1940 Constitutional Assembly* and that year he was elected member of the *Cuban House of Representatives*. Four years later he was elected to the *Cuban Senate* of which he was later President. On March 10, 1952, he went into exile and returned to Cuba to fight against the Batista regime. After the take-over of Cuba by the Communists, he went again into exile. He worked against the Castro regime and became General Coordinator of the *Frente Revolucionario Democrático*, spending the rest of his life lecturing at Universities and civic organizations in favor of a democratic Cuba.

*Photos above, left to right: **Carlos Márquez Sterling, Antonio de Varona** and **DEU students** at the University in 1933.*

Other distinguished Cubans in exile that died in the decade of the 1990s were **Goar Mestre, Roberto Agramonte** and **Andrés Rivero Aguero.**

Goar Mestre Espinosa (1912-1993) was born in Santiago de Cuba, where he lived until he turned 13. Seven years later he graduated from *Chestnut Hill Academy* in Philadelphia and later from *Yale University*. Upon returning to Cuba he founded *Mestre & Co.*, an advertising agency. In 1943 he bought **CMQ Radio** and hired Gaspar Pumarejo, who eventually would be his main competitor in TV in Cuba. At CMQ he hired the best technical and artistic talent in Cuba; by forging an alliance with NBC, CMQ was able to reach the entire island of Cuba. In 1946 he moved CMQ from Monte & Prado to 23 & L in *El Vedado*, to a brand new building modeled after **Radio City** in NY. Years later, in 1951, he opened **CMQ TV**; he lost his numerous businesses in Cuba in 1960 and moved to Argentina, where he died at age 81.

Roberto Agramonte (1904-1995) was a prestigious lawyer, philosopher, politician and Cuba's ambassador to Mexico. He attained the rank of Dean of the School of Philosophy at the *University of Havana*. He was the first *Foreign Minister* of the 1959 revolution and resigned once he realized the clear tilt of the government towards Communism. He went to Puerto Rico with his family and finally retired to Miami, where he died at age 91.

Andrés Rivero Aguero (1905-1996) was the last person to be elected President of Cuba. He was born to very poor parents in San Luis, Oriente, taught himself to read and worked to pay for his High School and a Law Degree from the *University of Havana*. He became *a leader of the Liberal Party and served as Minister* of Agriculture and *Education*, as well as *Prime Minister* and *Senator*. He tried to resolve the Cuban crisis in 1958, but the sudden triumph of the revolution thwarted his plans to reinstate Constitutional legality in Cuba. He went into exile in 1959 in Santo Domingo and later moved to Miami, where he lived an exceedingly modest life until he died at age 91.

Photos above: **Goar Mestre, Roberto Agramonte**
and **Andrés Rivero Aguero**

The **Holocaust Memorial**, a sculpture by Kenneth Treister erected at Meridian Avenue and Dade Boulevard in Miami Beach in February 1990.

Miami under the fury of a tornado in 1997.

The **Florida Gran Opera** premiered in 1997 a Robert Ashley opera-drama entitled **Balseros**.

On July 15, 1997, **Gianni Versace (1946-1997)**, the world famous designer, was about to enter his mansion at 1111 Ocean Avenue in Miami Beach when **Andrew Cunanan**, a drifter, murdered him before taking his own life.

Starting in the 1990s there has been a constant flux of artists from Cuba seeking contracts to perform in the US, particularly in Miami, New York, Los Angeles and other areas of heavy Cuban exile populations. Such has been the case with Silvio Rodríguez, Pablo Milanés, Omara Portuondo, Rosita Fornés, Alicia Alonso, Compay Segundo, Luis Fornell and the Van Vans, Ibrahim Ferrer and others. Groups of activist and militant anti-Castro Cuban exiles began to protest forcefully due to these artists' collaboration with the Cuban regime, as well as their open defense of the Communist revolution in cities where large numbers of Cubans have suffered from injustices and mistreatments by the Castros.

The main arguments of Cuban-based artists have always been that «the arts have no boundaries and no political affiliations.» Yet they called themselves "protest artists" without ever protesting the injustices —legal, economic, racial, political— and the abuses that the regime commits in Cuba. These visiting artists from Cuba have always alleged that «the true Cuban culture only flourishes in Cuba,» without considering the censured writers, painters and musicians that had to seek freedom of thought outside Cuba and the known loyalty to the revolution that the government requires to earn a living performing, painting or writing in Cuba. They have never been able to explain why is it, if the arts have no boundaries and are apolitical, that exiled artists have been called worms, scoria and traitors and are not allowed to visit or perform in Cuba; and why is it that they still compose ballads to the bloody adventures of Cuban Communism in Angola, the Congo and Namibia.

Photos above, top to bottom, left to right:
Pablo Milanés, Silvio Rodríguez, Compay Segundo, Luis Fornell, Rosita Fornés, Omara Portuondo, Ibrahim Ferrer and **Alicia Alonso**.

In spite of its fame as an intractable city controlled by recalcitrant and stubborn Cuban exiles, Miami—in the new millennium—opened its doors to Cuban artists that had long professed sympathy and loyalty to the Castro regime in Cuba.

Fading into memory were the years of aggressive reaction to Cuban artists living in Cuba that visited Miami but never supported the rights of Miami exiled artists to perform in the island. Starting around the mid 1990s, new waves of Cubans were settling in Miami taking advantage of the **Cuban Adjustment Act** (Public Law 89-732) of 1966. Most of these new Cuban immigrants arrived in the US as part of a lottery of 20,000 annual visas; others had by-passed the US Port-of-Entry regulations and, after a year, were eligible to become permanent US residents even if they became a public charge. Most of them arrived in Miami thinking that nothing unusual had happened in Cuba with the advent of the revolution; few had any desire to return Cuba to democratic principles.

These Cuban-based artists found welcoming promoters and tolerant venues to present their performances: the *American Airlines Arena*, the *Colony Theater* in Miami Beach, the *James Knight Center* in downtown Miami, the *Arsht Center*, the *Dade Country Auditorium*, as well as theaters, clubs and restaurants like *The Place*, *Club Aché*, *Grand Central Club*, *The Trail*, *The Place* and *Cuba Ocho Art Center*.

Photos above:
Cubans from the island performing in Miami in the 2000s

Veterans from the Escambray guerrillas that were defeated by Castro in the 1960s continued all around the world trying to restore Cuba to a system of democratic government and rule of law. In July of 1992, some 30 years after leaving Cuba and seeking refuge in the US and Latin America, they traveled in mass to Spain as soon as they learned that the dictator was to be present at the **Ibero-American Summit of Heads of State**. Everywhere in the streets of Madrid they hung signs and rented billboards denouncing Castro. Most busses in Madrid had signs reading *¡Cuba Si, Castro No!*

The year 1992 was especially important because the Ibero-American meeting was followed by the **Barcelona Olympics** and the **1992 Sevilla World's Fair**. It was also the year US Congressman **Robert Torricelli** presented to the US Congress the **Cuban Democracy Act**, which prohibited foreign-based subsidiaries of US companies to trade with Cuba, US citizens to travel to Cuba and Cuban exiles to send remittances to their families in Cuba.

Cuban exiles organized conferences, book sales, marches and expositions in many centric venues in Madrid and Barcelona. One of the Madrid organizers was **Carlos Alberto Montaner**, one of the most popular Cuban writers and analysts. *«Castro wants to receive the acclaim of the Spaniards but we will make sure they also listen to the abuses and mistreatments taking place in Cuba,»* Montaner said.

Photos below, left to right:
Madrid's **ABC** reporting on the **II Cumbre:** on top of the page, **Castro** arriving, below, left, **Costa Rica's Calderon** and **Spain's Felipe González,** on the bottom right, **Chile's Patricio Aylwin** and **Brazil's Color de Mello**; the **Barcelona Olympic Games** logo; US Senator **Robert Torricelli**.

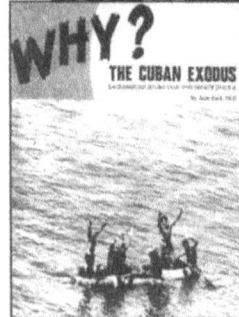

The facts and figures of the disaster that Castro and Communism have brought to the Republic of Cuba will forever be preserved by the efforts and lifetime dedication to scholarship of **Dr. Juan Clark**, Professor Emeritus of *Miami-Dade Community College*. A former leader of the *Juventud de Acción Católica Cubana* and a paratrooper in the failed *Bay of Pigs* invasion, Dr. Clark finished his doctorate in Sociology at the *University of Florida* in Gainesville. Almost immediately he joined the faculty at Miami-Dade College and continued his research on conditions in Cuba and among the Miami community of exiles. In 1992 he culminated his findings in an 800 page book entitled **Cuba: Mito y Realidad**, since then an indispensable library resource of information and data about Cuba's realities.

Cuba: Mito y Realidad is a monumental work, showing the criminal process that for over half a century has destroyed Cuba, subverting its most fundamental national virtues. Among the many figures included by Clark in his books and articles are sound estimates of Cubans that have perished attempting to flee the Communist regime in Cuba (30,000 to 40,000) as well as countless others (possibly as many as 110,000) that have died executed by Castro, by inhuman and deadly imprisonment practices, collectivist policies, malnutrition and the purposeful destruction and desolation of a once prospering republic.

Photos above:
Dr. Juan Clark; his best-seller **Cuba: Mito y Realidad**;
one of his writings about the Cuban exodus and a photo of Clark
in his days as *Miami-Dade professor.*

After **The Nation and the Emigration** first conference on February 14, 1994, a second conference was held in November, 1995. The first conference was aimed at creating a stable relationship between the Cuban exiles (now called in Cuba the *emigrants*) and their counterparts in Cuba (not Cubans on the island but the Cuban government). The emphasis in the first conference was, in the words of their organizers «*the promotion of constructive actions on the part of the emigrants...for the preservation of Cuba's sovereignty and independence... as well as* [spreading the word about the] *achievements of our people* [the government of Cuba] ».

The November 1995 conference had a larger number of Cuban exiles from outside Miami. It took place a few weeks after the approval in the US Congress of the **Helms-Burton Law**. During the conference, the Cuban government suggested that their doors had always been open to Cuban exiles since 1959, mentioning such events as the December of 1977 visits of the **Antonio Maceo Brigade**, the **1978 Dialogue**, when close to 100 Cuban exiles had talks with top members of the government and the efforts by the party to arrange for **Viajes de la Comunidad** (a new name for what they used to call the *Miami Mafia*) and the **Family Reunification Program** (a one way traffic of families of opponents towards the US). In the words of **Ricardo Alarcón** «*a Cuban policy favoring contacts with the émigrés has existed since 1959*».

Any aggressive acts by the Cuban government, it was explained, occurred when «*broad sectors of the emigrants began to attack the emerging Revolution. Confrontation became our policy to ensure the security of the country*». The rationale for Cuba torturing, incarcerating and executing opponents was that such events as *Playa Girón* and the «*gangs in the Escambray*» had forced the hand of the revolution. The view of the Cuban government *vis a vis* the exiles was clear, according to Alarcón: «*there are individuals in this world able to abhor their origin and their history, able to reach the point of looking for the protection of a foreign master to carry out actions that can harm even their nearest relatives left behind by them*». The same accusation had been presented by *Martínez Campos* in a letter to *Máximo Gómez* during the Independence War in 1895.

Photos below, left to right:

Magda Montiel, the anti-heroine of the First Conference when she was photograph kissing **Castro;** Cuba's UN Ambassador **Ricardo Alarcón**; **Andrés Gómez**, head of the *Antonio Maceo Brigade*; US Senator **Jesse Helms**.

On May 19, 1993, at 11:00 AM, 15 miles north of Cuban coasts, an American-registered single-engine Cessna, owned and piloted by **Brothers to the Rescue**, was buzzed by a Cuban MIG fighter plane in international airspace over the Straits of Florida.

It was the first time in more than 600 missions that a Cuban MIG had harassed this Good Samaritan pilots on a mercy mission. *Brothers to the Rescue* was a non-profit group of volunteer pilots scouring the Florida Straits searching for rafts of Cubans escaping the island. The encounter was so close (about 50 feet) that the Cessna pilot had eye contact with the pilot flying the MIG, who smiled and winked before taking off.

On February 24, 1994, the situation was different. Cuban MIGs downed two Brothers to the Rescue planes. Four men were dead:

- **Armando Alejandre**, 45, born in Cuba; a former US Marine who had seen combat in Vietnam.
- **Carlos Alberto Costa**, 29, US-born, son of Cuban parents.
- **Mario de la Peña**, 24, US-born; former NY resident.
- **Pablo Morales**, US-born; an amateur pilot.

The three Cessnas flying that afternoon had notified air traffic controllers as to their flight plans. Castro's response was to scramble 2 fighter jets from Havana. At 3:24 PM the pilot of one of the jets received permission and proceeded to shoot down one of the Cessnas, more than 6 miles north of Cuban territorial waters. Seven minutes later the pilots received permission to shoot a second Cessna, this time 18.5 miles north of the exclusion zone or 30.5 miles from the Cuban coast. The crew of the third Cessna, with **José Basulto** of *Brothers to the Rescue* and **Sylvia Iriondo** of *Mar por Cuba*, managed to escape the attack.

Photos below, left to right:
A **recreation of the shooting** of February 24, 1994; standing with **José Basulto** (with a cap) are the two spies that had infiltrated **Brothers to the Rescue**: Juan Pablo Roque (standing) and René González (kneeling).

After the murderous and remorseless action of Castro, President Clinton and White House aides met to discuss retribution. Cuban exiles insisted that the planes of **Brothers to the Rescue** were on a routine search and rescue mission, looking for people in rafts fleeing Cuban dictator Castro, as they had done more than 1,800 times before. Passengers on the cruise ship *Majesty* had watched the planes and the black smoke with bewilderment from a few miles away; they attested to the fact that it all happened in international waters. Passengers on the ship were shaken by what they had witnessed. The Cessnas were not armed and had no way to defend themselves against MIG fighters. Cuban officials stated *«the Cessnas were pirate planes; this must serve as a lesson to those who consider or carry out acts which tend to increase tensions between the United States and Cuba».*

Secretary of State **Warren Christopher** declared *«The actions the Cuban government took last Saturday were not justified under any circumstance.»* He requested that the U.N. Security Council meet Sunday night to consider punitive action against Cuba. According to transcripts released by Christopher, the following conversation had taken place between the MIG pilots and the control tower in Cuba:

> **Pilot One:**   *The target is in sight, the target is in sight.*
> **Pilot Two:**   *It's a small aircraft at a low altitude... give me instructions, hurry.*
> **Tower:**   *Fire... you are authorized to destroy.*

Minutes later, the Cuban MIG fighter pilot who blew one of the exile planes out of the sky could not contain his glee:

> **Pilot One:**   *We cut off their balls !*
> **Pilot Two:**   *This one won't mess around anymore.*

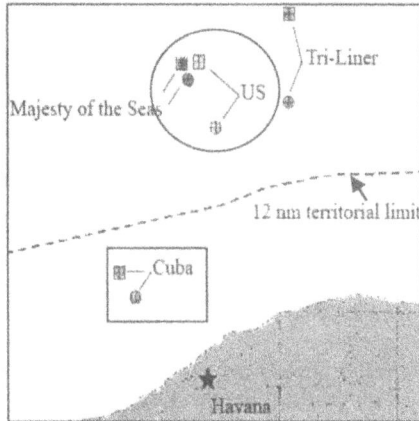

Photos above:
Warren Christopher, US Secretary of State; the map showing the location of the incident according to the **International Civil Aviation Organization (ICAO)**. The most likely location was declared to be that described by the ship **Majesty of the Seas** (circled) and not the one suggested by the Cuban government (squared).

Among Miami Cuban exiles and all across the US, the shooting of the Cessnas led to broad and intense condemnation of Cuba; months later it led to the adoption of the **Helms-Burton Act**, which strengthened the US embargo against Cuba. In addition, the *UN Security Council*, at the request of the US, passed *Security Council Resolution 1067 of 1996* condemning Cuba for its criminal act.

Photos above: the four pilots of *Brothers to the Rescue* (**Armando Alejandre, Mario de la Peña, Pablo Morales** and **Carlos Costa, Jr.**); on the right, **José Basulto**, the founder of Brothers to the Rescue.

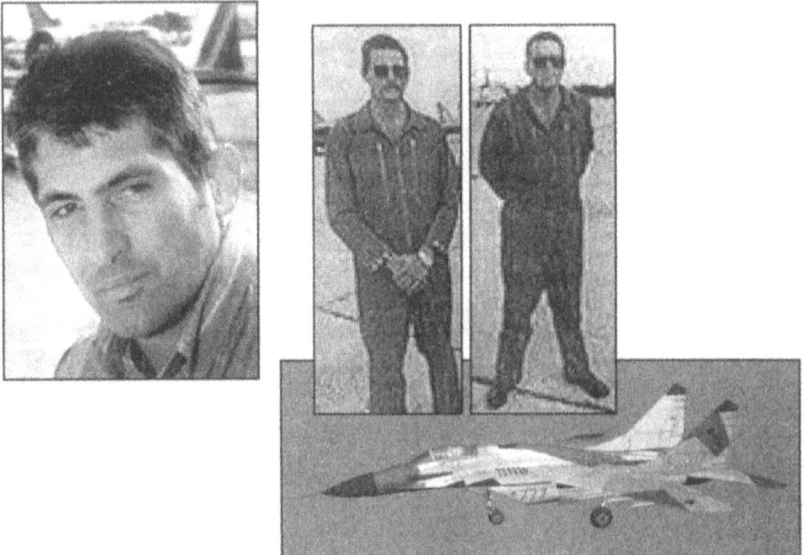

Photos above, left to right: **Juan Pablo Roque,** the spy and traitor inside *Brothers to the Rescue*; the criminal pilots, brothers **Francisco** and **Alberto Pérez y Pérez**, both Lieutenant Colonels of the *Cuban Air Force*; a **MiG-22**, the type of war plane piloted by each of the Pérez brothers.

In April of 1994, Castro greeted 223 Cuban exiles that had traveled to the island for a three-day conference aimed at exhorting the exiles to invest and participate in the Cuban economy.

Castro announced that travel and investment restrictions had been revised to facilitate the participation of exiles in Cuban life and that the conference demonstrated the seriousness of the government to ease relations with Cuban exiles (those that had lost their properties and way of life in the land they left and that years earlier he had characterized as *gusanos*). «*The conference primary success,*» he added, «*is the conference itself*».

Carlos Lage, Cuba's chief economic planner (later appointed President and finally defenestrated) told the exiles that they would have the same investment rights and policies that were enjoyed by foreign investors and any dollar-bearing capitalists. They could open factories, export (not import) businesses and invest in hotels for foreigners but could not open franchises or any businesses that dealt directly or indirectly with the Cuban consumers. His words sounded empty; all those present were Cuban exiles living in the US, which were restricted by laws that banned commercial business with Cuba. At the end of his words Lage intimated that in exchange for this opportunity, Cuba would welcome help in the campaign to lift the US embargo.

A second conference speaker was **Roberto Robaina**, at that time Foreign Minister and later defenestrated with Lage. He announced the creation of a new department to deal exclusively with travel and investments by exiles. In response to questions he declared «*Plans to allow exiles to invest in Cuba had to be approved on a one-to-one basis by a committee of the Cuban National Assembly*». He excused himself for not been able to discuss any developments about freeing political prisoners or the establishment of democratic reforms.

At the end of the conference, **Francisco Aruca**, leader of the exile visitors, stated «*The more the Cuban government can recognize legitimate interests that exist in our community, the more they are giving people concrete reasons to lobby in the US for changes on their side,*» adding, «*Castro has started down a route that is very serious and cannot be turned back*». Time proved him wrong.

Photos above, left to right:
Castro, **Lage**, **Robaina** and **Aruca**.

One of the most accomplished musicians in Cuba in the 1990s was **Arturo Sandoval (1949-)**, considered by critics to be one of the best trumpet players —and piano players— in the world. He was born in Artemisa, Cuba, at the heart of the best Cuban tobacco region. As a six year old child, knowing that he wanted to be a musician, he tried the trombone, bass drum, the flute, and the trumpet; he decided he wanted to play the trumpet for the rest of his life. In 1963 he joined the *Cuban National School of the Arts* and began to study music —but not the trumpet— for two years. In 1969 he became first trumpet at a professional orchestra.

In 1971 he was inducted into the Cuban army. After completing his military service —which he hated— he was back as first trumpet, this time playing Jazz at **Irakere**, a new band he had organized with some of his musician friends, two of whom also became famous musicians, **Paquito D'Rivera** on the sax and **Chucho Valdés** at the piano. By the 1980s the band had won a **Grammy** in the US with its creative combination of Jazz, Rock and Cuban rhythms. Not happy with the degree of personal and musical freedom he had in Cuba as a rhythm trailblazer, Sandoval made plans to go into exile with his wife Marianela and his children Leonel and Arturito. The opportunity to do so came with the help of **Dizzy Gillespie**, whom Arturo considered his spiritual father. The Castro government agreed to let him join Gillespie on a world tour, and Arturo and his family defected in London in 1993. He has since played solo and with *Dizzy Gillespie* and *Lionel Hampton*, from Tokyo to New York; he has recorded 15 solo albums and won four **Grammy Awards**, six **Billboard Awards** and a dozen Grammy nominations. His life story was played by **Andy García** in an HBO documentary titled *For Love of Country*; he has lectured at the *Conservatoire de Paris*, the *Tchaikovsky Conservatory* in Moscow and many other institutions.

*Photos above: **Sandoval** and a recording with **Guillespie**.*

¡Estas son las víctimas del remolcador! Víctimas... de un tirano cruel que afirma ser el defensor de las mujeres y los niños en Cuba.

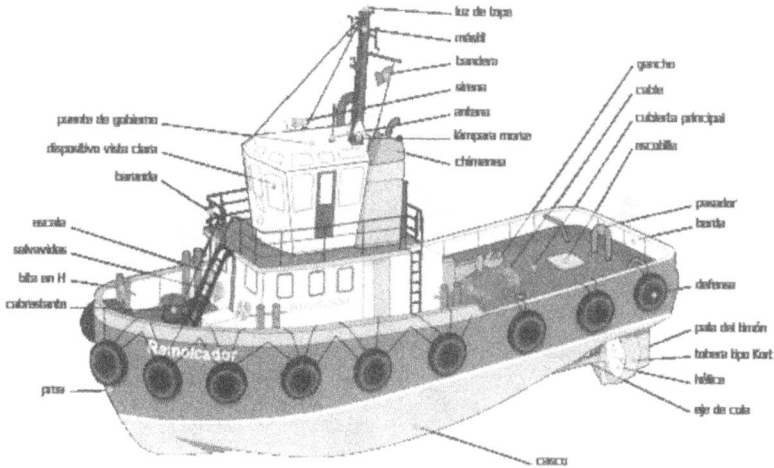

On July 13, 1994, at 3:00 AM, 72 Cubans were trying to leave the island aboard an old tugboat registered with the name "*13 de Marzo*," in memory of the day in 1957 when students from the *University of Havana*, under the leadership of José Antonio Echeverría, tried to assault the National Palace in Havana.

(Continued)

Photos above: pictures of the victims of the **13 de Marzo massacre** and a view of a tugboat similar to the *13 de Marzo*.

(continuation)

No sooner had the "*13 de Marzo*" exited from the port of Havana, two government vessels began to pursue it with the intention of sinking it. After 45 minutes of chase, when the tugboat was in "*la poceta*," 7 miles outside the Cuban coasts, two fireboats, equipped with powerful water hoses, began to block and ram the old tugboat, without ever trying to communicate with the passengers. Once the stern of the fragile *13 de Marzo* split in two, rendering it inoperative, the fireboats began to use their water hoses to throw people overboard and sink the ship. The screams and pleas of the escapees could not stop the attack. The *13 de Marzo* sank and 41 of its passengers died, without any assistance from the crews of the attacking ships. A Cuban coast guard cutter showed up during the assault and stood silent and passive, limiting its rescue effort to receive on board those survivors that could reach the cutter by themselves.

Photos below: some of the groups of Cuban exiles across the world denouncing the **massacre of the 13 de Marzo tugboat**. *From top to bottom*: Sancti Spiritus, Montreal, Montevideo and Miami.

On Friday August 5, 1994, a **Maleconazo** surprised Cuban exiles around the world. How was it possible that this act of protest could happen in Cuba? It was true that a few years before, in 1980, 10,000 Cubans had made a stampede for the *Peruvian Embassy* in Havana and 125,000 had gone to the port of *Mariel* to be picked up by their *gusano* friends or relatives and taken to the US, with absolute impunity. In July of 1994, however, 70 Cubans had been intercepted 7 miles from Havana in the old **13 de Marzo** tugboat where they were escaping; the boat was sunk under specific orders from Castro, with no regard for the lives of 10 children.

It started when, on July 26 of 1994, a small group of people kidnapped a *lancha de Regla* and took it to Key West; on August 3 another *lancha* with 120 Cubans successfully repeated the escape. Was the government hesitant to take violent action after the world-wide condemnation of the sinking of the **13 de Marzo** tugboat? Was this the time to escape safely from Cuba? Many theories were discussed by Cuban exiles yet nobody thought that a revolt inside Cuba could take place. But then the **maleconazo** occurred.

(continued)

Photos below: a popular rumor spurred hundreds of Cubans to the bayside **Paseo del Malecón** in Havana for the **maleconazo**, the first anti-Castro demonstration in 35 years. Most of them were hoping to commandeer a *lancha de Regla* like two previous groups had done.

On August 5, 1994, however, Castro's police was ready. Inside Soviet trucks stationed near the harbor were a dozen military men dressed as civilians, fully armed with pistols and assault rifles. Unlike other times, people began to chant *¡Libertad!* while running from the harbor to the malecón. At the corner of Malecón and Galiano Street, they began to throw stones at the *Hotel Deauville*, a symbol of the privileges that tourists enjoyed but the Cuban-born could not. They continued running until they reached the *Maceo Park*. There, a large group of military men were waiting for them, as well as a large contingent of **Brigadas de Respuesta Rápida**, the civilian militia of *sans-culottes* organized by the Castros. The entire area from Reina Street to the Malecón and from the Avenida del Puerto to Belascoain Street was full of demonstrators, police, the military, the militias and the members of the *Unión de Jóvenes Comunistas*. As the revolt lost its steam, Castro made an appearance. Days later he allowed a mini-Mariel to take place; hundreds of Cubans were allowed to go into exile to the coasts of Florida.

Photos and diagram above, top to bottom, left to right:

Two soldiers dressed in civilian clothes and a woman member of the **Brigadas de Respuesta Rápida** moving into the crowd; a map of Havana showing the areas of demonstrations; a policeman and a man of the *Brigadas de Respuesta Rápida* arresting a demonstrator; more militiamen in civilian attire with their weapons ready to attack.

Castro's decision in 1994 to allow Cubans to leave without any official obstacles produced indeed a second but smaller **Mariel exodus**. The American authorities panicked and began to redirect the *"exiles"* into Guantánamo base in Oriente. Nobody could really say if these new Cubans flowing towards the US were political exiles or not. The purpose of establishing a provisional stop at Guantánamo was to screen and vet the Cubans. In reality no one knew how to do that. Havana was, exactly like during the episode at Mariel, once more dictating the immigration policy of the US. Complicating things, President George H. Bush had decided, between October 1991 and June 1992, to intercept a total of 36.596 Haitian refugees and return them to their country or take them to Guantánamo.

By November 1994, the U.S. had invaded Haiti, restored **Jean Bertrand Aristide** to the presidency of his country and returned to Haiti the majority of refugees that had tried to enter the US. U.S. Attorney General, **Janet Reno**, after a new immigration agreement with Cuba in May 1995, allowed all Cuban refugees who were at the base into the US, with the exception of those with criminal records. By January 1996, the last Cuban refugee had left the "*safe haven*" of *Guantanamo*. In Miami, Cuban exiles were very reluctant to count them as genuine Cuban refugees.

Photos above: Cubans leaving the island and their perilous trip across the shark-infested Strait of Florida.

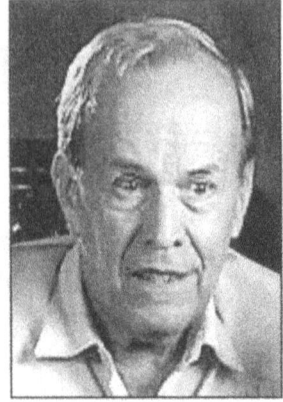

In September of 1996, a nationally televised debate, moderated by **María Elvira Salazar**, took place between **Jorge Mas Canosa (1939-1997)**, President of the *Cuban American National Foundation* and **Ricardo Alarcón (1937-)**, President-to-be of the *Cuban National Assembly*. According to the *Miami Herald*, «*María Elvira Salazar, a Miami-born Cuban American who often reports on Cuban issues, agreed to the task of securing Alarcon's participation; although Cuban officials had met with exile critics in the past, it had always been with relative moderates and only behind closed doors.*»

The reasons for Alarcón to participate in an event that all listeners perceived as a *de facto* recognition of Mas Canosa as a legitimate opposition leader, was never clear. As with all Cuban exiles in Miami, Más Canosa was considered in Cuba as a thug and right-wing zealot acting as a leader of the *Cuban Mafia*. *Telemundo*, the TV station broadcasting a political talk show hosted by María Elvira Salazar, advertised the event saying «*It's the first time* [Mas Canosa and Alarcon] *have agreed to a face-off.*»

After the debate was shown on TV in the US, Ricardo Alarcón stated publicly that «*he was tricked since, originally, he had been asked to be part of a broad range of individuals who would comment on a Dan Rather interview with Fidel Castro and not to participate in a debate with a Mafioso.*» In July of that year, *CBS* had run an hour-long documentary about Cuba, hosted by Dan Rather. On the other hand, the *Cuban American National Foundation* agreed to participate in the program after a commitment by *Telemundo* that the debate would be broadcast unedited on national TV in the US.

The overwhelming opinion of those who saw and scrutinized the debate was that Más Canosa had won handily; hence the complaints by Alarcón became moot. María Elvira Salazar was banned from ever reporting from inside Cuba, even though she had already established her journalistic credentials with a one-hour TV interview with Castro for *Telemundo*.

*Photos above: **Jorge Mas Canosa**, **María Elvira Salazar** and **Ricardo Alarcón Quesada**.*

Cubans launching a **raft** in Havana, on the way to Miami in 1993.

Cuban refugees' **camp** (all former raft people) in Guantánamo in 1994.

The campaign against the **Herald** organized by Jorge Mas Canosa during the 1990s.

Cuban-born **Magda Montiel Davis**, an unsuccessful candidate to the US Congress from Miami, spotted and taped in Cuba on April 24, 1994 as she was kissing and thanking Castro for all his «*good teachings and superb mentoring.*»

Photos above: scenes from the 1990s.

On top, an anti-Castro rally by **San Francisco Cuban exiles**, distressed about the culture of drug trafficking that dominated the regime in Cuba; *in the center*, the *ABC* newspaper in Madrid reporting the break *Havana-Moscow* in 1992 under the pressure from the *"gusanos rojos,"* a new brand of anti-Castro Cuban exiles living in Russia; *at the bottom*, some of the extraordinary Miami-based journalists who for years were committed to reporting the abuses of the totalitarian Cuban regime.

From top to bottom, left to right: **Alfonso, Connor, Cancio, Cao, Encinosa, Ferré, Montaner, Ninoska, Remos** and **Tamargo**.

On January 25, 1992, forty years after the Communist takeover in Cuba, supporters of the Castro regime organized a gathering at the *Jacob Javits Convention Center* in Manhattan. They were confronted by 15,000 Cuban exiles protesting the pro-Castro rally outside the Center; about 4,000 of them had traveled from Miami (at $400 airfare or $90 Bus fare) and chanted «**Cuba si, Castro no**» as they attempted to capture the attention of the press with testimonies that Cubans in the island had no rights and they have no way to express their disagreement with Castro's oppressive regime.

In Miami, hundreds of exiles took to the streets demanding to be heard by the US and Latin America; the thousands that marched in support of the counter-protesters of New York were asking for freedom for Cuba, condemning those who sympathized with Castro from the security of their free surroundings. In New York, on the other hand, the pro-Castro event, sponsored by *Peace for Cuba International Appeal*, was supported by Hollywood show business celebrities and international dignitaries opposed to the U.S. economic blockade of Cuba and what they called the US' anti-Communist imperialist propaganda. Their response to the opposing demonstrators was to chant «**Cuba si, blockade, no**».

(Continued)

Photos above: the three main sponsors of the **Jacob Javits pro-Castro rally in Manhattan in 1992.**

Ramsey Clark, former US Attorney in the Johnson Administration, defender at one time or another of Serbia's murderer *Slobodan Milosevic; Sheik Omar-Abdel Rahman*, the man who bombed the *World Trade Center* in 1993; *David Koresh*, the *Branch Davidian* leader; advisor to *Sadam Hussein* during his death trial in Baghdag, a notable leftist who lives in New York at one of the best 12th Street CO-OPs in Greenwich Village.

Harry Belafonte, the former *King of Calypso* turned left-leaning social activist and vocal critic of the US; he was inspired and mentored by actor, singer and social activist *Paul Leeroy Robeson*, a card-carrying member of the *Communist Party USA*. Belafonte became an apologist for Castro in the 1970s and a champion of socialist causes such as the reivindication of *Ethel and Julius Rosenberg*, the Soviet spies executed for treason in 1953.

Alice Walker is the author of *The Color Purple*, a 1982 Pulitzer Prize fiction winner novel. She participated in Martin Luther King's *1963 March on Washington* and since then has been associated with *Code Pink* and *Women for Peace*. She is the author of the phrase «*We Are the Ones We Have Been Waiting For*». She has described the *US government* as a **terrorist organization**.

(Continuation)

Fearing violence, the *Javis Center* management had cancelled the event two days before the gathering; a New York state judge over-turned the cancellation and the event was confirmed. As ten anti-Castro followers unfurled a banner inside the Center, enraged pro-Castro activists began to club these dissenters and drag them out of the premises, yelling *gusanos*, *scum* and other epithets and moni-kers. The organizers justified their violent reactions against the dis-senters by arguing that «*they could have been CIA agents posing as activists*». Similar pro-Castro events took place simultaneously in London, Manila, Stockholm and other cities, presumably to honor an anniversary of the birth of José Martí.

Few of the pro-Castro rally supporters in New York or other cities knew at the time that earlier on that very same week, the Castro government had executed **Eduardo Díaz Betancourt**, 38, a Cuban Exile from Miami, and condemned to 30 years two of his compan-ions, **Daniel Santovenia Fernández**, 36, and **Pedro Alvarez Pedroso**, 26, all accused of landing armed on a Cuban beach and trying to organize a similar gathering in Havana. For many years, while Cubans on the island were continually victimized by a brutally repressive Castro dictatorship, there have been Americans and Latin Americans in the U.S. who have shown no moral or ethical outrage and have been happily partying, drinking, and generally supporting and acclaiming the bloody and murderous regime in Cuba.

Photos above:
The front page of ABC in **Madrid** denouncing the execution of **Eduardo Díaz Betancourt** in 1992; Demonstration against the execution in front of the *Cuban Embassy* in Rome.

Salvador Díaz-Versón (1905-1982) was a Cuban-born crime reporter that took asylum in Madrid during the dictatorship of Gerardo Machado. In 1933, after the fall of Machado he became chief of the *National Police* during the days of Batista until he resigned and went back into journalism in 1948. He was Cuba's *Chief of Military Intelligence* in the government of Carlos Prío (1948-1952). He always was an implacable foe of Communism and began to document a file as *Chief of the Cuban Army Counter-Spy Bureau*. From 1954 to 1956 he lived as an exile in Miami; returned to Cuba after a general amnesty and became editor of the newspaper *Excelsior*. Researching for the paper, he visited every country in the Americas as President of the *Inter American Organization of Anti-Communist Journalists (OIPAC)*, based in Lima, Perú. On May 6, 1960, Diaz Versón was called to testify at the US Senate Committee of the Judiciary as **one of the most knowledgeable researchers about the Communist threat to the US**; Senators Keating (New York) and Dodd (Connecticut) took his testimony and praised him.

Elena Díaz-Versón Amos (1927-2000) was Salvador's Cuban-born daughter. In 1993 she was presented in the US Senate as «*a grand woman, well known to this house as a passionate champion of restoring democracy and human rights in her native Cuba.*» She and her husband **John Amos (1924-1990)** —a *University of Miami* alumnus she married in 1944— founded AFLAC in 1955, one of the largest health insurance businesses in the US. As a Cuban exile, she was active in educational, philanthropic, and political causes and was always very involved in anti-Castro activities. She was a director of the *Valladares Foundation*, a human rights organization. In 1992 she financed the flight of Major *Orestes Lorenzo Perez*, a Cuban exile, to Havana to rescue his wife and children; she also assisted *Alina Fernandez Revuelta*, Fidel Castro's daughter, to escape from Cuba.

*Photos above: **Salvador Díaz-Versón**; **Elena Díaz-Versón** and her husband **John Amos**.*

Watching movies have always been important to Cubans, as historically evidenced by the hundreds of theaters in Havana —many more per capita than in New York, Madrid, Paris or Mexico, even though Cuba was never an important producer of films like were the US, Spain, France and Mexico. Immediately after 1959 the revolutionary government created the *Instituto Cubano del Arte e Industria Cinematográficos (ICAIC)*, trying to capitalize on the large number of Cubans involved in the Cine-Club movement that flourished in the 1950s.

A large number of filmmakers, film technicians and actors and actresses took advantage of the ICAIC and began to launch a new wave of Cuban films. It all went well until the *P.M.* affair of 1960. Working independently from the ICAIC, a group of young creators —many of them affiliated with Carlos Franqui's magazine *Lunes de Revolución*— produced a short film for the magazine's TV program. The film presented the nightlife in the bars and waterfront night spots of Havana. The director was **Sabá Cabrera Infante** (brother to famous novelist Guillermo) and the cameraman was Cineperiódico's **Orlando Jiménez Leal**, who would earn fame a few years later with the exile-inspired production of **El Super**. The **P.M.** film received favorable reviews from **Néstor Almendros**, the movie critic of Havana's *Bohemia* magazine.

Within a few weeks, however, ICAIC refused to exhibit **P.M.**; Castro had made his famous *Words to the Intellectuals* speech (*Within the Revolution, everything; against it, nothing*), **Nestor Almendros** lost his job at *Bohemia* and a long line of movie makers began to leave the island: **Orlando Jiménez Leal** and **Sabá Cabrera Infante, Eduardo Manet** (writer), **Fausto Canel** (filmmaker), **Eduardo Moure** (lead actor in the film *Lucía*), **Edmundo Desnöes** (scriptwriter), among many others.

(Continued)

Photos, left to right: The introductory titles *of P.M.*; *Orlando Jiménez Leal* and *León Ichaso.*

They were followed in the 1970s by **Ramón Suárez,** cinematographer of *Las Doce Sillas*. **Tomás Gutiérrez Alea,** director of many extraordinary films like *A Woman, a Man, a City* and *Memorias del Subdesarrollo,* unlike others, never left Cuba. The exodus of the cinematographers was in large part due to Castro's declaration of the Socialist-Marxist character of his revolution. In fact, of the best ten top award winning filmmakers in 1965 five had chosen the route to exile five years later.

When he arrived in New York as an exile, **Orlando Jiménez Leal,** one of the most successful Cuban filmmakers, started his own production company, *Guede Films,* and in 1979 produced and directed *El Super,* the first Cuban exile fictional feature, winner of awards at film festivals in Manheim, Biarritz and Venice; *El Super* was based on a play by Iván Acosta. Married to newswoman **Mari Rodríguez Ichaso**, Orlando's co-director and writer was Mari's brother, **León Ichaso,** who would go on to make such successful films as **Bitter Sugar** in 1996.

The film brings to the screen the lives of Roberto (a former bus driver in Cuba) and Aurelia (a Cuban home maker), two Cuban exiles living in New York City with their 17-year-old daughter Aurelita. For ten years Roberto has been maintaining the boiler, repairing windows and disposing of the garbage as the *Super* of a boring apartment building. Roberto and Aurelia's everyday conversations are about the Bay of Pigs, Castro, and life back in Cuba. They are so depressed that are not even making love anymore. All of a sudden Aurelita is pregnant. Distress about her increasingly dominating Americanness, they decide to escape from New York and move to Miami. This decision, prompted by dreams of sun-drenched palm trees and the sounds of Spanish, brings new energy to their lives; the film ends without any suggestions about their new life among other Cuban exiles.

Photos: **Nestor Almendros** and **Tomás Gutiérrez Alea**; posters for the film **El Super**.

After producing **El Super** and **Bitter Sugar** (1996, an exploration of life in Cuba, a place with no easy physical or emotional escape from the disillusionment about Castro's revolution), filmmaker León Ichaso undertook the direction of **Paraiso**, 2009, closing his successful trilogy about Cubans and Cuban exiles after the revolution.

Paraiso is the story of a man (Iván) who has fled Cuba on a raft and lands in Miami, where he meets his father Remigio, a successful radio host living in a posh Key Biscayne condo. Through his father, Iván gets a job as a pool attendant at a South Beach hotel; he cannot control himself and shoplifts and gets friendly with drug addicts.

According to **Ichaso,** *«Iván is one of these new little Frankensteins that Castro makes and sets loose on the world,»* adding *«the idea for the movie coalesced after a series of encounters with recent Cuban exiles the world over... there is something visceral about the film that will connect with people. It might stun or bruise them for a second, but they will sense there is no lie here».*

According to film expert **Alejandro Ríos** *«Paraiso measures the damage that 50 years of dictatorship has wreaked in Cuba, a broken country. [Iván] the* **hombre nuevo** *(new man) that the revolution has created doesn't know how to deal with the codes and norms of another society. He didn't fit in Cuba, and he doesn't fit in Miami. He's in a very dark limbo, but that's not because he's wrong or evil. It's what he was taught».*

Photo at right:
León Ichaso and his camera; the official posters of **Paraiso** and Bitter **Sugar**; **Adrian Más** and **Tamara Melián** in Paraiso.

Half a century after Communism in Cuba had sent hundreds of Cubans to firing squads, had confiscated all private businesses, had closed all private schools and independent newspapers, had imprisoned all dissenting voices and had placed in every block of every city a committee of informers to supervise every aspect of the personal lives of citizens, the world continued to worship what the Castro brothers had accomplished in Cuba.

It became more important for the press and the news services to report about Jackie's marriage to a Greek shipping magnate, or the beaching of some whales in the California coasts, or the surprise that the gloves did not fit O.J. Simpson, or that Mitterrand's mistress had followed his death cortege alongside his wife, or that Maradona had begun his drug rehabilitation in Havana.

Cuban exiles, nevertheless, continued in their efforts to let the world know of the destruction of civil society in Cuba, even if the rest of the world did not care. What follows is a gallery of scenes in every corner of the civilized planet where Cuban exiles continued to protest what was happening in Cuba even with little or no support from the rest of their communities.

Nobody Listened was a documentary filmed in the US by Cuban exile directors **Néstor Almendros** and **Jorge Ulla** in 1987, presenting for the first time the summary executions, and the cruel, inhuman and degrading treatment of people that was occurring in Cuba.

The research was made by **Carlos Ripoll** and **Fausto Canel**, two early Cuban exiles. World class eye-witnesses and observers were presented in the documentary: **Ricardo Bofill, Angel Cuadra, Guillermo Estévez, Huber Matos, Roberto Martín Pérez, Luisa Pérez, Armando Valladares, Jorge Valls, Jean-François Revel, Yves Montand, Father Miguel Angel Loredo** and **Jorge Semprún** among others.

Photos at right: the movie poster and **Almendros** filming.

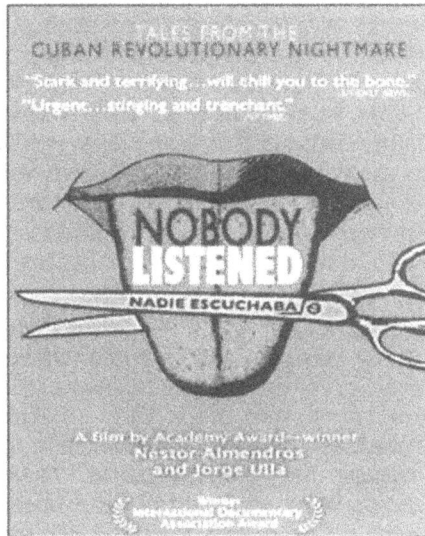

TALES FROM THE CUBAN REVOLUTIONARY NIGHTMARE

"Stark and terrifying...will chill you to the bone."

"Urgent...stinging and trenchant"

NOBODY LISTENED

NADIE ESCUCHABA

A film by Academy Award-winner Néstor Almendros and Jorge Ulla

Winner International Documentary Association Award

The **US Guantánamo Naval Base (GITMO)** covers an area of 71 square miles (35 of which are dry land) at the entrance of Guantánamo Bay, Oriente, Cuba. It was leased (about $6,000 per month in 2010 US currency) from the Cuban government in 1903, to be used as a coaling station by the US, under terms of «*complete jurisdiction and control.*» In 1991, President Reagan established a program to intercept refugees on the high seas to prevent them from reaching North American shores, and the base began to be known as **safe heaven**. President Bush the elder continued this policy and between October 1991 and June 1992 a total of 36,594 Haitian refugees were intercepted and sent back to Haiti. In 1994 President Clinton modified the policy and began to intern the Haitians into Guantánamo. In two years a total of 21,638 Haitians were in the camps at Guantánamo.

In 1994, when Castro began to allow Cubans to leave without any official impediments, President Clinton ordered the interception of Cuban refugees and their transfer to Guantánamo. During August and September, 32,362 Cubans were rescued from the high seas and transferred there. In the following two months 30,000 additional refugees were rescued and lodged at the Base. To accommodate the Cubans, **Joint Task Force-160** established 25 camps in several parts of the base, mostly near the coast. They were supplied with milk and hot meals, preventive medical care, facilities for pregnant women and newborn babies, regular mail service, public telephones to make calls to relatives (reversing the charges), recreational facilities, radios and newspapers, as well as facilities to publish their own papers.

On May 2, 1995, it was announced that all Cuban refugees in the base, with the exception of those with criminal records, would be able to go to the U.S. By January of 1996, **safe heaven** was closed as the last Cuban refugee departed.

(Continued)

Photos above, left to right:
An overall view of the **US Guantánamo** Base and the area of the
US Military Tent Camps, where Cuban refugees were housed.

After the last Cuban *balseros* left Guantánamo, the US government revised the **Cuban Adjustment Act of 1966** and established the **wet-foot-dry foot** policy: any Cuban reaching dry
ground in the US would be allowed to stay, but not those who
were rescued at sea. The new policy was so strict that in 2006,
when 4 women, 2 children and 9 adults climbed on a piling of the
old seven Mile Bridge in the Florida Keys, they were returned to
Cuba «*because they would need to get their feet wet to reach the
mainland*». After a hunger strike by *Ramón Saúl Sánchez* (of
Movimiento Democracia), the 15 were given migrant visas.

Photos above:
Camp Delta (former *Camp X-Ray*), set up in Guantánamo Base after the
Cubans left; in 2002 it became a penitentiary to house prisoners of the
War on Terror; the press informing about **Cubans in Guantánamo**.

Life in the US Guantánamo Base, 1994-1995

Photos above, top to bottom:
From the initial chaos in **August of 1994** to the organized living
in the last days of **December of 1995**.

One of the first Cuban exiles who reached an important position of power and influence in the city of Miami was **Cesar Odio**, appointed Miami city manager in 1978. He admirably became a «*low-key, nose-to-the-grindstone, penny-pinching public servant devoid of flash and artifice,*» according to the *Miami Herald* of July 31, 1988. Odio, after years of working in private industry, and after working as Miami's assistant manager for six years, became the manager of nearly 4,000 city employees with a budget close to $200 Million.

A lifelong sportsman —in Cuba and in exile— Odio's metaphor to his employees was the eight-man crew of rowing, his favorite sport. «*If the oars go into the water together, the boat is very light and moves very fast, but if the oars aren't in the water at the same time, it's a very heavy boat, and it doesn't move*».

Miami's businessmen, city fathers and civic leaders, praised Odio's virtues during his years of incumbency as the city leader: «*He is solid... has the ability to get things done without creating a lot of furor... When he decides to do something, he does it... he is a feisty, hands-on, tough-talking administrator who hangs to his job by mastering the art of knowing a lot but keeping his mouth shut... He's enormously energetic... Odio is a symphony of nervous energy... His office has a a lot of sport memorabilia but also photos of the Pope and Miss Universe... in moments of intense concentration, agitation or amusement, his lips purse, or his eyebrows soar and when he walks, his shoulders hunch slightly forward as if he were headed into an eternal strong wind... One-on-one he is capable of enormous warmth*».

Odio became famous for his quick telephone answers: «*If the question is money, the answer is no*». Deep down, Miamians knew Odio was a man that had «*washed dishes, pumped gas and sold truck parts to buy food and meet the mortgage payments,*» and these were very solid credentials.

In 1996, after 17 years of immaculate public service, Odio resigned as Miami manager after what seemed like an anti-Cuban strategy to bring him down fostered by the *Miami Herald* and local political interests.

In August of 1998, for the first time in history, the US charged a group of Cuban exiles in Puerto Rico with a plot to assassinate Castro. The exiles were identified as José Rodríguez, Alfredo Domingo Otero, Angel Hernández Rojo, Juan Bautista Márquez, all of Miami; Francisco Secundino Córdova, of Marathon Key; and Angel Alfonso Alemán, of Union City, N.J. The government argued that the group had attempted to kill Castro on October 27, 1997, during his visit to Isla Margarita, Venezuela, to participate in the VII session of the Cumbre Ibero-Americana. The plot failed when the 46-foot vessel **La Esperanza** began to sink on the western coast of Puerto Rico and radioed for help to the US Coast Guard. When the Coast Guard arrived, Angel Alfonso Alemán claimed ownership of the weapons and said «*I placed them there myself. These are weapons for the purpose of assassinating Fidel Castro*».

Two of the automatic weapons in the vessel were registered in the name of Francisco (Pepe) Hernández, President of the Cuban-American National Foundation. Spokesman John Russell from the US Justice Department acknowledged that there were several instances in the past when the CIA had tried to do away with Castro but the US Justice Department had never indicted Cuban exiles trying to do the same. US law barred military actions against a country with which the US is not at war.

On December 9, 1999, a jury in Puerto Rico acquitted all the defendants with a decision based on politics rather than evidence. The jury foreman explained «*This was a message to the Cuban people that we're with you, and not to lose hope*».

(Continued)

Photos below:

The fantasy of doing away with Castro perdured for many years, not only among Cuban exiles but also among spy and action writers around the world. On this and the next page are some of the dozens of books published on **How to Kill Castro**.

On December 2, 1961, Fidel Castro, an alumnus of the *Belén Jesuit High School* in Havana, declared himself a *Marxist-Leninist*, confiscated all Catholic Schools and forcibly expelled into exile 131 priests. A month later, on January 3, 1962, he was ex-communicated from the Catholic Church (he could be, as he was a baptized Christian and member of the Church) by **Angelo Giuseppe Roncalli, John XXIII (1881–1963)**, the *Good Pope*. John XXIII was acting under a decree by **Eugenio Maria Giuseppe Giovanni Pacelli (1876–1958), Pius XII** who, in 1949, established that Catholics supporting Communism would be ex-communicated. Cuban exiles were hopeful that this action would shorten the days of Castro in Cuba; Communism, however, consolidated its position in Cuba for close to half a century.

Forty years later, the decision did not dissuade **Karol Józef Wojtyła (1920–2005), John Paul II,** to visit Cuba in 1998, returning the courtesy of a visit from Castro to the Vatican in 1996. John Paul II offered a Mass at the *Plaza de la Revolution* on January 25, 1998, with Fidel Castro in attendance; he was given the peace greetings by **Cardenal Jaime Lucas Ortega Alamino, (1936-)**, Archbishop of Havana, who descended from the altar where he was acting as a co-officiant of the Mass. Castro later declared he had not been at Mass since his childhood.

As a result of John Paul II visit to Cuba, the Castros began to allow public religious processions, restored Christmas as a holiday, welcomed new priests to immigrate to Cuba and occasionally opened the Radio stations to Church announcements.

Neither in 1996 nor in 1998 was the ex-communication lifted. Aside from the concessions to John Paul II, the most Castro had agreed to, in 1992, was to replace «Cuba es un estado ateo,» in the Constitution, for the milder «Cuba es un estado laico».

Following the same presumed benefit to Communism in Cuba, **Raúl Castro** declared on December 18, 2011, that he would receive with «afecto y respeto,» Pope **Joseph Aloisius Ratzinger (1927-), Benedict XVI**, on the 400th anniversary of the finding of the *Vírgen of Charity*, patroness of Cuba.

Photos below, left to right: the four Popes during Castro's years:
John XXIII; Paul VI; John Paul II and **Benedictus XVI.**

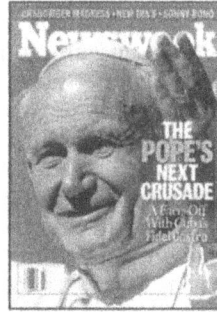

On December 20, 1997, deferring to pressure from Catholic Cuban exiles, Archbishop **John Favarola** announced his decision to cancel plans for sending the cruise ship *Norwegian Majesty of the Seas* to Cuba on a one-day pilgrimage to see Pope John Paul II. The pope's visit had been planed from January 21 to 25 and about 400 Cuban exiles had signed for the cruise, with fares ranging from $600 to $1,400 dollars.

«I truly believe that the archbishop made the decision in prayer last night. I believe somehow God indicated to him what was the right thing to do,» said **Carlos Saladrigas**, who had advised the Archbishop against sponsoring the trip. «I'm concerned that Catholics in Cuba will see this as those powerful Miami Cubans imposing their political views on a religious and spiritual affair,» said **Ely Chovel**, of Miami, who had bought a cruise ticket. At the time Saladrigas was President of *Vincam Group*, a human resources company and Chovel was president of the *Group Operation Pedro Pan (GOPP)*. From Cuba, dissident **Elizardo Sánchez** said: «I plan to discuss the decision with other Castro opponents but for the moment I can say that I think this is a step backward for the Miami Archdiocese.»

Without any doubt, many Cuban exiles viewed the papal visit to Cuba and the cruise plan as insensitive to their suffering. The cruise, they reasoned, would be traveling in luxury the same waters where thousands of Cubans had drowned or were eaten by sharks as they fled the Castro regime on fragile, improvised and insecure rafts. Many Cuban exiles also resented the public relations victory of Castro as he would be rendering homage to the pope and probably ceremoniously kissing his ring.

In the end, Pope John Paul II, during his visit to Cuba, delivered stinging condemnations of the U.S. embargo against Cuba, calling the policy «oppressive, unjust and ethically unacceptable;» he also urged Castro to open up his society. «A modern state cannot make atheism one of its political ordinances». His words fell on deaf ears in both instances.

*Photos above: **John Clement Favarola**, Archbishop of Miami from 1994 to 2010; **John Paul II** in the cover of Newsweek. When he died in 2005 Castro thanked him for having said that «the restrictive economic measures imposed from outside the country were unjust and ethically unacceptable,» during his 1998 visit to Cuba.*

At the end of January of 1998 Pope John Paul II visited Cuba, the only Latin American country he had never visited. Hundreds of Cubans, practicing Catholics or Communist loyalists, did not miss a step while the Pope was widely shown on the state-run TV. Cuban Cardinal **Jaime Ortega Alamino (1936-)** was for the first time allowed to broadcast his views in advance of the Pope's visit. He never made a reference to the Pope's role in the liberation of Poland in the 1980s and discreetly evaded the issue of John Paul II as a world known **anti-Communist**. Castro, on the contrary, was glad to reinforce the Pope's notion that the three decade old **US embargo** was an anti-Christian aggressive action against the suffering people of Cuba.

The Pope's objective was to bring about the resurgence of Cuba as a Catholic nation; it overlooked the fact that Castro had declared Cuba an atheist country in 1962, had expelled hundreds of priests from the island, closed down many churches and seized all Catholic schools and property. The pope's sense of outrage was tempered by the hope of a **Cuban glasnost**; not even the secretly planted microphones discovered in the Pope's accommodations were allowed to be a distraction. Likewise, the Cuban government veiled support of Afro-Cuban creeds such as *Abakua* and *Santería* did not affect the Pope's determination to make friends with the Communists in Cuba and secure a space for the Catholic Church in the island.

(Continued)

Photos above:
The **Popemovile** in the *Plaza de la Revolución*;
Castro publicly lecturing the Pope.

(Continuation)

In Miami and the Cuban exile *Diáspora* (from the Greek, διασπορά, scattering from the familial homeland) the Pope's visit to Cuba was interpreted in diametrically different ways. On one hand, the Archdiocese of Miami had to cancel the 1,200 passenger **cruise liner excursion** to see the Pope in Cuba. It received the protests of hundreds of exiles insisting that no one should return to the island while Cuba was under Communist rule. On the other extreme, an anti-Castro group, the *Democracia* movement, was instructed by the US State Department to refrain from sailing its **prayer flotilla** to a point across Havana in international waters.

The visit of Pope John Paul II to Cuba had been loaded with heavy expectations; Cubans and many Cuban exiles had high hopes it would mark the beginning of the end of Cuba's Communist government. Some even predicted popular uprisings. Nothing of the sort happened. John Paul's calls for national reconciliation, for religious freedom, and for Cuba's Marxist government to respect the inalienable rights of the individual, fell on deaf ears. Two hours after the Pope left Havana, the Cuban Government removed all vestiges of his presence in Cuba. Opponents and dissidents continued to be quickly crushed and neutralized, and most people continued to be afraid to speak freely.

In the end, the political accomplishments of the Pope's visit were small. The **US embargo** was not lifted; the Church did get a miniscule space for worship (six-blocks processions) but not access to the **airwaves** or the return of any of its properties and **schools**.

Castro, not surprisingly, was the only beneficiary. In 2005, the *Granma International* paper in Havana *commented:*

«*The leader of the Revolution [Castro] characterized the fundamental features of conflicts of the contemporary era as a basis for understanding the importance of the pontificate of John Paul II, whom he described as an exceptional man, a determined fighter, untiring, whose virtues should not be ignored. "These are our opinions from a human and social focus, in the light of fundamental questions for humanity, although we respect different opinions."*»

Photo above: John Paul II's mass at the **Plaza de la Revolución**, Sunday, January 25, 1989.

Cuban exiles in Miami, much to their distress, never had a close spiritual link to **Pope John Paul II**. It became evident during the pope's visit to Miami in September of 1987.

A public mass was organized at the *Miami Dade County Fairgrounds*. The weather was menacing and inauspicious but an enormous crowd had gathered; by the amount of small Cuban flags waved by the public it was evident it consisted mostly of Cuban exiles. Even in open air, the noise was deafening. When the Gospel reading was about to start, the Mass had to be cut short. It was lightening heavily; it forced the ceremony to be finished indoors. The Cubans in attendance stayed in place to listen to the Pope. *He never mentioned Cuba* in his homily; never made a single remark about the suffering of the exiles or the crimes being committed in Cuba; never took the time to visit the Miami's Shrine of the *Vírgen de la Caridad del Cobre*, patroness of Cuba; he *did not honor the request* of a group of Cuban Catholic leaders to be received in a special audience.

The next encounter of John Paul II with Cubans was during his visit to Havana in 1998. Mentioning Ché Guevara he said: «*He is now before God's Tribunal. Let us leave Our Lord to judge his merits. I am certain that he wanted to serve the poor.*» Did the Pope forget the words of Pius XI when his predecessor referred to Communism as «*a satanic scourge?*»

Years later, on January 8, 2005, **John Paul II**, while receiving the credentials of a new Cuban ambassador, praised «*the accomplishments of the Cuban government in the areas of health, education and culture.*»

(Continued)

Photos below:
Left, **TIME** Magazine published a cover article about the startling relationship of Castro with the Pope; *to the right*, **Lech Walesa** and **John Paul II**. Cubans were expecting the same support for their cause that he had offered the Polish people. It was an illusion.

(Continuation)

On the same occasion, the Pope praised the Castro regime for having «*erected pillars of excellence in the house of peace, promoting a harmonic growth of the body and the spirit among Cubans*».

The pope failed to mention the numerous martyrs within the Cuban youth that had faced the firing squads across the island and died shouting «***¡Viva Cuba Libre! ¡Viva Cristo Rey!***»

Moreover, he proposed to the Cuban regime at the *University of Havana* on January 23, 1998, to begin «*a fruitful dialogue between believers and non-believers —that is, Cuban Communists and Cuban Catholics— to seek a cultural synthesis under the premise that both shared the common goal of serving humankind.*»

For some unexplained reason, as recalled later by **Armando Valladares**, former US Ambassador to the UN Commission on Human Rights, Pope John Paul II ignored three filial messages written to him by several Catholic leaders of the Cuban exile community between 1987 and 1999:

- A 1987 letter entitled "*Holy Father, Free Cuba.*" addressed to him during his visit to Miami (*Diario las Americas*, August 7, 1987);

- A 1995 letter entitled "*Cubans in Exile Appeal to John Paul II: Holy Father, Protect Us from the Actions of Cardinal Ortega.*" (*Diario las Américas*, October 24, 1998);

- A third letter in 1999 entitled "*Holy Father, Save from Oblivion the Cuban Martyrs, Victims of Communism!*" (*Diario las Américas*, September, 1999).

Photos above:
The Pope in Santiago de Cuba in 1998; at the pedestal containing the
urn with the remains of **Father Félix Varela** at the *University of Havana*;
on the bottom, the papal coat of arms.

As the new century approached it became clear that the solution to the Cuban drama was as dependent on the US political life as the politico-commercial ambitions of Spain, the major influence on the European Union's opinions about Cuba. It seriously distressed most Cuban refugees, considering that many of them were descendants of Spanish émigrés to Cuba and that Spaniards were received in Cuba with open arms after the War of Independence.

Before and after the death of Generalissimo Franco, the Spanish government saw the Cuban revolution as the defender of Spain's legacy, heritage, culture and traditions against the imperialistic ambitions of the US. In spite of its limited condition as a second or third tier world power, Spain tried to occupy the moral, economic and ideological vacuum left by the dissolution of the USSR earlier in the 1990s. Hence Spain began a strong bid for a *reconquista* of Cuba and its politicians imbedded Cuban affairs in the daily narrative and concerns of Spanish politics. The EU's positions began to be influenced by the new Spanish *conquistadores* while, with the exception of the Czech and French governments, the nations of Europe maintained their traditional passive and disinterested diplomatic policy towards Cuba.

Photos: some evidence of the official Spanish half-century of support for the Castro regime. **Alfredo Guevara** in conversation with **Miguel Angel Moratinos**, the Spanish Foreign Minister; the signing of one of many *Spain-Cuba* commercial treaties; the shameful support of *Meliá Hotels* to Apartheid in Cuba; a huge bronze statue of *Ché* in the streets of Barcelona.

VI

«A genuine person goes to the roots. To be a radical is no more than that: to go to the roots.»

JOSÉ MARTÍ, FOUNDER OF THE CUBAN NATION.

«There may be times when we are powerless to prevent injustice, but there must never be a time when we fail to protest.»

ELIE WIESEL, AMERICAN NOBEL LAUREATE AND HOLOCAUST SURVIVOR.

The Unfinished Story of the Cuban Exile

A new Century not yet ready for Cuba's Freedom

IN A PREDAWN RAID on Saturday, April 22, 2000, federal agents under the direction of US Attorney General Janet Reno stormed the house of Juan Miguel González Quintana in Little Havana and seized his nephew, 6-year old Elián González, the child that for months had captured the imagination of Cuban exiles as a symbol of their own flight to freedom from the oppression in Cuba. Elián's relatives, the President of the University of Miami and several leaders of the Cuban exile community were sprayed with tear gas and held at gun point while Elián was swiftly removed from a closet in his own bedroom. A total of 130 Immigration agents participated in the operation; eight of them, from an elite BORTAC Border Patrol unit, were fully dressed with their SWAT uniforms.

Young Elián, his mother and twelve men had left Cuba on a small boat with an old engine. Elián's mother and ten of her friends drowned in the effort to reach Florida. The child and two escapees survived and were rescued by a fisherman on Thanksgiving day in 1999. Elián had been placed in an inner tube by his mother, who did not know how to swim; she sank in the sea and drowned a few minutes later. She had protected her son until she had no more strength to remain afloat. Rumors circulated that several dolphins had prevented the boy from falling from the inner tube.

Saving Cuba almost becomes a Dead-End Street

For Cuban exiles in Miami, the 21st century could not have started with a worst omen. The historical exiles of 1959 were getting on in years without any prospects of victory against the men who had ruined their country, sequestered all liberties and brutally murdered their opponents. The exiles had earned the respect of the Americans, had achieved substantial political clout and financial success, had excelled in their professions and trades, had helped to turn Miami into a thriving metropolitan area, had persevered in their *cubanismo* and had educated their children to love Cuba while being very American, without feeling to be exiles themselves. No small feat! Yet the dream of witnessing a free Cuba continued to elude them. To make matters worse, as of April 22, Elián was gone for good, back to the hands and the propaganda machine of Fidel Castro.

Not all Cubans in Miami lamented the loss of Elián. At the dawn of the new century there were quite a few former "exiles" in Miami sympathetic to Castro's regime, ready to forgive him. In their minds, the much touted social improvements of the Communists in Cuba more than compensated for the innocent lives taken. In their quest for enjoying occasional *mojitos* in Cuba while living in Capitalist America, they were rationalizing whatever excuses were necessary to justify the loss of freedom and life in the island. They were seeking mutual support in organizations like *Brigada Antonio Maceo, Asociación José Martí, Alianza Martiana, Miami Coalition Against the Embargo of Cuba, Alianza de Trabajadores de la Comunidad Cubana, Cuban Committee for Democracy, Asociación de Mujeres Cristianas en Defensa de la Familia, Cuban American Defense League,* and *Rescate Cultural Afro-Cubano,* to name a few. Shamelessly they were commenting on the Elián saga saying: «*This just might be the OK Corral for the hard-liners,*» or «*what we have is a bunch of stubborn old men on both sides of the Florida strait waiting for God to sort them out,*» or «*By now their anti-communist rants sound dated and shrill.*»

Unfortunately, the fact was that the Elián affair stroked a severe blow to Cuban exiles everywhere they lived and became a public relations nightmare. It had a depressing effect for Cuban-Americans, as stunning and devastating as the defeat of the *Bay of Pigs* invasion. It isolated exiles from the communities where they lived and had so carefully cultivated; all of a sudden few people could understand their passion for saving one child from the savage dictatorship in Cuba.

The only positive outcome of the entire incident was that it energized second-generation Cubans to share with their parents and grandparents the concerns for the oppression in Cuba. Cuban-American children protested and joined hands with their elders to demonstrate at Elián's temporary home at 2319 NW Second Street in Little Havana. Interestingly, the day after Delfín González, Elián's uncle, announced he was buying the house to turn it into a private museum, 192 players in Miami, in the best Cuban tradition, picked the numbers 2-3-1-9 in the *Cash Four Lottery* and won $5,000 each. It made some people think that the story of the dolphins saving Elián's life was not to be dismissed.

The Strange Marriage of Cuba and Venezuela

As this was happening in Miami and Cuba, Hugo Chávez Frías, a leftist military man in Venezuela, a failed leader of a *coup d'état* against Venezuelan President Carlos Andrés Pérez in February of 1992 and founder of a movement called the *Movimiento Revolucionario Bolivariano*, was elected in July 30, 2000 as President of Venezuela, with 60% of the vote. By October of that year he was tending a saving hand to Castro's Cuba with a *Convenio Integral de Cooperación Venezuela-Cuba*.

Under that treaty, «*inspired by the desire to strengthen the traditional friendship of Cuba and Venezuela,*» Castro agreed to provide goods, technical assistance and medical and health services to the Republic of Venezuela in exchange for oil products, frozen chickens and petroleum derivatives from Venezuela. The exchange rate and prices were to be determined later. Financial schemes for short and long terms, shipping rates, insurance and other details were also to be determined later. The treaty included a 5-year migratory clause that waived any and all restrictions for Cuban functionaries, specialists and workers to enter Venezuelan territory. Behind the business-like wording of the agreement, Cuba was assured of its energy needs by the people of Venezuela and Chávez could count on ideological, mediatic and military support from Cuba in his national and continental ambitions to be the revolutionary successor of Castro.

With Chávez' generosity, the Cuban revolution was able to float again. As an unknown blogger would write later «*The streets in Havana continued to feel the weight of buses, trucks and cars emitting stinking emissions that ruined with soot the laundered sheets hanging from the city balconies; the long lines of buyers continued to silently wait for their turns to receive a couple of eggs and a few vegetables every week; the leaders kept insisting that life in Cuba was tough and demanded sacrifice, but it was also full of prideful patriotism. They kept painting billboards proclaiming* Vas Bien Fidel, *instead of recognizing* Vamos Muy Mal Fidel...»

Empowered by Venezuela's economic assistance, Castro and the powers in Cuba continued during the XXI century to insist that socialism was still virtuous, and societies under Marxism-Leninism were superior to free market societies by virtue of their guaranteed employment security, an imaginary classless equality, powerful security nets for the poor and downtrodden, free access to health and education for revolutionaries, workplace peace, and non-competing political opportunities within the context of revolutionary and party loyalty.

The View of Young Cubans in the Island

Young Cubans in the island, however, were no longer agreeing, pointing to the authoritarian centralized decisions and staffing policies, lack of rewards for personal merits, a lackadaisical and apathetic approach to productivity, an extreme bureaucracy, an exorbitant distance "between Chiefs and Indians,"(common citizens and their leaders), as well as a total disregard for the psychological value of a sense of ownership. They were complaining about procrastination, lifeless organizations, indolent bosses, stagnant futures, and lack of space at the top. In other words, a prognostication and pretense of economic progress and opportunity in the face of an unmovable and failed communist rhetoric.

Young revolutionaries in Cuba were faulting party leaders for ignoring that in an environment of serious scarcity of resources, the pressure to *"resolve"* individual and family needs had to trump the will to contribute to *"solve"* institutional requirements. Cubans were also tired of having to be responsible for and protect property rights held only by the government (people could use houses, land, cars, tools, materials but could not own them). Even the revolutionary slogans were no longer making sense to the youth in Cuba. «*Socialismo o Muerte*» had replaced «*Patria o Muerte*» many years ago. They could go along with the price to pay for the fatherland, but could not stomach they had to give their lives for the failed doctrines of socialism.

They were also reproaching the old guard for its shortsightedness. Whenever the revolution had been at a critical point in its development (after the expropriation of American companies in 1960, after the breach of trust with the Soviets that followed the Missile Crisis in 1962, after the losses of know-how during the waves of expatriations, and more recently after the end of the Cold War in 1999), the Cuban government always sent people for training to Moscow to secure its authority and dominance over the island, instead of sending young professionals to business schools to get trained in the management of companies and resources. As a result Cuba has never lacked a well organized military force (Raúl's Castro power base, the most powerful institution in Cuba, controlling 60 percent of the economy) but does not have good professional managers.

In order to leave no doubts as to who was in command of the situation in Cuba, the Castro government set up a crackdown of Cuban dissidents on March 18 to 20, 2003. Seventy five dissidents were imprisoned (journalists, writers, poets, librarians, human rights activists, democracy activists, all accused as agents of the CIA, accepting bribes from the US government or conspiring with James Cason, the Director of the US Interest Section in Cuba. Quick trials were carried out between the 3d and the 7th of April. All 75 people (some of them organizers of the nationwide petition drive called the *Proyecto Varela*), were accused of "dangerousness" and received sentences from 6 to 30 years. They were seeking a legal and constitutional reform to make Cuba consistent with international human rights accords that the Cuban government had agreed to respect.

Together, the sentences added up to 1500 years in prison. None of the accused had incited violence or committed any criminal acts. Most were sentenced for violating Article 91 of the penal code, or Law 88, or both of them. At the time, the Iraq invasion was capturing the world's attention and the regime took advantage of it to carry out the *Primavera Negra* (Black Spring). Furthermore, three young black men were executed in those days for trying to escape the island. They had not hurt anyone during the attempt. Their death penalty was simply a message to any would be future-escapees.

Article 91 implied a sentence from 10 to 20 years in prison or a death penalty for committing actions that «*jeopardized the independence of Cuba, or its territorial integrity, in order to benefit a foreign country*». Law 88 called for years of prison for people that «*support US policy against Cuba in order to destabilize the country and jeopardize the socialist order and the independence of the country.*» Law 88, due to its open-ended language, was appropriately known as the *Ley Mordaza* (Gag Law). The European Union imposed brief sanctions to Cuba (that were lifted in 2008 at the behest of the government of José Luis Rodríguez Zapatero in Spain). The US government, in the hands of President Clinton, simply protested. The French politicians were outraged and began to send aid to the prisoners.

The conditions of the sentences to the 75 dissidents encouraged the organization of *Las Damas de Blanco* (The Ladies in White), a respected opposition group integrated by the wives and relatives of the jailed dissidents. They began weekly Sunday pilgrimages to attend Mass at the Church of Santa Rita in Havana, followed by marches through the city asking freedom for their loved ones. Over the next nine years they suffered harassment, beatings and detentions. They never ran away from their valiant resistance. Eight days before Pope Benedict XVI's arrival in Cuba on March 26, 2012, 70 of the Ladies in White were arrested by the Castro regime and taken to prison. They were detained while trying to attend Mass with his Holiness. The Pope never knew of it, and if he did, did not pay much attention.

The Views of Cubans Exiles in the Diaspora

On August 9, 2005 a 3-judge panel from the 11th US Circuit Court of Appeals rejected the convictions of five Cuban spies (Gerardo Hernández, Ramón Labañino, Antonio Guerrero, Fernando González, and René González, members of Havana's *Red Avispa*) alleging that seating an impartial jury in Miami had been an «*unreasonable probability because of pervasive community prejudice.*» These five men had been found guilty of collaborating in the 1996 shoot down by Cuban MIGs of two small unarmed recognizance planes belonging to *Hermanos al Rescate*, and were later convicted at a new trial in 2008.

Cuban-American leaders expressed outrage at the judicial rejection decision because of the reasons behind it. The commentary of an opportunistic and unnamed professor from the University of Miami Law School, for instance, was a sarcastic... «*Dade County is like Alice in Wonderland where up is down, down is up. As you drift out of Dade County this world ends at the Dade-Broward line.*» Richard Nuccio, a former Clinton man and frequent critic of Cuban exiles (because of their solid Republican loyalty), was delighted to write on several papers that «*people in other parts of the country are unsympathetic to Cuban-Americans because of the community's single-mindedness.*»

As mentioned by journalist Guillermo Martínez (author with San Verdeja of the 800 page book *Cubans: an Epic Journey*), «*Why does nobody recall the thousands of political prisoners who were jailed for decades in Castro's Cuba?... this is the same jailer who once had more political prisoners per capita than any other country in the world... the penalty for trying to leave Cuba was four years in jail...»*

The Eternal Issue of the Embargo

As the Cuban American population in Miami neutered its feelings with the influx of hundreds of economic and opportunistic new expatriates (the result of outdated migration US policies towards Cuba), the subject of the US embargo resurfaced with increased urgency.

The new immigrants, several Congressmen and some American companies claimed that if the embargo and the travel restrictions to Cuba were lifted, the Castro regime would topple and suppurate under the influence of a free market capitalistic presence in Cuba. This argument, of course, ignored the fact that for many years hundreds of Canadian, Italian, French, Spanish, British and American tourists had already been in Cuba without any positive effect on Cuba's ideological and totalitarian practices. In fact, nothing but positive cash flow had come to Cuba as 400,000 Cuban residents of Miami were vacationing in Cuba every year (even sending their children to summer camps) in nefarious complicity with the regime that had destroyed the republic.

The gullibility of those supporting free travel and no embargo to Cuba had no limits. It presumed an inexperienced leadership in Cuba (ignoring that 11 US Presidents had been successfully sidelined by Castro's government); it visualized an open arms, secure, unconditional and guaranteed welcome to US investments; it believed in a willingness on the part of Cuba to allow capitalists to keep control of their operations in the island; it ignored Castro's words to the 5th Communist Party Congress in 1997: «*We will do whatever is necessary but we will never renounce our principles. We do not like capitalism and we will not abandon our Socialist system.*»

The arguments of the opposing pro-embargo position were convincing and substantial: the end of the embargo would guarantee the growth of the regime by providing funds that would strengthen the state as owner of most business in Cuba; it would allow the Communists to suck funds from international organizations (the International Monetary Fund, the World Bank, and others) at a time when other lending sources (the former Soviet Union, the Club of Paris, Spain, Brazil) were reluctant to accept Cuba's credit worthiness; it would wipe out the last bargaining chip in the hands of those wishing to restore democracy in Cuba, which was to trade the embargo for a Cuban *Perestroika* and *Glasnost*.

New Approaches to "the Cuban Communities Abroad"

Finally, the first years of the 21st century were witness to renewed efforts of the Cuban government to recruit within the Cuban Diaspora an assembly of brokers and middlemen that would vouch for Cuba's good intentions and promote reconciliation under Castro's conditions.

These were not novel (or noble) efforts. In December of 1977 the *Brigada Antonio Maceo* had accepted the Communists' invitation to visit and work for the Castros. After several years of excursions they tired and discontinued the nonsense. During November and December of 1978 the infamous *Diálogo* took place in Havana. It was simply followed by 100,000 visitors from the *Diáspora* bringing cash and goodies to Cuba in 1979. Three meetings of *"La Nación y la Emigración"* took place in 1994, 1995 and 2004. The unsuspecting attendants were tortured with boring and long-winded speeches by Ricardo Alarcón and company, but nothing positive resulted in terms of rights, freedom, democracy or any other expectations.

On March of 2008 and on January of 2010, two *Isla-y-Diáspora* meetings took place in Havana under the hopeful denomination of *Cubanos Residentes en el Exterior contra el Bloqueo y el Terrorismo*. Both produced a final declaration that stated « *Comprometidos como estamos con la valiosa obra de la Revolución...*» (Committed as we are with the valuable achievements of the revolution...). Both ended with «*Exigimos el levantamiento del bloqueo... Fidel, usted será siempre nuestro Comandante*» (We demand the lifting of the blockade... Fidel, you will always be our leader). The names of the attendees were never provided.

They were also to remain anonymous in the *Primer Encuentro Nacional de Cubanos Residentes en Estados Unidos* held at the former Cuban embassy in Washington in April of 2012. All three conferences were attended by the same suspects: *Cuban Americans for Engagement (CAFÉ), Alianza Martiana: Brigada Antonio Maceo, Asociación José Martí, Asociación de Trabajadores de la Comunidad Cubana, Círculo Bolivariano de Miami* and *Asociación de Mujeres Cristianas en Defensa de la Familia.*

It is worth mentioning that two popes also visited Cuba in recent times: John Paul II in 1998 and Benedict XVI in 2012. Both asked for the end of the embargo. They joined their voices to Reverends Jesse Jackson and Al Sharpton, Minister Louis Farrakhan and Jaime Ortega Alamino, Cuba's Cardinal, who also opposed the embargo. When John Paul II made his last address in Cuba he said «*This rain during the last hours of my stay in Cuba may signify an advent.*» Other than the re-establishment of Christmas in Cuba the hopeful advent was reduced to nothing. After one of Benedict XVI's homilies in 2012, Marino Murillo, the Vice-President of the Council of Ministers, rebutted his Holiness with this words: «*We are updating our economic model, but we are not talking about political reform.*» Again, Good Friday was established as a holiday in Cuba, but no processions, marches or demonstrations, no Catholic schools or Catholic papers or radio stations would be allowed. Cuban Catholic exiles everywhere simply said: «*Big Deal.*»

All together six regional meetings were organized in Europe, three in South America, four in Central América and Mexico, one in the Caribbean and one in Spain; all seeking the unconditional end of the embargo and the normalization of relations between the *Comunidad Residente en el Exterior* and the politically immovable Marxist regime in Cuba. The end results: promises on one end; naiveté, candor, propensity to be seduced or stupidity on the other.

An Unfinished Story

The Cuban exile history will continue until the last women and men born in Cuba and living abroad dies. Those Cubans have been through CIA recruiting, the Bay of Pigs, the Missile

Crisis, the infiltration of terrorists, criminal elements and gangsters in the 1970s and the perplexing Mariel Boatlift. They were called heartless and insensible during the Elián Affair; for fifty years they received insults and unfair offenses from both sides: Cuba attacked them as members of the *Miami Mafia* while some US xenophobes insulted them as fanatical rightist zealots. They were part of the largest peaceful invasion of exiles in American history and made possible the extraordinary growth of the city they had chosen to inhabit. They had to endure hundreds of internal fights brought about by their powerlessness and the deaf ears of the rest of the world. They brought Cuban music, protests and their ethics not only to Miami but to cities like New York, Paris, Mexico City, Union City, Los Angeles, Chicago, London, Madrid, across five continents. Someday, probably too late, the world will honor their strength and their backbone, their generosity and their passion for freedom.

The
2000s
and
beyond

- On January 15, 2000, **Serge Lewish**, a French lawyer, backed by the **Asociación Europea Cuba Libre**, went to court accusing Castro and his cohorts of crimes against humanity and drug trafficking.
- On August 18, a group of Cuban exiles and Spanish citizens launched in Madrid the **Asociación de Españoles por la Libertad de Cuba**.
- On November 2, 2000, the signers of **La Patria es de Todos**, issued a new document entitled **Debates y Desagravios**, summoning the Cuban government to a debate centered in the political situation in the island. The document was the response of Roque, Bonne, Roca and Gómez Manzano to a speech by Castro where he invited the opponents to Chávez to come to Havana for a debate about the situation in Venezuela.
- Early in 2001, Cuban exiles across the US and Europe subscribed, reproduced and published a document entitled **Todos Unidos**, produced by several organizations in Cuba, including the **Movimiento Cristiano de Liberación**, the **Comisión de Derechos Humanos y Reconciliación**, the **Centro de Estudios Sociales de Cuba** and the **Partido Liberal Democrático**, among others.
- Starting on March 5, 2001, Cuban exiles the world over began to make available the document **Yo Acuso**, written by **Maritza Lugo**, a political prisoner in Cuba.

(Continued)

Photos above, top to bottom, left to right:
Gladys Ibarra Lugo, holding pictures of her father **Rafael Ibarra Roque**, founder of **Movimiento Noviembre 30 Frank País**, and her mother **Marit-za Lugo Fernández**, author of the document **Yo Acuso**, written from her cell in **Manto Negro**, one of the cruelest prisons in Cuba; the logotype of the **Asociación Europea Cuba Libre**; **Hector Maceda**, leader of **Partido Liberal Democrático de Cuba** and his wife **Laura Pollán**, who died in October of 2011, leader of **Damas de Blanco**; three of the signers of **Todos Unidos**, Payá, Roca and Sánchez Santa Cruz; the logotype of the **MCL**.

(Continuation)

- On March 30, 2001, **Jesús Díaz**, a Cuban exiled novelist and filmmaker, founder in 1996 of the magazine **Encuentro**, started to publish **Encuentro en la Red** electronically from Spain. Díaz had been a revolutionary and had written in Cuba the prize winning collection of short stories **Los Años Duros**, but took asylum in Europe in 1991.

- On April 1, almost every Cuban exile organization in the US and Europe expressed their preoccupation for the health of **Jorge Luis García Pérez (Antúnez)** and denounced the Cuban government for the rough treatment he was receiving in the **Nieves Morejón** prison in Cuba. As many as 70 Cubans protested in front of the prison in Sancti Spíritus, Cuba,

- Also in April, Cuban exiles launched the **Sociedad Cubano-Alemana** in the city of Cologne, Germany.

- Late in April, the **Consejo Económico y Social de Naciones Unidas (ECOSOC)**, once more, rejected the petition of the **Comité Cubano Pro Derechos Humanos** to be considered a non-Governmental organization. **Mar por Cuba**, under the leadership of **Sylvia Iriondo**, responded by holding an unofficial session about Human Rights at a Geneva Hotel.

- In Lima, Perú, late in April, a group of Cuban exiles launched the **Union de Cubanos Exiliados en Perú**.

- In Miami, on October 10th 2001, several former members of the **Cuban-American National Foundation** broke with **Jorge Mas Santos**, son of **Jorge Mas Canosa**, and founded the **Consejo por la Libertad de Cuba**. Its directors included **Alberto Hernández, Diego Suárez, Horacio García, Ninoska Pérez Castellón** and **Luis Zúñiga**, among others.

- On November 27, Cuban exiles in Madrid and the **Asociación de Españoles por la Libertad de Cuba** opened **La Isla Atrapada**, an exhibition of photos from Cuba provided by the **Fundación Elena Mederos**.

(Continued)

Photos below, top to bottom, left to right:

Jesús Díaz, publisher of **El Caimán Barbudo** and **Pensamiento Crítico** in Cuba (as a revolutionary) and **Encuentro in Madrid** (as an exile). He would die in Madrid, under strange circumstances, on May 2, 2001; **Jorge Luis García Pérez (Antúnez)**, suffered 17 years and 34 days in prison (1990-2007) for «*failure to respect Castro in public;*» three members of the **Consejo por la Libertad de Cuba**, **Ninoska Pérez, Alberto Hernández** and **Diego Suáez**; finally, the logo of the **Consejo**.

(Continuation)

- On March 13, 2002, the **Partido del Pueblo de Suecia** awarded **Gisela Delgado Sablón**, director of the **Proyecto de Bibliotecas Independientes de Cuba**, the **Pro Democracia Award**. The Cuban government did not allow her to travel to Sweden or her parents **Pedro Delgado** (76) and **Yolanda Sablón** (74) to travel to Cuba, arguing they were included in the government's *Black List of Undesirables*.
- On April 17th, the **Forum Paralelo de Derechos Humanos**, sponsored by **Mar por Cuba**, the **Comité Cubano Pro Derechos Humanos** and the **World Health Care Organization**, took place in Geneva.

    On May 20, 2002, the **Asamblea para Promover la Sociedad Civil en Cuba** took place in Rancho Boyeros, Havana. It was closely followed in Miami, New York, Paris, New Jersey, Puerto Rico and many other places with a Cuban exile population.

(Continued)

Photos above, top to bottom, left to right:
Gisela Delgado Sablón, the leader of the **Proyecto de Bibliotecas Independientes de Cuba**. The first free library was inaugurated on October 10, 1996. By 2002 the number of functional libraries surpassed 150, each with at least 300 books, two tables and 10 plastic chairs. A total of 255,000 readers had been served; the presidency of the **Asamblea para Promover la Sociedad** Civil en Cuba, showing **Gómez Manzano, Roque Cabello** and **Bonne Carcassé**; **James Cason**, the US diplomat in charge of the **Sección de Intereses de USA** is shown shaking hands with **Vladimiro Roca**, who was the fourth organizer of the meeting; finally a partial view of the 400 Cubans attending the very successful **Asamblea**.

(Continuation)

- On July 22, the **New York Academy of Sciences** granted **Martha Beatriz Roque Cabello**, director of the **Instituto de Economistas Independientes de Cuba**, its **2002 Heinz R. Pagels Award**.
- In San Juan, Puerto Rico, a large group of Cuban Bishops, Priests and other religious figures attended the **XXVIII Encuentro Internacional de la Fraternidad del Clero y Religiosos de Cuba en la Diáspora** on July 29 to 31.
- On August 10, the **Consejo Nacional del Presidio Político Cubano** was launched at the **Casa del Preso** in Miami. Its purpose was to secure the participation of former political prisoners in activities leading to the democratization of Cuba.
- On September 23rd Cuban exiles in Miami received the visit of **Václav Havel**, who exchanged strategies and tactical moves with several groups of Cuban exiles.
- On October 1st, **Osvaldo Payá Sardiñas** received the **W. Averel Harriman Award** from the **National Democratic Institute for International Affairs (NDI)**, an organization created by the US government through the **National Endowment for Democracy**. On October 23 he received the **Andrei Sajarov Award** for **The Defense of Human Rights and Freedom of Conscience** from the **European Parliament**.
- In New York, on October 8th, the **Northcote Parkinson Foundation** granted **Vladimiro Roca** the **2002 Civil Valor Award** for his having signed the document **La Patria es de Todos**. It was the first time a Cuban had obtained this award. Vladimiro was the son of Blas Roca, one of the most important traditional Communist leaders of Republican Cuba.

(Continued)

Photos below, top to bottom, left to right:
Martha Beatriz Roque Cabello, **Vladimiro Roca**,
Václav Havel, and **Osvaldo Paya**, all award winners for their defense of freedom in Cuba and around the world in 2002, for their dedication to democracy and their steadfast opposition to the Communist ideology.

(Continuation)

- On November 15th, 167 organizations inside Cuba, under the umbrella of **Todos Unidos**, with the help of Cuban exiles, addressed a document to the **XII Cumbre Iberoamericana de Jefes de Estado y Gobiernos**, meeting in Bávaro, Santo Domingo, demanding solidarity with the struggle of free men and women in Cuba and their support to the **Proyecto Varela**. Rather than attend to this petition, the XII *Cumbre* produced a document entitled the **Declaración de Bávaro**, asking the «*US government to drop the Helms-Burton Act and open their markets to Cuba.*»

- On December 17th, in the city of Strasbourg, seat of the European Parliament, **Hans-Gert Pöttering**, on behalf of the European Community, invested **Osvaldo Payá** with the **2002 Andrei Sararov Award for Human Rights**. Pöttering would later be Chairman of the **Conrad Adenauer Foundation**, through which he continued to help Cubans in the island and Cuban exiles to claim their rights to democracy in Cuba.

- In the US, the **National Republican Institute**, based in Washington DC, awarded **Oscar Elías Biscet** with its **2003 Democracy Promoters Prize** on February 6, 2003.

- During the month of February Cuban exiles launched two organizations in pro of the restoration of human rights in Cuba: in Rome, the **Unión de Cubanos en Italia** and in the Canary Islands, Spain, the **Comité Canario de Solidaridad con la Disidencia Cubana**. In March, the **Partido Nacionalista Democrático** was also founded in Miami.

- In March of 2003, the **Asociación Europea Cuba Libre** began to hold in Paris the **Martes por la Democracia en Cuba**, a series of protest meetings every Tuesday at 6:00 PM in front of the Cuban embassy, to denounce the 75 political prisoners jailed during the spring of 2003.

(Continued)

Photos above, top to bottom, left to right:
Osvaldo Payá receiving the **Premio Sajarov** in Strasbourg;
Cuban exiles and French sympathizers in 2002 protesting in Paris for the lack of human rights and freedom in Cuba;
The logo of the **XII Cumbre Latinoamericana de Jefes de Estado**.

(Continuation)

- On March 28th, most Cuban exile organizations in Miami joined forces and organized a march along *Calle Ocho* demanding the release of the 75 political prisoners captured in **Cuba's Primavera Negra**. They were joined by many family members of Cuban political prisoners in the island. In Cuba a document called **Declaración Conjunta Urgente** was signed by **Gustavo Arcos, Elizardo Sánchez, Félix Bonne Carcasses, Vladimiro Roca, René Gómez Manzano** and **Martha Beatriz Roque.**

- Cuban exiles in New York, Miami and other capitals made public across the world the executions on April 11, 2003, after a flash trial, of **Lorenzo Enrique Copello, Bárbaro Leodán Sevilla** and **Jorge Luis Martínez Isaac**, three young Blacks that had stolen a small boat to escape Cuba.

- In April, in Geneva, the **Comisión de Derechos Humanos de la ONU** continued to reject all motions to admit a Cuban exile delegation, and they held a second **Foro Paralelo de Derechos Humanos en Cuba**.

- On May 25th, the **Directorio Democático Cubano** organized a **Día Mundial de Reclamo de Libertad para Cuba**, honoring **Pedro Luis Boitel,** the Cuban student leader murdered in the Castro prisons. There were marches and protests in Mexico City, the Dominican Republic, Argentina, Puerto Rico, El Salvador, Perú, Costa Rica, Chile and Guatemala.

- Early in June of 2003, Cuban exiles in Puerto Rico attempted and failed to create an organization that would represent all Cuban exiles in the world.

(Continued)

Photos below: Some of the political prisoners that were jailed by the Cuban government in March 2003, during the **Primavera Negra;**

(Continuation)

- In July of 2003 the **Congreso Nacional Cubano** was organized in Miami to act as a parliament elected by Cuban exiles.
- In May of 2003 Cuban exiles circulated around the world the process by which the three men trying to escape Cuba in a **Lancha de Regla** ended up executed. They were captured on April 5, 50 Kms north of Havana; they ran out of fuel, and were captured and presented in front of a **Tribunal del Pueblo** on the same day. As the Tribunal was trying to indoctrinate them to drop their attitude, Castro himself showed up and ordered that they be charged with treason. On April 11 they were tried and given the death sentence. The Cuban government never contested this story.
- On July 3rd, *Columbia University* granted the **Sociedad de Periodistas Manuel Márquez Sterling (SPMMS)** its **2003 María Moors Cabot Award** in recognition to their defense of freedom of the press. At that point in time, the society had most of its members in exile.
- Also in July, the **Sociedad Interamericana de Prensa (SIP)** granted collectively to all independent journalists in Cuba the **Gran Premio a la Libertad de Prensa**, an award not ever given before in the Americas.

(Continued)

Photos above, top to bottom, left to right:

Lorenzo Enrique Copello Castillo (31), **Bárbaro Leodan Sevilla García** (21) and **Jorge Luis Martínez Isaac** (43), the three young Blacks sentenced to death in secret summary trials for attempting to leave Cuba. A similar crime had been denounced in 1963, when *The New York Times* reported that three Protestant ministers had left Cuba by boat and arrived at Anguilla Key, Bahamas, where the Cuban Coast Guard staged a raid. Returned to Cuba, Reverends **José Durado**, **Pablo Rodríguez** and **Antonio González** were swiftly executed for exiting the country illegally; The **María Moors Cabot Award in Journalism** from *Columbia University*, the oldest international award to journalists. It *was given to José Ignacio Rivero in 1941, Pedro Cue in 1944, Miguel Angel Quevedo in 1958, Raúl Rivero in 1999, the Sociedad de Periodistas Manuel Márquez Sterling (SPMMS) in 2003 and Yoani Sánchez in 2009; the magazine* **De Cuba**, *published by the* **SPMMS** *in Havana in the 2000s.*

(Continuation)

- In November of 2003, 71 American businesses from 18 states and Puerto Rico opened booths in **Havana's Trade Fair**; in December over 125 US agribusiness executives were hosted by the Cuban government in Havana. Cuban exiles tried unsuccessfully to control the ambition of American businesses to start operations in Cuba or export their products there.

- Agribusiness giants **Archer Daniels Midland** of Illinois, **Tyson Foods** of Arkansas, **Splash Tropical Drinks** of Florida, **Marsh Supermarkets** of Indiana and **White Rose Foods** of New Jersey were among 125 American companies participating in this weeklong International Fair in Havana.

- Early in 2004 a similar situation occurred with the Orthodox Christian Church. Ecumenical Patriarch **Bartholomew** visited Cuba to consecrate St. Nicholas Cathedral on January 25. Cuban exiles sought and obtained from President Bush **tighter travel and trade res**trictions against Cuba.

- Through the influence and presentation of Cuban exiles in Paris, **Raúl Rivero** was awarded **UNESCO's Press Freedom Prize** in 2004.

- In April Cuban exiles denounced the sale to Cuba of **$23 million in farm goods** (not foodstuffs but tools and equipment) by US companies.

- In June the US government imposed **restrictions for academic institutions to travel to Cuba**; these popular excursions for presumed academic studies had turned into drinking and brainwashing sessions. **Harvard University** was one of the schools that turned Cuba into a *spring fête*.

Photos below, top to bottom, left to right:

Ramón Castro, brother of Fidel and Raúl, talking with a Florida rancher during the **XII Feria Internacional de la Habana**; the Orthodox Christian **Patriarch Bartholomew** thanks Castro for his warm welcome to Havana; **Raúl Rivero** the day he was released from prison after considerable pressure from Cuban exiles in the US and Europe; advertising at **UCLA** for **Academic Trips to Cuba**.

Raúl Rivero talks with reporters shortly after his release from prison.

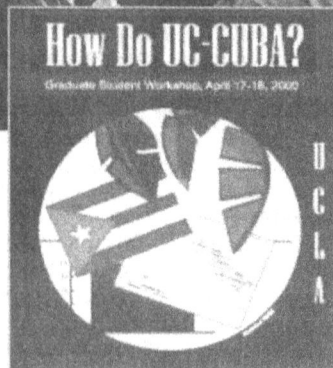

How Do UC-CUBA?
Graduate Student Workshop, April 17-18, 2000

(Continuation)

- Cuban exiles protested publicly in New York on October 28, 2004, when for the 13th straight year the **UN General Assembly** urged, by a large vote, that the US end its four decade old embargo against Cuba.
- On November 8, Cuban exiles that made **remittances to their families** in Cuba found out the dollar was eliminated from circulation in the island.
- At the end of 2004 most members of the **Havana Night Club Review**, a Cuban dance troupe playing Las Vegas, were granted asylum in the US.
- On November 30, after international pressure from Cuban exiles, poet and writer **Raúl Rivero**, writer **Oscar Espinosa Chepe**, **Marcelo López** and **Margarito Broche** were freed from prison in Cuba and became exiles.
- After three days of talks, on December 17, 2004, Castro agreed to buy $125 million in agricultural products from US companies, **paying in cash**.
- To the dismay of Cuban exiles, New Year 2005 opened with the news that France, Britain, Germany, Italy, Austria, Greece, Portugal and Sweden **would no longer invite Cuban dissidents** to celebrations of their National Day festivities at their Havana embassies. The US reaffirmed that they would. The same European countries announced on January 15th that they would ignore their objections to the crackdown on dissidents and the firing-squad executions of the three Black men that were trying to leave the island and **resume formal diplomatic ties with Castro's Cuba.**

(Continued)

Photos above, top to bottom, left to right:

Some of the heavy propaganda published by the Cuban government to influence public opinion about the US embargo to Cuba; the Cuban government unfair exchange of **$1 dollar for a Cuban peso** in 2005; **Dennis Savigne** and **Iván Ramos,** two of the stars from the show **Havana Night Club Review** at the *Stardust Casino* in Las Vegas who defected with the rest of the troupe; the **US Interest Section in Havana**, the only diplomatic representation inviting, welcoming and helping Cuban dissidents in 2005, under **Jim Cason**, the US diplomat in charge.

(Continuation)

- On April 17, 2005, Cuban exiles denounced the **one-party elections** to the **Municipal Assemblies** in Cuba, which Castro considered «*the most democratic elections in the world*».
- On July 10, Cuban exiles began to send help to Cubans in the island after the disastrous impact of **hurricane Dennis**. 15,000 homes were destroyed and 16 people killed; property damage amounted to $1.4 billion.
- In August, a three-judge panel of the US 11th Circuit Court orders a new trial for the **Cuban Five**. All confessed being Cuban intelligence agents.
- On October 13th, in spite of intense lobbying by Cuban exiles, the **Ibero-American Summit Conference** meeting in Spain approved a motion calling for the end of the US embargo against Cuba.
- On February 3rd 2006, the **UNESCO José Martí International Prize**, originally established by UNESCO to be awarded to individuals or institutions contributing to the integration of Latin American countries, was granted to **Hugo Chavez**. Castro personally gave the diploma to Chavez.
- The traffic of **Cuban immigrants to the US** began to strengthen in 2006. On April 6, the US captured 39 migrants on a US registered speedboat ran by a Cuban migrant that had left the island three weeks earlier.
- On May 5th, **Forbes Magazine** in an article entitled **Fortunes of Kings, Queens and Dictators** placed Fidel Castro as the 7th richest world ruler with «a *lofty position and a vast fortune*.» It estimated Castro's wealth at **$900 million**, both in Cuba (a convention center, several retail conglomerates and factories of Cuban-produced pharmaceuticals) and abroad (land and buildings in Spain, France, England, Italy, Venezuela and Chile).

(Continued)

Photos below, top to bottom, left to right:

The Cuban five spies of the **Red Avispa** and the federal prisons where they served their terms; Castro on TV, on May 15th 2006, complaining and denying the allegations on **Forbes Magazine** about his personal wealth.

(Continuation)

- On June 30, 2006, after pressure from a large number of Cuban exiles, **Miami-Dade County School Board** retired **Vamos a Cuba**, a children's book presenting a positive depiction of life in Cuba.

- Bolivian doctors staged a one-day strike to protest the presence of 600 Cuban physicians hired by president Evo Morales. Cuban exiles accused Morales of allowing an **infiltration of Cuban indoctrinators** in Bolivia.

- Cuba attempted to boycott communications between exiles and dissidents by **cutting power to the US embassy in Havana**. Power was restored after a day of serious admonitions by the US.

- On July 31st, Castro temporarily ceded power to his brother Raúl. Cuban exiles showed this to the world as evidence of the **totalitarian a nature of the Cuban government**. The only governments taking note and criticizing the move were from recently liberated Eastern Europe countries.

- Cuban exiles gave up lobbying the UN on November 8 when the **General Assembly**, once again, urged the US to **end its embargo against Cuba** but defeated an amendment calling on the Castros to **free political prisoners and respect human rights**.

- On December 22nd, Cuban exiles protested the visit of 10 US legislators from the Black Caucus to Cuba; it was the first such visit in over 40 years.

(Continued)

Photos below, top to bottom, left to right:
The book **Vamos a Cuba**, an expert means of portraying a false reality of human rights in Cuba to American children; two pictures showing the unconditional support of US legislators from the **Black Caucus**; Castro asked them «*How can we help President Obama?*», according to **Los Angeles Times.** The visit would be followed in 2009 by representatives of the Black caucus **Barbara Lee** (D-Oakland), **Bobby L. Rush** (D-Ill., on the microphone in the picture above), **Emanuel Cleaver II** (D- Mo.), **Melvin Watt**(D-N.C.), **Marcia L. Fudge** (D-Ohio), **Michael M. Honda** (D-San José) and **Laura Richardson** (D-NY).

(Continuation)

- **Mario Chanes de Armas**, a comrade in arms of Castro before the **Moncada attack** and his companion in the adventure of the **Granma** and the fight in **Sierra Maestra,** died in Miami at age 80 on February 24, 2007. He became a 30-year prisoner of Castro when he began to conspire in Cuba once he disagreed with Castro's «*megalomaniac speeches and his vehement irrationality.*» He was imprisoned longer than **Nelson Mandela** and was freed thanks to Cuban exiles in Chile and the good offices of its government. His first action was to go to the cemetery and place flowers on the grave of his son, whose funeral he had not been allowed to attend.
- On April 6, US District Judge Kathleen Cardone ruled that **Luis Posada Carriles** could be released on $250,000 bond. He was freed on the 19th of April and travelled immediately to Miami.
- Also in April, with the help of Cuban exiles, **Yoani Sánchez** began to post her blog **Generation Y** in Havana.
- On June 11th, the Canadian firm **Sherritt International**, the largest producer of coal in Canada and energy, nickel and cobalt in Cuba (30% owner of **Energas** and control of Cuban gas fields in Varadero, Canasí, Yumurí and Puerto Escondido, as well as control of **Moa Mining**), signed a $1.2 billion contract to expand its operations in Cuba. Cuban exiles in Toronto picketed their Headquarters in protest.
- On July 23rd, Cuban exiles in Brazil helped **Guillermo Rigondeaux** to desert. He was a two-time Olympic Boxing Champion (2000 and 2004), and had signed in Rio a contract with German based **Arena Box Promotion**. In August, inexplicably, possibly after threats to his family, he returned to Cuba.

(Continued)

Photos below, top to bottom, left to right:

The poster for the film **Libre tras las Rejas**, a documentary about **Mario Chanes de Armas**; *Sherritt International Corporation's* CEO **Ian Delaney** and Raúl Castro in 2007, during the opening of a gas plant. Delaney declared «*For us things have always been good. The operating environment in Cuba is really good*;» **Yoani Sánchez** at the time she opened her blog **Generation Y**; **Guillermo Rigondeaux**, the deserting Cuban boxer who, after signing a juicy contract to fight in Europe, mysteriously returned to Cuba.

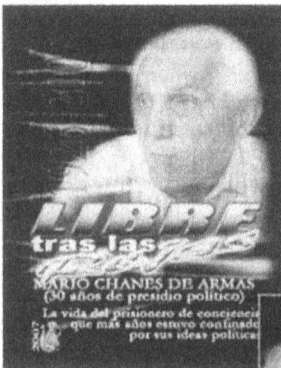

(Continuation)

- In February of 2008 **Raúl Castro** became the new President of Cuba as his 81 years old brother Fidel, after half a century in power, resigned as Cuba's top leader. Cuban exiles tried to highlight the **hereditary quasi-monarchical nature** of this succession but no government in the world paid any attention. In fact, to celebrate the occasion **Mexico resumed full diplomatic relations** with Cuba.

- In April Cuban exiles began to introduce **hundreds of cell phones** in Cuba; long lines stretched outside phone centers when Raúl Castro allowed Cubans to sign up for cellular phone service. In May a similar situation occurred with **laptop computers** also brought by Cuban exiles.

- In June Cuban exiles denounced people smugglers that were **outflanking the Coast Guard** bringing Cuban immigrants to the US and charging $10,000 a head. Few of them were ever stopped and sanctioned.

- Also in June, through the efforts of **Prime Minister Zapatero of Spain**, the European Community lifted its 2003 diplomatic sanctions against the Cuban regime. Neither Zapatero nor the CE demanded **changes** in Cuba.

- In August 2008 Cuba defaulted on its debt payments. **Hurricane Gustav** roared across the island; Cuba declined any disaster assistance from **Cuban exiles**, rather asking they lobby Washington to lift the embargo. In September hurricane **Ike** struck Cuba with similar results and reactions.

- On March 11, 2009, the US, under President Obama, rolled back all of the Bush administration restrictions to Cubans in the US visiting Cuba. By 2010 they were making a total of **400,000 annual trips** to Cuba.

(Continued)

Photos below, top to bottom, left to right:

Time Magazine cover on the failure of the 50-year Castro regime in Cuba; at the Coast Guard Marina in Miami, boats confiscated from **people smugglers** bringing Cuban immigrants to Florida; **Spain's P.M. Zapatero**; **Cuban immigrants traveling to Cuba** after Obama's lifting of restrictions.

Juanes Cuba Concert Study

Do you support or oppose the Juanes concert that will take place in Havana?

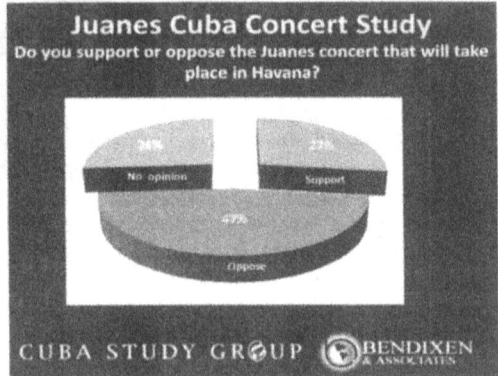

CUBA STUDY GROUP   BENDIXEN & ASSOCIATES

(Continuation)

- In March of 2009 the US Government Accountability Office reported that Cuba, through the US State Department, had received **$11 million** from 1997 to 2007 under a program of technical cooperation for **peaceful uses of nuclear energy**. The news was hardly reported in the US press.

- In April Fidel Castro received yet another delegation of the **Democratic US Congress Black Caucus**, which made promises to improve US-Cuba relations. Almost immediately thereafter **Luis Posada Carriles** was charged by the US Justice Department for terrorism and President Obama *eased curbs on money transfers to Cuba*. At no time did the Black Caucus ask for the freedom of Black Cuban opponent **Oscar Elías Biscet**.

- Also in April, **Walter** (72) and **Gwendolyn** (71) **Kendall Myers** were arrested as Cuban spies working inside the **US State Department**.

- Cuban exiles, on August 25th, denounced talks by New Mexico governor **Bill Richardson** with **Ricardo Alarcón**, President of Cuba's National Assembly, as they sought to improve US commercial relations with Cuba.

- On September 20, Cuban exiles denounced the concert offered by Colombian rocker **Juanes** in Havana's *Plaza Cívica*. Juanes later found, as exiles in Miami had predicted, that his presence had been used to present a favorable image of Cuba. He was even **scuffled by Cuban police**.

- In February of 2010, **Orlando Zapata Tamayo**, an activist imprisoned since 2003, died after a lengthy hunger strike in prison. Cuban exiles protested worldwide for this premeditated murder and received support from all civilized quarters. The US Congressional Black Caucus ignored it.

(Continued)

Photos above, top to bottom, left to right:

Dr. Oscar Elías Biscet, a Cuban Black man and Castro opponent, never supported by the Black Caucus in the US Congress; Castro sympathizer and frequent visitor to Cuba **Bill Richardson**, former governor of New Mexico; **Amnesty International** denouncing the murder of **Orlando Zapata**; the Cuban exiles opinions about the Juanes concert in Havana in 2001, as measured by Bendixen for the Cuba Study Group.

(Continuation)

- In June 11th of 2010, the Cuban government unexpectedly released political prisoner **Ariel Sigler Amaya** from jail; he is received in Miami by hundreds of Cuban exiles; the same day **Amnesty International**, released a report stating «*Cuba used repressive laws, a well-oiled state security apparatus and complicit courts to stifle political dissent as it spied on and imprisoned those who openly opposed its Communist system*».

- On July 13, several former Cuban political prisoners arrived in Madrid following a Castro's policy to **release prisoners** and banish them from Cuba, like the Spanish Colonial government had done in the 1800s.

- On October 21, the *European Parliament* awarded its **2010 Sakharov Prize** to **Guillermo Fariñas** (48), the Black man whose 134-days hunger strike drew attention to the plight of all political prisoners. As in the case of Zapata, the **Black Caucus of the US Congress** had never approached the Castros on **behalf of Fariñas.**

- In December, **Guillermo Fariñas** was not allowed to fly to Strasbourg to receive the **Sakharov Prize for Freedom of Thought** and Jerzy Buzek, President of the European Parliament arranged to have an empty chair at the ceremony to represent his absence. Fariñas thanked the Parliament through a recording made in Cuba and taken to France by Cuban exiles.

- In January of 2011 President Obama increased the **remittances** that Cubans in the US could send to Cuba from $300 to $2,000. It increased the potential support to Cuba from residents of the US to a possible $1 billion.

- Former US President **Jimmy Carter** made one more futile trip to Cuba and met on March 30 with Raúl Castro.

Photos below, top to bottom, left to right:

Ariel Sigler Amaya the day he was released from jail in Havana; the empty chair of Fariñas at the **Sakharov Prize ceremony**; **Andrei Sakharov** in TIME; President Carter **joyfully sharing a laugh** with Raúl Castro.

Few Cuban immigrants to the US in the years after 1990 understood the reasons for the obstinacy of older Cuban exiles to any arrangements or concessions to the Cuban regime other than its complete dissolution and disappearance. That unwavering determination was the result of having witnessed numerous acts of inhuman cruelty perpetrated by the Communists during a half century of control in Cuba.

One such barbarous act was the shooting on December 15th, 1961, of six young students in the *Batey* of **Central Adela**, north of Las Villas, near the town of *Remedios*. Poorly armed, they had been captured the day before inside a cave; they offered no resitance and surrendered to the revolutionary army under the command of Raúl Castro. They were taken to *Central Adela*, the commanding post of Castro's troops, with their hands tied and their heads covered with hoods. On the way there, they were attacked by Castro's followers shouting **¡Paredón! ¡Paredón!** It was one of the first times the regime made use of those miserable bullying crowds later known as the **Rapid Response Brigades**.

Once the six youngsters were in the *Batey* of *Central Adela*, an order was received by a man landing from a helicopter: **death penalty**. Without trial or the opportunity to speak, the men were taken to a mound of industrial ash by the side of the road and shot. Those witnessing the event mentioned the deep silence that followed the execution, when only the faint murmur of a nearby stream could be heard. The bodies were immediately buried on a common pit in the cemetery of the town of *Buenavista*. Their names were never recorded, the event never made the news. People in the area retired to their homes and wept in silence. Only with the pasage of time the names of the six martirs have been known: **Norberto Camacho Guerra**, **Julio Guevara Domínguez**, **Luis Guevara**, **Jerónimo Camacho**, and brothers **Juan** and **José González**. Most of them were members of the **Juventud Estudiantil Católica (JEC)**; they died shouting **¡Viva Cuba Libre! ¡Viva Cristo Rey!** They were from the group of *Jecistas* that were following the «*Insurrection Line*» rather than the «*Pure Apostolic Line*» that Cuban Bishops had prescribed for the entire *Juventud Católica* leadership. All records of this event were made to disappear: the death registrations from the *Department of Health* in Santa Clara province as well as from the *Ministries of Public Health* and *Justice in Havana*. It was also one more time that the *Catholic Church* in Cuba remained silent and did not mention the massacre. After their deaths, many young couples in Las Villas baptized their new sons with the name **Julio Norberto**.

Photo above:
Norberto Camacho Guerra and **Julio Guevara Domínguez**, with the seal of the **Juventud Católica Cubana**.

In the new century, more than ever before, the US, Spain, the EU and even the Cuban exiles began to realize that the final solution of the Cuban dilemma was the natural death of Fidel Castro. Such an event would resolve the unsolvable predicament of Cuba, although it would open another enigma. What would happen next?

Unlike the **Generalisimo Franco**'s events that followed his death in 1975 (according to him «*todo está atado y bien atado*,» meaning everything is taken care of), Castro's immortality complex never allowed him to resolve the need for a clear succession strategy in Cuba; except the passing of the torch to his brother Raúl, a colorless figure, a documented mass murderer, barely six years younger. The rumors and false reports of Castro's death abounded for many years and required constant photographic evidence by the Cuban regime to attest to the life of its aging leader, particularly after 1996.

Photos below: some of the many times fabricated evidence about the demise of the Cuban dictator showed up in the press.

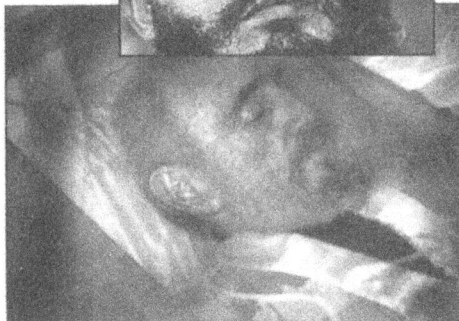

Even before the full development of the Cuban nationality in the nineteenth century, Cuba was fully immersed into the poetry of the banished. *José María Heredia, Gertrudis Gómez de Avellaneda, José Martí, Félix Varela, Domingo del Monte, José Antonio Saco, Cirilo Villaverde, Juana Borrero*, the poets of the *Laúd del Desterrado* and *Bonifacio Byrne*, among others, were some of the predecessors and models for exiled poets of the XX and XXI centuries. These centuries were no exception. An exile poetry was produced after the demise of the Republic that was nostalgic, rich in the ways in which loneliness was phrased, always mourning for the lost days away from Cuba and from the family, rather than for any personal material loss; always optimistic or grateful for an inevitable return and very passionate in describing the human condition.

Poets in exile like **Roberto Cazorla** (*Soneto a mi Abuelo*), **Belkis Cuza Malé** (*Summertime in Princeton*), **José Kozer** (*Divertimento*), **Gustavo Pérez Firmat** (*Entre Hermanos*), **Antonio José Ponte** (*Juguetes Puritanos*), **Rossardi** (*Elogio de mi Locura*), **Pio Serrano** (*El Espejo*), **Nivaria Tejera** (*Panteras Búfalos Cocodrilos*), **Pepe Triana** (*Soñé*) y **Zoé Valdés** (*Montparnasse*), among many others, attest to the enduring nature of poetry as the best vocabulary of the soul of Cuban exiles.

Photos below, top to bottom, left to right:
Cazorla, Cuza, Kozer, Pérez Firmat, Aponte, Rossardi, Serrano, Tejera, Triana and **Valdés.**

For half a century Cuban exiles had to dispel and cast off notions that the revolution of 1959 had launched Cuba, for the first time, as a land of world class athletes. It became a mantra of the Castro regime, starting in the early 1960s, to say that «*Cuba is now a world power in sports because the interest and opportunities of the government in the wholesome education of youngsters*».

This propaganda failed to recognize that the emphasis in sports since 1959 was a concealment for the lack of progress in the economic well-being of the nation. It also ignored a past history of competition and successes of Cuban sports figures throughout the entire republican life. Some examples follow:

- *José Raúl Capablanca* (1888-1942), World Chess Champion.
- *Ramón Fonst* (1883-1959), World Fencing Champion.
- *Kid Chocolate* (1910-1988), World Featherweight Champion; *Kid Gavilán* (1926-2003), World Welterweight Champion. Retired with a record 107-30-6 and 28 KOs; *José (Mantequilla) Nápoles*, World Welterweight Champion, with a record of 77-7 and 54 KOs; *Benny Paret* (1937-1962) World Welterweight Champion, died with a record of 35-12-3 with 10 KOs; *Ultiminio (Sugar) Ramos* (1941-), World Featherweight Champion, with a record of 55-8-3 and 40 KOs;
- *Adolfo Luque* (1890-1957), twice Major League Champion Pitcher; *Miguel Angel González* (1892-1977), one of the top Major League catchers for 20 years; *Martin Dihigo* (1907-1971), Baseball Hall of Fame inductee; *Conrado Marrero* (1911- 2010), Napoleón Reyes (1919-1955), *Orestes (Minnie) Miñoso* (1925-), Gold Glove Awardee in 1957 and head coach for the Chicago White Socks; *Edmundo (Sandy) Amorós* (1930-1992), *Camilo Pascual* (1934-), *Mike Cuellar* (1937-2010), Cy Young Award; *Preston Gómez* (1923-2009), manager, San Diego Padres; all superstars in the US Major Leagues.

«*The deterioration of the capital's major athletic center, Ciudad Deportiva, is an embarrassment, while gold hangs from the necks of dozens of Cuban athletes who have barely any food and school children spend many semesters without a Physical Education teacher,*» as pointed out by several bloggers from Cuba in recent times.

Photos above, left to right: *Kid Chocolate; Kid Gavilán; Ramón Fonst; Adolfo Luque* and *Martín Dihigo*.

The **Cuban American National Foundation (CANF)**, the organization founded by **Jorge Mas Canosa** in 1981, was shaken by the exodus of 22 of its directors on October 10th, 2001, when they broke away and set up a splinter group called the **Cuban Liberty Council (CLC)**. Their reasons for the schism were explained as «evidence that CANF was going soft on Castro,» and that, with the death of Jorge Mas Canosa and the leadership falling on his son Jorge Mas Santos, «the acorn had fallen very far from the tree,» i.e., the very nature of the organization had been changed.

Among the founders of **CLC** were some of the most prominent, recognized and successful businessmen, intellectuals, lawyers and journalists from the **CANF**, who had earned the respect and support of most of the Cuban democratic opposition inside and outside Cuba: Paul Alcázar, Remedios Díaz Oliver, Marcell Felipe, Esq., Ninoska Pérez Castellón, Feliciano Foyo, Horacio S. García, Dr. Alberto M. Hernández, Elpidio Núñez, Raúl F. Pino, Esq., Diego R. Suárez, Felipe Valls and Luis Zúñiga.

Both **CANF** and **CLC** continued to seek and support candidates from the Republican and Democratic parties that would embrace and promote a US active role on behalf of a free Cuba. But their styles were very different.

Jorge Mas Santos, as the head of **CANF**, began to convey the notion that there was a trailbrazing movement among second and third generation Cuban-Americans who were not fearful to break with their elders and continue to support human rights in Cuba while seeking an accommodation with the Cuban Marxist government. They began to spouse easier travel to Cuba, the end of the embargo and the start US investments in the island. The leadership of the **CLC** was unyielding in its determination to sustain a hard economic embargo on Cuba to bring about the collapse of the Marxist regime. They advocated a continuation of hard-line policies, tougher economic sanctions against the Cuban regime and increased support for human rights and opposition groups in Cuba. The **CLC** established a close relation with the Republican Party while the **CANF** endorsed Obama in his 2008 presidential bid.

Photos above, left to right:

Jorge Mas Santos and **President Obama**; the logotype of the **CLC**; **Diego Suárez** and **Paul Alcazar**, from the Board of the **CLC**.

The year 2001 saw a record number of arrivals from Cuba reaching the US. Analysts attributed the increase to several important causes:

- The constant blackouts and food and other shortages in Cuba;
- the dismal economic prospects;
- the government taking a much larger bite (up to 18%) from every dollar sent by relatives in the US;
- the US imposing a remittance limit of $100 a month;
- a demoralizing continuing crackdown on dissidents; and
- the continuing empty messages of false hope by the Castro brothers;

US authorities interdicted almost twice as many Cubans at sea in 2005 than in 2004; in fact, more interdictions that any year since 1994, when 37,000 Cuban immigrants had prompted the US to implement the *wet foot-dry foot* solution. We*t foot-dry foot* was a controversial new immigration policy that allowed Cubans who made it to dry land to stay in the US but decreed repatriation for those picked-up at sea.

Soon, however, the policy became murky. Several Cubans had arrived at the old Seven Mile Bridge, closed since 1982 and disconnected to the mainland. Their feet were dry but... where they in American territory or did they have to get their feet wet to get to the mainland? The Department of Homeland Security ruled that the artificial structure was not US soil.

The latest trend in migrant smuggling from Cuba became the super fast boats. It was a risky proposition since it left the Cubans taking that route at the mercy of smugglers who had more interest in the cash than in the safety of those whose relatives in the US had paid several thousand dollars to be smuggled into American territory.

Photos below, left to right:
Ramón Saúl Sánchez during a hunger strike in Miami to protest the **Wet Foot Dry Foot** ruling in the case of the old Seven Mile Bridge. The Cubans were deported but later, after numerous protests, they were admitted to the US; a 33-foot speedboat **smuggling** Cuban migrants and/or drugs as it became stuck on a bed of mangroves in Miami after an 80 miles-per-hour race with the Coast Guard.

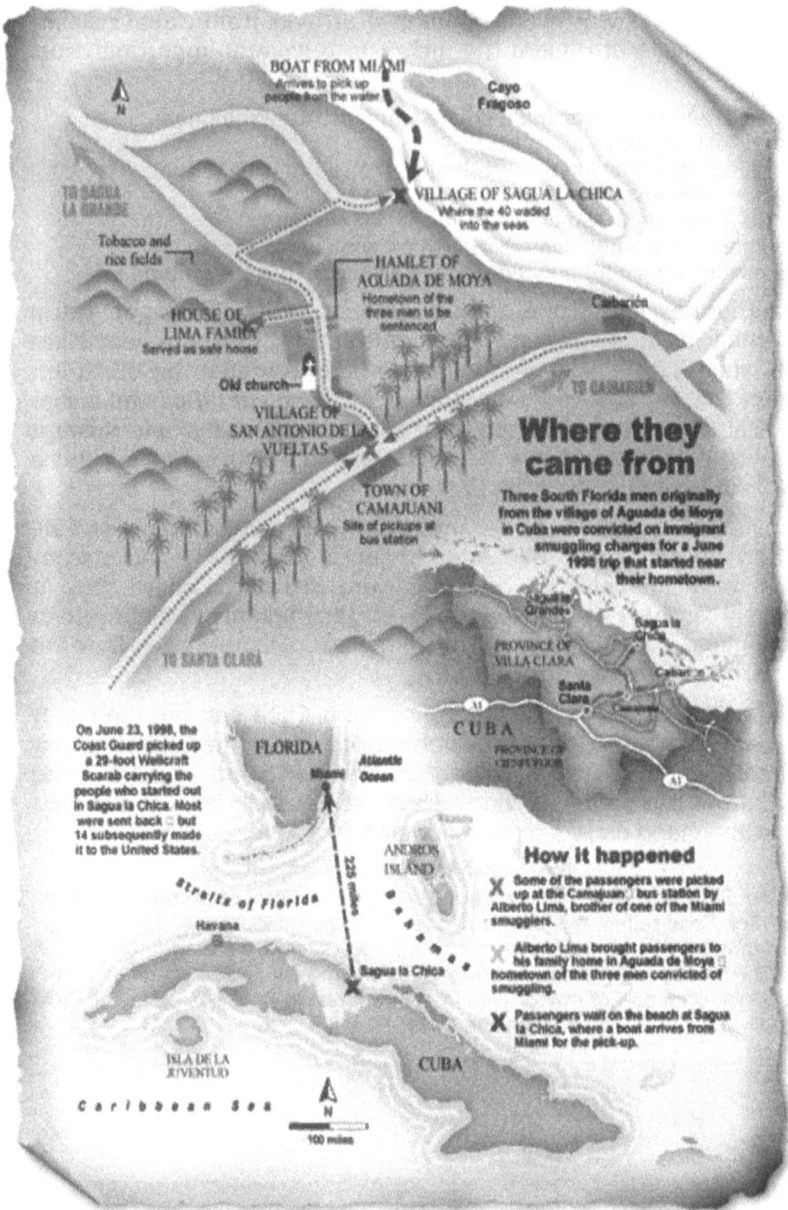

BOAT FROM MIAMI
Arrives to pick up people from the water

Cayo Fragoso

N

TO SAGUA LA GRANDE

Tobacco and rice fields

VILLAGE OF SAGUA LA CHICA
Where the 40 waded into the seas

HAMLET OF AGUADA DE MOYA
Hometown of the three men to be sentenced

HOUSE OF LIMA FAMILY
Served as safe house

Caibarién

Old church

VILLAGE OF SAN ANTONIO DE LAS VUELTAS

TOWN OF CAMAJUANI
Site of pickups at bus station

TO CAIBARIEN

Where they came from

Three South Florida men originally from the village of Aguada de Moya in Cuba were convicted on immigrant smuggling charges for a June 1998 trip that started near their hometown.

TO SANTA CLARA

Sagua la Grande

Sagua la Chica

PROVINCE OF VILLA CLARA

Caibarién

Santa Clara

On June 23, 1998, the Coast Guard picked up a 29-foot Wellcraft Scarab carrying the people who started out in Sagua la Chica. Most were sent back — but 14 subsequently made it to the United States.

FLORIDA

Miami

Atlantic Ocean

CUBA

PROVINCE OF CIENFUEGOS

Straits of Florida

225 miles

Havana

ANDROS ISLAND

Sagua la Chica

How it happened

X Some of the passengers were picked up at the Camajuani bus station by Alberto Lima, brother of one of the Miami smugglers.

X Alberto Lima brought passengers to his family home in Aguada de Moya, hometown of the three men convicted of smuggling.

X Passengers wait on the beach at Sagua la Chica, where a boat arrives from Miami for the pick-up.

ISLA DE LA JUVENTUD

CUBA

Caribbean Sea

N

100 miles

A typical people-smuggling operation from Cuba to Miami in the 1990s. Smugglers (themselves recent immigrants from Cuba) often charged $8 to $10 thousand dollars a passenger, paid in advance by Miami relatives. In December of 1997, **Orlando (El Duque) Hernández**, a future Mayor League pitcher, used this route to escape from Cuba. He made it on a 29 foot Scarab speedboat to Anguila Cay, 50 miles north. As with other smuggled Cubans, all passengers were promised a free second voyage if the one their relatives had paid for did not succeed.

To the dismay of Cuban exiles in the US, Miami became in the 2000s the region where most *Medicare* frauds were committed. Out of a total US expenditure of $500 billion a year, *Medicare* fraud was consuming $50 Billion; Miami accounted for 10 to 20% of that figure. It was was larger than drug smuggling, with a lesser chance to be detected and civil, rather than criminal penalties if discovered.

Fraud on the Medicare program was relatively easy to do because the program was based on an *"honor billing system,"* counting of honorable physicians submitting honorable claims for medical services; speed rather than time consuming confirmation was the focus of Medicare's management system.

Unfortunately most of the Medicare fraud in Miami was perpetrated by unscrupulous and criminal elements in the Cuban exile community masquerading as upright citizens. They perfected a system of **Phantom Billing** (unnecessary or unperformed tests and procedures); **Patient Billing** (a recruited patient provided his/her Medicare number and was ready to admit having received a treatment); and **Upcoding Billing** (inflating invoices and expenses).

A typical example of this blight among Cuban exiles was the case of **Caridad** and **Clara Guilarte** who, after being under federal investigation in Miami, fled to Dearborn, Michigan, and opened *Dearborn Medical Rehabilitation Center*, from which they performed their frauds. Their *modus operandi* was to use all three types of billing frauds in costly HIV therapy claims. The Guilarte sisters had come to the US in early 1980 and fleeced more that $6 million from the Medicare program between 2005 and 2009.

In 2011 US District Judge **Cecilia Altonaga**, a Cuban exile, gave the Guilarte sisters, Caridad, 54, and Clara, 57, 14 year prison terms, five more years than the plea agreement they had agreed to. Altonaga's admonition on the day of sentencing was «*the US welcomed you with "open arms" from Communist Cuba and you have returned the privilege by stealing millions from the government's healthcare program for the elderly and disabled*».

Photos below, left: the convicted pair, **Caridad** and **Clara Guilarte**; *On the right*, the prestigious US District Judge **Cecilia Altonaga**.

Cuban Theater in Miami: 1960 - 1980

As far as back as 1981, the New York Times reported that «*Cuban theater is thriving in Miami,*» adding «*this town is not only the political headquarters for anti-Castro Cubans, it also has become the exile's cultural center.*» In 2005, the crafting of good theater in Miami was strenghened with the founding of the **Instituto de Cultura Rene Ariza (ICRA)**, an effort led by poet, critic and playright **Matías Montes Huidobro**, author of "*Las Cuatro Brujas*" and "*Sobre las Mismas Rocas*" in the days of *Teatro Prometeo* in Cuba, by literary critic and scholar **Yara González Montes**, member of the Board of the Institute, and many other writers, actors, directors and theater devotees like Yvonne López Arenal, Mario García Joya, Orlando Rossardi, Carlos Rodríguez, Juan Roca e Iván Cañas.

By 2012, the local scene included the *Hispanic Theater Guild, Teatro en Miami Studio, El Ingenio Teatro, Teatro Cómplice, Havanafama, Centro Cultural Español, Sala de la Calle Ocho, Jerry Herman Ring Theater, Akuara Teatro, Hybrid Scene, Teatro Trail, Maroma Players y Teatro, Teatro Avante, Artspoken, Arsht Center for the Performing Arts, Coral Gables' Actor's Playhouse, Dade County Auditorium, Sociedad Pro Arte Grateli, Teatro Bellas Artes, Teatro Manuel Artime, Academia de las Luminares de las Bellas Artes (ALBA), South Miami Cultural Art Center, Area Stage de Miami Beach*, as well as the important plays presented regularly at the annual *International Hispanic Theatre Festival.*

Photos above: **Matías Montes Huidobro** and some of the announcements for theatrical news and presentations in Miami (Continued on next page)

Some Cuban Exiles' Theatrical News and Events in Miami

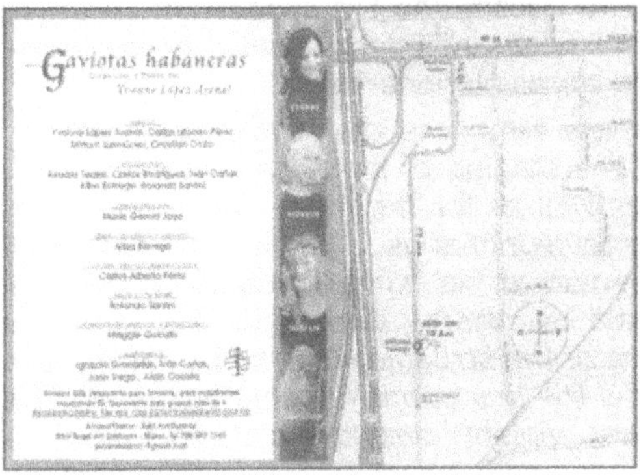

Photos above, top to bottom, left to right:

The play **Diente por Diente**, presented in May 2012 at *Teatro en Miami Studio*; **Caminos y Esplendor del Teatro Cubano** an event presented at FIU, honoring *Eduardo Arrocha, Antón Arrufat, Carucha Camejo, Abelardo Estorino, Eduardo Manet,Matías Montes Huidobro and Rafael Mirabal* in March of 2010; **Gaviotas Habaneras**, a play by Ivonne López Arenal at *Akuara Teatro*; **Cuba detrás del Telón** (so far a 4-book series on Cuban Theater) by *Matías Montes Huidobro*; the poster for **Las Monjas**, the international aclaimed play by Eduardo Manet, at *Teatro Estudio* in 2011; presentation of the book **Teatro Cubano de Miami** by *Luis de la Paz* in 2010 (published by Editorial Silueta).

Exiles from Cuba, knowing as they did the real nature and history of **Ernesto (Ché) Guevara (1928-1967),** tried for years to present the world with the true identity of **Ché**. It was always a rather difficult task. Promoted by the Castro government (and Robert *Redford*, the capitalist Hollywood movie producer turned devoted "silk revolutionary"), **Ché Guevara**, who worked almost his entire life to destroy capitalism, became after his death a capitalist brand; his famous photo by *Alberto Korda* (official photographer of Castro) adorns everywhere baseball caps, coffee mugs, key chains, hats, T–Shirts, jeans and every conceivable artifact. He grew after death into the world's heart-throb and turned into the logo of the "*capitalist chic*". The best recent examples of Ché as an exalted assassin-hero are the tattoo on the right upper arm of the Argentinian soccer star *Maradona*, the shirt of crooner *Carlos Santana* at the Oscars and the suggestion by the Brazilian priest *Fray Bretto* that images of Trotsky should be replaced by those of Ché in the homes of all revolutionaries.

Guevara, for those who knew him, was the revolutionary leader in Cuba most responsible for the staging of summary trials without the opportunity of a defense, as well as for the mass executions of those who were deemed counterrevolutionaries. This is his most quoted phrase, erased from the memory of his contemporaries of the "*velvet left*" but to this date learned by rote by Cuban primary school children: «*Hatred as an element of the struggle; unbending hatred for the enemy, which pushes beyond the limitations of being human and turns revolutionaries into effective, violent, selective and cold killing machines*».

Photos above, left to right:

Maradona and his tatoo; the book by **Jacobo Machover** that has devastated the image of **Ché** in Europe; **Carlos Santana** with his **Ché T-Shirt**; the **counter-image** used by Cuban exiles in Paris;a **pop soda** with the image of **Ché**.

This is the copyright protected photo taken by legendary Cuban photographer Alberto Korda Guitterez. It depicts Che Guevara, legendary and romantic hero of the Cuban revolution on the 5th of March, 1960. Little did he know that it was destined to become one of the world's most famous and recognized images, revered by Cubans, Central and South Americans and young idealistic Americans alike. Che has come to symbolize the epitome of the struggle of the working class and the oppressed everywhere. Even those who don't know who he is know and recognize the image, adding to this "coolness factor". The image is now available for licensing for a number of product categories and has been the subject of a very successful licensed apparel program in the United States and Europe, among many others. The excitement grows monthly as new image treatments are developed and new categories are added. Noted rap and hip hop artists have worn clothing with the Che image in the past year. Numerous international companies have licensed the image to symbolize the revolutionary nature of their company's vision. It appeals to a wide spectrum of demographics for different reasons, and now it is available to enhance your licensing program.

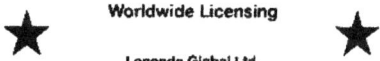

Photos above, top:
The **Ché** marketed as merchandise by the Castro government in a three language brochure published in France.

Bottom left and right:
An ad for **Mercedes Benz** in 2012, for which the company had to apologize; **Der Spiegel** mocking the Mercedes Benz Advertisement by presenting **Ché** as it would look in the 2000s.

The worldwide successful marketing of the Ché Brand

One of the most frustrating concerns of Cuban exiles since 1959 was the functionality, relevance and fairness of the United Nations and all its commissions, forums, councils and specialized agencies when it came to the repetitive, flagrant and unrepented **violations of human rights in Cuba**.

In 1945, when the UN officially came into existence, it consisted of 51 member States. At that point its main concern was *colonialism* and not *human rights*. It was not until 1964 that the *UN Commission on Human Rights (UNCHR)* was created by the UN General Assembly; it consisted of 53 of the UN member States, elected from the entire and then much expanded UN membership. This Commission met in March/April of each year in regular sessions in Geneva to deal with all sorts of human rights situations worldwide.

By 2006, the UN had a total membership of 192 States, and the *UN Commission on Human Rights (UNCHR)* was dissolved and replaced by a *UN Human Rights Council*, with a membership of 53 States **elected from six regional groups**: Africa (15 member States to be elected), Asia (12), Western Europe (10), Eastern Europe (5), Latin America (11). This new Commission would also meet yearly in Geneva for six weeks during March/April. The focus of their charge was now: minority rights, transnational corporation's issues, administration of justice, anti-terrorism, contemporary forms of slavery, indigenous populations, communications and social issues, as well as other human rights concerns.

(Continued)

Photo below:
The **UN Human Rights Council** in Geneva after 2006.

(Continuation)

From the start the new Commission was criticized because several of its member countries had **dubious human rights records** and could use their membership as a way to deflect accusations of abuse. Such was the case of China, Zimbabwe, Saudi Arabia, Cuba, Pakistan, Libya, Syria and Uganda. The most egregious example was the election of *Sudan* to the Commission in spite of its ethnic cleansing in the *Darfur* region. The Commission was also criticized because of its bias against Israel, failing to include stoning of women, mutilations, honor killings and apostasy killings in Muslin-Arab countries among its investigations.

Since its inception in 2006, the *UN Human Rights Council* adopted an explicit policy to *«work quietly with abuser nations to convince them to end the murder, torture, maiming and political imprisonment of dissident citizens»* rather than a more effective severe policy of *name-and-shame* of the offending nations.

Among the Cuban exile communities, the denunciation of abuses in Cuba was advocated and championed by the exiles in Miami and Paris as they protested and appealed for changes and reforms to the UN Commissions. For many years, groups of exiles travelled to Geneva to make presentations before the *UN Commission on Human Rights (UNCHR)* and the *UN Human Rights Council.* These groups were inspired and organized in Miami and Puerto Rico by *MAR por Cuba* under the leadership of **Sylvia Iriondo**, in Paris by the *Association Européenne Cuba Libre*, under the leadership of **Laurent Muller** and by the *Action Droits de l'Homme*, under the leadership of **Françoise Hostalier**. In one such visit in April 15, 2004, Cuban exile leader **Frank Calzón**, a tireless defender of human rights in Cuba as executive director of the *Center for a Free Cuba*, was aggressively attacked by representatives of the Castro regime after the *Human Rights Council* voted to censured Cuba by a margin of one vote; there was little or no action taken by the UN Human Rights Commissioner.

Photos above:
Sylvia Iriondo, President, MAR por CUBA; Laurent Muller, President, Association Européenne Cuba Libre; Françoise Hostalier, President , Action Droits de l'Homme and Frank Calzón, Executive Director of Center for a Free Cuba

The Cuban exile community never lacked the presence of many Priests, Pastors and Rabbies that generously tended to their spiritual needs. Only a brief selection is presented here:

From left to right, top to bottom :

Msgr. Agustín Román, Father Francisco Santana, Rev. Martín Añorga, Father Armando Llorente, SJ.

Father Francisco Villaverde, OP, Msgr. Pedro Luis Pérez, Father Mario Vizcaino, SchP, Msgr. Emilio Vallina.

Father Antonio María Entralgo, SchP, Rev. Marcos Antonio Ramos, Father Vicente Fernández Mariño and **Msgr. Gilberto Fernández.**

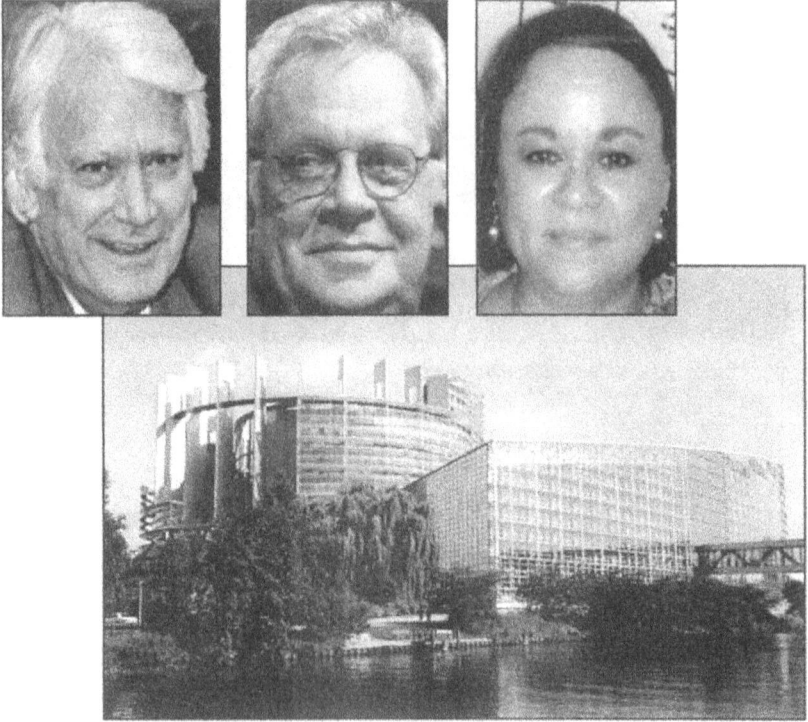

As part of the continuing denunciation of terror and violations of Human Rights in Cuba, Cuban exiles in France regularly organized activities in the city of **Strasbourg**, the capital of the *European Parliament* and headquarters of the *European Court of Human Rights*. One such event took place on June 18, 2004, under the title **A Night of Freedom**. It consisted of a tribute to **Raúl Rivero**, a poet and journalist sentenced to 20 years in prison in March 23, 2003, who was confined to the maximum security prison at *Canaleta*, near the city of *Ciego de Avila*. The activity was jointly organized by the *City of Strasbourg, Reporters Without Borders* and the *Solidarity Collective Free Cuba (Cuba SI, Castro NO)*, with the participation of the writer and former Spanish Minister of Culture **Jorge Semprún (1923-2011)** and exiled Cuban best-selling writer **Zoé Valdés**.

Throughout the night, poems by Raúl Rivero were read by actors Catherine and Frederic Solunto-Javaloyes as well as texts from Antonio Machado, Federico Garcia Lorca, Octavio Paz and Pablo Neruda. During the event, the minutes of the summary trial of Cuban poet Rivero were also read and the documentary **The Cuban Spring** (produced by Carlos González and Pablo Rodríguez), was shown. Five French members of Parliament were present and spoke during the meeting: *Philippe Richert, Hubert Haenel, Jean-Luc Reitzer, Armand Jung* and *Yves Bur*.

Photos above:
Jorge Semprún, Raúl Rivero and **Zoé Valdés**; the building of the
European Parliament in Strasbourg, France.

For many years the most notable support in Miami for Cuba's Castro Communist regime was **Max Lesnik (1930-)**, a man who had fled Cuba in 1960 but never ceased to be a friend of Castro and an una-bashed socialist. He created *Alianza Martiana* in January of 2001. As with the *Brigada Antonio Maceo,* the *Miami Coalition against the Embargo of Cuba,* the *Cuban-American Defenses League* and *Rescate Cultural Afro-Cubano,* among others, these organizations were the refuge of pro-Castro advocates —many of them unques-tionably infiltrated into the exile community as Castro's agents.

Alianza Martiana's leaders were not only Max Lesnik and his daughter Miriam, but also other leftist sympathizers like Juan Zamo-ra, Blanca Cuza, Carlos Rivero, Harold Morales, Pedro Villalonga, Ramón Coll and Juan Betancourt. Their open support for Communist Cuba in the streets of Miami became a convincing refutation of the presumed intransigence and extreme rightist and intolerant ideology of the Cuban exiles. Some of the very unpopular but permitted and respected actions of these pro-Castro groups in Miami were...

- Their support for the unconditional *lifting of the US embargo*;
- Their recruiting of rabid anti-Americans from the ranks of other Latin-American groups, for the purpose of blindly *accusing the US for every misery* that occurred in their countries;
- The *indoctrination of youngsters* with the mantra that «*the US was the worst terrorist nation in human history*»;
- Broadcasting *vitriolic broadsides* against the US through the radio, which included lambasting Abraham Lincoln for his «*false emancipation of the American Blacks*» and the sanctioned killing of Black leaders such as Martin Luther King and Malcolm X;
- The accusation of the US for the events in *Hiroshima* and *Nagasaki*; the US support of the criminal activities of the *State of Israel*; the US invasion of *Iraq*, the destruction of the *Maine* in 1898 and the US fak-ing of a staged *landing on the moon* in 1969;
- The unconditional support for Cuban spies such as the *Cuban Five*, all members of a cell called *Avispa* (wasp) that penetrated the US and was caught, tried and convicted for espionage and conspiracy to commit murder in 2005.

Photos above:
Max Lesnik in the year 2005; **Lesnik** visiting **Castro** after renewing their friendship in the late 1970s; the active propaganda in Miami to free the five Cuban spies from the **Red Avispa**.

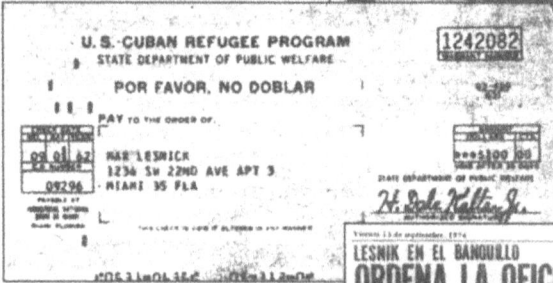

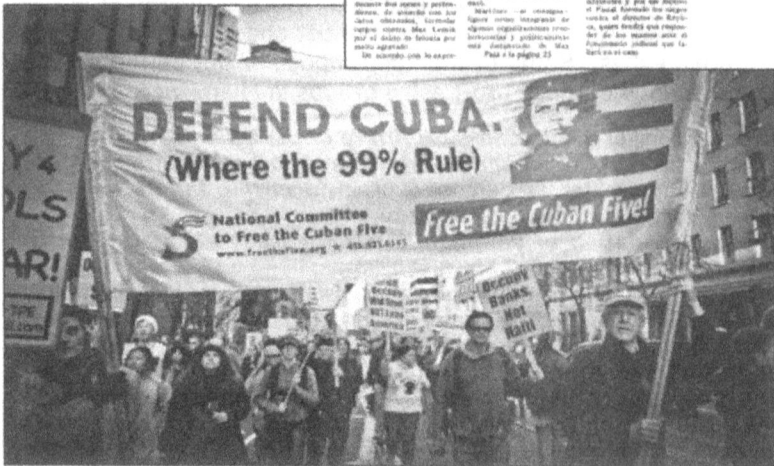

Photos above top to bottom:
Max Lesnik in 1958, as a pro-Castro activist in Cuba; Lesnik with other armed revolutionaries and his daughter **Miriam** with a toy gun; a **US Refugee Program ckeck** Lesnik allegedly received (like all Cuban refugees) upon his arrival as an exile in Miami; a 1974 Miami newspaper with the news of **Lesnik's arrest** after he threatened a political adversary with a gun after a discussion; a 2011 rally defending the **Cuban Five** and also supporting the *Wall Street Occupiers.*

In the pre-dawn hours of April 22, 2000, US Immigration forces, at the urging from Attorney General Janet Reno and her assistant Eric Holder, entered a house owned by a Cuban exile, **Lázaro González**, in Little Havana at 2319 N.W. 2nd St., corner of N.W 23rd Avenue. Fully equipped with SWAT equipment, the soldiers pepper-sprayed and maced the occupants and seized **Elián González**, the 7 year old boy who had been rescued from the high seas after her mother, escaping from Cuba, had drowned by his side in late 1999. She had Elián's father promise to follow her and escape to Miami. Pressured by Castro, the father later recanted.

Elián and twelve others, including his mother, had escaped from Cuba in November of 1999. All but two died in the crossing of the Florida straits. Elián had been placed in an inner tube and he drifted from the sinking aluminum boat where the others were after the boat's engine failed and a storm had sealed their fate. Elián was rescued by **Donato Dalrymple**, a local fisherman who found him by sheer luck.

The decision to leave the child in the US (as his Miami family, many Miami Cuban exiles, Barry University's President **Sister Jeanne O'Laughlin**, Dade County Mayor **Alex Penelas** and others requested) and the petition of his father in Cuba to get his son back (supported by the Castro regime, President and Mrs. **Clinton**, VP **Al Gore**, the Rev. **Jessie Jackson**, Spanish Foreign Minister **Abel Matutes**, and others), became a serious inter-national incident. Eventually Elián was returned to Cuba, where he joined the *Young Communist Union*. His father was made a member of the *Cuban National Assembly* and began to take Elián regularly to the events of the *Cuban Communist Party*. The affair became a factor in the 2000 US presidential elections: **Al Gore** lost the State of Florida and possibly the presidency of the US.

Photos: for months **Newsweek Magazine** and many other US publications kept track of the Elián affair during 2000; on the right, the **Pulitzer Prize** winning photo of an INS agent seizing with an automatic weapon a terrified Elian, hiding in a closet in his room.

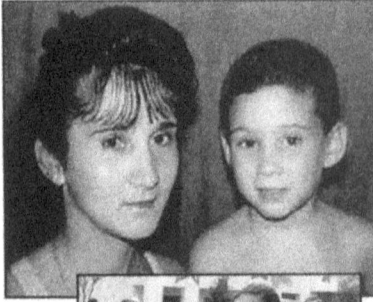

When Elián was finally sent back to Cuba, Cuban Exiles in Miami called for a general strike. Workers stayed home, students skipped school, businesses closed, honking cars and Cuban flags flooded the streets of Miami. Cuban American players and coaches in the Major Leagues benched themselves in protest: one in Tampa Bay, six from the Florida Marlins, two from the San Francisco Giants and two from the NY Mets. In solidarity, three non-Cuban American players of the Florida Marlins chose to sit out a game in solidarity.

Photos above, top to bottom, left to right:
Elián González and **Elizabeth Brotons**, his mother; Elián and his Miami cousin **Marisleysis González** during a visit to *Disneyworld*.
Hundreds of Cuban exiles marched and prayed for weeks to prevent the US government to return Elián to Cuba; several conspicuous defenders of his right to stay in the US were **Sister Jeanne O'Laughlin**, President of *Barry College*, TV commentators **Sean Hannity**, **Rush Limbaugh** and **Brit Hume;** and **Alex Penelas**, Mayor of *Miami-Dade County*.

The national press agreed that if Elián had been a Jewish boy from Nazi Germany, with parents in Berlin who wanted him to stay there, those claiming parental rights trumping freedom would have been much less enthusiastic. There were indeed precedents for freedom prevailing over parental rights, such as the Polovchak case in 1980. The parents of **Walter Polovchak** and his sister Natalie wanted to take them back to the Ukraine after a long visit to Chicago. The US family of these two Ukrainian children wanted to keep them in Chicago. The courts agreed the children had the right to remain in freedom, over the objections of their parents, if they wanted to return them to a totalitarian country.

Photos above, top to bottom, left to right:
The protests of Cuban exiles in **Miami** (in front of Elián's house); public demonstrations in **Miami** (in front of the federal courthouse), **Washington, D.C.** (in front of the Cuban Embassy), **Union City** (down Bergenline Avenue) and **New York City** (in front of the Cuban UN delegation building).

A gallery of advocates of sending Elián back to Cuba. They were, invariably, old supporters of Castro or celebrities awestruck by Castro's fame and power. Opting out for Elián's return was one more chapter of their disdain for Cuba's suffering under Communism.

Photos left to right, top to bottom:
US V.P. **Al Gore**, **President and Mrs. Clinton**, the Rev. **Jessie Jackson**, US Representative **Charles Rangel** (D-NY); Attorney Generàl **Janet Reno** and her Assistant **Eric Holder; Barbara Walters,** TV anchorwoman; INS Commissioner **Doris Meissner; Gregory Craig**, Mr. Clinton's impeachment defense lawyer; **Lucia Newman**, CNN correspondent in Havana; US Senator **Tom Daschle** (D-ND), US Representative **Maxine Walters** (D-Cal); **Joan Brown Campbell**, leader of the *National Council of Churches*; US Representatives **Sheila Jackson Lee** (D-Tx); **Barney Frank** (D-Mass); **Diane Sawyer**, TV anchorwoman; **Michael Moore**, radical cinematographer.

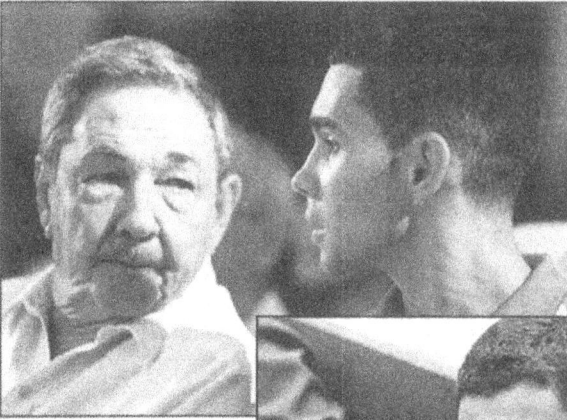

Once Elián González was returned to Cuba, his indoctrination to make him a hero of the revolution began. Ironically he would eventually be defending the regime from which his mother had escaped and gave her life in order to set him free.

*Photos above, top to bottom: **Elián** with **Fidel Castro**, who became his "mentor and adoptive father"; **Elián** with **Raúl Castro**, years later, when a sick Fidel Castro turned him over to his brother; finally **Elian** at 16, wearing the uniform of the Cuban army, the day of his initiation in the Cuban Communist Party.*

Some facts about the Elián González saga:

- **Doris Meissner**, Immigration and Naturalization Service (INS) Commissioner, rejected on her own Elian's standing to apply for political asylum (PA). The INS lawyers, however, had declared that the U.S. government could «*accept the child's asylum's application, since there were no prohibitions on age to a child filing application and any such PA should proceed.*»

- **Doris Meissner** also ordered many documents related to the Elián González's affair to be destroyed.

- According to **Judicial Watch**, the public interest law firm that investigates and prosecutes government corruption, copies of documents that survived Meissner's order to destroy, showed that «*the U.S. government knew and discussed the fact that Elian's father had sought to leave Cuba for the United States prior to the arrival of his son in Miami and that he was being coerced by the Castro regime.*» In fact, he had taken action to that effect including the request for a visa to the *U.S. Interest Section* in Havana.

- At the time, **Sister O'Laughlin**, President of Barry College, declared: «*It was clear from my observations that the Cuban government was exerting control over Elián's grandmothers and the National Council of Churches.*»

- In 1999, **Dr. Robert Edgar**, Secretary General of the *US National Council of Churches* asked an audience in Havana, with Fidel Castro beaming in the front row, to «*forgive the American people for the US embargo against your Country.*» During the Elián affair he declared «*Castro himself is calling the shots.*»

- After the Elián saga was finished **TIME** magazine editorialized «*Happily reunited with Dad and going home to family, friends and an adoring nation, the worst of his ordeal is over.*»

- At the same time, almost flippantly, **President Clinton** said, «*If the boy and his father decided they wanted to stay here, it would have been fine with me.*»

- The **National Review** editorialized «*Most Americans do not know what life is like in a Communist country. 90 miles from Florida lies the only Communist state in the Western Hemisphere. Fidel Castro is portrayed as a grandfatherly figure with a big U.S. chip on his shoulder, rather than the brutal, evil thug he is.*»

Photos below: the logos of two institutions that distinguished themselves in the fight for **Elián Gonzalez'** rights to live in freedom:
Judicial Watch and **MAR por Cuba**.

On **October 20, 2004**, after leaving the rostrum at a graduation ceremony in the City of Santa Clara, Castro tripped on a step, tumbled to the ground and fractured a knee and an arm. He had banged his knee, hip, elbow and arm into the first row of chairs. He was 78 at the time, not a good age to hit the ground in pain, and had been in power for 45 years. He immediately left the city in his *Mercedes Benz* limousine for the 3 hour ride to Havana, not even considering an emergency treatment anywhere else but in his private one-patient personal clinic.

The incident followed one on **June 23, 2001**, when he fainted during a two-hour speech under a scorching Cuban summer day before a crowd of thousands. The moment his body began listing to the side, the cameras pulled away and focused on the crowd until Foreign Minister Pérez Roque took the microphone to state «Sorry, *the commander in chief cannot finish his presentation*».

To the delight and hope of Cuban exiles, the *US State Department* made the following statement:

«We heard that Castro fell and we guess you'd have to check with the Cubans to find out what's broken about Mr. Castro. We, obviously, have expressed our views that what's broken in Cuba is Castro himself.

The situation in Cuba is of primary concern. The situation of Mr. Castro is of little concern to us, but, unfortunately, of enormous importance to the people of Cuba, who have suffered very long under his rule.

The US thinks that the kind of rule that Cubans have had should be ended. The Cuban people deserve democracy. They, like everybody else in the world, deserve a chance to choose their own fate and future. There is an administration effort (Bush's), led by Secretary of State Colin Powell, to identify what we can do to hasten that day and what we can do when that day comes to support the people of Cuba as they find their own democracy, which is something we have strong confidence that they will someday be able to do».

On November 21, 2005, *Santiago* Alvarez, a wealthy Cuban developer, US Army veteran and staunch supporter of Cuban exile militant *Luis Posada Carriles*, was arrested at his *Belle Meade* home in Miami. He was charged with possession of several automatic weapons, among which were four *AK-47* assault rifles, one *M-3* rifle with a silencer not properly registered, a *Heckler & Koch* grenade shooter and three *Makarov* pistols with their serial numbers erased. Also confiscated during his arrest were several passports. The weapons and passports were found at his Hialeah office according to Alvarez' high profile lawyer *Kendall Coffey*.

This arrest placed the US administration of President Bush in a disconcerting position. On one hand, Castro and many leftists in the US, including some Cuban exiles, were accusing the US of harboring Posada, a man waging a personal unrelenting war on Castro who had many times be accused but never convicted of terrorism. On the other hand, Cuban exiles were faithful and dependable supporters of Bush's style of anti-Communism and the US was in the middle of a campaign to eradicate terrorism.

Alvarez' arrest send shock waves within the Cuban exile community in Miami. The arrest had taken place the day after a Cuba-based leftist group had run a full page in the *New York Times* pointing to Posada as the man who masterminded the 1976 bombing of a Cuban jetliner and had directed a series of bomb attacks in Havana hotels during 1997-1998. In all probability, the man setting these bombs in Havana was posing as a Posada partisan in Habana but was in effect an agent of the Castro government.

A year later, in 2006, Santiago Alvarez was sentenced to four years in prison and a $10,000 fine. After sentencing, US District Court Judge *James Cohn* expressed «*This court recognizes that Mr. Alvarez is a perfect gentleman and a patriot. His ultimate goal has been a free and democratic Cuba, but we are a nation of laws*».

Photos below, left to right:
Santiago Alvarez at the time of his arrest; years later, *Santiago Alvarez*, accused by the Castro regime as an unconditional supporter of the *Damas de Blanco* in Cuba; the 2005 New York Times page against *Posada Carriles*.

Manifestación del exilio cubano en París

Este domingo habrá una gran marcha de exiliados cubanos en París, culminación de las que semanalmente se han llevado a cabo frente a la embajada de Castro en la capital francesa con el lema Martes por la Democracia en Cuba. El Colectivo Solidaridad Cuba Libre prepara la marcha para recibir "como se merece", al canciller castrista Felipe Pérez Roque. La convocatoria fue hecha por Laurent Müller, de la Asociación Europea Cuba Libre y el Dr. Raúl Chao.
La foto es de una reciente marcha en París.

As the *Assembly to Promote Civil Society in Cuba* (a coalition of 365 independent civil society groups within Cuba led by Martha Beatriz Roque Cabello, René Gómez Manzano, Félix Bonne Carcassés and Vladimiro Roca Antúnez) proceeded in Havana during May of 2005, hundreds of Cubans in exile joined forces to denounce to the entire world the tyranny that ruled Cuba.

Photos above, top to bottom:
A view of the members of the Assembly **meeting in Cuba** on May 21st, 2005; A view of the **rally in Paris**, in front of the Cuban Embassy, in support of the meeting in Cuba, on the same day, as reported by the **Diario las Americas**.

Celia Cruz (1925-2003) and **Guadalupe Victoria Yoli Raymond (La Lupe) (1939-1992)** are probably the most original and notable Cuban divas of the 20th Century.

Celia Cruz, the *Guarachera de Cuba*, was born in Havana, the daughter of a railroad man, and at age 19, in 1948, debuted in Havana in *Radio García Serra*. She became the main singer of *Sonora Matancera* (the most popular orchestra in Havana) in 1950. It was then that she started her trademark shout *¡AZUCAR!* After the 1959 revolution she left Cuba for the US with her husband Pedro Knight and became a US citizen. She has performed at *Carnegie Hall* as well as at every prestigious popular venue in Europe and Latin America. She won seven *Grammys* and was awarded the *National Medal of the Arts* in 1994 by President Clinton. After her death she was honored by the *Smithsonian Institution* with an exhibit celebrating her life and music. She recorded more than 80 LPs.

La Lupe was a Cuban-American singer of *boleros, guarachas, salsa* and *soul,* best known for her energetic and almost frenetic performances. She was born in Santiago de Cuba, the daughter of a worker at the *Bacardí Rum* plant. She debuted in 1954 when she won a contest to imitate *Olga Guillot's* bolero *Miénteme.* Soon she was performing on Radio and at nightclubs and was recorded by *RCA Victor* for a gold album. She went into exile in 1962, was discovered by *Mongo Santamaría* and made fans of *Ernest Hemingway, Tennessee Williams, Jean-Paul Sartre, Simone de Beauvoir* and *Marlon Brando.* In the late 1960s she sang at *Madison Square Garden*, where they called her the *Cuban earthquake.* She retired (destitute) in 1980, abandoned *Santería* and died a *born-again Christian* at age 52.

Photos above, top to bottom: **Celia Cruz** *as a young woman and with her husband of 43 years;* **La Lupe** *and some of her recordings.*

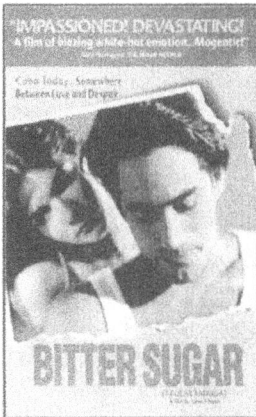

Photos above, top to bottom, left to right:
Some of the best films produced by Cuban and Cuban-American directors.

First row, those produced in Cuba: **Memorias del Subdesarrollo**, **Fresa y Chocolate** and **Guantanamera**.

Second row, those produced in exile: **Bitter Sugar**, **Lost City** and **Conducta Impropia**.

Third row: the directors: **Tomás Gutierrez Alea**, **Juan Carlos Tabío**, **Andy García**, **Nestor Almendros** and **León Ichaso**.

Woodland Park North Cemetery and Mausoleum in Miami has been the final resting place for many prominent Cuban exiles:

- **Edmundo (Sandy) Amorós (1930-1992).** Major League Baseball Player; for seven years with the *Brooklyn Dodgers* and later for the *Los Angeles Dodgers* and the *Detroit Tigers*.

- **Manuel Artime (1932-1977).** Leader of the unsuccessful *Bay of Pigs* invasion of Cuba in 1961. Member of the *Agrupación Católica Universitaria*.

- **Fernando Bujones (1955-2005).** International Ballet performer. Student of Alicia Alonso. Principal figure of the *New York City Ballet* from 1974 to 1990, and *Ballet Theater* at the *Metropolitan Opera House* until his death at 50 years old.

- **Jorge Mas Canosa (1939-1997).** Leading businessman and millionaire in the US Cuban-American community. A friend and influential advisor of US presidents Reagan, Bush and Clinton. Founder of the *Cuban American National Foundation*.

- **Rafael Guas Inclán (1896-1975).** Lifelong member of the Cuban *Liberal Party*, President of the Cuban *Chamber of Representatives*, VP of Cuba, *Mayor of Havana*. His son Carlos Guas Decal died in combat at the *Bay of Pigs* invasion.

(Continued)

Photos above, top to bottom, left to right: **Sandy Amorós, Manuel Artime, Fernando Bujones, Jorge Mas Canosa** and **Rafael Guas Inclán.**

(Continuation)

- **Gerardo Machado Morales (1871-1939).** General of the *Cuban War of Independence* in 1895 and *President of the Republic* from 1925 to 1933, when he was violently ousted.

- **Carlos Prío Socarrás (1903-1977).** President of Cuba from 1948 to 1952. Leader of students in the revolution of 1933. The charismatic *"Presidente Cordial"* was overthrown during a *coup-de-état* by Fulgencio Batista.

- **Antonio Prohías (1920-1998).** Famed Cuban cartoonist that, once in exile in 1959, created *"Spy vs Spy,"* the popular series published by *Mad Magazine*.

- **Ramón (Mongo) Santamaría (1922-2003).** Composer and Latin-jazz virtuoso percussionist, winner of six *Grammys* awards from 1975 to 1985.

- **Unknown Patriot (Bay of Pigs).** A grave with the legend «*Here rests in Glory a Cuban Freedom Fighter known only to God*».

Photos below:

Gerardo Machado, Carlos Prío Socarrás, Antonio Prohías, Mongo Santamaría and the grave of an **Unknown Cuban Patriot** that sacrificed his life at the *Bay of Pigs* invasión.

Woodland Park North Cemetery, at 3250 SW Eighth St. in Miami.

Since 1993, Cuban exiles in Sweden have been organized under the **Cuban Union of Sweden (UCS)**, the oldest independent exile group established in the Scandinavian countries. Over the years they have been very active in demonstrations outside the *Cuban Embassy* demanding the release of Cuban prisoners of conscience. Most Cuban exiles in Sweden are former students and residents of the Soviet Union who have escaped from the reach of the Communists. Very often the activities of the UCS are interrupted by attempts to repress freedom of speech by small groups of individuals, defenders of the regime in Havana, who attack them armed with sharpened umbrella tips and belts with hard and heavy buckles. On July 26, 1997, to mention one instance, they physically attacked a group of Cuban exiles at a rally including a pregnant woman which they mistreated and forced to the ground.

In 2007, during a meeting of the *Human Rights Council*, held in Geneva from 12th to 30th March, Swedish chancellor **Carl Bildt** strongly denounced Cuba of violating human rights not only inside the island but also in many capitals around the world. In his address he expressed: «*The UN has a responsibility to supervise respect for human rights and human freedoms. Both are rather restricted in Cuba and it is our duty to say so. It should not lead to the sort of hysterical attack on an entire nation such as that made by the Cuban regime to Sweden*».

Bildt also complained that most of the incoming mail for the Swedish embassy in Havana was routinely opened by Cuban officials before it left the island. He ended his presentation saying, «*There are many Cuban exiles that have been living in Sweden for years as freedom of speech and freedom of the press are not at the top of Cuba's bill of rights. After all, everybody knows that Cuba's government is a dictatorship*».

Photos above: Cuban Exiles demonstrating against Castro in Stockholm.

Cuban exiles were not naïve or unaware that most academic institutions in the US leaned far to the left, even in such apparent bastion of conservatism as Miami. It was not then a surprise that two Cuban exile professors from *Florida International University (FIU)*, were found to be spying for the Castro regime: psychology professor **Carlos Alvarez** (associate professor in the Educational Leadership and Policy Studies Department since 1974, and a frequent traveler to Cuba), and **Elsa Alvarez**, his wife (a psychology counselor specializing in psychological treatment, crisis intervention and group psychotherapy, member or sympathizer of the Antonio Maceo Brigade). They were spies in the novel fashion world of shortwave radios, numerical-code language and computer encrypted files. For 30 years they had been supplying Castro with detailed notes about the Cuban exile community. Carlos Alvarez was sentenced to five years in prison and his wife Elsa to three years.

Not long after that, on June 7, 2009, **Walter** (aged 72) and **Gwendolyn Myers** (aged 71), also a husband and wife spy team, were indicted as the most significant Castro spies within the US government. For 30 years they concealed their treason by living in a well-to-do apartment complex in Washington DC as neighbors of two cabinet members, 31 Congressmen, 121 Senators and 14 Federal Judges. Walter Myers was the great grandson of Alexander Graham Bell, inventor of the telephone, and appropriately he received and sent messages to Cuba in Morse code. At the time of their arrest Walter was a Visiting Professor at *Johns Hopkins University*.

(Continued)

*Photos above, left to right: **Carlos Alvarez**, **Elsa Alvarez**; **Walter** and **Gwendolyn Myers**.*

(Continuation)

Prior to the indictments of the **Alvarez** and **Myers** couples, the most important case of Cuban espionage among Cuban exiles in the US had been the cases of **Ana Belén Montes** in 2001 and the spy network known as the **Avispa Red** (Wasp Web) in 1998.

Ana Belén Montes was a senior analyst at the *US Defense Intelligence Agency (DIA)*. On September 1, 2001, she was arrested for espionage for the Castros. She had obtained a Master's degree at *Johns Hopkins*, coincidentally at the time **Walter Myers** was an adjunct professor there. She began to work at the DIA in 1985 and in 1992 was commissioned to go to Cuba to study the Cuban military. It has been speculated that by that time she was already in Castro's payroll. In time she reached the highest DIA position for Cuban analysts and began to *«communicate with the Cuban Intelligence Service through encrypted messages, receiving her instructions through shortwave encrypted transmissions from Cuba,»* according to federal prosecutors. All her notes were on water-soluble paper that could be rapidly made to disappear.

The feds also stated at her trial that *«Montes passed a considerable amount of classified information to Cuba's government, including the identities of four spies, and information which caused the death of a U.S. special operations soldier in Central America (SGT Gregory Fronius on March 31, 1987)»* She was sentenced to 25 years in 2002, after declaring that *«She felt the Cuban revolution was treated unfairly by the U.S. government»*.

(Continued)

The U.S. Department of State believed that Montes' role in the DIA *«was the rule and not the exception since Cuban intelligence services had numerous spies and moles within U.S. intelligence units and among Cuban exiles»*. A 1998 report concluding that *«Cuba did not represent a significant military threat to the United States,»* for instance, was entirely conceived, written and presented by Ana Montes. The unrepentant spy, upon receiving her sentence, declared: *«Espero que mi caso, en alguna manera, estimule a nuestro gobierno para que abandone su hostilidad en relación con Cuba»*. (I hope my case would make our government abandon its hostility towards Cuba).

Photos above, left to right: **Ana Belén Montes** as presented by the press in Cuba and as presented by the press in the US.

Fernando González   Ramón Labañino   Antonio Guerrero   Gerardo Hernández   René González

(Continuation)

The Cuban Five (shown above) were the celebrated spies from the **Red Avispa** (Wasp Web), sentenced to long prison terms on **June 8, 2001**, convicted of spying for the Cuban government. Three of them had been born in Cuba and had fought in Angola; the other two were born in the US. For many years, all five had been pretending to be **Cuban exiles**.

- On **August 9, 2005**, their convictions were overturned by the US 11th Circuit Court in Atlanta, based on a possibly unfair trial in Miami.
- On **August 9, 2006** the 11th Court reinstated the convictions.
- On **June 4, 2008**, a three judge panel of the 11th Court sent back to Miami the sentences of three of them, Labañino, Guerrero and René González.
- On **January 30, 2009**, the defense team asked the *US Supreme Court* to take their cases under appeal.
- The Court refused on **June 15, 2009**.
- On **October 13, 2009**, the US District Court of Southern Florida imposed new sentences to Guerrero (21 years and 10 months).
- On **December 8, 2009**, the United States District Court in Southern Florida imposed a new sentence of 17 years and nine months to Fernando Gonzalez, and 30 years to Ramón Labañino; they were serving life sentences plus 19 and 18 years.

Ever since their sentences were confirmed, they received the support of many US leftist organizations. The city of San Francisco was the epicenter of protests in their favor. Shown above are public gatherings organized by the **National Committee to Free the Cuban Five**, the **Bay Area Latin American Solidarity Coalition (BALASC)**, **Bay Area Farabundo Martí National Liberation Front (FMLN)**, the **Act Now to Stop War and End Racism (A.N.S.W.E.R.)**. *ANSWER*, in particular, is a well-known front group for the **Stalinist Workers World Party**.

Cuban exiles back to Cuba?

A return to Cuba of the Cubans in Exile, even when they persisted in toasting «*next year in Havana*,» became more a sweet dream that a reality by 2000. No one continued thinking that US Cuban exiles would follow the traditional biblical patterns of a come back to the Promised Land. The reliance on external forces to solve the Cuban tragedy and the impotence at overpowering the murderous and unscrupulous Castro regime led most Cuban exiles to split in two ideologically different communities: those who felt that it was **unpatriotic** to visit their land while the scoundrels that had destroyed it were still in power and those that —for different reasons— believed in visiting occasionally even if it meant **submitting** to Castro's rules during their stay.

For many, the humane reasons adduced for such visits were to see again their (aging?) kin, to bring them items that were not available in Cuba (medicines, food, clothing, small appliances, dollars, gifts) or even to seek treatment in Cuba's free hospitals. For others the unavowed reasons were to **show-off** their prosperity in the land of the dollar, to **profit** from the black market for American goods or to satisfy their **nostalgia** for things Cuban.

(Continued)

Photos: Cubans living in Miami traveling to Cuba with their hands full of merchandise as gifts for their families, or to "*do some business there*" due to the lack of essentials in the central planned economy of Cuba.

(Continuation)

In addition to the physical visits to the island, Cuban exiles —more or less for the same purposes— began to send remittances to their families in Cuba. By 2010 it amounted to more than $1.0 billion a year of unearned net cash flow to the Cuban regime. 80% of remittance senders were from pre-1990 Cuban exiles; 75% from non-US citizen exiles; 70% of senders were from families earning less than $45,000 a year; almost all were using either Western Union or some Cuban-operated companies (approved by the Castro's) in Miami, New York or Paris that were taking usury level commissions. For the Castro regime the exile remittances covered almost 25% of the annual budget and —for years— substantially contributed to the economic viability of the regime. So sure were the Castro brothers of the stability of this income that they began to surcharge all sorts of fees to the remittances sent by the exiles.

By 2006, in support of the growing numbers of Cuban exiles sending cash and visiting Cuba, several exile organizations joined forces in what was called **Consenso Cubano**. Its purpose was to lobby the US government to go a step beyond remittances and facilitate more and easier travel to Cuba. Their reasoning was that the "*blockade*" had not resulted and to limit remittances or travel would «*violate fundamental rights of Cubans, damage the Cuban family, and constitute an ethical contradiction*». The split between *Consenso Cubano* and other traditional Cuban exile organizations was presented as «*a fundamental rift between hard-line conservative old exiles and moderate Cuban Americans in Miami allied to Cuban dissidents in the island*».

The stalwarts and main supporters of *Consenso Cubano* were the **Cuba Study Group,** the **Institute of Cuban Studies** of Florida International University, the **Cuban American National Foundation,** the **Christian Democratic Party of Cuba**, and several others, i.e., the same organizations that for years had been lobbying for a "*diálogo*" with Castro's Cuba.

Photo above, sitting: leaders of *Consenso Cubano*, **Roland J Bejar, Carlos Saladrigas** and **José Antonio Blanco.** *Standing, left to right:* **Marcelino Miyares, Julio Pich, Siro del Castillo, Carlos Manuel Estefanía, Tomás Rodríguez** and **Eduardo Ojeda Camaraza.**

For close to half a century Cuban exiles were the best and always unconditional supporters of Cuban dissidents and opponents to Communism in the island. In addition to the authors of **La Patria es de Todos**, other important voices in Cuba protested, risked their lives and their personal freedom in defense of liberty and respect for Cuba's traditions of democracy and free expression. Three such voices were Father José Conrado Rodríguez Alegre, freedom activist Osvaldo Payá Sardiñas and magazine publisher Dagoberto Valdés Hernández.

Father José Conrado Rodríguez (1953-), many times called *The People's Cardinal*, became well known in 1994 after he wrote a public letter to Fidel Castro blaming him for the disaster of the Cuban economy and the suffering of Cubans, both in the island and in the *Diáspora*. The Catholic Church removed him from Cuba in 1996 and sent him to study in Spain, from where he returned in 1998, on occasion of the visit of Pope John Paul II to the island. In 2007 Cuban security agents violated the integrity of *Santa Teresita*, his modest Church in Santiago de Cuba in what he characterized as «*a pachanga terrorista*». After many other interventions in defense of Cuban freedom, Father José Conrado was transferred by his superiors to the rural parish of *El Cristo*, a small town near Santiago de Cuba.

(Continued)

Photos below:**Father José Conrado Rodríguez**; the Church of **Santa Teresita** in Santiago de Cuba;**Osvaldo Payá** denouncing **EcuRed**, the Cuban Web Page dedicated to the spread of misinformation among exiles.

La Wikipedia cubana inyecta veneno contra disidentes y opositores

EcuRed, la llamada Wikipedia cubana, se encarga de brindar la versión oficialista de los principales líderes de la oposición en Cuba. En declaraciones a martinoticias, el activista Oswaldo Paya Sardiñas dijo que se trata de "una perversión para destruir la mente"

(Continuation)

Osvaldo Payá (1953-), the founder of *Movimiento Cristiano de Liberación* and main promoter of *Proyecto Varela*, was awarded the *2002 Sakharov Prize* by the European Parliament; he has been nominated for the *Nobel Peace Prize* in more than one occasion and was received in a public audience by John Paul II in 2003. He is an engineer and works in Cuba as a medical equipment repairman.

Dagoberto Valdés (1955-) is an intellectual and former editor of *Revista Vitral* in Pinar del Río, Cuba. Unlike Payá, who has some support from the Church in Cuba, Valdés always found resistance within the Church for his direct political crashes with the government and with some Church leaders. At one time he was characterized as «*a Cuban dissident who takes advantage of the Church to promote his political ideas*». Valdés was fired from his government job in 1996 when he started publishing *Vitral* with the support of **Mons. José Siro González**, the Bishop of Pinar del Río. It was rumored that in 2007 Cardinal Ortega forced him out of *Vitral* when Mons. Rodríguez retired and **Bishop Jorge Serpa** replaced him. Valdés began to publish *Convivencia*, in digital format, adding «*both Jorge Serpa [the new Bishop of Pinar del Río] and Cardinal Ortega Alamino are loyal to the Cuban regime and should not be trusted*».

Photos above, top to bottom, left to right:

Dagoberto Valdés, founder and director of the **Revista Vitral** in Cuba; a copy of *Vitral*. **Mons. Pedro Meurice** (In the presence of Raúl Castro, 100,000 Catholics and the Pope in 1998, the **León de Oriente**, as he was known, launched a harsh criticism of the Communist system for «*its lack of freedom that had turned Cuba into a country torn by exile, ideological confrontations and false mesianism*»), **Mons. José Siro**, **Mons. Jorge Serpa** and **Cardenal Ortega Alamino**.

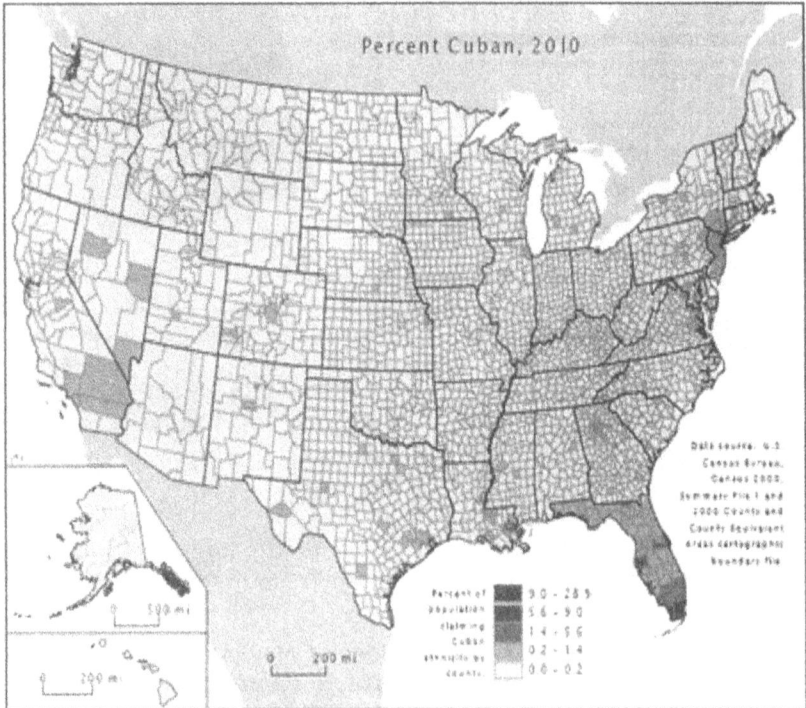

Percent Cuban, 2010

Data source: U.S
Census Bureau,
Census 2005,
Summary File 1 and
2000 County and
County Equivalent
areas cartographic
boundary file

Percent of population claiming Cuban ancestry by county	
	9.0 - 28.9
	5.6 - 9.0
	1.4 - 5.6
	0.2 - 1.4
	0.0 - 0.2

By 2010, the extent of the *Cuban Diáspora* had achieved unimaginable and unpredictable dimensions.

- **South Florida** was the home of close to 1,400,000 Cuban exiles, the largest community of Cubans outside the island.

- In the **Houston** area of Texas there were 10,000 Cuban exiles; 6,000 in **New Orleans**, 180,000 in **New York**, 145,000 in **Southern California**, 90,000 in **New Jersey**, 70,000 in **Chicago.**

- In Europe the largest communities were in **Spain** (possibly 25,000) and **Paris** (about 2,000).

- In **Sweden** there were about 2,000 exiles, many of them young Cubans studying in Moscow in the early days of Perestroika that instead of returning to Cuba went to Stockholm. There were known as the "*gusanos rojos*".

- In **Venezuela**, even after the ascent of Chávez, there were over 4,000 Cubans left.

- In **Perú** were 1,500 Cubans, most of them originally the occupants of the Peruvian Embassy in Havana in 1980. It is probably the least adapted group of Cuban exiles.

- The **Australian** government sponsored about 200 Cuban families to move in. They live mostly in Sydney and Melbourne.

Lore has it that if you wish to rent a *camel* to get close to the Pyramids in **Egypt**, or if you wish to have your children riding a *burrito* at the *Gardens of Luxembourg* in **Paris**, you will be dealing with a Cuban refugee.

Diagram: the presence of Cuban exiles in the US as of 2010.

Cuban exiles were never able to erase the devotion of many world leaders to the totalitarian regime the Castro brothers had implanted in Cuba. First they sided with the Castros because of the ongoing Cold War; later it was a reaction against the condition of the US as the world's most powerful nation. It did not matter that Cuba did not have **freedom of the press** or **freedom of expression**; that Cubans could not **freely leave or return to their country**; that **schools, TV, radio and all news media were government-controlled**; that the **economy was in ruins**; or that there were **no political parties** allowed other than the *Communist Party*.

Photos, top to bottom, left to right:

Castro handholding *Libya's* **Muammar Gaddafi** and *Nicaragua's* **Daniel Ortega**; with *Venezuela's* **Hugo Chávez** and *Bolivia's* **Evo Morales**; with *Brazil's* **Luiz Inácio Lula da Silva**; with Panama's **Manuel Noriega**; *with South Africa's* **Nelson Mandela**; *with PLO's* **Yasser Arafat**; with Poland's **Wojciech Jaruzelski**; with *US'* **Louis Farrakhan**, finally, with **Malcolm X** and **Jimmy Carter**, also from the US.

Two Great Cultural Institutions run by Cuban Exiles in Miami

The organization that has most effectively presented the reality of Cuba to the world and has most persistently contributed to the cultural life of Cuban exiles in Miami has been for many years the **Institute of Cuban and Cuban-American Studies (ICCAS)** at the University of Miami. Some of their senior research staff and administrators are presented above.

Photos above: **Dr. Jaime Suchlicki**, Emilio Bacardí Professor, Director of ICCAS; **Dr. Andy Gómez**, Senio Fellow; **Dr. José Azel**, Senior Research Associate; **María del Carmen Urizar**, Administrator.

Cuban Cultural Heritage (CCH) was founded in Miami in 1994 with the purpose of saving Cuba's cultural, patrimonial and historical roots. It publishes *Herencia*, a magazine that documents Cuba's history, art and culture. Since its founding, CCH has been the custodian of numerous original Cuban documents, rare books, pictures and historical items that record in detail the glory of the Cuban nation.

*Photos: **Drs. Marcos Antonio Ramos**, **Luis Mejer** and **Bertie Bustamante** presenting the 2011 Herencia Award to historian **Enrique Ros**. On the right, recent copies of Herencia Magazine.*

The Cuban exiles living in New York City had in many ways a greater challenge than exiles living in other cities: Harlem was the only community in the US that openly proclaimed an admiration for Castro. It had started in 1960 when the Cuban delegation to the UN had been evicted from Manhattan's *Shelburne Hotel* and welcomed by Harlem's *Hotel Theresa*.

On October 24, 2006, a group of pro-Castro activists talked Connecticut sculptor **Daniel Edwards** *into producing a colossal sculpture of Castro at rest (25 feet in size)*, to be exhibited at *New York's Central Park*, near Wollman rink, just a few feet north of the equestrian statue of José Martí. The title of the exhibition would be **"Fidel Castro's Deathbed Portrait,"** honoring the man the Blacks of Harlem revered as a «*true champion of civil rights*».

The plan stirred a hornet's nest of emotions among the Cuban exiles in New York. So much that Edwards had a change of heart and decided to change the venue of his show to Miami; the aim of the exhibition was also changed. It now consisted of burning and burying a Castro's clay effigy, or at least his head, as an **anti-monument**, highlighting the coming end of the Castro regime.

The title of the exhibition, rescheduled for November 8th in Miami was changed to **"Deconstruction and laying to rest of Fidel Castro."** Edwards made a declaration stating «*I'm only sorry I wasn't aware of all that pain before my project started. After hearing all these painful accounts, in good conscience, as a friend of the Cuban-American communities, I cannot show the sculpture in Central Park*».

Photos below: **Daniel Edwards** and his **"Castro's Death Mask"**.

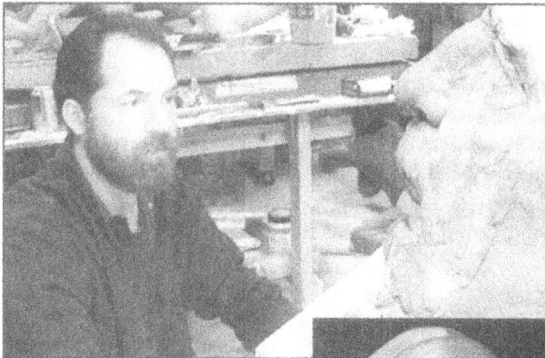

Many of the Cuban exiles that arrived in the US after 1980 involuntarily became the strongest allies of Castro's regime in Cuba by means of the "*humanitarian remittances*". The rationale of the exiles that were behind these transfers of funds to Cuba was only a shade different from the opinions of the US liberal media that characterized Cuba as a «*victim of an inhuman US blockade*». All along, however, Castro's Cuba was classified by the US State Department as «*a state sponsor of terrorism*». By 2010, cash remittances by exiles to Cuba, on a yearly basis, were over *$1 billion*, in the same range as China's foreign aid to Cuba. Incredibly, the individual recipients of remittances in Cuba were receiving from their exile families over four times the typical Cuban salary for a physician.

During the years of the Cold War, Czechs, Russians, Polish, East German and Hungarian refugees were never asked to send cash to those left behind or expected to have the opportunity to visit the countries they had fled. They never anticipated or demanded to be able to support their families from their places of exile abroad. In the US, however, many Cuban exiles, after kissing the ground of the country in which they had found refuge, immediately began to *plan their return* to Cuba with gifts and cash, or perhaps on a summer or *Christmas holiday vacation*.

Miami, in addition, became a free zone for swindlers stealing funds from the bureaucratic and lightly protected US welfare and medical programs. FBI's investigations revealed that in the 2000-2010 decade, over $450 million of fraudulent funds from Medicare had gone to "*Cuban exiles*" that had fled back to Cuba to escape prosecution. Most of them still had Cuban passports and the Cuban regime welcomed them back, evidently shielding them from justice in the courts of the country where they had been sent to steal in the first place.

Photos: **CADECA**, the offices set up in Cuba to receive the **remittances**
from the Cuban exiles; an explicit cartoon presenting the
dilemma of the exiles' **cash transfers** to Cuba.

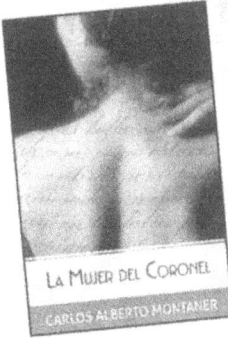

Cuban exiles have sustained for many years a loyal readership to **Carlos Ripoll (1922-2011)** and **Carlos Alberto Montaner (1943-)**.

Carlos Ripoll was the best and most prolific scholar on the life of José Martí during the second part of the 20th century, probably second to only *Félix Lizaso* or *Jorge Mañach*. He had obtained his PhD at the *University of Miami* in his sixties, after arriving from Cuba, and remained in academe for the rest of his life, absorbed and touched with Martí's life and writings. He researched and wrote about the Apostle, as well as about many Cuban themes, well into his nineties. **Carlos Alberto Montaner**, one of the best analysts of Cuban successes and misfortunes, has published more than 25 books, written hundreds of newspaper articles and delivered equal number of addresses and lectures in Europe, Latin America and the US. He is also a graduate of the *University of Miami*. In the 1970s he founded the *Editorial Playor* in Madrid. Over the years he has received numerous prizes, honorary degrees and appointments to important newspaper editorial boards in three continents.

Photos, top to bottom: **Carlos Ripoll** *and* **Carlos Alberto Montaner** *with some of their most popular best-sellers.*

Photos above, left to right, top to bottom:
The literary critics of the Cuban exile; judicious and industrious arbiters and crafters of the written word, both in the island and the *Diáspora*.

Ariel Remos, lawyer and journalist, worldwide defender of human rights; **Olga Connor**, PhD in Romance Languages, scholarly journalist, traces her filiation to *Orígenes*; **Luis Mario**, first class poet, journalist professor at *U of M*; **Manuel C. Díaz**, writer, star literary critic of *El Nuevo Herald*; **Luis de la Paz**, journalist, dramatist, former editor of *Mariel*, VP of the Pen Club; **Guillermo Cabrera Leiva**, writer for *Diario las Américas* for more than 50 years, abstract painter and poet; **Armando Alvarez Bravo**, poet, essay writer, editor, journalist, numerary of the Academia Cubana de la Lengua.

Shamefully, as **Castro** aged, 11 US presidents came and went. After 50 years of Communism, Cuba began to make preparations for "*economic reforms*," meaning pink-slipping citizens (every Cuban on the island was a government employee) by the thousands and asking them to fend for themselves to find sustenance, which Cubans had been doing fairly well before 1959. It also meant taxes, professional and service licenses, higher rents and electrical bills and possibly even fees to attend schools. The Castros began to sound more like Bush and Clinton than Marx and Lenin.

Finally, on September 7, 2010, the ultimate confession emanated from the heart of Castro into the ears of **Jeffrey Goldberg**, a journalist from *The Atlantic*. «*The Cuban model* [of government] *does not even work for us anymore*». Days later a western diplomat stated for the press in *The Economist* «*One day we might well look back on this as Cuba's "perestroika" moment*».

Photos, first row: an aging **Castro** lingered to power in Cuba longer than any other dictator in the history of the American continent. *Bottom rows*: US Presidents **Eisenhower, Kennedy, Johnson, Nixon, Ford, Carter, Reagan, G.H.Bush, Clinton, G.W.Bush** and **Obama**. All had to include Castro in their presidential agendas.

By the time Castro resigned as Cuba's Maximum Leader in April of 2011, the world was already tired of him. College students no longer had posters of him in their rooms; Cuba was no longer the island where social classes disappeared and the utopical world of socialism had been reached. The executions, the brutality of the regime's repressions, the Brigades of Quick Response against dissidents, the censorship, the hunger, the authoritarian disposition of the new class, the blessing of Castro to the Russian tanks crushing the Czech revolt, the boring marathons of Castro's speeches, the flight from Cuba of over 15% of its citizens, and hundreds of other disappointments, were blemishes in the face of the revolution.

Cuban exiles, however, knew that it was not going to be easy to bury the semi-mummified Dictator. The adulation continued as his worldwide leftist devotees increased their pilgrimages. A photo with the prophet, now in *Adidas* paraphernalia, was more indicative of a close friendship with the Supreme Leader than when he posed for the cameras dressed with the old military fatigues. As Castro withered so did the hopes of most Cuban exiles.

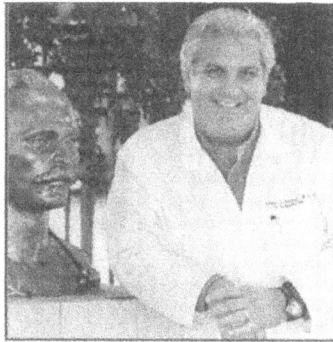

Pedro Jose Greer Jr., M.D. is an Assistant Dean at the *University of Miami* Medical School who has dedicated his career to improving the health of those without access to health care. He is Medical Director of **Mercy Mission Services**, Medical Director of **San Juan Bosco Clinic**, a Miami health care facility that serves 6,000 patients a year which he founded in 1991, and the Medical Director of the **Camillus Health Concern**, a clinic he founded in 1984 where over 100 voluntary physicians provide medical services to more than 10,000 homeless patients per year.

Greer is a physician trained in hepatology and a 1980 graduate from the *University of Miami* School of Medicine. He was born in Florida by accident. His mother, a native of Cuba, traveled to the United States in 1956 for a family birthday celebration; she was only six months pregnant, but little Joe decided to be born in America. Mother and son returned to Cuba in two weeks but four years later, in 1960, the entire family decided to leave Cuba upon Castro's start of the revolution. Joe's US citizenship was crucial to secure a safe exile in the US. They have never considered going back to Cuba under the circumstances of the last half century.

Greer's proudest accomplishments have been his 30 years of service at the **San Juan Bosco Clinic** and **Camilus House**. He has received three presidential awards, two papal awards and the coveted *MacArthur "genius" Fellowship*, which is given to individuals who «*show exceptional merit and promise for continued and enhanced creative work*». He has been honored as **Outstanding Young Men of America** (1987); **Excellence in Leadership Award** from the Organization of American States (1990); a Tribute in the **US Congressional Record** (1990); Time Magazine's **50 Future Leaders of America** (1994); **Ellis Island Medal of Honor** (2001); **Hero of the Americas Award** from the Pan American Health Organization (2005), and about some other fifty awards.

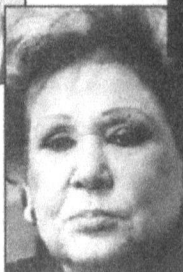

Time began to take a toll in the longest active political exile in recent times as more and more Cuban exiles around the world began to die after half a century of hope and despair. In the first years of the 21st century, several exiles from different walks of life became a memory of dignity and sacrifice for their friends.

Carlos (Patato) Pascual (1931-2011), the great right hand pitcher for the Washington Senators, older brother of all-star pitcher Camilo Pascual, died in Miami at the age of 80. He had been an exile in Miami since 1960.

Rosendo Rosell (1918-2010), a master of comedy, movies, radio, TV, journalism and music, also went into exile in 1960, when he left Cuba with his wife Marta and their daughter. In a lifetime of devotion to the artistic world he recorded his humor in 20 LPs, composed many well known songs, wrote extensively for the *Diario las Americas* and worked on several films in Mexico and Cuba. He died in Miami at the age of 92.

Olga Guillot (1922-2010) was born in Santiago de Cuba; after 73 years of a worldwide successful career as the "*queen of bolero,*" "*Olga de Cuba*" died in Miami Beach at the age of 87. She had gone into exile in 1961. She had established herself as an international figure in Mexico in 1948 and in 1958 in Europe, where she became a friend of Edith Piaf.

José Ignacio Rivero (1920-2011), grandson of Don Nicolás Rivero, the founder of *Diario de la Marina* and son of Pepín Rivero, his successor, was first a newspaper publisher and later an admired journalist until the day of his death in Miami, where he had been writing for many years in the *Diario Las Américas*. He went into exile in 1960 upon confiscation of his newspaper by Castro. He was the recipient of numerous awards for his lucid articles and his defense of journalism in the Americas.

Photos above: **Patato Pascual, Rosendo Rosell,**
Olga Guillot and ***José Ignacio Rivero*** at the time he assumed
the direction of the *Diario de la Marina* at age 25.

Carter's skills can smooth U.S.-Cuban hostilities

Nothing short of perplexing to Cuban exiles was the Castro-Carter congeniality since the time of Carter's presidency. Former President **Jimmy Carter's** first relations with Cuba were in the late 1970s, when the Cuban newspaper *Granma* mocked his background as an ignorant peanut farmer. Following this unfair characterization of Carter, Castro launched 125,000 Cubans to American shores, including criminals and mental patients, in the belief that Carter's brain was smaller than his. Also, within a few weeks, Castro began to deploy his "**Repudiation Brigades**," mobs throwing stones, eggs, and spit on the "traitors" abandoning Cuban shores.

In May of 2002, at a first personal encounter, Castro received the American ex-President at Havana's airport tarmac during Carter's visit as a private non-governmental man with a mission. Upon his return to the states Carter referred to Castro not as a Communist leader but as an "*old friend*." Within a few weeks after Carter's visit Castro launched a series of arrests known as the "*Primavera Negra*," (Black Spring) sentencing 75 dissidents and journalists to hundreds of years in prison.

The second personal encounter in the Castro-Carter saga occurred in March of 2011. Carter showed up once more in Havana, this time to be greeted at the airport not by Fidel or Raúl but by two second tier Cuban government figures: Foreign Minister Bruno Rodriguez and the head of the U.S. diplomatic mission in DC, Jonathan Farrar. Carter's position was made clear to the Castros:

- the 50 years long US trade embargo and travel ban damaged the Cuban people and hindered rather than helped reform;
- keeping Cuba on a list of state sponsors of terrorism was counterproductive;
- Free the Cuban Five? Sure! they're no threat to the United States and they've served long enough;
- He wanted to learn about new economic policies and the themes of the upcoming (Communist) Party congress, as well as to discuss ways to improve U.S.-Cuba relations.

It seemed that the visits of Carter to Castro always reinforced the notion that doing Castro's bidding invariably brought painful consequences to the Cuban people.

DIARIO LAS AMÉRICAS

The Spanish daily *Diario las Américas* (founded on July 4th, 1953) has been, for six decades, the strongest voice for freedom and democracy in South Florida and the rest of the US. It has been the dean of Spanish language journalism in the US and an unconditional supporter of Cuban exiles and every cause that needs defending in the American continent, the US nation included. By 2012, *Diario las Américas* has presented close to 20,000 editorials in the only bilingual section of the paper. No noble cause in the US has ever found a more powerful and effective advocate than the *Diario*. The depth, power of analysis and honest intellect of its columnists has rarely been matched by other papers in the US.

The paper was founded by Nicaragua-born **Don Horacio Aguirre Baca**, a lawyer by profession (Panamá, 1947-1950) who emigrated to the US in 1953 with his brother Francisco, co-founder of the paper. Don Horacio's children **Alejandro, Helen** and **Carmen María** joined him in the direction of the paper as *Newspaper Director, Director of the Opinion* pages and *Director of the Revista del Diario*. By all accounts, a remarkable complement of talents.

Photos above, top to bottom, left to right:

Horacio Aguirre Baca and his brother **Francisco** (†2008); the seal of the *Interamerican Press Society;* **Alejandro, Helen** and **Carmen María Aguirre Craigie**; the logo of **Diario las Américas**.

Cuban Exiles in the 2000s

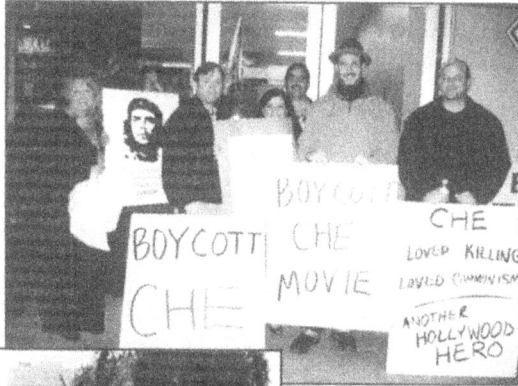

Cubans in Los Angeles boycotting Soderberghs' Movie **Ché** on Dec 12, 2008.

Cubans in **Calle Ocho**, Miami, in February 2011.

Cuban exiles participate as members of the *US Commission for Assistance to a Free Cuba*, presided by US Secretary of State **Condoleezza Rice** in 2007.

Cubans exiles protesting at the **Plaza Mayor de Madrid** in 2008.

Cuban Exiles in the 2000s

Cubans exiles protests at the Cuban consulate in **Barcelona** in 2005.

Cubans exiles organized an **International Marathon** pro-human rights in Cuba in 2009.

Cuban exiles demonstrating in front of the Cuban delegation in **Washington** in 2005.

Cuban exiles demonstrating in **Madrid** in 2010.

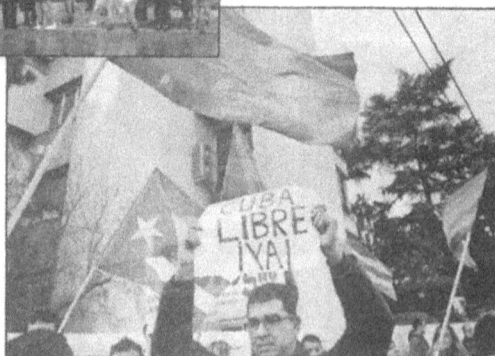

Cuban Exiles in the 2000s

Cuban exiles
demonstrating
in **Madrid**
in 2010.

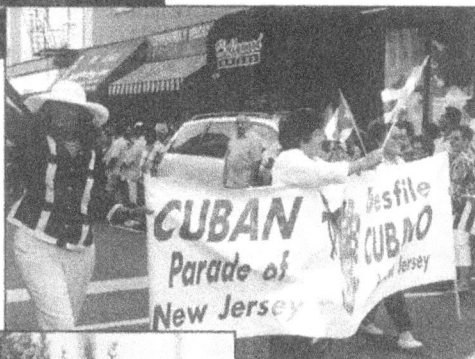

A march of
Cuban exiles
in **New Jersey**
in 2009.

Cuban exiles
in Paris got
permission from the
Prefecture of Paris to
temporarily
change the name of the
street in front of the
Cuban Embassy to **Rue
Raúl Rivero**, the
imprisoned Cuban
poet, in 2003.

A demonstration
of Cuban exiles
in front of the
UNESCO building
in Paris
in 2005.

Cuban Exiles in the 2000s

Cuban exiles in **Barcelona** in 2009.

Poster for a rally of Cuban exiles in **New York** in 2010.

Cuban exiles in **Palencia**, Spain in 2011.

Cuban exiles at a demonstration in front of the Capitol in San Juan, **Puerto Rico** in 2001

Cuban Exiles in the 2000s

Cuban exiles in **Norway** in 2006.

Cuban exiles at a demonstration in **Barcelona** in 2001.

Cuban exiles at a meeting in **Union City** in 2010.

Poster for a Convocation to a concert for the freedon of Cuba in **Madrid**, Spain.

Cuban Exiles in the 2000s

Cuban exiles in **Madrid**.

Cuban exiles in **Milán**, Italy in 2010.

Cuban exiles in *Queens College*, **Canada**, in 2009.

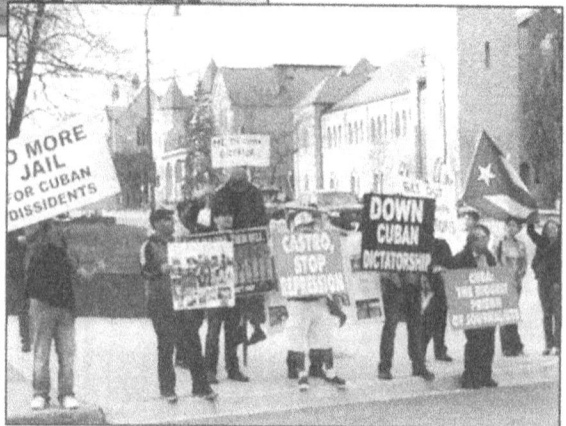

Cuban Exiles in the 2000s

A full page Ad placed by Cuban exiles in *Los Angeles*, US, in 2011.

God Bless America march organized by Cuban exiles in *Miami* in 2001.

Poster announcing the film *Guevara: Anatomía de un Mito* (*Guevara: Anatomy of a Myth*) by the *Institute of the Historical Memory of Cuba*, under the leadership of its founder *Pedro Corzo*.

Cuban Exiles in the 2000s

Cuban exiles
at a demonstration in
La Puerta del Sol,
Madrid, Spain, in
2009.

Cuban exiles
in **Miami** in 2009.

March by Cuban
exiles
in *Calle Ocho*,
Miami, in 2008.

Cuban exiles
marching in **Miami**,
February 24, 2011.

Cuban Exiles in the 2000s

Cuban exiles marching in Miami in support of **Brothers to the Rescue** in 2004.

Cuban exiles In **Miami**, March 26, 2010.

A demonstration by Cuban exiles in **Buenos Aires**, Argentina.

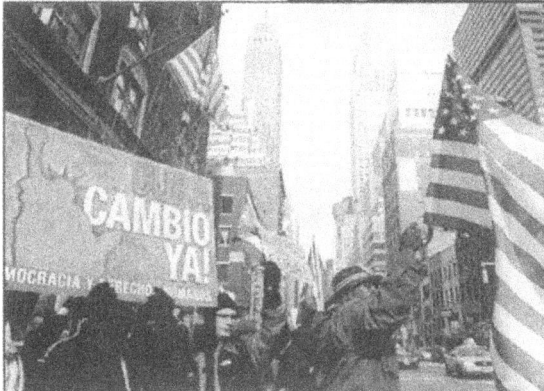

Cuban exiles protesting in **New York** in 2010.

Cuban Exiles in the 2000s

Cuban exiles boycott (see circle) the tourist Ads placed by the Castro government in almost every bus in **Paris** in 2003.

Employees of the *Cuban Embassy* in **Paris** threatening Cuban exiles protesting in front of the Embassy on October 14, 2003.

Cuban exiles at *Trocadero* in **Paris** during a protest for the lack of human rights in Cuba in 2003.

Cuban exiles at a protest in **Paris** in 2004.

Cuban Exiles in the 2000s

Fernando Arrabal, the famous dramatist, joining Cuban exiles waving a Cuban flag at the **Bruselles** *European Union Headquarters* in protest for the lack of freedom in Cuba.

Cuban exiles at the European Union auditorium in **Brussels** in 2004 presenting evidence of the violations of human rights in Cuba.

Union City, New Jersey, Cuban Patriotic Parade in 2002.

A **Miami** parade of Cuban exiles with the theme *Yo No Coopero con La Dictadura* in 2011.

Inspired by Paul Éluard's poem *Liberté*, Cuban exiles living in Paris, under the leadership of Zoé Valdés, gathered on May 18, 2010, in front of the *Hôtel de Ville* to pay homage to the *Damas de Blanco* in Cuba. The international press covered it; all electronic screens across Paris advertised it, and Parisians were informed about not only the *Ladies in White* but also about *Orlando Zapata Tamayo*, all Cuban dissidents, the current hunger strikes in the jails in Cuba, Castro's totalitarism and the urgent need to pay attention to what was happening in Cuba. The two statues in front of the *Hôtel de Ville* (representing **science** and **art**) were dressed in white for the occasion.

Present in the activity was **Gina Pellón**, the greatly admired painter who, in spite of her years and her fragility was always ready to demand freedom in Cuba. Also the writers **Eduardo Manet** and **Jacobo Machover**, both Cuban-born best-sellers in France and the cinematographer **Ricardo Vega**. Representing the French government, the following dignitaries spoke during the meeting: **M. Pierre Shapira**, Deputy Mayor of Paris for International Relations, Europe and the Francophone, **M. Jean-François Julliard**, secretary general of *Reporters Without Borders*, **Mme. Sophie Bessis**, secretary general of the *International Federation of Human Rights* and **Mme. Geneviève Garrigos**, president of *Amnesty International*. Éluard's poem **Liberté** was recited by Eduardo Manet to bring the activity to a close.

Photos below: **Zoe Valdés** speaking in friont of the *Hôtel de Ville* in Paris; *top left*: the message in the many electronic boards all across Paris; *bottom right*: the two statues at the *Hôtel de Ville* dressed as **Damas de Blanco**.

Reporters Without Borders (RWB) is an organization founded in Montpellier, France, in 1985, by Robert Ménard, a French journalist. Its purpose is to defend freedom of the press everywhere in the world. It draws its inspiration from Article 19 of the 1948 *Universal Declaration of Human Rights*, according to which everyone has «*the right to freedom of opinion and expression, as well as the right to seek, receive and impart information and ideas regardless of frontiers.*»

RWB has been highly critical of the lack of freedom of the press in Cuba, describing the Cuban government as «*totalitarian and engaging in recurrent actions against the freedom of its citizens to express their opinions.*» In their campaigns RWB has been supported and assisted by Cuban refugees. In April of 2003, for instance, RSF occupied the *Cuban Tourism Office* in Paris to discourage the French from visiting Cuba for the sexual exploitation of minors, as the Cuban government was indirectly advertising in their tourism propaganda. RSF organized a demonstration in front of the Cuban Embassy and also distributed postcards at *Orly Airport* to tourist boarding flights for Havana. The Castro government, of course, has accused RSF of receiving support from Cuban exiles and anti-Castro organizations.

Photos above, left to right, top to bottom:
Robert Menard, founder of RSF; the façade of the French **Cuban Tourism Office** taken over by RSF in April 2003; a **postcard** showing a likeness of Ché Guevara during the campaign to discourage Europeans to travel to Cuba in 2004; a **poster** of RSF placed all over Paris; **Menard** with **RSF** picketing the Cuban Embassy in Paris.

Bacardí is a family-controlled spirits company, headquartered in Hamilton, Bermuda, selling over 300 million bottles a year, in 100 countries; its 2011 sales exceed US$6.5 billion.

The company was founded in *Santiago de Cuba* in the 1860s by **Don Facundo Bacardí Massó (1814-1886),** a Catalonian wine merchant who moved to Cuba in 1836. **Emilio Bacardí (1844-1922),** Don Facundo's eldest son was a generous contributor to the Cuban War of Independence in the 1890s and was imprisoned by the Spaniards several times. In 1899 US General Leonard Wood appointed him Mayor of Santiago de Cuba. The Bacardí firm had been managed during the 1895 War by **Enrique Schueg (1863-1951),** Emilio's brother-in-law, considered by many as a business genius; after World War II, management of the company fell in the hands of **José (Pepín) Bosch (1899-1994),** Schueg's son-in-law. Pepín Bosch served as *Minister of the Treasury* in Cuba in 1949 and became the man who straightened out Cuba's finances; he managed *Bacardí* until his death in 1994.

Bosch was an original supporter of Castro's revolution until it became a pawn of the Soviet Union in 1960; the family and the company became fierce opponents of Communism in Cuba and left for exile, moving their headquarters to Bermuda. Bacardí's products became so popular in the 1960s that Hemingway mentioned *Hatuey Beer* in three of his novels: *For Whom the Bell Tolls, To Have and Have Not* and *The Old Man and the Sea.*

Half a century after leaving Cuba, **Bacardi Limited** counts among its over two hundred brands: Rum **Bacardi**, **Hatuey** Beer, Italian Vermouth **Martini**, French Vermouth **Noilly Prat**, Vodka **Grey Goose**, Scotch Whisky **Dewar's**, single Malt Scotch **Aberfeldy**, **Bombay** Gin, **Cazadores** Tequila, Cognac **Otard**, Brandy **Viejo Vergel**, Liqueurs **Bénédictine** and **B&B** and Sparkling Wines **Martini**. The firm and the family have continued to contribute to support and promote the genuine Cuban culture and Cuban freedom causes all over the world.

Photos above, left to right: the **Bacardí Art Deco building** in Havana, built in 1930; the **Bacardí building in Miami**, designed by **Henry Gutierrez**, a Cuban exile, in 1963, today housing the *Bacardí Museum.*

Radio Reloj was a radio station opened by the Mestre brothers in the old CMQ building in *Monte* and *Prado* Streets in Havana in 1947. Originally it only had a table, a microphone and two chairs in a dark inside room of a small and uncomfortable building. By 1959 it had become one of the stations with the largest audience in Cuba.

At 6:00 AM on October 14, 1960, the station announced that all sugar mills and rum factories had been nationalized the night before, including the world famous *Bacardí* distillery. At that time, a one-page document was presented to the firm's office in *Monserrate* Street in Havana. Unknown to the law clerk and the *milicianos* presenting the document, the headquarters of *Bacardí* were in Santiago de Cuba and not in Havana.

By the time the legal team and its escorts had reached Santiago de Cuba at 2:00 PM that day (they travelled commercial airline), *Bacardí's* most precious possession had been sacrificed rather than surrendered. A few days earlier the unique strains of yeast that produced **Bacardí Rum** had been taken to the Bahamas, leaving in Cuba only less than 100 milliliters, barely enough to propagate itself and ferment sugar molasses on a daily basis. Once the yeast strains in Cuba were thrown down the sink, the exclusivity of the yeasts developed over the last 150 years by the *House of Bacardí* continued to be exclusively in the hands of the heirs of Don Facundo Bacardí. It was an extraordinary victory for **José (Pepín) Bosch**, president of *Bacardí* and a member of the family by marriage.

The occupation of the Santiago distillery made Castro feel triumphant, until his men discovered that there was no yeast to ferment anything. They brought to Santiago yeasts from other rum refineries and even attempted to bottle a *Bacardí* product, until they lost the trade mark in the international courts of law and the loyalty of the Bacardí followers in the palate of its devoted consumers.

Photos above:
The **Bacardi** plant in Santiago de Cuba in the 1950s, the old
Bacardi **Logo** and the interior of the 1880 factory.

For half a century, Cuban exiles have been the only source of information about the abuses of the Communist regime in Cuba and the heroism of Cubans in the island resisting the destruction of the traditions and culture of the republic. While the rest of the world looked elsewhere, the exiles have made public the impositions, mistreatments and inhumane assaults by the mobster gangs that hijacked Cuba's political life. It has been by the testimonies of the exiles that events such as these are known:

- In the fourth floor of building 3 of the *Isla de Pinos Prisión Modelo*, a prisoner known as **Mayinbe** was attacked with a soldier's bayonet that split one of his eyes in two. Screaming and almost fainting from the pain, slipping on his own blood, full of desperation, he tried in vain to replace a fragment of his eye into his almost empty eye socket. (***El Nuevo Herald***, Miami, December 30, 2008).

- ***Pedro Luis Boitel***, former leader of the students of the *University of Havana*, went 31 days into a hunger strike in the *Cabaña fortress* in Havana, followed by 21 days in the *Boniato Prison* in Oriente province, concluding at the *Mijial* near the city of Holguín. He died in 1972, after 53 days of protest.

Over the years, witnesses to these crimes founded the ***Casa del Preso*** in Miami (Luis González Infante and Padre Loredo), the ***Ex Club*** (Rolando Borges and Angel Cuadra), the ***Sisters and Brothers Forever*** (Jorge Sánchez Villalba), the ***Ex Confinados Políticos de la UMAP*** (Francisco García), the ***Unión de Ex Presos Políticos Cubanos*** (Jorge Dulzaides), the ***Consejo del Presidio Político Cubano*** (Roberto Martín Pérez and Pedro Fuentes Cid), the ***Coordinadora Internacional de Ex Presos Políticos*** (Guillermo Rivas Porta and Nelly Rojas) , the ***Federación Mundial de Ex Presos Políticos*** (Marta Lima and Eugenio Llamera), the ***Grupo de la Memoria Histórica Cubana*** (Pedro Corzo) and the ***Plantados Hasta la Libertad y la Democracia*** (Angel de Fana).

Photos below, left to right:
Angel Cuadra, **Pedro Corzo**, **Angel de Fana** and the
Casa del Preso in Miami.

The participation of women in the social, political and cultural life of Miami from the 1960s to the present has been nothing short of outstanding. Many of these women were Cuban exiles; some of them came to the US as children in the *Pedro Pan* program. Others were born in the US. In one way or another, they have secured their place in the history of the city and made Miami a captivating place to live. Some of these women are presented above.

Photos, left to right, top to bottom:

Helen Aguirre Ferré, an award-winning journalist, writer, radio hostess, TV political analyst, and editor of *Diario Las Americas*.

Mikki Canton, leading legal, business, civic and political force in South Florida, former partner at *Holland and Knight*.

Remedios Díaz Oliver, business leader and an untiring worker for charitable and civic causes; leader of the powerful *Cuba PAC*.

Olga Connor, art and literary critic and author of numerous essays on the cultural life of Miami; long time columnist at *El Nuevo Herald*.

Katherine Fernández Rundle, a remarkable jurist, for many years has been a State Attorney for the 11th Judicial Court of Florida.

Sylvia Iriondo, founder of *MAR por Cuba*. A tireless international advocate of freedom, democracy and human rights in Cuba.

Marijean Miyar, art historian, teacher, lecturer and collector; a prominent voice in cultural Miami for many years.

Olga Nodarse, founder of *The Cuba Corps*, an influential exile organization; art and political lecturer and writer; former business executive.

Ileana Ros-Lethinen, US Representative for Florida's 18th Congressional district, Chair of the *House Foreign Affairs Committee*.

Maria Elena Villamil, entrepreneur, college professor and administrator, business executive and community leader.

For almost half a century, a newspaper and a magazine published by Cuban exiles in Miami have been stedfast bearers of news and information for the exile community. **Ideal** and **Libre**, the work of **Lorenzo del Toro** and **Demetrio Pérez**.

Ideal started publication in 1971 and is in many ways the successor of **La Quincena** magazine, published by the Franciscan fathers in Cuba (Fray Ignacio Biain OFM) for many years. A common motto plausibly links both publications: "A Christian perspective to today's problems." According to **Lorenzo del Toro** what prompted him to open **Ideal** was to read an issue of *Daily Planet* with its favorable treatments of pornography and abortion directed to youngsters.

Libre has been a weekly newspaper since 1966. It provides news and information of interest to Hispanics in Greater Miami, with a circulation of 5,000 copies and subscriptions all over the US. **Demetrio Pérez**, who also founded the *Lincoln Martí* child care centers and private schools, was prompted to publish **Libre** by the need to have a vehicle to honor the legacy of hard work and ethics of traditional Cuban parents.

Photos, top to bottom:
Lorenzo del Toro and his magazine **Ideal**;
Demetrio Pérez and his newspaper **Libre**.

For over fifty years, Cuban exiles in Miami have been exposed to radically different views and interpretations about their role, strategies and even the legitimacy of their thinking and tactical approach to Communism in Cuba. No other positions reflect those opposite views better than the actions of two men: *FIU* professor **Darío Moreno** and *Democracy* leader **Ramón Saúl Sánchez**.

Darío Moreno (*above on the left*) has journalism degrees from the *University of Southern California* and *Harvard*. He has been a professor at FIU since 1987 and has been widely presented and quoted in the *Wall Street Journal*, the *New York Times* and even *Agence France Presse* in Paris. His comments are generally offensive to many Cuban exiles: «*Subtropical sleaze is slathered all over Miami*». On occasions he has advocated for the abolition of Miami as a City. He characterized Miami as a «*banara republic*» on the national TV show *60 Minutes,* adding «*Professors give lectures no one listens to. It is fun to see your name in print.*» Later on he opined that «*the only likely goal of the Cuban exiles is to get a reaction from the Cuban government.*» He implied that «*the demonstrations* [of the exiles] *led to the shoot-down of the airplanes in 1996... the Brothers to the Rescue airplanes ignored the demands not to fly over Cuban airspace.*»

Ramón Saúl Sánchez (*on the right above*) was born in Cuba in 1954 and has been a US resident since 1967. In the 1970s he was linked to *Alpha 66* and *Omega 7* but he renounced violence when he joined Huber Matos' *Cuba Independiente y Democrática (CID)*. He is the founder and leader (since 1995) of the *Movimiento Democracia*, whose vessel has been taken frequently in front of Cuban waters, as he protests the crimes of the revolution. Sánchez has been involved in many hunger strikes to advance his goals of «*promoting a peaceful and democratic transition in Cuba.*» He has been quoted as saying «*The Cuban people are trapped between a cruel dictator in Cuba and nonsense policies on this side of the Straits of Florida*». He has been a champion denouncing Cuba for its violation of Article 13 of the *UN Declaration of Human Rights*: «*citizens have a right to leave their countries and to return to it.*» He lives a very frugal life: «*two suits, two pair of shoes, a pair of work boots, a job paying $300 a week and no savings,*» he declared to David Lawrence, the Herald publisher, in 1996.

By the end of the first decade of the 21st century, given the demographic realities in Miami, Union City, New York, Madrid, Paris and the rest of the world, very few exiles who had opposed the Cuban revolution from its initial years were left alive. Most exiles organizations continued their opposition to Castro but events that would move public opinion and kept the Cuban drama in the news were rare. Regardless of strategical or conceptual differences with other groups of Cuban exiles, the **Movimiento Democracia** distinguished itself for its persistence in its peaceful demonstrations against tyranny in Cuba.

Photos above, top to bottom:
The page of the **Movimiento Democracia** on the Web; a poster with a **convocation** for a fleet of small crafts to go in front of the coasts of Cuba; **Ramón Saul Sánchez** in one of his hunger strikes; a **flotilla** (fleet) as it leaves Miami in the direction of Havana.

Cuban exile humor across half a century of expatriation

Castro and Khrushchev **burying** alive the Republic.

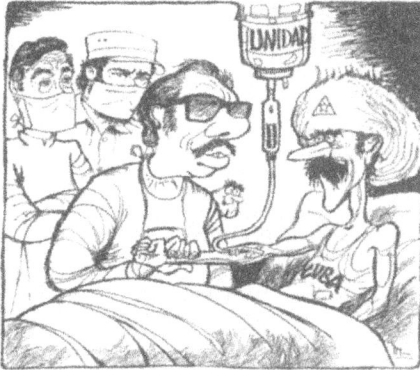

Huber Matos and others trying to save Cuba with a dosis of **unidad**.

A naïve Carter trying to **deal** with Castro.

Life in Cuba and in exile.

Cuban exile humor across half a century of expatriation

Cubans in the island happy to have **permission** to sell their houses.

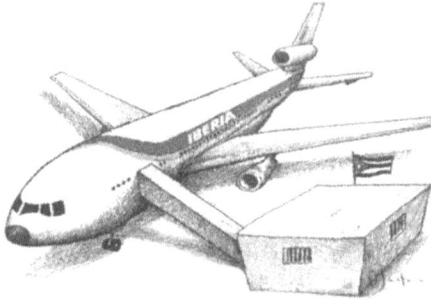

Political prisoners going from their jails to Spain and **not allowed** to stay in Cuba.

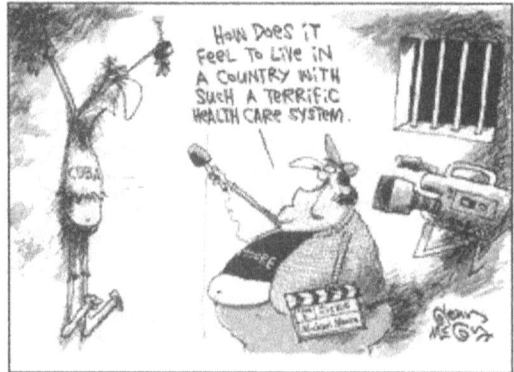

Michael Moore's praise for **Castro's health system**.

Fidel steps down and Raúl steps up while **Cuba asks for help**.

Cuban exile humor across half a century of expatriation

ELITE CUBAN ESPIONAGE TEAM INVADES MIAMI

¡TREMENDO PAQUETE!

Dile a tu padre, Marielito, que lo que hace falta son HUEVOS

Over the years, many entire Cuban families have immigrated to the US as exiles and reached important achievements in their new communities. It has been a clear evidence of the loss of human talent and know-how that the Cuban revolution produced as it forced from the island its best talents; the Communist regime excluded from participation all who did not agree with its social and political policies. A case in point has been the **Valdés-Fauli-Pedroso** family.

Resting on a firm tradition of service and attainment, Raúl J., José, Gonzalo and Teresa Valdés-Fauli Pedroso, the children of **Raúl Ernesto Valdés-Fauli Juncadella** and **Margarita Pedroso Aróstegui**, have for many years projected an image of talent, natural endowments, integrity and business acumen and expertise in the US.

The Valdés-Fauli family traces its Cuban roots back four centuries. The family patriarch in the 20th century, **Raúl Ernesto** represented sugar and banking interests in Havana until he went into exile with his children in 1960. His wife **Margarita**, a member of an affluent Havana family, died in 1985. Raúl Ernesto was one of the first Cuban lawyers to pass the Florida bar, went on to practice law past his 80th birthday and died in 2003.

Raúl J., became an expert in corporate law, security, finances and international litigation, and has held several elective offices, including *Mayor* of the City of *Coral Gables*. He is a *Chevalier of the French Legion of Honor* among many other distinctions; **Gonzalo** has been Vice Chairman of *Barclays Capital PLC* and Group CEO for Latin America, as well as a Trustee of the *University of Miami*; **José** has served as President and CEO of *Colonial Bank*, *Eastern National Bank* and *Beach Bank* in Florida, as well as Chairman of the *Miami Opera*; **Teresa** has been President and CEO of *Fiduciary Trust International*, a trust and investment management company, as well as a lawyer for *Exxon Corporation*.

Photo above, left to right:
Gonzalo, José, Teresa and **Raúl J. Valdés-Fauli**

For well over half a century, many Cuban exiles in the US were witness to the deterioration of the relations between Cuba, their country of origin, and the US, their adopted country. In spite of their best efforts and aspirations, the political reality in Cuba never changed and the US, rightly choosing their best interests, preferred a stable **status quo** than to have an unpredictable instability near their shores. Here is a summary of US-Cuba relations over 50 years of Cuba's Communist regime in Cuba.

- President Eisenhower recognized the Cuban revolutionary government early in 1959 but worried about the **agrarian reform** and the **nationalization** of US industries.
- In April 1959 Castro visited the US in a **charm offensive** and laid a wreath in the statue of Lincoln in Washington, DC.
- As takeovers of US citizens' property continued, the US **stopped buying Cuban sugar**.
- President Eisenhower secretly authorized the CIA to organize Cuban exiles as an **anti-Castro military force**.
- On January 3, 1961, the **US broke relations with Cuba** and closed its Havana embassy.
- On April 16, 1961, Cuba resisted an armed force of 1,500 CIA trained Cuban patriots at the **Bay of Pigs**.
- Cuban exiles get involved in **Operation Mongoose** (known in the US as the "Cuban Project").

(Continued)

Photos above, left to right:
Castro at the **Lincoln Memorial** in April of 1959; Cuban **Women's Militias**, ready to fight the US, on a parade in Havana in 1962.

(Continuation)

- In October 1962, US aircraft documents intermediate range missile Soviet bases in Cuba, producing the **Cuban Missile Crisis.**
- Late in 1962 all US travel and trade with Cuba is discontinued and an **embargo** is established.
- Khrushchev and Kennedy sign a pact by which the missiles are retired with the **US promise never to invade Cuba.**
- A sustained period of **US passenger aircraft hijackings** to Cuba runs through the 1960s and 1970s, finally abetting by the 2000s.
- In the 1980s, thousands of Cubans seek political asylum in Havana, turning into what became known as **the Mariel boatlift.** It resulted in the US tightening the embargo, and the beginnings of **Radio and TV Marti.**
- On February 24, 1996, two unarmed Cessna 337s flown by **Brothers to the Rescue** were shot down by Cuban Air Force MiG-29s, killing four Cuban-Americans, three of them **American citizens.**
- At a UN Millennium Summit in September 2000, **Fidel Castro and Bill Clinton shook hands.** No known results occurred.
- In 2001 **five Cuban spies** in the US (la *Red Avispa*) were convicted of espionage.
- In 2005, President George W. Bush declared Cuba to be one of the few **"outposts of tyranny"** remaining in the world. No known results occurred either.
- In January 2006, **James Cason**, Head of the US Interest Section in Havana began to display **democratic messages and news on a scrolling electronic billboard** in the windows of the top floor of the building.
- In April 2009, President **Obama announced a softer policy towards Cuba**, stating he was open to a dialogue with the Castro brothers. Cuba responded by signing new pacts with Venezuela's Chavez and Iran's Ahmadinejad. Nevertheless, the Obama administration eased travel and other restrictions to Cuba in January 2011.

Photos below, top to bottom:

Newspapers worldwide reporting about the **Missile Crisis** in 1962; the logo of **Brothers to the Rescue**; Cuba alliances with **enemies of the US**.

James Cason (1945-) was the principal officer of the *US Interests Section in Havana* from 2002 to 2005. Prior to that he had been Deputy Chief of Mission at the *U.S. Embassies* in *Tegucigalpa, Honduras,* and *Kingston, Jamaica*, as well as Political Advisor to the Commander of the *U.S. Atlantic Command (USACOM)* and to NATO's *Supreme Allied Commander Atlantic (SACLANT)*. Cason's experience in the world of diplomacy included having served the U.S. in missions in Milan, Italy; Lisbon, Portugal; San Salvador, El Salvador; Panama City, Panama; Maracaibo, Venezuela; Montevideo, Uruguay; and La Paz, Bolivia.

Mr. Cason graduated from *Dartmouth College i*n the class of 1966 and has an M.A. from the *School of Advanced International Studies (SAIS)*, Johns Hopkins University (JHU). During his tenure as principal officer of the *US Interests Section in Havana*, Mr. Cason supported the work of the Cuban dissidents as no other American diplomat had ever done. He turned the front of the old US Embassy into a gigantic **news board** where Cubans in the island could read news from around the world; he opened the embassy grounds to dissidents and offered them free and regular **access to the Internet** and distributed close to **30,000 long wave radios** to Cubans in the island so that they could listen news bypassing the captive Castro's censored radio stations.

For all his consistent and dedicated efforts to the cause of freedom in Cuba —invariably with the help of private donors from the US and Latin America— Cason, after his retirement, was soundly elected as **Mayor of Coral Gables**, Florida, with the spontaneous help in his political campaign from hundreds of grateful Coral Gables Cuban exile residents.

Photos above:
Jim Cason at a *4 of July celebration* in Havana, 2004; the **news ticker** Cason installed on the US building in Havana.

For 50 years, in the midst of thousands of Cuban exiles, the Castro regime operated "***front companies***" to steal industrial technology from the US and other European countries (technology marketable to countries like China, Venezuela, Iran and Syria) and to provide cover for its spy operations, against the US as well as the Cuban exiles. After the fall of the Soviets, these companies became one of the most important sources of hard currency for Havana; sometimes they produced operational profits by themselves, other times they simply provided support for one of the most sophisticated networks of industrial spying in the world.

An important collateral benefit of these companies was to keep the functionaries of the Communist government in Cuba loyal to the Castro brothers. Many high officials of the Cuban army and the ministries were granted a stake in the economic operations of the companies; they had a considerable personal financial benefit to protect. A combination of profits, corruption allowances and the threat of heavy reprisals insured their loyalty to the revolution.

After 1979, when the Castros decided to allow Cuban exiles to visit their relatives in the island, the number of *front companies* (initially operating only out of Mexico and Panamá) increased dramatically in the US and Europe. Cuban exiles knew this but it was not possible to refrain them from their emotional and deeply felt need to visit Cuba; the US and European press, by the way, never focused their eyes on such blatant infiltration of spies, delinquents and Communist agents into their territories.

(Continued)

Photos, *left top*: **General Julio Casas Regueiro**, head of the holding companies that operate the *Cuban Armed Forces* business empire;
Top right: **Fidel Castro**, exposed as a billionaire by *Forbes Magazine*;
Bottom right: **General Ulises Rosales del Toro**, member of the Politbureau, top manager of the front companies and Chief of Staff of Raúl Castro.

(Continuation)

Early in 2011, the US press uncovered several front companies of the Castros operating in the US: corporate names such as **Telefónica Antillana S.A.**, **La Casa del Habano**, **Universal Trade & Management Corporation S,A (Utisa)**, **Banco Financiero Internacional**, **Negocios en Telecomunicaciones, S.A.** and **Banco Internacional de Comercio** were revealed as well as **Rafin, S.A.**, supposedly a financial arm of the Cuban military, with the unsavory and hard to digest full name of Raúl and Fidel Investments.

Among the Castro's officers directing these front companies the following military men have been mentioned at one time or another: **Gen. Ulises Rosales del Toro**, **Col. Librado Reina Benitan**, **Gen. Julio Casas Regueiro**, **Lt. Col. Sergio Sanchez**, a **Col. Alonso** and a **Brig. Gen. Milián**, to mention the best known.

A notable example of the power of these front companies is the relationship between Castro's **Havana Club Company** (which illegally used a brand owned by *Bacardí-Martini Ltd.*) and the French liquor conglomerate *Pernod-Ricard*. The French company shares, with a Castro personal front company, $45 million in profits annually and generates $170 million in hard currency for Cuba's treasury, according to a *Forbes Magazine* report in 2004.

Photos above, top to bottom:
La **Casa del Habano** in *Hamburgo*, Alemania and in *Quatar*, the sovereign Arab state in the Middle East. The **Havana Club** rum.

Fidel Castro as portrayed outside Cuba

Raúl Castro as portrayed outside Cuba

Cuban exiles in the US were never surprised by the support that Hollywood celebrities always lent to the totalitarian regime in Cuba. They were the most visible part of the **velvet left**, i.e., the very rich that favored Communism for everyone but themselves.

Photos below:
Top row: **Morgan Freeman, Juan Manuel Serrat** and **Barbra Streisand**.
Middle row: **Will Smith, Woopy Goldberg** and **Steven Spielberg**.
Bottom row: **Tom Hanks, Sean Penn** and **Woody Allen**.

All along half a century of Cuban exile, many important public figures had consistently supported the rights of Cubans to affirm the democratic principles of the republic. What follows is a brief recognition of their sustaining defense of freedom for Cuba.

Photos above, top row:

Václav Havel, President of Czechoslovakia and the Czech Republic; **José María Aznar**, President of Spain, defender of Cuba's dissidents; **Charles Krauthammer**, political analyst, denouncer of Castro; **Brit Hume**; smart anchorman of Fox News for many years;

Center row:

Sean Hannity, political commentator in TV and radio; **Rush Limbaugh**; top political analyst and commentator of US radio; **Shepard Smith**, main defender of the rights of Elián González; **Robert Torricelli**, US Senator, friend of Castro's opponents;

Bottom row:

Claude Pepper, Florida Senator in the 1960s, benefactor of exiles; **Maurice Ferré**, Miami Mayor in the 1960s, friend of Cuban freedom; **Fernando Arrabal**, Spanish playwright, Castro's main foe in Europe; **Madeleine Albright**, former defender of exiles, *US Secretary of State*.

Quite a few important public figures had also consistently supported the Cuban government in spite of their dreadful record on civil rights, the total elimination of a civil society in Cuba and their failed but persistent attempts to export terrorism and undemocratic principles across Latin America and Africa and even the US.

Photos above, top row:

Barbara Walters, TV personality, Castro long time admirer;
Charles Rangel, US Congressman, always pro-Castro;
Gregory Craig, Clinton's lawyer, always for Castro's favorite causes;
Bill Richardson, frequent pro-Castro visitor to Castro's Cuba.

Center row:

José Serrano, US Congressman, Castro's enduring defender;
Diane Sawyer, delighted to adore, meet and interview Castro;
Maxine Waters, pro-Castro US Congresswoman, always on his side;
Michael Moore, defender of Castro's health *"achievements."*

Bottom row:

Sheila Jackson Lee, visitor to Castro, permanent apologist;
Diego Maradona, soccer player, had a tattoo of *Ché* on his upper arm;
J.L. Rodríguez Zapatero, Castro's favorite European President;
Hugo Chávez, the President who sold Venezuela to the Castros.

From 1990 to 2011 Cuba presented to the UN General Assembly multiple resolutions to «*end the economic, commercial and financial **blockade** imposed by the United States of America against Cuba*». Given the composition of the UN General Assembly, the resolutions were always approved by the international community, sometimes almost unanimously, with the sole exceptions of the US and Israel. The Cuban government always argued that the embargo violated international law and the U.N. Charter, and constituted **genocide** according to the *1948 Geneva Convention on the Prevention and Punishment of the Crime of Genocide*.

During those years, every President of the US continued the embargo under the *Trading with the Enemy Act*, arguing that it was «*in the national interest of the United States and a just response to a nation that supported worldwide terrorism*». The US also imposed heavy sanctions to the countries that carried supporting financial transactions with Cuba, such as a $500 million fine forced upon the *Dutch Bank ABN Amro* in 2009.

The *Cuban Democracy Act of 1992* and the *1996 Helms-Burton Act* added further restrictions seeking to prevent individual US citizens and US corporations and their worldwide affiliates from doing business with Cuba; they codified the embargo into law to sanction Cuba until the Castro brothers «*began to respect human rights in Cuba*». Adding to this, President Clinton in 1999 expanded the embargo seriously enforcing the prohibition that foreign subsidiaries of US companies would trade with Cuba, with the exception of humanitarian sales to Cuba on cash terms.

The measure was forcefully opposed by Cuban-American apocryphal exiles who wanted to visit Cuba regularly and by some US business leaders and agricultural producers who alleged that the embargo caused harm to American farmers, port workers and others. The Cuban government continued to rebuff all requests by friends and foes to slacken the tight grip on rights in Cuba; evidently it was not interested in a relaxation of the embargo rules.

Photos below: the UN on the day of the **vote about the embargo to Cuba** in 2000; **Castro's propaganda in Cuba** about the embargo.

On Thursday, October 10, 2002, **Carlos Mauricio Castañeda Angulo (1932-2002)**, publisher emeritus of Miami's **El Nuevo Herald** and former editor and publisher for 28 years of Puerto Rico's **El Nuevo Día**, died in Lisbon while on vacation with his family, due to severe complications of an aggressive form of Leukemia. During his years with *El Nuevo Herald*, Castañeda reformulated the nation's largest Spanish-language daily, changed its editorial content and increased circulation, advertising while improving its relations with the Cuban exile community in South Florida.

Castañeda was born in Havana; by the time he was 16 he became host of **La Voz del Aire**, a popular sports radio show. At age 22 he joined the popular Cuban weekly magazine **Bohemia**, and **El Mundo**, a daily Havana newspaper; in both publications he became one of the star writers. In the years around 1959 he interviewed both **Fulgencio Batista** and **Fidel Castro**. His journalistic career spanned half a century and included consulting for two dozen Latin American newspapers. In 2001 he won the **Ortega y Gasset Journalist Award** for the *El Nuevo Herald*, a prize given to the best Spanish Language daily newspapers in the world.

Castañeda and his family left Cuba in 1960 and established themselves in New York. Carlos, after working as the political correspondent in Washington for **Bohemia Libre**, worked his way to the top editing responsibilities for **LIFE Magazine**. He was recruited as the first editor of *El Nuevo Día* in Puerto Rico in 1969 and as editor of *El Nuevo Herald* in Miami in 1998, a paper with a staff of 425, including reporters in many important capitals of Latin America. Among his many journalistic interests, he was a longtime member of the *Inter-American Press Association (IAPA)*, and Chairman of the *Committee on Freedom of the Press*. As such, he denounced abuse and intimidation of Cuban journalists by the Castro regime on the island to the IAPA's 1,500 member newspapers.

Photos above:
Carlos Castañeda and two issues of the Miami paper from which he relentlessly defended the right to a free press in Cuba.

Cuban exiles in the US have had to struggle for half a century against Castro's friends and agents placed in important US government positions. The Cuban regime, for many years, had entertained and patronized (with propaganda and electoral backing) many individuals that have consistently shored up the presence and legitimacy of a long totalitarian regime in Cuba. Two cases in point are the relentless support to Cuba of US Congresswoman **Maxine Waters** and US Congressman **José Serrano**.

Maxine Waters was a Democratic Member of Congress who represented the 35th District of California. She was born in 1938 in St. Louis, Missouri. In 1984 she was co-chair of **Jesse Jackson's** presidential campaign. During the Los Angeles riots in 1992 (**Rodney King** affair, resulting in 58 dead people), she described the violence as «*a spontaneous reaction to a lot of injustice,*» and justified the looting of Korean-owned stores as «*mothers taking milk, bread and some shoes for their children.... They were not crooks*». During the **Elián González** affair she flew to Cuba to support the boy's father and grandmothers. In 1998 she wrote Castro to oppose the extradition from Cuba of **Joanne Chesimard** (aka *Assata Olugbala Shakur*), a US fugitive who had shot twice in the head and killed, execution style, a *New Jersey Turnpike* patrolman with his own weapon; instead she asked Castro to grant her «*political asylum*». Among her frequent oppositions to US House resolutions dealing with Cuba were:

- April of 2003; only member abstaining to a unanimous resolution supporting **free elections** in Cuba;
- May of 2005; voted against supporting the **Assembly to Promote the Civil Society in Cuba** (it passed 392 to 22);
- July of 2005; voted against condemning the **repression** in Cuba (it passed 393 to 31).

(Continued)

Photo above, on the left: **Maxine Waters**, (D-Cal), Chairman of the *Congressional Black Caucus*; she visited Cuba in 1999, sponsored by *Pastors for Peace* and the Rev. Lucius Walker. The group met *Castro* for six hours, as well as *Robaina, Alarcón* and *Lage*, and ended up protesting «*the US aggressive actions against Communist Cuba.*»

Photo above, on the right: **Maxine Waters** with other frequent visitors and supporters of Castro; **Jessie Jackson** and **Michael Moore**.

(Continuation)

José Enrique Serrano was a Democratic Member of Congress who represented the 16th District of New York, the South Bronx, which was the most densely populated Puertorrican district in the US. He was born in Mayagüez, Puerto Rico and in 1950 moved to New York. He described Puerto Rico as a **US colony**. In 1961 he sponsored in the House a **Foreign Assistance Act** that failed to repeal the US embargo to Cuba. He repeatedly tried to pass this law; the last time in 2009. During many sessions of the US Congress he tried to pass laws proposing **trade normalization, free trade** and **foreign aid** to the government of Cuba. In 2005 he was one of the five US Congressmen voting to withdraw the troops from Iraq immediately.

Among his frequent oppositions to US House resolutions dealing with Cuba were:

- September of 1992; voted against promoting a **transition to democracy** in Cuba (it passed 276 to 135).
- April of 2001; voted against condemning the **human rights** situation in Cuba (it passed 347 to 44).
- May of 2005; voted against supporting the **Assembly to Promote the Civil Society in Cuba** (it passed 392 to 22);
- July of 2005; voted against condemning the **repression** in Cuba (it passed 393 to 31).

Both Waters and Serrano consistently defended the government of Cuba, even though it harbored over 70 fugitives from US law, including several in the FBI most wanted lists.

Photo above, on the left: **José Serrano**, founding member of the *Young Lords* in the Bronx, New York. Originally, in 1969, the group had the purpose of «*defending the rights of the Latino community*». In 1970 it created an armed division and discarded its commitment to peaceful action. In 1971 it became the Maoist-inspired *Puerto Rican Revolutionary Workers Party*. **Serrano**, then 26 years old, felt that the *Young Lords'* philosophy was his inspiration for public life.

Photo above, on the right: the Young Lords marching through **el Barrio** in 1969; 40 years later **Ricardo Alarcón** wrote Serrano that «*Defending The Cuban Revolution was not easy in those days... we will always be united... hasta la Victoria siempre...*»

Most Cuban refugees living in Miami share to this day warm and pleasant memories from a City landmark intimately linked to their few moments of amusement and recreation when they first came to the US as exiles: the **Miami Marine Stadium**. The Stadium was built in 1963, just when the first wave of Cuban exiles was reaching its *crescendo*. Its original designer was **Hilario Candela**, a Cuban-born architect who at age 27 conceived a stadium that 50 years later would be considered a masterwork of civic architecture and an icon of modern design. Every one of its seats offered a beautiful view of downtown Miami; its sculptural zig-zagging roof floated gracefully over the water of Biscayne Bay, magically supported by a few columns that levitated over its waters.

The stadium sat on **Virginia Key**, on land donated by the *Matheson family*, in front of a 6,000 by 1,400 foot water basin in the shape of *Circus Maximus*, and had the presence of both a *marine hippodrome* and an *opera house*. It fact, it normally accommodated an audience that would be entertained from a floating stage where orchestras, musical groups, Hollywood plays and concerts would come from points unknown and anchor at its feet. Needless to say, dozens of owners of small boats usually saved the entrance fees and watched the performances from the surrounding waters, in the privacy of their crafts. During the day, political rallies, boxing competitions, regattas, speedboat races, water skiing, canoeing, hydroplane and swimming competitions and even religious baptismals and revivals were performed by all faiths. One celebrated occasion was when President Richard Nixon hugged Sammy Davis Jr. during a rally for his Presidential election.

(Continued)

Photos above:
Young Architect **Hilario Candela** supervising the construction of the Stadium in 1963; a **speed boat race** in the 1970s.

(Continuation)

In 1992 the stadium was believed to have been damaged by *Hurricane Andrew* and it was temporarily closed to the public. The damage was very modest, requiring only $2 or $3 million for repairs. Yet it was never fixed and a long period of deterioration, neglect and graffiti began to make it more expensive to restore this extraordinary landmark to its grandeur.

After years of neglect and the countless visits of hobos, drifters, drug addicts, vagrants and vandals, as well as threats of collapse, the **Miami Marine Stadium** was finally approved for historical renovation by the Miami-Dade County in February of 2010.

Photos below:

Two views of the **Marine Stadium** after 20 years of graffiti and neglect; two renderings of its **new look** after renovation as a historical monument.

The controversial dialogue of some Cuban exiles (handpicked by Cuban officials, who claimed the exiles had not been able to pick their own representatives for the last 20 years) with the Cuban government in 1978, resulted on a big fiasco and a serious propaganda *coup* favoring the Cuban regime. Fifty four exiles from Miami, New York, Puerto Rico, Mexico, Venezuela and Spain participated. A letter signed by 138 political prisoners from the *Combinado del Este* prison in Havana characterized the meeting as a «*farce staged by Mr. Castro in order to deceive the people of Cuba and the world at large.*» Among the signers of the protest letter were **Ramón Grau Alsina, Huber Matos, Francisco and Mario Chanes de Armas, Angel de Fana** and **Andrés Vargas Gómez**.

The 1978 meeting was followed from 1994 to 2010 by several **Nation and Migration** conferences, tightly controlled by the Cuban government under the pretense of «*reuniting and soothing historical wounds.*» These conferences always ignored the overhaul of Cuban government regulations destined to punish those who left Cuba (such as handing over their properties); they also highlighted the need for increasing remittances from those wishing to help their friends and family left in Cuba. Those Cuban exiles seeking a *dialogue* were also asked to support the end of the US embargo to Cuba. The **Nation and Migration Conferences** took place in 1994, 1995, April 11-13, 2003 (postponed due to the "*black spring*" in Cuba) and May 21-23, 2004.

After an interval of eight years, the Cuban government announced in February of 2012 that it would host a meeting of «*respectful*» Cubans living in the US to take place in Washington DC on April 28th, 2012; it was a new and explicit effort of Raúl Castro to warm up a relationship with close to 2 million Cubans living abroad.

(Continued)

Photos below: **Bernardo Benes**, the organizer of the 1978 dialogue of Cuban exiles with the Cuban government; **Francisco González Aruca,** founder of *Marazul Travel* and the top financial beneficiary of the expanded US-Cuba travel; **José Orlando Padrón**, owner of *Padrón Cigars*, one of the negotiators in the 1978 dialogue; **Gustavo Godoy**, Executive Editor of *Vista Magazine*, the main journalist-witness of the 1978 dialogue.

(Continuation)

Old Cuban exiles saw the new Conference as one more Cuban government ploy to extract more remittances from those it had sent into exile. Recent Cuban immigrants to the US applauded it as a decided step towards reconciliation by the new Cuban president Raúl Castro. Simultaneously, it was announced at the *International Book Festival* in Havana that Cuba would be publishing the works of artists who live abroad and have been «*discreet in their criticism of the Cuban government*».

The two most enthusiastic supporters of these two events were **Carlos Saladrigas**, the wealthy Cuban-American businessman ... «exiles should *board the trains of change in Cuba. If one hopes to influence, or be part of the solution, one has to be part of the process,*» and *Nuevo Herald* columnist **Alejandro Armengol**... «*Cuban artists on both sides of the revolution should look forward and not lock themselves in the past.*»

«*Not very original*», commented **Orlando Gutiérrez**, head of the Miami-based *Cuban Democratic Directorate*, «*this approach to Cubans living abroad is a fraud and a repeat of what Cuban governments have tried before, whenever they were hit with economic crisis in the 1970s, 1980s and 1990s. Every time they need money, they milk the exiles*».

Photos above, left to right:

Carlos Saladrigas as a child in Cuba aged 12, when he was sent to the US via *Pedro Pan*. Upon arriving he «*sold shoes by mail, Encyclopedia Britannica and hand bags, delivered newspapers, mowed lawns and washed cars; went to school at night while his mother picked tomatoes and his father washed dishes at a hospital,*» a remarkable hard work success story that led him to build a fortune many years later.

Alejandro Armengol, engineer and nuclear physicist turned political commentator for the *Nuevo Herald*; grew up in Cuba but took the route of exile in 1983 and later became a resident in Madrid.

Orlando Gutierrez Boronat, born *in 1965*. He has a PhD in International Studies from the *University of Miami*; co-founder and National Secretary of the "*Directorio*" (*Cuban Democratic Directorate*), «*a movement of popular affirmation in the face of those in power in Cuba.*»

Si limitan los viajes a Cuba,
van a afectar a la familia
cubana...

I AGREE WITH MY BROTHER'S REFORMS

3 Cartoons by Garrincha

Fidel transfers POWER to his Younger Brother

'I CAN'T BELIEVE MY EYES!'

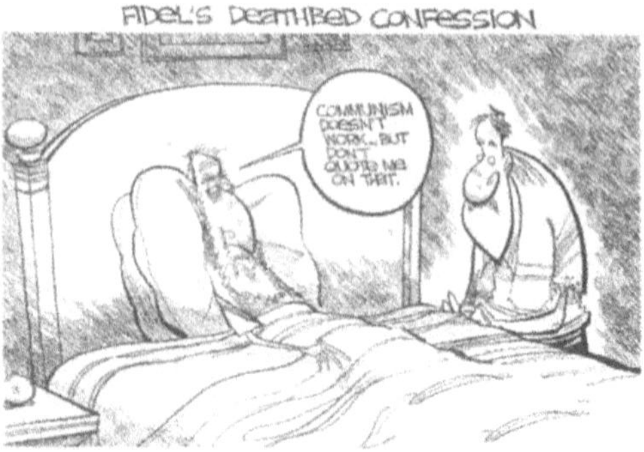
FIDEL'S DEATHBED CONFESSION
COMMUNISM DOESN'T WORK... BUT DON'T QUOTE ME ON THAT.

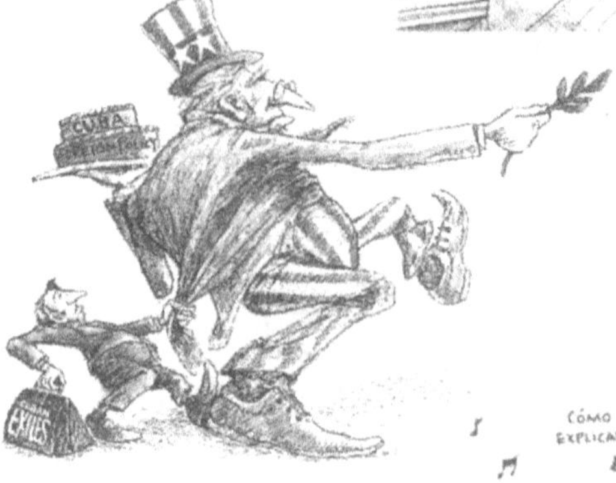
CUBA
EXILES

The Exiles look at Cuba through the polítical cartoons of the 2000s

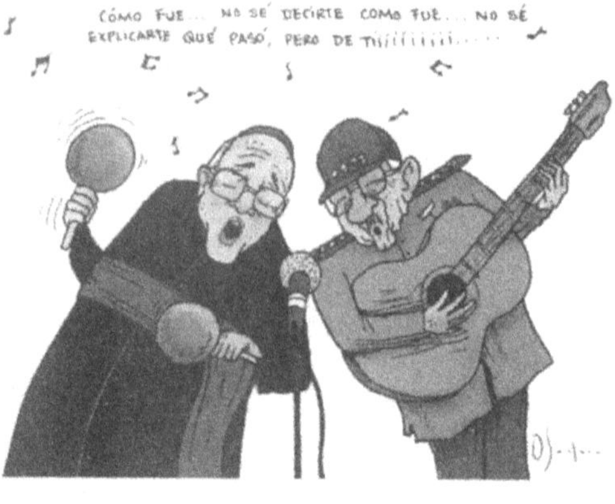
CÓMO FUE... NO SÉ DECIRTE COMO FUE... NO SÉ EXPLICARTE QUÉ PASÓ, PERO DE TIIIIIIIIII......

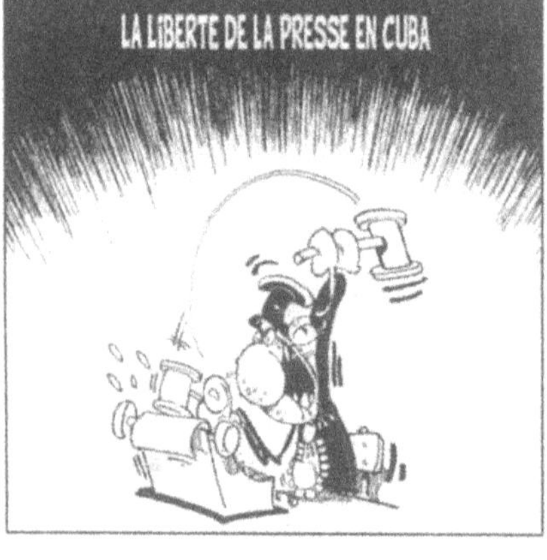
LA LIBERTE DE LA PRESSE EN CUBA

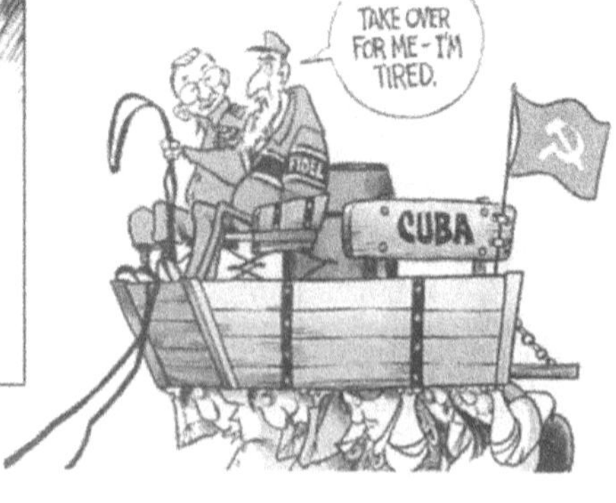
TAKE OVER FOR ME - I'M TIRED.
FIDEL
CUBA

After half a century of dominance and absolute control in Cuba, the remains of the Communist regime had nothing to offer to Cubans or to any other citizens of the world but pleas for survival. The political aims of the Castros were reduced to bringing about disharmony among Cuban exiles, securing larger and larger remitances from them, facilitating their visits to the island under severe controls and obtaining their support and their persuasive powers to lift the US embargo. In hot pursue of these aims the regime created the mythical goals of "*national reconciliation*" and "*economic reforms,*" both of which ran concurrent with campaigns to discredit the exiles abroad and abuse the dissidents at home. Those deceptive games attracted a few participants eager to "*do something for Cuba.*" Some American diplomats and businessmen, the Catholic Church hierarchy in the island, several leftist-leaning exiles, most recent immigrants from Cuba and practically all US academics that looked at Cuba from a distance, played the game with the Castros. They were, in the terminology of the 1950s, the new generations of "*fellow travelers.*"

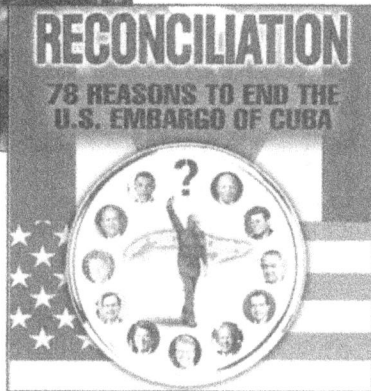

Photos above: the **Damas de Blanco**, the world known Cuban dissident group, under aggression from Castro's para-military forces; propaganda for "**reconciliation-lifting of embargo,**" showing Castro and the 11 US Presidents he has *fooled*; a cartoon showing **Cardenal Ortega Alamino** as the "*front*" for the Castros.

Nothing polarized more the Cuban exiles than the subject of traveling to Cuba. For many exiles the memories of their efforts to make it in Miami and the austerity of those initial days in exile did not diminish their fervor and were never forgotten. They would not travel to Cuba until the tyrant was gone. They belittled the Cubans that had arrived since the early 1990s and traveled frequently to Cuba bearing gifts and packages. In their minds «*they just wanted to make money, carve a future or a present for themselves, ignoring those suffering in the island while looking forward to having a good vacation in Cuba*». These historic Cuban exiles followed to the letter the words that **José Martí** wrote in 1887.

Why would we go to Cuba?

We were brought here by war, and here we remain in our abhorrence of tyranny, so ingrained in us and so essential to our nature that we could not get rid of it but by getting rid of our own flesh.

Why would we go to Cuba if we cannot live there with dignity and it does not seem that the time has come to die again? ... Why would we go to Cuba? To hear the cracking of the whip on the backs of men, the backs of Cubans and, even if the only weapons there were tree branches to be nailed to a tree trunks, as an example to the hand that punishes us?

To watch the repugnant consortium of the sons of heroes flaunting their unclean prosperity in front of those who should turn their backs on them dwarfed as they are by their impurity and their vices?

To greet, beg, smile and salute with our hand the herd that thrives on our distress, much like the black and yellow butterflies that feed on the manure along the roads?

To watch an insolent bureaucrat rambling with his luxury, his carriage, his lady, before a venerable thinker who is walking alongside, not knowing, in his own land, where to find sustenance for his family?

To watch the illustrious in their embarrassment, the honest in their homelessness, the talented in their shameful complicity, the women without the bounty of their own land, having to keep company with evil men; and the peasant yielding even the growth of his own crops to the soldier who will be chasing him tomorrow?

To watch an entire people, our people, dishonoring themselves with cowardice or dissimulation, as shame replaces today what was yesterday courage?

A dagger is not enough to say how it hurts. To go there... to shame oneself! Others could: WE CANNOT!

José Martí
October 10, 1887

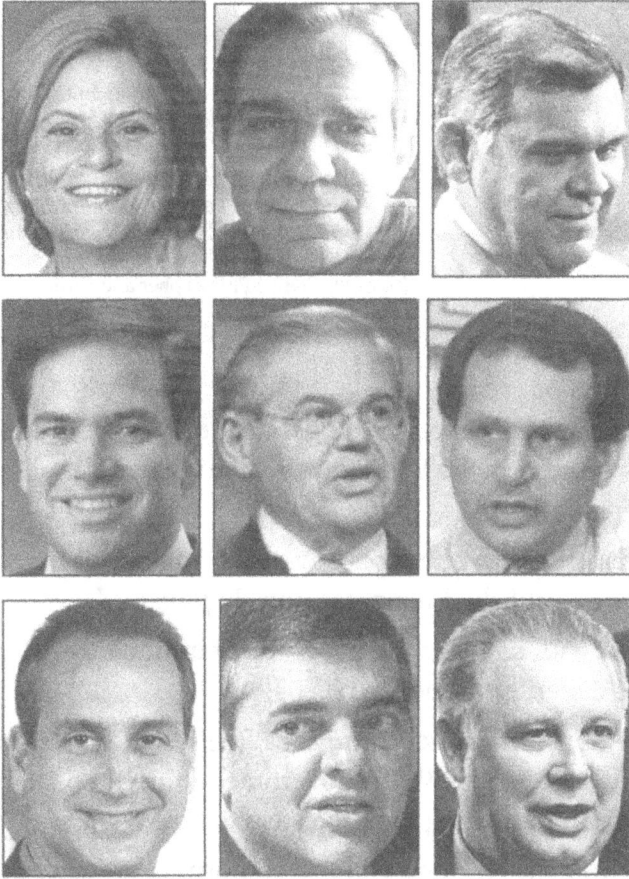

The highly political maturity of US based Cuban exiles, their territorial concentration and their high voter turnout, together with their resolve to have influence over those making decisions about Cuba, have resulted in 20 years of significant levels of Cuban political representation at all levels of the US federal government. Detailing their resourceful and persistent efforts on behalf of a free Cuba would take many more pages than can be summarized in this book. But a chronicle of **Exiled Cuba** would not be complete without rendering a tribute to their virtuous and generous efforts.

Pictures above, top to bottom, left to right:

Ileana Ros-Lehtinen, first Cuban-American (from Florida) elected to the US Congress in 1989; **Xavier Suárez**, first Cuban-born Mayor of Miami; **Mel Martínez** and **Marco Rubio** (from Florida) and **Bob Menéndez** (from New Jersey), elected US Senators; **Lincoln** and **Mario Díaz Balart**, **David Rivera** (from Florida) and **Albio Sires** (from New Jersey), elected to the US House of Representatives.

Epilogue

*«Nations never die a natural death. They die
because their leaders did not know
how to fulfill their promises and
replenish their strengths.»*
VOLTAIRE, French Philosopher and Writer (1694-1778)

As things stand when this book went to press, Cuba remains the only country in the Western world that represses all forms of political dissent.

- Any difference of opinion, controversy, debate or disparity with the established regime is quickly *punished*;

- At their will, forces of the government inhumanly *attack* the public dissenters as needed;

- The regime's organized *Comités de Respuesta Rápida* jump on those disagreeing with the government official positions, beating and reducing the protesters to *forced silence*;

- Those citizens resisting political conformity are *restricted* in their employment, travel and places of residence; they become non-citizens in what is a new *Apartheid*;

- Those freed from jails (where they have been abused for many years) are confined to their homes or are *forcibly banished* to Spain;

- Arbitrary and *"preventive"* arrests and short-term detentions can be imposed onto any citizen with no explanations;

- Criticizing the government is punishable and subject to *criminal charges*;

- An *Acta de Advertencia* (an official warning of political misbehavior) is issued to dissenters to facilitate further prosecution of those participating in unregulated meetings;

- Block by block spies in all towns (*Comités de Defensa de la Revolución*) keep an eye on all citizens;
- *Due process* guarantees are non-existent, just like public hearings, impartial tribunals and writs of *habeas corpus*;
- The judiciary system and the legislative bodies are *subordinate* to the non-freely-elected executive power;
- There is no *freedom of the press*, no freedom of *movement*, no freedom of *education*, and only the level of *religious* freedom tolerated by the government, as per secret compromises with the Catholic Church hierarchy;
- Any *internet communications* have to be sent abroad using memory sticks to upload files at a secure transmission point, typically a friendly non-complicit embassy; in recent times the embassies that would support dissidents are only those from the Czech Republic, the US, Poland and Hungary;
- *Press credentials* and visas are only given to friendly journalists who would portrait a positive image of the regime. Visas are cancelled for any non-complying news person;
- No international human rights *monitoring* is allowed in Cuba. International observers are not granted entry permits, even if they work for the United Nations.

In spite of this record, Cuba was elected in May of 2009, for a period of three years, as a member of the *United Nations Human Rights Council.*

The Cuban regime record speaks for itself.

The 1959-to-present Cuba exile is probably one of the longer lasting proscription phenomena of recent times. As the numbers of Cubans feeling as exiles has decreased over the years, the nature of their claim to the category of exile continues, mostly because an unfailing immersion in emotional, inquisitive or political activism. For those Cubans that felt like exiles when they left Cuba, the day when they would turn into immigrants is still over the horizon. Memories have not disappeared, identities have not been lost, values have not changed much, traditions have continued to be respected, the language and the preference for certain foods are as vivid as they were on the day they started their wearisome journey. Even when time has faded away the hope of returning to Cuba and the ties that anchored Cuban exiles to their land have been dissolved, the anxiety, fear and apprehensions of exile have simply turned into sadness, reverence and warmth for the land where they were born. For many Cuban exiles, Cuba will never be forgotten.

HOW NOT TO BE AN EXILE
A cartoon by Garrinche

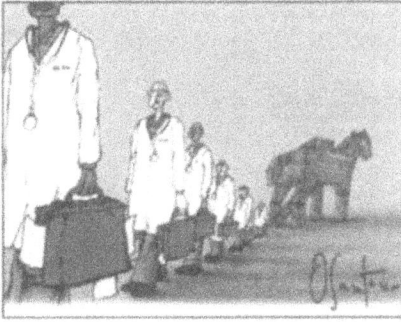

**The Cuban exiles
view of the Castros
in the late 2000s**

Appendices

I - The Cuban Exile Experience: a lifetime of Commitment.

Never has the world seen a group of exiles more committed to its history and traditions than the **Cuban exiles**. Overwhelmed as they were for half a century in the thick of the Cold War and beset by the sacrifices imposed by their own survival, they never forgot their country of origin and relentlessly continued working in myriad ways to bring freedom to Cuba.

The entries that follow show a brief selection of Cuban exiles; artists, politicians, writers, sportsmen, businessmen, activists, men and women of all classes, shown as they were in the days they became exiles and many years later, when they were still thinking of Cuba and doing their best to bring about a better future for those trapped in the island.

José Basulto, founder and leader of *Hermanos al Rescate*, the organization that spotted and helped rescue Cubans in the high seas on the Florida Straits, on the way from Cuba to Miami.

Cundo Bermudez, one of the best Cuban painters and muralists; lived in Puerto Rico much of his exile, moving later to Miami.

Bishop Eduardo Boza Masvidal, former pastor of *Iglesia de la Caridad* in Havana; he was one of the priests sent into exile by the Communists in 1961. Traveled throughout the world helping Cuban exiles from his home in Venezuela and founded *the Union of Cubans in Exile (UCE).*

(Continued)

Dr. Juan Clark, former leader of the *Cuban Catholic Acti*on; best-selling author of many important studies about Cuban exiles and the Communist regime in Cuba. Professor Emeritus of *Miami-Dade College.*

Willie Chirino an extraordinary and popular composer, musician, band leader and crooner; his music has found enormous popularity in Cuba, even though the government will not allow him to perform there or allow his records to be sold to the public.

Guillermo Cabrera Infante, former writer for *Lunes de Revolución*, a magazine suppressed by the Castro regime in 1961. He is one of the best known Cuban writers in exile. In 2009 he received from the King of Spain the *Premio Cervantes.*

Angel Cuadra, widely *translated* poet, writer, president of the *PEN Club* of Cuba. In 1967 became a prisoner of conscience after he was sentenced to one of Castro's gulags for conspiracy. He has been in exile since his release in 1982.

(Continued)

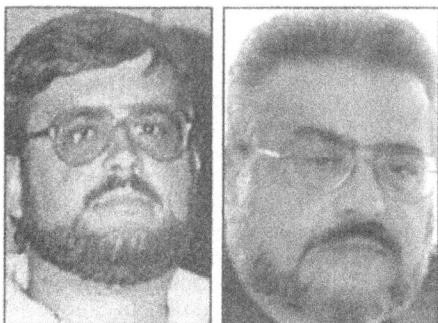

Enrique Encinosa, a *Purdue* alumnus; best seller writer of the definitive book about Cuban boxers, as well as three other books about Cuba. Script-writer and radio personality. Producer, director, writer and actor of serious films about Cuba.

Andy García, popular Cuban-American actor, an international acclaimed star, very successful in Hollywood; an alumnus of *Miami Beach Senior High School* and *Florida International University*. Has won many awards and was nominated for an Oscar for his role in *Godfather III*.

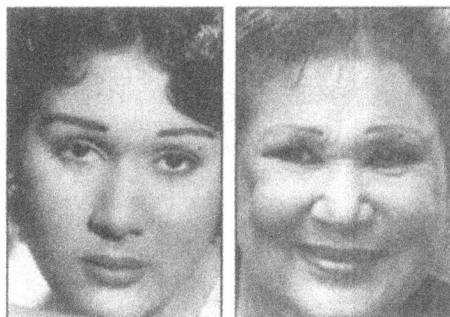

Olga Guillot, known in Cuba and among exiles as the *"Queen of Bolero"*. Her professional career started in 1948 in Mexico; for many years she regularly toured Europe and the Americas. Was admired by *Edith Piaf*, who sang with her in 1958. She has performed at *Carnegie Hall* and earned many awards. Went into exile in 1961.

Yara González Montes, an extraordinary researcher and prolific writer, Professor Emeritus of the *University of Hawaii*. Expert in Spanish *Siglo de Oro* literature; obtained her PhD at the *University of Pittsburgh*. Her writings and citations can be found in many important literary journals throughout the Spanish speaking world.

(Continued)

Eduardo Manet is a world re-nown writer, dramaturgist, thea-ter director, novelist and teacher. He was born in Santiago de Cuba and moved to the US and France during his youth. After returning to Cuba in 1959 he left the island disillusioned by the Castro regime. He has received many prizes and decorations in France and is a recognized best-seller author throughout Europe.

Luis Mario left Cuba in 1967 as an exile. He has taught journal-ism at the *University of Miami* and has written for the *Diario las Americas* for a long time. Start-ing in 2002 he collaborated with *Radio Martí*. He is a member of the *American Academy of Span-ish Language*, the *Cuban Acade-my of History* and the *PEN Club*, and has published 13 books of his poetry.

Guillermo Martínez Márquez, who twice debated Castro on Cuban TV in 1959, has been an exile since 1960. He was a founding member of the *Interamerican Press Society* (SIP) and was a featured writer in *La Prensa* de Buenos Aires; his news column was syndicated in two dozen Latin American news-papers.

Jorge Mas Canosa was a Cuban American activist best known for his strong opposi-tion to Fidel Castro as founder and president of the *Cuban-American National Foundation (CANF)*. As a young man he volunteered for the *Bay of Pigs* invasion. Years later he became a millionaire as the founder and head of the *MASTEC Corporation*.

(Continued)

Huber Matos was a Cuban revolutionary and founder of the *26 of July Movement* presided by Castro. He reacted against the government of Castro when it began to turn towards Communism, was condemned for treason and spent 20 years in jail. When he was released in 1979 he went into exile in Miami.

Carlos Alberto Montaner is probably the most prolific author in Latin America and a Cuban exile since 1960. He has written over 25 books and hundreds of articles, as well as several novels. It is estimated that more than 6 million readers read his weekly columns; he is a political analyst for CNN in Spanish.

Matias Montes Hudobro is a well known poet, critic, playwright and lecturer. He taught at the *University of Hawaii* as a professor of European Languages. He has published extensively in Cuba, Spain and the USA and his theater works has been on stage in many countries. He has received numerous awards throughout his career.

Emilio (Millo) Ochoa is a former Senator from Cuba, and was the last living member of the *1940 Cuban Constitutional Convention*. A dentist by profession he became founder of two Cuban parties: the *Auténticos* and the *Ortodoxos*. He went into exile in 1960 and taught at *Wayne State College* in Nebraska.

(Continued)

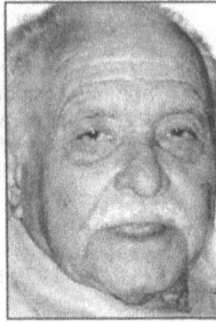

Rolando Ochoa was the first *Mr. Television* in Cuba, a true idol of Cubans, both in his country and in exile. He performed with his wife *Pepita Berrio* in most countries in Latin America. Once in exile he lived by painting windows until he found a job in the radio stations. Later he worked in movies with Juan Orol and other Spanish stars.

Erneido Oliva was the Deputy Commander of the failed *2506 Brigade* that tried to rescue Cuba from the hands of Communism in 1961. After the *Bay of Pigs* he joined the US Army, where he reached the rank of Brigadier General in the *US Army Reserve* in 1984. He retired as a Mayor General in 1993 and continued his anti-Castro work.

Armando Pérez Roura has been associated to radio since his days in Cuba as a youngster. He went into exile in 1959 and became a leader of *Unidad Cubana* and *Consejo por la Libertad de Cuba*. For many years, he has directed *Radio Mambi*, the most popular exile radio station in Miami and has organized mass rallies to keep up the spirits of the Cuban exiles.

Carlos Prío Socarrás was President of Cuba from 1948 until 1952, when he was deposed in a military coup by Fulgencio Batista. He was identified as *El Presidente Cordial* and was the most dedicated Cuban president for the ideals of civility and freedom of expression. He had been a student leader in Havana in the 1930s and a very successful politician in the 1940s.

(Continued)

José Ignacio Rasco was for many years an activist of freedom and cultural developments in Cuba, first as lawyer and professor at the *University of Villanueva* in Havana and later as head of the *Movimiento Demócrata Cristiano (MDC)* in exile. He founded and was president of Miami's *Instituto Jacques Maritain* and was a member of *Consenso Cubano*.

Tomás Regalado is a former broadcast journalist elected *Mayor of Miami* in 2009. He worked many years as reporter for *Univisión* and news director for *Radio Mambí*. He was a member of the White House press corps for ten years. His father was the last president of the *Cuban Association of Reporters* and was a political prisoner of Castro during 22 years.

Ariel Remos was a philosophy student in Cuba who turned to the law and became an attorney. In exile he wrote on economics, international politics and music, particularly opera. He was a consummated guitar virtuoso and liked to write about Cuban exile success stories. For years before his retirement he wrote regularly for *Diario las Américas*.

José Ignacio Rivero was a notable Cuban exile and journalist, grandson of Don Nicolás Rivero, the founder of Havana's *El Diario de la Marina* in 1832. He received many honors for his work in defense of freedom of the press, both from Cuban and international organizations. He went into exile in 1960 as *El Diario* was confiscated by the Castro regime.

(Continued)

(Continuation)

Félix Rodríguez participated in the *Bay of Pigs* invasion and became a member of the CIA during the early 1960s. He fought in Vietnam and was shot down five times while flying his assault helicopter. Later he became famous as the man who hunted, wounded and captured *Ché Guevara* in the Bolivian jungle. He was later President of the *2506 Brigade* in Miami.

Enrique Ros is a Miami-based Cuban-American businessman and activist, as well as a writer, radio host and lecturer. He is related to another *Enrique Ros* that took part in the assault to the *Hotel Nacional* in Cuba in 1933. He is one of the best researchers and historians of Cuba in exile, having authored over 15 books.

Ileana Ros Lethinen is a Cuban-American US Representative for Florida's 18th district, having been elected for the first time in 1989. She graduated from *Florida International University* (Bachelor's and Master's) and the *University of Miami* (PhD). For many years she has had a prominent role in the fight for Cuba in Washington, DC.

Rosendo Rosell was a famous actor, composer, radio and TV producer and journalist who excelled in all of these activities both in Cuba and in exile. Before discovering his acting talents he had been a tobacco factory worker. He made movies in Cuba (*Casta de Robles* and *Siete Muertes a Plazo Fijo*); in exile he became a top-notch journalist and raconteur.

(Continued)

(Continuation)

Juan Manuel Salvat is the founder and director of *Ediciones Universal*, one the most successful publisher of books in Latin America, with over 1500 titles as of 2012. As a youngster he was director of the *Cuban Student Directorate*, «*the most militant and deeply motivated*» of all the Cuban exile organizations according to the American press.

José (Pepe) Triana has been a poet and dramatist for over 50 years: 50 volumes of poetry and 11 dramas for theater. He began writing in Havana in the 1940s and left Cuba after his disillusionment with the revolution during the *Padilla Affair*. He has lived and worked in Paris since leaving for exile and has been published and translated frequently in Europe and the US.

Zoé Valdés is, without doubt, the most prolific and successful of all the writers exiled from Cuba. She has been a consistent, inspired and recurrent best-seller in the Spanish, US and French worlds. Aside from her novels and critical articles against the Castro regime, Zoé writes for Madrid's *El Pais and El Mundo* and for Paris' *Le* Monde, *Libération* and *Le Nouvel Observateur*.

Armando Valladares is a former political prisoner in Castro's Cuba (1960-1982) turned US ambassador to the *United Nations Commission on Human Rights* (1988-1990). He is the founder of New York's *Human Rights Foundation*. In 2004 the Cuban government accused him of terrorism and complicity with *Carlos Alberto Montaner*, another writer accused by Cuba of the same felonies.

II – Cuban Exile Organizations

A

Abdala
Academia de la Historia de Cuba
Acción Cívica Cubana
Acción Cubana
Acción Democrática Cubana
Agenda Cuba
Agrupación Católica Universitaria
Agrupación de Infantería de Combate
Agrupación Montecristi
Agrupación Católica Universitaria
Agrupación Patriótica Calixto García
Alacrán
Alianza Cubana
Alianza Fraternal José Martí
Alpha 66
Alianza de Jóvenes Cubanos
Alianza Democrática
Alianza Nacional Cristiana
Alianza para la Libertad de Cuba
Asamblea de la Resistencia Cubana (ARC)
Asociación de Amigos de Aureliano
Asociación de Amigos de Aureliano -
   Independiente
Asociación de Caballeros Católicos
Asociación de Contadores Cubanos
Asociación de Contratistas Cubanos
Asociación de Ex Confinados de la UMAP
Asociación de Músicos Cubanos Libres
Asociación de Productores de Arroz ECA
   Escambray
Asociación del Patrimonio Nacional
   Cubano
Asociación Democrática de Profesionales
   del Servicio Exterior
Asociacion Félix Varela
Asociación Integral Mambisa
Asociación Médica Pachá
Asociación Medioambientalista Cubana
Asociación Nacional de Colonos
Asociación Nacional de Ganaderos de
   Cuba
Asociación Nacional de Hacendados de
   Cuba
Asociación Patriótica José Martí
Asociación por la Paz Continental
   (ASOPAZCO)
Asociación Pro Cuba (New Jersey)
Association Européenne Cuba Libre (Paris)

B

Batallón de Brigada
Bibliotecas Independientes
Bloque de Organizaciones
   Anti-Comunistas
Brigada de Asalto 2506
Buró Internacional de la Legión
   Anticomunista

C

Cámara de Comercio Latina (CAMACOL)
Camagüeyanos Ausentes
Center for a Free Cuba
Centro De Derechos Humanos y
   Democracia (Brigada 2506)
Centro de Información y Documentación
   de Estudios Cubanos
Centro Histórico Cultural Cubano
Círculo Cubano de Puerto Rico
Club de Leones Cubanos en el Exilio
Club de Rotarios Cubanos en el Exilio
Club Patriótico Villaclareño
Coalition of Cuban-American Women
Colegio de Abogados de la Habana
Colegio de Farmacéuticos Cubanos
Colegio de Ingenieros Agrónomos
   Azucareros
Colegio de Ingenieros Civiles
Colegio de Notarios Públicos Cubanos
Colegio de Veterinarios Cubanos
Colegio Nacional de Periodistas Cubanos
Colegio Médico Cubano
Colegio Nacional de Arquitectos de Cuba
Colegio Nacional de Abogados Cubanos
Colegio Técnico Rubi Feria
Comandos F-4
Comandos L
Comandos Libres Nacionalistas
Comandos Pedro Luis Boitel
Comando Martiano
Comando Revolucionario Marcelino García
Comité Anti-Comunista de Ayuda a la
   Liberación Cubana
Comité Coordinador de Organizaciones
   Democráticas Cubanas (PR)
Comité Cubano Pro Derechos Humanos
Comité de Santiagueros en el Exilio
Comisión Cubana Pro-Derechos Humanos
Confedeeración Campesina de Cuba
Confederación de Trabajadores de Cuba
   en el Exilio
Confederación Profesionales Cubano
   Americanos en el Exilio
Confederación Profesionales Universitarios
   Cubanos en el Exilio
Consejo por la Libertad de Cuba
Consejo Militar Cubano-Americano
Consejo Revolucionario Cubano
Consenso Cubano
Coordinación de Organizaciones
   Revolucionarias Unidas (CORU)
Coordinadora Internacional de
   Ex-Prisioneros Políticos Cubanos
Coordinadora Social Demócrata
Corriente Agramontista
Criterio Alternativo
Cruzada Educativa Cubana
Cruzada Femenina Cubana
Cuba Acción 13 de Marzo
Cuba Democracia Ya
Cuba Democratique
Cuba Independiente y Democrática (CID)
Cuba Study Group
Cuba Unida
Cuban American Veteran Association
Cuban American Workers Coalition
Cuban Democratic Coalition
Cuban Defense League
Cuban Independent Party

Nueva Generación

O

Observatorio Cubano de Derechos Humanos
Omega
Operación ALFA 66
Organización Auténtica
Organización de Masones Anticomunistas
Organización del Ejercito Secreto Anticomunista
Organización de Jóvenes Exiliados Cubanos (O-JEC)
Organización La Voz Anticomunista de Cuba
Organización Libertadora de Cuba
Organización Nacional de Liberación Anticomunista
Organización Occidental Anticomunista
Organización Patriótica Cubana
Organización pro Libertad, Equidad y Justicia
Organización Revolucionaria Anticomunista
Organización Revolucionaria Cubana
Organización Revolucionaria del Transporte
Organización Revolucionaria La Estrella Solitaria
Organización Revolucionaria Militar
Organización Revolucionaria Patriótica
Organización Revolucionaria Secreta
Organización Telefónica Anticomunista
Organizaciones Cubanas del Exilio (PR)
Organizaciones Cubanas Unidas
Organizaciones Revolucionarias Unidas
Ortodoxos Revolucionarios

P

Partido Acción Nacionalista
Partido Cubano de Renovación Ortodoxa
Partido del Pueblo Cubano (Ortodoxo)
Partido Demócrata Cristiano de Cuba
Partido Demócrata Cubano
Partido Independentista Cubano
Partido Liberal
Partido Nacionalista Democrático de Cuba
Partido Social Demócrata Cubano
Partido Revolucionario Cubano (Auténtico)
Partido Revolucionario Cubano en el Exilio
Partido Unidad Nacional (PUN)
Partido Unión Nacional Democrática
Plataforma Unitaria Cubana
Presidio Político Histórico Cubano
PEN Club
Plantados hasta la Libertad y la Democracia en Cuba
Plataforma Democrática Cubana
Poder Cubano
Policía Nacional Cubana en el Exilio
Presidio Político Histórico Cubano
Pro-Gobierno Constitucional de Cuba en el Exilio

Pro-Unidad Cubana (México)
Puente de Jóvenes Profesionales Cubanos

R

Raices Cubanas
ReRescate Revolucionario Democrático
ReRescate Democrático Revolucionario
Rescate Obrero
Rescate Revolucionario Nacional
Resistencia Agramontina
Resistencia Anticomunista Nacional
Resistencia Cívica 7 de Diciembre
Resistencia Nacional Anticomunista
República de Cuba en el Exilio
Rosa Blanca
Rosa Blanca Independiente

S

Salve a Cuba
Sector Aéreo Cubano
Segundo Frente Nacional de Escambray en el Exilio
Servicio Clandestino
Sociedad Cubana de Pediatría en el Exilio
Sociedad Económica de Amigos del País
SOS Justicia

T

The Cuba Corps

U

Unidad Anti-Comunista de Cuba
Unidad Cubana
Unidad Cubana de Acción Libertadora
Unidad Cubana Revolucionaria Anticomunista
Unidad de Liberación Nacional de Cuba
Unidad de Unidades Revolucionarias
Unidad Revolucionaria
Unidad Revolucionaria (Tampa)
Unidad Insurreccional Revolucionaria
Unión Cubana Anticomunista
Unión de Cubanos en el Exilio (UCE)
Unión de Ex-Presos Políticos Cubanos
Unión de Mujeres Anticomunistas
Unión de Soldados y Oficiales Libres
Unión de Trabajadores Cristianos
Unión Democrática Militar
Unión Familia Escolapia Cubana (UFEC)
Unión Liberal Cubana
Unión Nacional de Instituciones Revolucionarias (UNIR)
Unión Nacional de Profesionales Anticomunistas
Unión Nacional Democrática "Movimiento 20 de Mayo"
Unión Nacional Democrática Libre
Unión Republicana Democrática

V

Vanguardia Cívica Constitucional
Veteranos de Misiones Especiales
Vigilia Mambisa
Voz de la Fundación

W

Women Fighters for Democracy

III — Cuban Intellectuals in Exile

A quick overview of the human talent lost to Cuba after the imposition of Communism in 1959: **the top 500.**

A

Ada Mirta Mendoza
Adela Serra
Adolfo Fernández
Adolfo Franco
Adolfo Rivero Caro
Agustín Acosta y Bello
Agustín Gaínza
Agustín Román
Aida Levitán
Alberto Alonso
Alberto Baeza Flores
Alberto González
Alberto Gutiérrez Solana
Alberto Hernández Chiroldes
Alberto Lauro
Alberto Muller
Alberto Roldán
Alberto S. Bustamante
Alberto Zarraín
Alejandro Anreus
Alejandro F. Pascual
Alejandro Ríos
Alexander Aznarez
Alexander Domínguez
Aleyda Cruz Espineta
Alfredo M. Cepero
Alicia G. Barrionuevo
Alis García
Alvaro Alba
Álvaro de Villa
Amado Rodríguez
Amalia de la Torre
Amalio Fiallo
Amelia del Castillo
Ana María Alvarado
Ana María Simó
Ana Rosa Núñez
Andrés Candelario
Andrés Cao Mendiguren
Andrés Reynaldo
Andrés Rivero Aguero
Andrés Valdespino
Andrés Valerio
Andrés Vargas Gómez
Andy Gómez

Ángel Aparicio Laurencio
Anolán Ponce
Angel Cuadra
Ángel Gaztelu
Ángel Martín Rodríguez
Ángel Pérez Vidal
Anita Arroyo
Antonio A. Acosta
Antonio de Varona
Antonio J. Molina
Antonio José Ponte
Antonio Jorge
Antonio Orla
Ariel Hidalgo
Ariel Remos
Arístides Sosa de Quesada
Armando Álvarez Bravo
Armando Casín
Armando Chávez Rivera
Armando Cobelo
Armando P. Ribas
Armando Pico
Arturo Pino
Aurelio de la Vega

B

Beatriz Bernal
Beatriz Varela
Belkis Cuza Malé
Benigno S. Nieto
Berta G. Montalvo
Byron Miguel

C

Calixto C. Masó
Carlos Alberto Montaner
Camilo Venegas
Carlos Alfonso
Carlos Bermúdez
Carlos Eire
Carlos Franqui
Carlos M. Luis
Carlos Márquez Sterling
Carlos Paz Pérez.
Carlos Ripoll
Carlos Saladrigas
Carlos Victoria
Carmelo Mesa-Lago
Cecilia La Villa de
    Fernández-Travieso
Cecilia Molinero Flores
Celedonio González
César A. Mena
César Leante
Cesar Mena
Ciralina Quijano
Concepción T. Alzola
Cosette Alves Carballosa
Cristina Rebull
Cristóbal Díaz Ayala

D

Daína Chaviano
Daniel Fernández
Daniel Román
Delia Fiallo
Delfín Rodríguez Silva
Delia Díaz de Villegas
Demetrio Pérez

Diosdado Consuegra
Dora Amador
Doris de Goya
Dosinda Pérez
Dulce María García

E

Edilberto Marbán
Edmundo García
Eduardo Boza Masvidal
Eduardo Cuenca García
Eduardo García Moure
Eduardo G. Noguer
Eduardo J. Tejera
Eduardo Lolo
Eduardo Manet
Eduardo Michaelson
Eduardo Rodríguez
Eduardo Zayas-Bazán
Efrén Córdova
Eladio Secades
Elena Iglesias
Elías Miguel Muñoz
Elio Alba Buffill
Eliseo Alberto
Ellen Lismore Leeder
Eloy A. González
Eloísa Lezama Lima
Emilio Cueto
Emilio Ichikawa
Emilio Martínez Paula
Ena Curnow
Enildo García
Enrico Mario Santí
Enrique Baloyra
Enrique de Armas
Enrique Del Risco
Enrique Encinosa
Enrique Huertas
Enrique J. Ventura
Enrique José Varona
Enrique Labrador Ruiz
Enrique Ovares Herrera
Enrique Ros
Enriqueta del Pino
Ernesto Ardura
Ernesto F. Betancourt
Ernesto Fernández
    Travieso S.J.
Ernesto Hernández Busto
Ernesto Montaner
Esperanza Figueroa
Esteban Fernández Jr.
Estéban J. Palacios
Esteban Luis Cárdenas
Esther Sánchez-Grey
Estrella Bustos Ogden
Eugenio Florit
Eusebio Mujal-León

F

Fausto Canel
Fausto Masó
Favio Murrieta
Federico Arvesú SJ
Felicia Guerra
Felipe J. Préstamo
Felipe Lázaro

Felipe Martínez-Arango
Felipe Pazos
Félix González
Fermín Peinado
Fermín Peraza
Fernando Palenzuela
Fernando Villaverde
Florinda Álzaga
Francisco Alabau Trelles
Francisco Morín
Francisco Villaverde OP
Frank Falcón
Frank Fernández
Fray Miguel Ángel Loredo
OFM

G

Gastón A. Fernández
Gastón Álvaro Santana
Gastón Baquero
Gastón Fernández de la
Torriente
Gemma Roberts
Gerardo E. Martínez-
Solanas
Germán Barrios
Germán Guerra
Gilberto Marino
Gilberto Ruiz
Gina Montaner
Gladys M. Varona-Lacey
Gladys Zaldívar
Goar Mestre
Gonzalo Fontana
Grisel González
Grace Piney Roche
Guillermo Arango
Guillermo Cabrera Infante
Guillermo Cabrera Leyva
Guillermo de Zéndegui
Guillermo I. Martínez
Guillermo Martínez
Márquez
Guillermo Milán Reyes
Guillermo Rosales
Gustavo Godoy
Gustavo Pérez Firmat
Gustavo Valdés Rivera

H

Heberto Padilla
Hector Lemagne Sandó
Héctor Santiago
Herminio Portell Vilá
Hilda Perera
Hortensia Ruiz del Vizo
Hugo J. Byrne
Hugo Consuegra
Humberto J. Peña
Humberto López Cruz
Humberto López Morales
Humberto Medrano
Humberto Piñera Llera

I

Idolidia Darias
Ignacio Berroa
Ignacio Ortiz Bello
Ileana Curra

Isaac Delgado
Isabel Castellanos
Isis Wirth
Israel Rodríguez
Israel Vera
Iván Acosta

J

J. A. Albertini
Jacobo Machover
Jaime Suchlicki
Janisset Rivero
Javier de Castro Mori
Javier Figueroa
Jesús Angulo
Jesús Bravo Espinosa
Jesús Díaz
Jesús García
Joaquín Clavería
Joaquín de Posada
Joaquín Estrada
Montalván
Jorge A. Sanguinetty
Jorge Castellanos
Jorge Domínguez
Jorge F. Pérez López
Jorge Febles
Jorge Fernández Fonseca
Jorge Guillermo
Jorge Hernández
Jorge Marbán
Jorge Mañach
Jorge Salazar Carrillo
Jorge Vals Arango
José A. Escarpanter
José A. Madrigal
José Ángel Buesa
José Antonio Arcocha
José Azel
José de Jesús Planas
José Duarte Oropesa
José Gómez Sicre
José Hidalgo Gato
José Ignacio Lasaga
José Ignacio Rasco
José Ignacio Rivero
José Kozer
José Miró Cardona
José M. González Llorente
José M. Hernández Puente
José Manuel García
José Mármol
José Olivio Jiménez
José Pardo Llada
José Prats Sariol
José Ramón Villalón
José Sánchez-Boudy
José Sánchez-Priede
José Triana
Josefina Inclán
Joseph I. Dixson
Juan Abreu
Juan Alborná-Salado
Juan Antonio Blanco
Juan Arcocha
Juan Barturen
Juan Boza

Juan Clark
Juan Cueto
Juan F. Benemelis
Juan José López Díaz
Juan J. Sosa
Juan Manuel Salvat
Juana Rosa Pita
Julián Izquierdo
Julio C. Pita Jr. M.D.
Julio César Gálvez
Julio Fernández-León
Julio Ferreiro Mora
Julio Hernández Millares
Julio Hernández Rojo
Julio Matas
Julio Rodríguez-Luis
Julio Venegas
Julito Martínez
Justo Carrillo

K

Karla Barro

L

Laura Luna
Laureano Batista
Lázaro J. Abreu
León Ichaso
Leonardo Fernández
Marcané
Leonel de la Cuesta
Leonor Zamora
Leovigildo Ruiz
Lesbia O. de Varona
Levi Marrero
Lino Novas y Calvo
Lorenzo García Vega
Lourdes Gómez Franca
Luis A. Gómez
Domínguez
Luis A. Jiménez
Luis Aguilar León
Luis Ángel Casas
Luis Bofill
Luis David Rodríguez
Luis de la Paz
Luis Felipe Díaz Galeano
Luis Felipe Marsans
Luis F. González Cruz
Luis Fernández Caubí
Luis Mario
Luis Nodal
Luis Ricardo Alonso
Luis Vega
Luis Zúñiga
Lydia Cabrera

M

Madeleine Cámara
Magaly Agüero
Manolo Blanco
Manolo Feral
Manolo Pozo
Manuel Antonio de Varona
Manuel C. Díaz
Manuel Cereijo
Manuel Fernández
Santalices
Manuel Márquez Sterling

Manuel Matías
Manuel Mijares
Manuel Ray
Manuel Reguera Saumell
Marcelino García S.J.
Marcos Antonio Ramos
Marcos Miranda
Margarita Camacho
Mari Rodríguez Ichaso
María Cama
María Carmen Zielina
María Elena Villamil
María Julia Casanova
María Vega de Febles
Maricel Mayor Marsán
Marcelo Alonso
Mariela Gutiérrez
Marifeli Pérez-Stable
Marijean Miyar
Marino Martínez Peraza
Marino Pérez Durán
Mario E. Dihigo
Mario G. Mendoza III
Mario Llerena
Mario P. Landrián
Mario Vallejo
Mario Vizcaino SChP
Marlén Urbay
Marta Moré de Fiallo
Martha Strada
Martín Añorga
Mateo Jover Marimón
Matías Montes Huidobro
Mauricio Fernández
Mercedes García Tudurí
Mercedes Muriedas
Mercedes Sandoval
Migueal Angel Quevedo
Miguel Chávez
Miguel Correa
Miguel Figueroa Miranda
Miguel A. Loredo, Pbro.
Miguel Ordoqui
Miguel Sales Figueroa
Miguel Uría
Miriam Morell
Manuel Serpa

N

Nancy Pérez Crespo
Nazario Vivero
Nelson Franco
Néstor Almendros
Néstor Carbonell Cortina
Nicasio Silvero Saínz
Nicolás Abreu Felippe
Nicolás Pérez Diez Agüelles
Ninoska Pérez Castellón
Noel Silva-Ricardo
Norberto Fuentes

O

Octavio R. Costa
Ofelia Martín Hudson
Olga Connor
Olga Isabel Nodarse
Olga Rosado

Omar Moynelo
Onilda A. Jiménez
Orestes Ferrara
Orestes Miqueli
Orlando Gómez-Gil
Orlando Jiménez-Leal
Orlando Rossardi
Oscar Echevarría
Oscar Hijuelos
Osvaldo de Tapia-Ruano
Osvaldo Rodríguez
Otto Olivera
Ovidio Mañalich

P

Pablo Cano
Pablo López Capestany
Pancho Vives
Paquito D'Rivera
Patricia Gutiérrez-Menoyo
Paul Alcazar
Pedro Corzo
Pedro Damián
Pedro Juan López Díaz
Pedro Monge Rafulls
Pedro Roig
Pedro Tamayo
Pepe Carril
Pío Serrano
Pura del Prado

R

Rafael A. Aguirre
   Rencurrell
Rafael B. Abislaimán
Rafael Díaz-Balart
Rafael Rojas
Ramón Bonachea
Ramón Ferreira
Ramón Humberto Colás
Ramón J. Santos
Raquel la Villa
Raúl Acosta Rubio
Raúl Chibás
Raúl de Cárdenas
Raúl Eduardo Chao
Raúl García Iglesias
Raúl Gómez
Raúl Mestre
Raúl M. Shelton
Raúl Rivero
Raúl Tápanes Estrella
Reinaldo Arenas
Reinaldo Bragado Bretaña
Reinaldo García Ramos
René Ariza
René Cifuentes
Rey Batista
Reynerio Lebroc Martínez
Ricardo Bofill
Ricardo Eddy Martínez
Ricardo Menéndez
Ricardo Pau-Llosa
Ricardo Rafael Sardiña
Rita Geada
Rita Martín
Roberto Agramonte

Roberto Cazorla
Roberto Goizueta
Roberto González
   Echevarría
Roberto Luque Escalona
Roberto Marín
Roberto Martín Pérez
Roberto Valero
Rodolfo Martínez
   Sotomayor
Rodolfo Valdés Sigler
Rogelio de la Torre
Rogelio Menéndez
Rolando Sánchez Mejías
Rosa Bella
Rosa Dihigo Beguiristain
Rosario García Tudurí
Rosario Hiriart
Rosario Rexach
Rudy Pérez

S

Salvador Blanco
Salvador Díaz Versón
Salvador E. Subirá-Turró
Salvador Larrúa Guedes
Samuel Nodarse
Sam Verdeja
Sergio Ramos
Sergio San Pedro
Severo Sarduy
Silvia Pedraza
Sylvia Iriondo

T

Tamara Álvarez-Detrell
Tania Quintero
Tatiana Vecino
Teresa Escandón
Teresa Fernández Soneira
Teresa María Rojas
Teresita Diego
Teté Casuso Morín
Tomás Fernández Travieso
Tomás García Fusté

U

Uva de Aragón

V

Valentín Arenas
Vicente Echerri
Víctor Gómez
Víctor Vega Ceballos
Virgilio F. Beato

W

Waldo de Castroverde
Wenceslao Cruz
Wilfredo Cancio Isla
Wilfredo Méndi

X

Xiomara J. Pagés

Y

Yara González Montes
Yolanda Cuellar
Yolanda Ortal Miranda
Ysrael A. Seinuk

Z

Zoé Valdés

IV —
Alphabetical
Index

As this book was going to press, news of the death of **Osvaldo Payá Sardiñas (1952-2012)** reached Cuban exiles across the world. Payá was the founder of the *Christian Liberation Movement (CLM)* and the organizer of the *Varela Project,* for which he received the *2002 Sakharov Prize* from the European Parliament. He died in a car crash on July 22 at 1:50 PM near Bayamo, on Cuba's Eastern province. With him died **Harold Cepero (1981-2012)**, Chairman of the *CLM Youth League*. Politicians **Jens Aron Modig** of Sweden and **Angel Carromero** of Spain, traveling with Payá and Cepero, only suffered minor injuries in what was a rather suspicious accident. Payá's death followed the passing of **Laura Inés Pollán Toledo (1948-2011),** a prominent Cuban opposition leader, founder of the dissident group *Ladies in White*, who died of cardiorespiratory arrest, also under suspicious circumstances, on October 4, 2011.

During Payá's funeral in the *El Salvador del Mundo Church* in the Havana neighborhood of *El Cerro*, over 200 Cuban security agents began roughing up the mourners and bundling them into buses. More than 40 persons were arrested, including dissident journalist **Guillermo Fariñas**.

Photos above: Cuban exiles in Madrid honored Payá's memory by projecting his image on the *façade* of the Cuban Embassy on the day of his funeral. The car were Payá was traveling, showing damages that suggest a rear end collision from another car rather than a front or side crash against a tree, as reported by Cuban authorities.

Raúl Eduardo Chao received his PhD from Johns Hopkins University and after a brief stint in industry spent 18 years in academe, as Full Professor and Department Chairman at the **Universities of Puerto Rico and Detroit.** *In 1986 he founded a very successful management consultancy, assisting companies and government agencies to develop positive work environments and process improvement techniques as the means to secure improvements in productivity and quality.* **The Systema Group** *had as clients many Fortune 100 companies and Federal and State organizations, both in the US and abroad. As its Chairman, Chao wrote a dozen books and numerous articles in newspapers and reviewed journals. He and his wife Olga live in Coral Gables, Florida and spend long periods of time in Paris.*

(His picture in a circle on page 10 of this book)

The author wishes to thank **Olga Nodarse, Sara Marina** and **Sergio García** for their thorough and thoughtful editing and proofreading of this book. He also wishes to express his gratitude to **Juan Manuel Salvat** of *Ediciones Universal* for his always wise advice and his valuable and timely help in nursing this book to completion; to **Gustavo Rodríguez** (Garrincha) and other Cuban caricaturists for their genial cartoons; to **Gustavo Acosta** for the painting that shown at the back cover; finally, to all the scholars, journalists and Cuban exiles that have generously contributed their ideas and experiences to this work.

This book was printed in the United States.

The font used throughout the text
has been **Palatino Linotype**, one of the classic old style
serif typefaces inspired by designs of the 16th century Italian
calligrapher **Giambattista Palatino**. The font was reissued in 1948 by
Hermann Zapf for the Linotype Foundry, the company created by Ottmar
Mergenthaler, a German immigrant to the U.S. who invented the revolutionary
line typesetting machine that was first used in 1890 by the **New York Tribune**.

The font used in the covers, title pages, headings and ornaments is **P22 Franklin
Caslon**, a faithful interpretation of the type used by Benjamin Franklin in the 1750's in
his printing shop and particularly in his **Poor Richard's Almanac**. This font was developed in 2006 by the International House of Fonts for the Philadelphia Museum of
Art to commemorate the 300th birthday of our most remarkable Founding Father.
The font accompanying the photos and illustrations is **Verdana;** a humanist sans-
serif typeface designed by **Matthew Carter** for *Microsoft Corporation*, with hand-hinting
done by **Tom Rickner**, then at *Monotype*. Demand for such a clear and easy to read
type-face was recognized by **Virginia Howlett** of *Microsoft's* typography group.
The name "**Verdana**" is based on a mix of *verdant* (something green,
as in the Seattle area and the Evergreen state of Washington),
and *Ana* (the name of Howlett's
eldest daughter

www.ingramcontent.com/pod-product-compliance
Lightning Source LLC
Chambersburg PA
CBHW060302030426
42336CB00011B/911